H. H. ARNASON

THE SCULPTURES
OF HOUDON

The Sculptures of
HOUDON

by H.H. Arnason

New York · Oxford University Press · 1975

First published in the United States of America 1975
by Oxford University Press, Inc.
200 Madison Avenue, New York, New York 10016
All rights reserved
ISBN 0 19 519782 8
Library of Congress Catalog Number 75-10186

Text printed in Great Britain by R. & R. Clark Ltd., Edinburgh
Plates printed in Great Britain by Westerham Press Limited

CONTENTS

PREFACE

JEAN-ANTOINE HOUDON is widely considered the foremost French sculptor of the eighteenth century, and by many as one of the outstanding portrait sculptors in history. Much research has been devoted to him during the last two centuries, and almost all the known facts about his life and career have been published and discussed frequently. But there still remain unanswered a substantial number of questions having to do with the identification and authentication of sculptures associated with him. As a consequence there are further problems concerning his style, his quality, and his final achievement as a sculptor. It is to these problems specifically that I address myself in this essay.

We have records of some three hundred subjects of sculptures by Houdon. For many of these it was his custom to make replicas and variants. Of his portrait of Voltaire he may have made more than a hundred busts in different materials; we know that he gave plasters of it to all forty members of the French Royal Academy. Although the *Voltaire* is an extreme instance, it is very likely that he produced some two thousand sculptures during his long career. Since most of these were portrait busts, easily portable, frequently of historic figures, they have been scattered over Europe and the Americas. Many have been destroyed or have simply disappeared, perhaps into private collections or institutions where they are no longer recognized.

Unfortunately the most serious problem is not that of lost works. Because of his reputation and the prestige of his subjects, replicas and forgeries of his sculptures began to be made during his lifetime, and the process has continued ever since. Aside from the deliberate falsifications there has been the equally pernicious custom of attributing to Houdon any eighteenth-century and some nineteenth-century portrait busts that need a distinguished father. There are even twentieth-century replicas of figures such as his *Washington* or *Benjamin Franklin*, made in all innocence for some commemorative purpose, and now installed in museums as original Houdons.

It is then my hope in this book to establish the basis for a canon of quality and authenticity in the sculptures of Houdon. To this end I shall concentrate on those works which I feel to be unquestionably from his hand and to illustrate these with the best photographs available, including details of individual pieces. The arrangement is chronological, following the Salon exhibitions in which the artist participated between 1769 and 1814, with the exception that later replicas are usually placed with the first model, and certain busts, such as those of his family, are grouped together. Works which did not appear in a Salon are treated with the Salon closest in date. Although each sculpture is discussed in terms of its style, technique, subject and, where pertinent, historical background, more space is devoted to his earlier portrait busts, not because they are inevitably better, but for the obvious reason that the continuing questions of Houdon's character and quality as a portraitist are posed at the very beginning of his career and must be examined at this point. Since some one hundred and fifty works are described, to avoid undue repetition these descriptions become progressively more summary.

For almost all the sculptures discussed I have studied and photographed the actual work in detail. In the few instances where it is necessary to mention a piece of which I have only seen photographs, this fact is noted. In such cases I have reserved judgement—even on works I have no reason to question. My own experience with photography has taught me how incredibly a sculpture can be distorted in a photograph.

Although examples of most of Houdon's surviving sculptures are included in this book, it is not a *catalogue raisonné*. It is an attempt to describe and illustrate the authentic and best works by the artist. When there are many replicas of a given work, I have selected the one or ones I believe to be of the highest quality and have listed two or three others which are comparable. There is no attempt to be inclusive. In some instances there exist other casts of comparable quality to those I include. Except in one or two cases that relate to a larger problem, I have not included sculptures on which I have reservations. This is a matter for the *catalogue raisonné*, which, hopefully, will soon follow the present study. Others may differ with some of my inclusions and exclusions; this I welcome.

During my stay in France, in 1955 and 1956, I completed most of the documentary research on the sculpture, and studied and photographed most of the works in French museums and many in private collections. The documentary research was not onerous, since the material is easily available. Most surviving documents are in the Archives Nationales in Paris and many of them have been published by a distinguished series of French scholars, extending from Montaiglon and Duplessis in the mid-nineteenth century to Gaston Brière, André Michel, Paul Vitry, Louis Réau, and others in the twentieth century. An unexpected problem was that photographs available from museums and official photographic services, while plentiful, were generally old and inferior in quality. (Many of these have latterly been improved.) As a consequence I was forced to learn how to photograph sculpture and, whatever the results, I discovered that a telephoto or close-up lens was an excellent way to see sculpture. Many photographs in this book I have taken myself; some have been taken by museum photographers in accordance with my directions. Where good museum photographs were available I have used them, since I have more faith in a professional photographer than I have in myself.

In 1955 I learned that Louis Réau, the chief scholar of Houdon during the previous fifty years, was about to publish his definitive study of the sculptor. Towards the end of my stay in Paris, 1955–6, I had the privilege of meeting Monsieur Réau, who informed me that his book was to all intents completed and would appear within the next year or two. In the light of this statement it would have been both foolish and presumptuous for me to rush into print, even though I had the mistaken idea that much of my work had been completed.

Réau died, sadly, in 1961. Although I heard indirectly that he had completed his work on Houdon before his death, I was not immediately able to learn what plans had been made for publication. My own researches continued sporadically, principally in the form of collecting and photographing other examples of sculptures by or attributed to Houdon. It was at this period that I became more and more aware of how many forgeries, late replicas, and doubtful attributions existed. Works were continually referred to me by museums, collectors and dealers in Europe and the United States. My photographic file grew to two or three thousand negatives (for each work I take twelve to twenty views and details); and problems of attribution and authenticity developed correspondingly. In 1963 I was invited to organize an exhibition of sculptures by Houdon for the Worcester Art Museum, Worcester, Massachusetts, and to write a detailed catalogue. The catalogue was published at the beginning of 1964 and the exhibition was held January 16 through February 23, 1964. The catalogue is a prototype for the approach and organization of the present book. I have used passages from it where they seemed pertinent and have cited it immodestly in the notes. I have also attempted to correct errors.

Later in 1964 I learned that Réau's book was finally in process of publication and I secured a copy early in 1965. It is a monumental study, encyclopedic in its learning, certainly the most important work on Houdon ever to appear. I would like here to record my great debt to it. It is immensely valuable as a compendium of documentation and Houdon scholarship for the last hundred and fifty years.

The principal criticisms that may be made of Réau's book arise in part from his at times over-enthusiastic authentications and, even more, from the fact that the book was published posthumously. Although the editors performed a dedicated task in carrying out Réau's design, they could not, understandably, achieve all his intentions. There are, thus, included in the catalogue a substantial number of works to which I must take exception: some thirty which

I have actually seen and another twenty where the photographs look dubious. On the latter group, of course, I can give no firm opinion. Nevertheless it will be apparent that there are many differences between Réau's attributions as published and my own.

THIS book opens with a background summary of French sculpture from the sixteenth to the eighteenth century. The account of Houdon is chronological. After discussion of his youth and the four years spent at the French Academy in Rome, the *livrets*, or catalogues, of the Salons form the basis on which his career is studied between 1769 and 1814. Since most of Houdon's work was submitted to the Royal Academy, these biennial exhibitions provide a framework which makes it possible to follow his progress as an artist. Although biographical details are few and frequently of little interest, these are all noted in their appropriate places.

Finally, may I reiterate the fact that this is a selective study of Houdon's sculpture and that the emphasis is placed on those works which I feel to be from his hand. The principal contribution of the book may well be in the photographic details, from which it is hoped that some idea of Houdon's style and quality as a sculptor will be gained.

I DEDICATE this book to RENSSELAER W. LEE, who first introduced me to the study of art history.

H.H.A.

ACKNOWLEDGEMENTS

RESEARCH for this study of Jean-Antoine Houdon was initiated in 1955–6 with a fellowship to France under the Fulbright Program. My first acknowledgements are to that Program and to the Graduate Department of the University of Minnesota, which aided me with various supplementary research grants. During the long period from 1956 to 1970, when other commitments of research and administration in the area of modern art delayed the completion of the book on Houdon, I was nevertheless continually accumulating material from museums, collectors and dealers in the United States. The number of those who have aided me by bringing to my attention works attributed to Houdon is so great that it is impossible to list them all by name. I simply express my thanks to them. Specifically, I must thank those who have welcomed me to their collections and have given me every cooperation in studying and photographing sculptures. I owe a particular debt to Messieurs Pradel and Gaborit of the Louvre, Gérard Hubert, Curator of the Château de Malmaison, John Goldsmith Phillips of the Metropolitan Museum, Daniel Catton Rich, Director Emeritus of the Worcester Art Museum, the late Monsieur Courty, perhaps the most dedicated of all contemporary collectors of eighteenth-century portrait sculpture, notably of Houdon.

In the early 1970s I resumed work on Houdon in detail under a grant from the National Endowment for the Humanities and grants from the Samuel H. Kress Foundation and from the American Philosophical Society. To all of these I express my appreciation.

Specific thanks are due to many research assistants, notably to Mary Ann Bieter, Barbara Burn, Anna Golfinopoulos, and Dorothy Anderson. Since a most important part of this book consists of the photographs, I must also express my appreciation to the professional photographers who have guided me: Joseph Lyons of the Frick Collection, Eric Sutherland of the Walker Art Center, Robert Mates and Paul Katz of the Guggenheim Museum, Monsieur Gassman of Pictorial Service, Paris, and many others.

To my editors at Phaidon Press, Keith Roberts, who waited with enormous patience and gentle encouragement for the manuscript, and Dr I. Grafe, who guided the book through the press with great knowledge and sympathy, my most special thanks are due.

Finally, I have a debt impossible to evaluate to all those scholars who have worked on Jean-Antoine Houdon over the last one hundred and fifty years. The list of those who have contributed to Houdon scholarship is far too extensive to be recounted here, but the bibliography gives a sufficient indication. Special mention must be made of Paul Vitry and Louis Réau. Anyone who works on Houdon, or for that matter on almost any aspect of eighteenth-century sculpture, owes an enormous debt to these scholars.

A SUMMARY OF FRENCH SCULPTURE, SIXTEENTH TO EIGHTEENTH CENTURY

FRENCH Gothic sculpture, one of the noblest traditions in the history of sculpture, continued well into the sixteenth century and beyond, despite the ever-increasing influence of Italian Renaissance art on France. In fact, elements of the Gothic style are evident in French religious sculpture of the seventeenth and eighteenth centuries. French Renaissance art was indebted to the Italian artists imported by Francis I—Benvenuto Cellini, Primaticcio, Rosso, not to mention Leonardo da Vinci—but soon produced its own masters—Jean and François Clouet among the painters, and Jean Goujon and Germain Pilon among the sculptors. Ligier Richier, a sculptor of comparable stature, illustrates the struggle of styles between French Gothic and Italian Renaissance; but even so classical an artist as Pilon could produce one of the masterpieces of late Gothic sculpture, the *Virgin of Sorrow* in the Louvre; a work, incidentally, that dramatizes the continuity that existed in religious sculpture between late Gothic and seventeenth-century Baroque.

A few examples of sixteenth- and seventeenth-century French sculpture should be mentioned as pertinent to the course of eighteenth-century sculpture, and in one or two instances, perhaps even to the sculpture of Houdon. Especially significant were the tomb sculptures, which testify not only to the growth of a new, classical-architectural tradition, but also, emerging directly from late Gothic, to a continuing fascination with the problem of the portrait. It was in the effigies of princes and prelates on medieval tombs that the strength of the French tradition of specific portraiture is most evident, a tradition that continued without interruption until the end of the eighteenth century. Pilon collaborated with Primaticcio on PILON the architectural-sculptural tomb of Henri II at Saint-Denis (1563–70), in which the kneeling figures of Henri and his queen, Catherine de Medici, surmount the recumbent corpses, the Fig. 3 *gisants*, rendered with gruesome fidelity. In the tomb of René de Châlons (*c.* 1550, church of Saint-Pierre, Bar-le-Duc), attributed to Ligier Richier, this accent on the macabre is carried RICHIER even further in the standing Death, to which cling shreds of flesh, horrible yet imbued with Fig. 1 life and hope in the gesture with which he holds up the heart of René to the forgiveness of God.

That the elegant elongation of Italian Mannerist figures had a particular appeal to French Renaissance sculptors is evidenced by Goujon's naiads from his *Fountain of the Innocents* (Paris, 1548–9), and the *Diana of Anet* (*c.* 1550, Louvre), associated with the circle, if not the GOUJON person, of Pilon. Even the theme of Diana and her nymphs, perhaps popularized by Cellini's Figs. 2, 4 *Nymph of Fontainebleau* (*c.* 1545), and by the Italian painters of the Fontainebleau School, was to have an unbroken popularity in French painting and sculpture until the end of the eighteenth century. Pilon was also a master of the portrait bust and medallion. His marble bust of a child in the Louvre is remarkable in French sculpture of the period for its serious but genuinely childlike quality.

During the first half of the seventeenth century French sculpture declined from the heights attained by Goujon and Pilon. While the tendency to import sculptors continued, now from Flanders as well as from Italy, none of these had the impact of Primaticcio and his school. The chief names are Simon Guillain, Jean Warin, Jacques Sarrazin, and the brothers François and Michel Anguier, all of whom continued to be influenced by Italian sculpture of the late Renaissance or early Baroque. Guillain's most notable surviving work is the life-size group GUILLAIN of Louis XIII, Anne of Austria, and the child to become Louis XIV, impressive examples of Fig. 6 seventeenth-century official portraiture in bronze (1647, Louvre). Warin continued the tradition of the bronze medallion, as his portrait of Cardinal Richelieu (Bibliothèque Mazarine, Fig. 5 Paris, *c.* 1640) continued and elaborated that of the portrait bust. Sarrazin, who spent some fifteen years in Rome during the last stages of Renaissance and the first of Baroque classicism, in effect created the sculptural style of Louis XIV, the style given authority by the founding of the French Academy, and opportunity by the enormous patronage of the king and the great nobles.

This style was the peculiarly French adaptation of Italian Baroque; in it the formal and emotional extremes of a Bernini were held in check by a precise and even historically-based classicism. The brothers Anguier also practised a less extreme version of the Baroque, in which the continuing force of late Renaissance classicism is clearly evident. The reign of Louis XIV, extending from 1643 to 1715, saw in painting, sculpture, and architecture, a continuing dialogue between Renaissance and Baroque classicism. The great commissions from the king for the Louvre and Versailles, and from those nobles who dared emulate the king, were composites of painting, sculpture, and architecture, formulated on the principles laid down by the Academy of Painting and Sculpture, which was established in 1648. This was the first of the specialized French Royal Academies, which within the next twenty years were to encompass all the arts and sciences. Like its prototypes, the Italian Academies that had grown up during the sixteenth century, the Academy of Painting and Sculpture in France originated as an attempt by the court artists to liberate themselves from the restrictions of the town guilds and also to stop the visual arts being thought of as mere crafts or trades. The timing was opportune since the idea of centralized institutions for the arts fitted well with the concepts of absolute rule generated by Richelieu and consolidated by Louis XIV's ministers, Mazarin and Colbert.

THE ACADEMY

By the end of the seventeenth century the Academy of Painting and Sculpture dominated the lives of artists, controlled their total education with a tightly prescribed curriculum based on the tradition of classical antiquity, established hierarchies through which the artist slowly advanced within the system, from *agréé*, to academician, to professor, to officer. Hierarchies were even established of suitable subjects for the artist, from noble historical and mythological themes down through portraiture to genre and still life. The royal commissions were transmitted through the Academy, and private commissions were certainly affected by the academic prestige of the individual artist.

In practice there was much more variety in painting, sculpture, and architecture than one might expect under so authoritarian a system. While the models for painting might be Raphael and Poussin, painters could not ignore the great Venetians or Rubens. When the favored students went to Rome to study ancient statuary they found themselves surrounded by the overwhelming sculptures of Bernini.

During the reigns of Louis XIV and Louis XV sculptors were engaged in decorative ensembles with painters and architects, a fact that conditioned style and frequently subject matter. One art necessarily affected another, although in French seventeenth- and eighteenth-century art, exterior architecture usually maintained a relatively classic simplicity and clarity contrasted with the pictorial elaboration of the interiors.

GIRARDON
Fig. 7

The three great sculptors of the later seventeenth century were François Girardon, Antoine Coysevox, and Pierre Puget. Girardon was the most consciously classical of the three. His group of *Apollo and the Nymphs of Thetis* (1666, Versailles), transferred in the later eighteenth century into a romantic rock grotto designed by Hubert Robert, was originally the central group in a series of three architectural niches. The figures are a fascinating pastiche of Roman sculpture and the paintings of Raphael and Poussin. The *Apollo* derives from the *Apollo Belvedere*, the nymphs are taken from Hellenistic prototypes, the idea and composition from Raphael's *Apollo and the Muses* and from the late classic paintings of

Fig. 8

Poussin. Girardon's *Rape of Persephone* (1677–79, Versailles) is a synthesis of Giovanni da Bologna's *Rape of the Sabines* and Bernini's *Persephone*, controlled again by the formal principles of Poussin.

COYSEVOX

Although Coysevox probably never visited Rome, whereas Girardon and most of the other major French sculptors of the seventeenth century did, his sculpture is closer to Bernini and Italian Baroque than is that of Girardon. Much of his best work is to be found in the decoration of the interiors of Versailles, most notably the equestrian relief of Louis XIV (c. 1678) in the Salon de la Guerre. Whereas Girardon in his equestrian portrait of Louis for the Place Vendôme, Paris (1663–99, destroyed in the French Revolution; bronze reduction at Versailles), had followed closely the classic repose of the Roman equestrian statue of Marcus Aurelius, Coysevox's *Louis XIV* is conceived in the tradition of Bernini. In fact, the closeness of the concept leaves little doubt that Coysevox had seen drawings or maquettes for Bernini's ill-fated equestrian portrait of the king (maquette, Borghese Gallery, Rome). The rider with rearing, rampant horse, conceived by Leonardo da Vinci in his *Sforza* monument, explored by Bernini in his *Constantine*, once more realized by Coysevox in his *Horses of Marly* (1702, Tuileries, Paris), further perfected by Guillaume I Coustou's *Horse Tamers* (1740–5, Tuileries, Paris), was finally almost liberated from earth in Falconet's *Peter the Great* (c. 1782, Leningrad).

Fig. 9

Fig. 18
Fig. 19
Fig. 35

Coysevox could achieve a sense of classical restraint when the project demanded it. Whereas Girardon's tomb of Richelieu (1675–94, Sorbonne, Paris) shows the cardinal on his deathbed supported and mourned by Virtues in a manner almost neo-classical when compared with Italian Baroque, the tomb of Mazarin by Coysevox, while more elaborate in its contrast of colored marbles and bronze, is also classical rather than Baroque in the balanced frontality of its organization and the serenity of the figures.

Fig. 10

Fig. 11

The range of Coysevox's achievement is so great that in one form or another it touches on most phases of eighteenth-century French sculpture with the exception of the extremes of rococo decoration. A late work such as *Marie-Adélaïde of Savoy as Diana* (1710, Louvre), based on the Hellenistic sculpture of *Diana with the Stag*, is rococo in its mannered charm, the delicate modeling of the draperies, the lightness of the movement. It provides an effective transition between the *Dianas* of the sixteenth and eighteenth centuries in France.

Fig. 15

In the last years of his life Coysevox devoted himself extensively to portrait busts. Girardon had executed some fine portraits, notably his less official characterizations of artists and men of letters, such as the painter, Pierre Mignard; but Coysevox was the finest portrait sculptor before Houdon. His portraits of Louis XIV, while necessarily official, are certainly the best sculptured likenesses of the king. *Le Grand Condé* (1688, Louvre) is a wild and savage interpretation. But it is in his informal studies, in which the man rather than the position is the theme, that he makes his unique contribution. Here he creates a new genre that is to mature in the eighteenth century. His portraits of the architect, Robert de Cotte (1704, Bibliothèque Sainte-Geneviève, Paris) and of himself (1678, Louvre), despite the necessary formula of the long, heavy, seventeenth-century perruque, show definite individuals caught informally at a specific moment. The question that now began to be asked was not, 'What is this man's station?', nor even, 'Who is this man?', but, 'What kind of a man is this?'

Fig. 12

Fig. 13

In contrast with Girardon and Coysevox, Pierre Puget was out of the main stream of French seventeenth-century sculpture. Much of his early life was spent in Italy, where his style was formed by the tradition of Michelangelo and Pietro da Cortona. His herm figures for the portal of the Hôtel de Ville at Toulon (1656) are close, in their sense of strain and inner conflict, to Michelangelo's *Slaves*. His *Milo of Croton* (1671–83, Louvre), a strange and immensely powerful sculpture, is Baroque in its outward emotion and its organization in diagonals, but still Michelangelesque in its violent tension of opposites. This work not only inspired Falconet's *morceau de réception* for the Academy in 1754, but influenced, more or less directly, half a dozen others.

PUGET

Fig. 14

Fig. 32

Puget's great relief sculpture of *Alexander and Diogenes* (1671–93, Louvre) is a curious, clumsy, and disturbing accretion of details from Roman triumphal arches. In its crowded and confused intensity it is a remarkable assimilation of late Roman sculpture and Baroque painting.

Fig. 16

Since the portrait busts of Coysevox, particularly the informal studies, his *Horses of Marly* and his *Marie-Adélaïde of Savoy as Diana*, effected the transition to the eighteenth century,

Fig. 18

it is appropriate that eighteenth-century sculpture should have been inaugurated in France by the brothers Guillaume and Nicolas Coustou, sons of Coysevox's sister; thus initiating the pattern of artistic dynasties so characteristic of the new century. The elder, Nicolas, belongs as well to the age of Louis XIV and was one of the earlier sculptors to go through the French Academy system, rising through the various stages of student, *Prix de Rome*, *agréé*, academician, to that of chancellor. His brother, Guillaume, was almost twenty years younger, but the brothers collaborated, notably on the *Apollo* and *Daphne* in the Louvre with Nicolas doing *Apollo* and Guillaume, *Daphne* (c. 1713–14). The two figures were inspired by the group by Bernini in Rome, and in turn, Nicolas' *Apollo* may have been the initial inspiration for Houdon's *Priest of the Lupercalia*.

Guillaume's *Maria Leczyńska as Juno* (c. 1726, Louvre), a companion piece to Nicolas' rather prosaic *Louis XV as Jupiter*, derives from Coysevox's *Marie-Adélaïde as Diana*, and thus belongs in the sequence of ideal-mythological portraits of noble ladies so popular in eighteenth-century painting and sculpture. Although elegant in the new mode, the handling of the draperies is somewhat more cumbersome than in the earlier work, perhaps appropriate to Juno *vis-à-vis* Diana. Guillaume's masterpiece is his version of the *Horse Tamers*

Fig. 19
(1740–5, Tuileries, Paris), based on the concept of Coysevox, but enlarging that concept with a new freedom, dramatic sweep, and naturalism. In his portraits he also continued

Fig. 22
the experiments of his uncle. His tomb of *Cardinal Dubois* (c. 1725, Saint-Roch, Paris), simplified to the single, kneeling figure, is a precise, even satiric characterization. The tradition of the informal portrait is exemplified in the sensitively observed, freely handled study of his brother, Nicolas, sketched in his working clothes (Louvre).

As the French Academy consolidated its position in the later seventeenth century, minutes of meetings were kept and catalogues (*livrets*) of the Salons—named after the *Salon carré* in the Louvre where they were held—began to be issued. Sculptors' and painters' *morceaux de réception*, the works required for acceptance into the Academy, have been preserved in the Louvre as a miniature history of eighteenth-century French art. Thus, even lesser artists begin to be better documented and, perhaps for this reason, perhaps because of the general expansion of French art as it gained maturity and independence, the artists of some quality seem to proliferate. Robert Le Lorrain's (1666–1743) relief of the *Horses of the Sun* (Hôtel de Rohan, Paris) is a unique work of wild energy, handled with all the freshness of a first, terra cotta maquette. With Le Lorrain's students, Jean-Baptiste Lemoyne (1704–78) and Jean-Baptiste Pigalle (1714–85), the main line of French sculpture continued. Lemoyne was the outstanding member of another distinguished family of French artists. While his uncle,

Jean-Baptiste I, was less noted, his father, Jean-Louis Lemoyne (1665–1755) was a fine portraitist, a transitional figure between Girardon, Coysevox, and his more talented son. Jean-

Fig. 17
Louis' bust of the architect, *J.-H. Mansart* (1703, Louvre), is one of the last, splendid exemplars of seventeenth-century Baroque portrait sculpture. Mansart is shown as a kingly figure, assured to the point of arrogance, whose powerful face is in no sense dominated by the elaborate swirl of perruque and draperies that encompass it. Jean-Louis' *Nymph of Diana* (1724, National Gallery, Washington) carries the concept of Coysevox's *Marie-Adélaïde as Diana* further in the direction of the rococo ideal of fluttering femininity. This ideal is per-

fected in the classic-mythological figures of Jean-Baptiste II, who in terms of his total work must rank as one of the greatest French sculptors of the eighteenth century. He is the century's master of the portrait bust before Houdon. In his portraits most of the questions on the nature of portrait sculpture were raised and many brilliantly resolved.

There are two problems central to the study of Jean-Baptiste II Lemoyne's large output of portrait busts, as they are to the study of Houdon. These are the problems of attribution and of reproduction. Since Lemoyne, like Houdon, portrayed many of the distinguished men and women of his time in remarkable characterizations, his busts have remained almost comparably popular; and consequently were reproduced many times, both by the artist himself and by others. The reproduction of portrait busts in different materials, terra cotta, plaster, bronze, or marble, began to be practised by Lemoyne on a large scale, particularly busts of men of letters, philosophers, and scientists who, with the emerging spirit of the French Enlightenment, became symbols of that spirit. Unfortunately, as in the case of Houdon, there are also many later reproductions of varying degrees of quality. Reproducing a portrait bust by taking a cast of an existing bust is not difficult and greatly complicates the problems of attribution.

In general Lemoyne's portraits share a quality of theatricality. His portraits of Louis xv, when compared with Coysevox's portraits of Louis xiv, reveal a greater elegance in concept and a sense of individual characterization suggested largely by the alert lift of the head. Studies of the dramatist, *Crébillon* (c. 1761, Dijon), and the actress *Mademoiselle Clairon* (1761, Comédie Française, Paris), are theatrical delights, and that of the painter, *Noël-Nicolas Coypel* (1730, Louvre) is a fascinating piece of bravura. Lemoyne most frequently sought the particular expression—in his men the smile, the knowing look, even the grimace— in his women, wherever appropriate, the sidelong glance, the coquettish turn of the head, anything to emphasize their womanliness.

Fig. 23
Fig. 24

During his long life Jean-Baptiste II achieved a position of great power. He was a favorite sculptor of Louis xv and, when Houdon first exhibited in the Salon of 1769, Lemoyne was Director of the Academy of Painting and Sculpture, the senior sculptor in the hierarchy. As a chief representative of the rococo in sculpture he came under attack from the classicists of the later century. They preferred an artist like Edmé Bouchardon (1698–1762), who adhered to classical antiquity. The art of Bouchardon illustrates how impossible it is to try to categorize French eighteenth-century sculpture sequentially, except in terms of the relative predominance of given tendencies at given moments. A contemporary of Lemoyne, he spent nine years in Rome and for the rest of his life represented the purist-classical opposition to the rococo. His portrait bust of *Philipp Stosch* (1727, Berlin-Dahlem Museum) is a remarkable exercise in antiquarianism and could be mistaken for a neo-classical sculpture of the end of the eighteenth century. On the other hand his marble bust of *Pope Clement VII* (1730, Prince Corsini, Florence) is an equally remarkable essay in precise naturalism within the tradition of Roman Baroque. Bouchardon's fountain on the Rue de Grenelle, Paris (c. 1739), although difficult to comprehend as a unit on the narrow street, is a sculptural-architectural organization of the greatest purity, with the severity of the architectural frame enlivened by the figures of *Seasons* and, below, by the famous frieze of abstractly composed putti. These, incidentally, are very much in the rococo spirit which Clodion continued to the end of the century. This quality is also apparent in Bouchardon's *Amor Carving a Bow from the Club of Hercules* (c. 1750, Louvre), whose erotic classicism anticipates comparable figures by Canova.

BOUCHARDON

Fig. 26

Fig. 28

Fig. 27

The three Adam brothers and René-Michel Slodtz (1705–64) (known as Michel-Ange) all came from dynasties of craftsmen-sculptors and represented, particularly Slodtz, the closest approximation of French eighteenth-century sculpture to the Roman Baroque. Lambert-Sigisbert Adam (1700–59) is best seen in his decorative Baroque fountain of *Neptune and Amphitrite* (c. 1740, Versailles) and Nicolas-Sébastien Adam (1705–78) in his tomb of Queen Catharina Opalinska (c. 1749, Notre-Dame de Bon Secours, Nancy). While Nicolas uses every conceivable device of Roman Baroque in this tomb—colored marble and bronze contrasts, illusionistic smoke effects, the sweeping diagonal of the figure group, the eternal pyramid—it is a tame accumulation of cliché accessories. However, it does illustrate the impact of seventeenth-century Roman tomb sculpture on the tombs of eighteenth-century France.

ADAM

Much more significant than the Adam brothers, although until recently little recognized in France, Michel-Ange Slodtz might almost be considered an Italian artist of the late Baroque. In his monuments to Archbishop Montmorin (1740–4, Cathedral, Vienne) and to

SLODTZ

5

Fig. 25
Fig. 29

ALLEGRAIN
Fig. 30

COUSTOU
Fig. 31

FALCONET

Fig. 32

Fig. 33

Fig. 35

CLODION
Fig. 34

Languet de Gergy (*c.* 1753, Saint-Sulpice, Paris), Slodtz brought to France two notable variants of the Roman Baroque tomb. The Montmorin monument is relatively restrained, balanced and frontalized, precise in the portrayal of living and dead archbishops. That of Languet de Gergy on the other hand is all elaborate allegory and coloristically contrasting materials, close to the excessive side of Roman Baroque. This side, combined with a peculiarly eighteenth-century elegance, is seen in Slodtz's *Saint Bruno* (1744, Saint Peter's, Rome), discussed below with Houdon's *Saint Bruno*.

The mid-century saw the emergence of a new generation of sculptors, contemporary with or somewhat senior to Houdon. It also saw the increasing impact of that remarkable group of thinkers and propagandists for the rights of man, the *philosophes* who created the French Enlightenment, revolutionized French ideas and strongly affected French and world history.

The norm of later rococo sculpture is represented by works such as the *Venus at the Bath* (1766, Louvre), or *Diana Surprised by Actaeon* (1777, Louvre), of Gabriel Allegrain (1710–1795); and the climax by the intimate *sculpture d'appartement* of Falconet and Clodion. Guillaume II Coustou (1716–77), son of Guillaume I, is noted principally for his Tomb of the Dauphin (1766 *et seq.*, Sens Cathedral), a work of little distinction in the design of the figures but remarkable in its total concept. It departs from the Baroque tomb tradition in that there is no effigy of the dauphin (son of Louis XV and father of Louis XVI), no accent on Death as a tangible presence, merely the four mourning figures of Religion, Immortality, Time, and Conjugal Love, grouped in the free-standing monument about the urns for the hearts of the dauphin and dauphine. The figures are cold and heavy in execution, but relatively restrained in emotion (Conjugal Love does agonize somewhat); the ensemble is remarkably suggestive of neo-classical historical classicism.

The two masters of rococo sculpture, Falconet and Clodion, were active in the second half of the century at a time when the decorative court tradition was losing ground in the face of the new accents on nature and neo-classicism. Étienne-Maurice Falconet (1716–91) was so devout an admirer of Puget that he adapted the *Milo of Croton* for his own *morceau de réception* to the Academy, only to be accused of plagiarism. This *Milo* (*c.* 1754, Louvre) is a brutal, powerfully Baroque sculpture, very different from the sweetly erotic marble nudes in which he shortly began to specialize. These latter arose not only from his own love for the subject expressed through the sensuous qualities of marble, but also from the patronage of Madame de Pompadour, a staunch supporter of the decorative, rococo approach until her death in 1764. In the latter part of the century a new class, the rich bourgeois, provided a significant audience for such *sculptures d'appartement*. These new patrons are important for the development of intimate sculpture, small figures, and decorative objects, and particularly for the increased interest in the portrait bust. Falconet's *Bather* and *Love Menacing* (both 1757, Louvre) demonstrate what became known as the Pompadour style. As director of the Sèvres porcelain factory together with the painter François Boucher, he was able to multiply such figures indefinitely for a broad public.

Falconet's selection by Catherine the Great of Russia to execute a monumental equestrian statue of Peter the Great for Saint Petersburg may seem surprising, but it can be understood as a result of the encyclopedist Diderot's influence on Catherine and Falconet's passion to be recognized by some great sculptural project. He spent the years 1766 to 1778 in Russia and produced one of the masterpieces in the history of the equestrian portrait. He not only solved brilliantly the technical problems of casting the rearing horse supported essentially on the hind legs and the sweeping tail, but he also created a superb image of Peter as Roman emperor, as a benevolent ruler rather than simply a conqueror.

Rococo art achieved a lovely close in sculpture—as it did in the paintings of Fragonard—with the little terra cotta figure groups of Claude Michel known as Clodion (1738–1814). Clodion's life-span closely parallels that of Houdon (1742–1828); they were even at the Academy of Rome during the same period. But no two sculptors could have been more

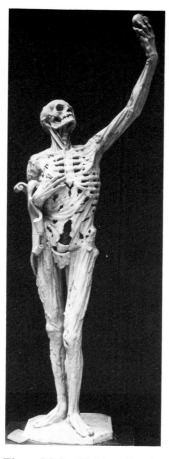

Fig. 1. Ligier Richier: *Death*,
from the Tomb of René de Châlons.
About 1550. Bar-le-Duc, Saint-Pierre

Fig. 2. Jean Goujon: *Two Naiads*, from the Fountain
of the Innocents, Paris. 1548–9

Fig. 3. Germain Pilon: *Gisants* (*Recumbent Corpses*), from the Tomb of Henri II and Catherine de' Medici. 1563–70.
Paris, Saint-Denis

Fig. 4. *Diana of Anet*. About 1550. Paris, Louvre

Fig. 5. Jean Warin: *Cardinal Richelieu*. About 1640. Paris, Musée
Jacquemart-André

Fig. 6. Simon Guillain: *Louis XIV
as a Child*. 1647. Paris, Louvre

Fig. 7. François Girardon: *Apollo and the Nymphs of Thetis*. 1666. Versailles

Fig. 8. François Girardon: *The Rape of Persephone*.
1677–9. Versailles

Fig. 9. Antoine Coysevox: *Louis XIV on Horseback*. Relief. About 1678.
Versailles

Fig. 10. François Girardon: *Tomb of Cardinal Richelieu.* 1675–7. Paris, Sorbonne

Fig. 11. Antoine Coysevox: *Tomb of Cardinal Mazarin.* 1689–93. Paris, Louvre

Fig. 12. Antoine Coysevox: *Le Grand Condé*. Detail. 1688. Chantilly, Musée Condé

Fig. 13. Antoine Coysevox: *Robert de Cotte*. Detail. 1707. Paris, Bibliothèque Sainte-Geneviève

Fig. 14. Pierre Puget: *Milo of Croton*. 1671–83. Paris, Louvre

Fig. 15. Antoine Coysevox: *Marie-Adélaïde of Savoy, Duchess of Burgundy, as Diana*. 1710. Paris, Louvre

Fig. 16. Pierre Puget: *Alexander the Great and Diogenes.* 1671–93. Paris, Louvre

Fig. 17. Jean-Louis Lemoyne: *Jules-Hardouin Mansart.* Detail. 1703. Paris, Louvre

Fig. 18. Antoine Coysevox: *Fame on Horseback.* 1702. Paris, Jardin des Tuileries

Fig. 19. Guillaume Coustou: *A Horse-Tamer.* 1740–5. Paris, Place de la Concorde

Fig. 20. Guillaume Coustou: *Daphne*. About 1713–14. Paris, Louvre   Fig. 21. Nicolas Coustou: *Apollo*. About 1713–14. Paris, Louvre

Fig. 22. Guillaume Coustou: *Tomb of Cardinal Dubois*. About 1725.
Paris, Saint-Roch

Fig. 23. Jean-Baptiste II Lemoyne: *Noël-Nicolas Coypel*. 1730. Paris, Louvre

Fig. 24. Jean-Baptiste II Lemoyne: *René Antoine Ferchault de Réaumur*. 1751. Paris, Louvre

Fig. 25. Michel-Ange Slodtz: *Tomb of Languet de Gergy*. Detail. About 1753. Paris, Saint-Sulpice

Fig. 26. Edmé Bouchardon: *Philipp Stosch*. 1727. Berlin-Dahlem, Staatliche Museen

Fig. 27. Edmé Bouchardon *Amor carving a Bow from the Club of Hercules*. About 1750. Paris, Louvre

Fig. 28. Edmé Bouchardon: *Summer*. After 1739. Paris, Fontaine de la rue de Grenelle

Fig. 29. Michel-Ange Slodtz: *St. Bruno*. 1744. Rome, St. Peter's

Fig. 30. Gabriel Allegrain: *Venus at the Bath*. 1766. Paris, Louvre

Fig. 31. Guillaume II Coustou: *Tomb of the Dauphin*. Detail. Begun 1766. Sens, Cathedral

Fig. 32. Etienne-Maurice Falconet: *Milo of Croton*. About 1754. Paris, Louvre

Fig. 33. Etienne-Maurice Falconet:
Love menacing. 1757. Paris, Louvre

Fig. 34. Clodion: *Amor and Psyche.* London, Victoria and Albert
Museum

Fig. 35. Etienne-Maurice Falconet: *Peter the Great on Horseback.* Completed 1782. Leningrad

Fig. 36. Jean-Baptiste Pigalle: *Mercury fastening his Sandal.* 1744. Paris, Louvre

Fig. 37. Jean-Baptiste Pigalle: *Love and Friendship.* 1758. Paris, Louvre

Fig. 38. Jean-Baptiste Pigalle: *Tomb of the Maréchal de Saxe.* 1753–76. Strasbourg, Saint-Thomas

Fig. 39. Jean-Baptiste Pigalle: *Voltaire*. 1776. Paris, Louvre

Fig. 40. Clodion: *Baron de Montesquieu*. 1783. Paris, Institut de France

Fig. 41. Pierre Julien: *Nicolas Poussin*. 1804. Paris, Louvre

Fig. 42. Félix Lecomte: *Jean Lerond d'Alembert*. 1808. Paris, Institut de France

Fig. 43. Jean-Baptiste Pigalle: *Denis Diderot*. 1777. Paris, Louvre

Fig. 44. Jean-Jacques Caffieri: *Jean de Rotrou*. 1783. Paris, Comédie Française

Fig. 45. Jean-Baptiste Pigalle: *Citizen (Self-Portrait)*, from the Monument to Louis XV. Rheims

Fig. 46. Augustin Pajou: *Comte de Buffon*. Detail. About 1775. Paris, Museum of Natural History

Fig. 47. Augustin Pajou: *Madame du Barry*. 1773. Paris, Louvre

Fig. 48. Félix Lecomte: *Queen Marie-Antoinette*. 1783. Versailles

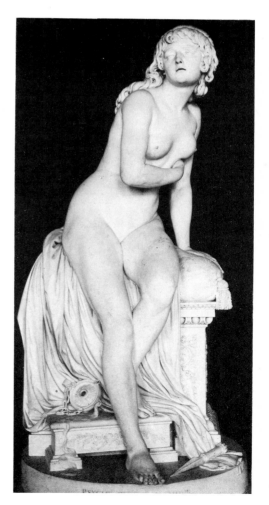

Fig. 49. Pierre Julien: *Girl with a Goat*. 1786–7. Paris, Louvre

Fig. 50. Augustin Pajou: *Psyche abandoned*. 1783–90. Paris, Louvre

Fig. 51. Charles-Louis Corbet: *Napoleon*. Detail. 1799. Lille, Musée des Beaux-Arts

Fig. 52. Claude Ramey: *Napoleon*. Detail. 1813. Paris, Louvre

Fig. 53. Joseph Chinard: *Madame Récamier*. 1802. Lyons, Musée des Beaux-Arts

Fig. 54. Joseph Chinard: *The Empress Joséphine*. 1805–6. Château de la Malmaison different. Clodion's career was devoted to the production of miniature terra cotta sculptures of nymphs, youths, satyrs, and children: *sculptures d'appartement*, figures pursued and pursuing, running, dancing, loving, and eternally filled with a spirit of laughter and abandon wonderfully communicated. Although they seemed out of step with the new seriousness of the reign of Louis XVI, with the new naturalism, the new morality, and the growth of neo-classicism, they were enormously popular during Clodion's lifetime and have continued to be so ever since. Clodion was capable of other things. He produced some impressive religious sculpture, and his statue of *Montesquieu* (1783, Institut de France) in d'Angiviller's series of Great Men, is one of the finest in the series, conceived entirely differently but inviting comparison with Houdon's *Seated Voltaire*.

Fig. 40

There remain two major sculptors other than Houdon to be discussed in this summary; and a number of lesser but still competent men to be mentioned. The first two are Jean-Baptiste Pigalle (1714–85) and Augustin Pajou (1730–1809). Pigalle, as a consequence of the popularity of his *morceau de réception*, the charming figure of *Mercury Refastening his Sandal* (1742, terra cotta, Metropolitan Museum, New York; 1744, marble, Louvre), attracted the patronage of Madame de Pompadour and for ten years produced allegories celebrating her substitution of *Amitié* for *Amour* in her relations with Louis XV. In these and other mythological subjects or portraits of the marquise there is, however, little of the decorative-erotic associated with the Pompadour style. There is rather a straightforward, even unflattering quality of unsentimental observation somewhat at odds with the rococo tradition, in which they supposedly belong. Even Pigalle's deservedly famous *Infant with a Cage* (1750, Louvre) renders the baby with a peculiar intensity of rapt attention reminiscent of Pilon, or Donatello, or Houdon.

PIGALLE

Fig. 36

Fig. 37

Nevertheless the patronage of the marquise and the king led to great commissions, notably the monument to the Maréchal de Saxe (1753–76, Saint-Thomas, Strasburg) and the monument to Louis XV (c. 1765, Place Royale, Reims). The tomb of the great marshal is one of the last and probably the most dramatic in the tradition of Bernini and Roman Baroque. With all its Baroque symbolism, its allegorical appurtenances, this is an impressive work, in which the proud, disdainful figure of the Field Marshal rises triumphantly above his conquered enemies, the open tomb, and Death himself. This is a powerful concept, superbly modelled and designed and placed within the church, all its diverse elements integrated with and under the control of the central figure. Although very different in its total structure, in concept it does have relationships with the French tombs of the Renaissance, such as that of Henri II and Catherine de Medici.

Fig. 38

Very much of the same ruthlessly realistic vision is the figure of the *Citizen* from the monument to Louis XV at Reims (the original statue of the king was destroyed). In the *Citizen*, one of the attendant figures, we have a full-length, nude self-portrait, depicted with a precision that makes it one of the great portraits of the century. It may well have been the recollection of this figure that prompted Pigalle, when given the commission for a statue of Voltaire, to conceive of the aged philosopher in the role of the *Dying Seneca*, naked but not unashamed. Despite the hostile criticism that greeted this interpretation, not to mention the embarrassment of the subject, it has great merit as a work of sculpture. It exemplifies the qualities of hard, direct observation, of uncompromising honesty of vision, which made Pigalle, like Diderot, like Rousseau, or like Voltaire himself, one of the most perceptive critics of the world—in his case specifically the art—that surrounded him.

Fig. 45

Fig. 39

While by no means so prolific a *bustier* as Jean-Baptiste II Lemoyne, Pajou, or Houdon, Pigalle's particular vision resulted in a number of the finest portrait busts of the century. This is particularly true of his terra cottas, a material in which he was able to achieve—like Clodion in his particular métier—the directness, freshness, and informality of a momentary mood or expression. His *Self-Portrait* (1780, Louvre) and the portrait of *Desfriches* (Museum, Orléans), which is shown together with the terra cotta of his servant, the negro,

Fig. 43

PAJOU

Fig. 50

Fig. 47

Fig. 46

CAFFIERI

Fig. 44

LECOMTE

Fig. 48

DEFERNEX

JULIEN

Fig. 46

Paul, have all the unselfconscious immediacy of Houdon's *Diderot*. In eighteenth-century France, as seldom elsewhere, the qualities of terra cotta as a medium for sculpture were fully realized, not only for maquettes but for finished works. Pigalle's *Diderot* in bronze (1777, Louvre), showing the *philosophe* as a somewhat older, heavier, more reflective individual than did Houdon in 1771, merits comparison with the earlier work as a superb portrait study.

Augustin Pajou (1730–1809) was a favorite sculptor of Madame du Barry and official sculptor of Louis XVI. His abilities as a decorative artist are apparent in his designs for the opera house at Versailles; and his prolific production included innumerable portrait busts, historical portraits, classical, mythological, and allegorical subjects. He adapted so easily to changing styles that his sculpture constitutes a one-man history of the rapidly changing scene from Louis XV to Napoleon. An early relief of the *Princess of Hesse-Homburg* (1761, Hermitage, Leningrad), still a student work, is for the time an unusually successful classical relief. The Versailles opera decorations are gay and flamboyant examples of late rococo; while the *Psyche Abandoned* (1783–90, Louvre) combines rococo sensuousness with the new sentimentality. *Maria Leczińska as Charity* (1769, Louvre), elaborately allegorical and delicately erotic, should be compared with the chastely neo-classical *Madame de Noailles* (1792, Duc de Mouchy, Paris). For the Salon of 1802 Pajou produced a literally neo-classical bust of *Caesar* (Senate, Paris).

In his portrait busts this same pattern of stylistic change can be followed from the delightful representation of *Madame du Barry* (1773, Louvre)—so different from Pigalle's honestly unflattering portrayal of *Madame de Pompadour*—to the equally charming though more vitally youthful eighteen-year-old *Madame Vigée-Lebrun* (1783, Private Collection, Paris), to the late bust of a *Young Girl* (1789, Private Collection, Paris), shown undraped, *à l'antique*. Of the men he portrayed, his teacher, *J.-B. Lemoyne* (1758, Louvre) is one of the most lively and personal, his *Buffon* (c. 1775, Museum of Natural History, Paris) the most dramatic. Pajou also carved the marble statue of *Buffon* for the Museum of Natural History (c. 1775), showing the great naturalist draped in a toga, very much *à l'antique*. In general, however, the portraits, both male and female—with a few notable exceptions—suffer from a certain similarity, suggestive of a formula. As the ranking sculptor of his time, Pajou received four of the commissions for the Great Men series, and produced respectable but generally not very inspired solutions. His statue of *Turenne* (1783, Versailles) seems to be attempting to outdo Houdon's *de Tourville* (1781, Versailles) in the elaboration of its seventeenth-century costume and accessories.

Many other sculptors of the later eighteenth century in France deserve further study. Jean-Jacques Caffieri (1725–92), member of a family of sculptors and goldsmiths, slightly senior to Houdon, was also a specialist in the portrait bust. In this field he frequently achieved brilliant, dramatic effects, and, in fact, became almost the official portraitist of the Comédie Française. His posthumous portrait of the actor *Jean de Rotrou* (1783, Comédie Française, Paris) is a marvellously caught piece of melodramatic acting; his study of the astronomer, *Pingré*, might also be that of a character actor. Felix Lecomte (1737–1817), favorite portraitist of Marie-Antoinette, would probably have been somewhat annoyed if he had known how often his portrait of the queen (1783, Versailles) is attributed to Houdon.

Jean-Baptiste Defernex (1729–83) particularly warrants a re-evaluation for his straightforward, unadorned portrait busts, in which the characteristic, unflattering presentation of the model, the subordination of the torso, and even details like the undercutting of the eyes, anticipate Houdon's approach. Pierre Julien (1731–1804) pursued a generally successful career within the academic system, being entrusted as evidence of his prestige—and seniority—with three of the Great Men statues. These statues, incidentally, provide an interesting document of the gradually increasing classicism at the end of the century. Pajou's statue of *Buffon* (c. 1775), which is not in the series, showing the great naturalist as a half-nude Roman athlete, was, to say the least, unusual at this date. It had, nevertheless, general approval, although not from Buffon himself. Pigalle's decrepit old *Voltaire* (*c.* 1776) in the nude was, as noted, treated with derision, perhaps because of its painful exposure of an aged, unheroic body. Houdon, in his *Seated Voltaire* (1781), settled for a somewhat ambiguous but reflective *robe de chambre* with classical overtones. He also wished to portray *Washington* (1785 *et seq.*) draped *à l'antique*, but the general showed no enthusiasm.

Of d'Angiviller's Great Men series proper, now divided between Versailles, the Louvre, and the Institute of France, Clodion's original concept of *Montesquieu* (1783) was *à l'antique* but he modified it in the face of adverse criticism. Julien's *La Fontaine* is in modern dress of the seventeenth century; his *Poussin* (*c.* 1789) is half-draped in a rather peculiar concept of a toga; and Jean-Baptiste Stouf's *Montaigne* (1800) is virtually nude. By 1808 Canova could present Napoleon as an Olympian Mars, completely nude.

Julien is principally remembered for his statue of a *Girl with a Goat* (1786–7, Louvre) designed originally for Marie-Antoinette's Rambouillet dairy. This is a rather heavy, rustic piece, with the maiden modestly shielding her charms in a manner appropriate to the new puritanism of the court of Louis XVI. She has some affinity to Pajou's *Psyche* (against whose 'immodesty' there was an outcry), and is principally of interest as representing a norm of proto-neo-classicism; as well as for the romantic rocky grotto, conceived by the painter, Hubert Robert, that originally framed her.

Mouchy, Moitte, Boizot, Stouf, the brothers Deseine, are sculptors little regarded today except as showing the varying stylistic trends that marked the last years of the old regime. With Charles-Louis Corbet (1758–1808), Denis-Antoine Chaudet (1763–1810), and Joseph Chinard (1756–1813), although all of them were formed under the old, royal, academic tradition, the triumph and nature of neo-classical sculpture under Napoleon became evident. Corbet's portrait bust of *Napoleon* (1799, Museum, Lille) is a sensitive, even inspired work, more romantic than classic in its interpretation. With Chinard the official, Napoleonic, neo-classical bust was established; frontalized, blank eyes, coldly carved, set on a solid, herm block base. An exception to this formula is Chinard's delightfully sentimentalized portrait of the coyly modest *Madame Récamier* (1802, Museum, Lyon), which reveals how much of the rococo spirit survived in the seeming austerity of neo-classicism. Chaudet, a painter and talented draughtsman as well as a sculptor, carried a strong linear quality into his decoratively handled classic myths. His *Eros and Butterfly* (plaster 1802, marble finished after his death, Louvre) is close in its adolescent grace to the rococo-classical side of Canova, and even closer to the more linear classicism of the Dane, Bertel Thorvaldsen (1770–1844). With the Italian, Antonio Canova (1757–1822), Napoleon's favorite sculptor, French sculpture was dominated by a foreign artist for the first time since the sixteenth century and the School of Fontainebleau.

Fig. 39
Fig. 111

Fig. 40

Fig. 41

Fig. 49

CORBET
CHAUDET
CHINARD

Fig. 51

Fig. 54

Fig. 53

JEAN-ANTOINE HOUDON

ON June 24, 1784, the Assembly of the State of Virginia in the United States of America voted for a commission of a marble statue of General George Washington. Since there was then no sculptor in the United States who could be entrusted with the commission, Benjamin Harrison, Governor of Virginia, transmitted it to Thomas Jefferson in Paris. Jefferson, who was American Minister to France between 1785 and 1789, following Benjamin Franklin, wrote Harrison in January 1785: 'There could be no question raised as to the sculptor who should be employed, the reputation of Mons. Houdon, of this city, being unrivalled in Europe.'[1] Houdon's pre-eminence specifically within the genre of portrait sculpture, established within his lifetime, seems never to have declined, and only briefly gone out of fashion.[2] It is conceivable that his continuing reputation is in part due to his sitters, the great individuals of the eighteenth century who created the systems and attitudes of the modern world— Voltaire, Rousseau, Diderot, Buffon, Franklin, Jefferson, and Washington. On the other hand, though his most notable subjects were all portrayed by other artists it is the image created by Houdon that persists.

The life of Houdon includes little of drama or the spectacular. He simply worked prodigiously, creating remarkable sculptures and interpreting the great figures of his age in a way rarely if ever equalled by any other sculptor. He advanced slowly but steadily through the system of the Royal Academy of Painting and Sculpture. He married late but apparently successfully and produced three lovely daughters, who also seem to have married well.[3]

Although Houdon's stature as a sculptor was soon recognized, he seems in his personal life to have been simple and even uneducated. His concerns, as expressed in his infrequent letters, had largely to do with day-to-day matters of commissions, finance, hope for recognition, and rivalry with other artists.

HOUDON'S EARLY LIFE

JEAN-ANTOINE HOUDON was born on March 25, 1741, at Versailles, the son of Jacques Houdon and Anne Rabache.[4] Jacques Houdon came from peasant stock, and Anne's father and brothers were gardeners in the parks of Versailles. Thus the sculptor did not have the advantage of belonging to one of those great dynasties of sculptors, such as the Lemoynes, the Coustous, and the Adams, who dominated so much of eighteenth-century French sculpture. Jacques Houdon at the time of his son's birth was a simple concierge at the Versailles *hôtel* of the Comte de Lamotte, controller-general of the king's parks. Of Jacques' three sons and four daughters, only Jean-Antoine, the fourth child, achieved fame as an artist, although the eldest son, Jacques-Philippe, did have some reputation as a designer and decorator. Since Jacques-Philippe served his apprenticeship in the decorative arts with the sculptor, Michel-Ange Slodtz, he may have had some influence in Jean-Antoine's choice of a career.

The determining factor, however, was the fortunate accident that in 1749 the Comte de Lamotte's house in Paris was leased to the Crown to serve as the *École des élèves protégés*, a highly select school for those students of the Academy who had taken a first prize in painting or sculpture and were preparing for a sojourn at the French Academy in Rome. Jacques Houdon was permitted to continue as concierge of the new school, and as a consequence Jean-Antoine literally grew up among artists. By 1756 Houdon, officially enrolled in the school of the Royal Academy of Painting and Sculpture, received a third prize in sculpture; and in 1761 at the age of twenty, a first prize for a bas-relief entitled *La Reine de Saba apportant des présents à Salomon*. His principal master was René-Michel (known as Michel-Ange) Slodtz, but he also worked with other academicians such as Jean-Baptiste Lemoyne and Jean-Baptiste Pigalle. The award of first prize enrolled him in the élite group of six students at the *École des élèves protégés* for the years 1761–4 before he went to Rome.[5] The curriculum included not only the study of techniques (for the sculptors particular attention was paid to the carving of marble), but also lectures on history and mythology designed to enlarge the cultural background of the students, particularly for the period of classical antiquity.[6]

When Houdon began his studies in sculpture under the system of the Academy, he was set upon a course already rigidly defined, dominated by its French exemplar, but practised throughout Europe. In fact, his life was lived within this system, as was that of almost every artist who hoped to gain patronage or to advance in any manner. Before proceeding to Rome in 1764 on his *Prix de Rome* fellowship, he had been studying at the *Académie Royale de peinture et de sculpture* and its élite offshoot, the *École des élèves protégés*, for some eight years. During much of this period, according to the prescribed system, he worked as a student apprentice in the studios of several of his academician-sculptor masters. Although Michel-Ange Slodtz is the only name mentioned in surviving documents, the pattern of teaching within the Academy, with its regular rotation of professors, exposed the artist to the works and ideas of other sculptors and painters; as visits to the Louvre and other royal and private collections exposed him to works of art from other countries and past traditions. Nevertheless, it must be emphasized that nothing is known of Houdon's personal style until late in his stay at Rome. All the earlier student works, as might be expected, have disappeared, even his *Queen of Sheba*, for which he had received the first prize in 1761.

FEW documents survive from the Roman sojourn either; but these, together with the sculptures of the period that have come down to us, are crucial in their indications of the sculptor's training, his talents, and his specific interests. There are five surviving statues, some in different versions, known from the Roman period. These are: the *Vestal*, c. 1767–8 (of this there are several examples in different materials, which may be later replicas by the artist of the original statue); *L'Écorché* (the *Anatomical Figure*), 1766; *Saint Bruno*, 1766–7, Santa Maria degli Angeli, Rome (reduced plaster sketch, Schlossmuseum, Gotha); *Saint John the Baptist*, 1766–7, plaster sketch, Villa Borghese, Rome (plaster sketch of head, Gotha); *Priest of the Lupercalia*, c. 1768, Gotha. Other works, such as the *Peasant Girl of Frascati* (Gotha), recorded in the Salon of 1769, and two heads of young men in the Salon of 1771, may very well date from the Roman period.[7]

The French *Prix de Rome* fellows were required to make copies of classical works of art as part of their training and also in order to enrich the collections of the French Crown. The *Vestal* as well as a lost *Centaur* would probably come under this category, but what is notable in the *Vestal* is how freely Houdon seems to have interpreted his mandate. Throughout his life he returned periodically to themes from classical myth or history, but he almost invariably treated these in a personal manner owing more to the spirit of classical art than to its surface appearance.

The *Vestal* illustrates a classical thread that runs through Houdon's sculptures, although it is frequently lost sight of in the emphasis on his achievement as a portrait sculptor; in fact, this classicism contributes to the quality of many of his portrait busts. The *Vestal* also illustrates his tendency to return to a subject at different stages of his career; sometimes simply producing new casts in different materials, but frequently, as in this case, playing subtle variations on a theme and from time to time restudying it to create a new work.

Although the first known mention of the *Vestal* is in 1774 it seems certain that Houdon's original version dates from his Roman years. He first exhibited a bronze version in the Salon of 1777 (No. 255). The entry in the catalogue (*livret*) of the Salon includes the note: 'A Vestal in bronze, the idea is taken after a marble which is to be seen in Rome, popularly known as Pandora, this figure of 23 inches is intended to serve as a night lamp.' The antique prototype may be identified as a statue of *Psyche* in the Capitoline Museum.[8] From this date forward different versions of this small *Vestal* in various materials are mentioned frequently in catalogues and other lists—evidence of its continuing popularity.[9] Why Houdon should have delayed exhibiting the *Vestal* in the Salon until 1777 is not known, but there is nothing mysterious about the fact. This is a small sculpture, a student work, specifically a free copy from the antique; and the artist was obviously more interested in showing his new works after his first Salon of 1769. Although he sold plasters and terra cottas of the *Vestal*, he exhibited it only after he had cast it in bronze and then, obviously thinking of it essentially as a decorative piece, with the canny note that it could serve as a night lamp. But this little piece is perhaps more significant than even Houdon realized at the time. Even if it is not the earliest surviving work by the sculptor, it embodies features that make it appropriate to be the first discussed.

The small *Vestal* survives in several examples in different materials, plaster, marble, terra cotta and bronze. A plaster in the Frick Art Museum, Pittsburgh, Pa., includes a small triangular altar placed against the right leg. Gabriel de Saint-Aubin, whose drawings in the margins of his copies of the Salon *livrets* provide an invaluable record of these exhibitions, drew the *Vestal* in the 1777 Salon with this altar. On the other hand a terra cotta in the Fig. 55   Wildenstein Gallery, New York, signed on the front of the base in cursive script, *houdon. f.* but not dated, does not include the altar. Neither does the antique *Psyche* (popularly or vulgarly known as *Pandora*) in the Capitoline Museum; so we may assume the terra cotta to be closer to Houdon's original model, although the cursive signature is more common in his works after 1780. All of this confirms—what we know to be the fact—that the artist continued to make replicas of the *Vestal*, as he did of many other sculptures, throughout his life.[10]

In all known versions of this *Vestal* the figures are to all intents identical. The bases vary—the terra cotta square, the plaster oval, and the bronzes circular—as does the disposition of the libation bowl. In all versions she holds the bowl with her hands covered by drapery, high against her breast; but in the plaster the bowl is more completely covered by the drapery than in the other versions. The weight rests on her right leg, over which the drapery falls in vertical, columnar folds. The left leg is bent to reveal its form through the garment. The uncovered head is slightly inclined to the left, the eyes blank, the features delicately classic; the hair, parted in the center, is combed back softly over the ears; the nose is Grecian and somewhat pronounced, the mouth small with full lips and the chin fully rounded. In every way the face and the figure conform to their classic prototype, but they transcend it in quality. The Hellenistic original is a rather dull and inferior work, upon which Houdon has improved incredibly, retaining a specific classic spirit while giving to his version a rococo delicacy and femininity. Even the draperies in his *Vestal* are thin, structural and form-revealing in a manner that transcends his prototype.

A plaster *Vestal* listed in the inventory of the Schlossmuseum at Gotha has been lost or mislaid or shattered; but it may be assumed to have been of the type under discussion. The collection of Houdon sculptures in the Gotha Museum is of crucial importance, since it includes a number of unique or initial versions of some of the earliest works. The Duke of Saxe-Gotha, Houdon's first important patron, not only ordered many portrait busts and commissioned the first *Diana*, but also bought from the artist's studio most of his original plasters from the Roman period or immediately thereafter. These included not only the small full-length *Vestal*, but also a bust of a *Vestal*, the so-called *Peasant Girl of Frascati*, *Saint Bruno*, a head of *Saint John the Baptist*, the *Priest of the Lupercalia*, *L'Écorché*, and the life-sized *Morpheus*, executed *c.* 1769–70, shortly after the artist's return to Paris.

Fig. 56   The plaster bust of a *Vestal*, which differs from the small figure in that the head is covered, may also be assumed to be a copy or adaptation of an ancient bust, made while in Rome. The features are, if anything, more immaculately classic than those of the figure; the irises and pupils of the eyes are lightly indicated in the manner that became customary in Roman sculpture during the reign of Hadrian. The head is frontalized, slightly inclined, the eyes wide and unfocused, the features abstractly idealized. All elements make this one of the most impressive recreations of an ancient priestess or goddess from the hand of any eighteenth-century sculptor. Houdon obviously kept the terra cotta model or the plaster moulds of this work, since much later he made an almost identical marble, the bust now in the Louvre, signed and dated: *houdon f. 1788*. The marble differs in small details—the torso is slightly lengthened; there are adjustments in the drapery; the base is square rather than round. The most important change is that the eyes are now completely blank in the manner favored by the neo-classicists at the end of the eighteenth century. The square base was also more favored at this time. It may be that it was Houdon's consciousness of changing styles which inspired him to bring out this convincing demonstration of his own prior classicism.

The *Peasant Girl of Frascati*, from its title, would seem to derive from the Italian sojourn and also to be a specific portrait. In fact, like the bust of the *Vestal*, it is an idealized classical head, in its abstract chastity a *Diana* or one of her nymphs. If it was a portrait of a peasant girl from Frascati, what caught the artist's attention was undoubtedly the strongly classic features, the reminiscence of antiquity in a contemporary peasant. The form of the bust, with nude, abbreviated torso, frontalized, *à l'antique*, is again adapted from one of the innumerable ancient portrait busts to be seen in the Capitoline Museum in Rome. The eyes are once more lightly incised; the hair is pulled back tightly and fastened at the back with an elaborate ornament. Here, as in the *Vestals*, Houdon already demonstrates his manner of modelling the hair to suggest its soft, natural mass.

The belief that the sculptor saw in this bust a generalized study from the antique is supported by the fact that he later repeated it twice in marble, with the lightly sketched eyes of the original abandoned, as in the marble bust of a *Vestal*, in favor of the blank eyes of the neo-classical ideal. Although the two marble versions of the *Peasant Girl* are signed and dated respectively: Houdon Sculpsit 1774 (Cognacq-Jay Museum, Paris), and: HOUDON. F. 1775. (Hermitage Museum, Leningrad), and were unquestionably made in those years, they are here grouped with the plaster bust, since they are virtually exact replicas. The marbles reveal better than the somewhat worn plaster the delicate precision and abstract beauty of the portrayal.

Still another classical bust should be grouped with these first works of Houdon, even though its history and provenance are somewhat uncertain.[11] This is the so-termed head of a *Roman Youth*, signed and dated: HOUDON F. 1775. Despite the broken nose—which may enhance its air of antiquity—this is an authentic early work by the sculptor; and contemporary references relate it to the Roman period. Whereas the busts already discussed are frontalized, the torso of the youth is tilted and the head is turned to his right. The principal difference lies in the treatment of the hair. The hair of the *Peasant Girl* and her marble replicas is pulled back and lightly rendered; that of the youth is a dense mass of curls encircled by myrtle (?) leaves. The treatment of the hair is close to that of Houdon's *Morpheus*, of which he exhibited the large plaster in the Salon of 1771 (No. 279) and a reduced marble in the Salon of 1777 (No. 256). Even closer is the treatment of the hair of the youth in the group of *Le Baiser donné* (1778, New York), which is encircled by a plain band.

On first examination *L'Écorché*—the *Flayed Man*—the famous anatomical model, of which casts and copies have been used in art schools in Europe and America for the last two hundred years, is a dramatic contrast to the *Vestal*. The origins of this remarkable work are known in some detail through the circumstance that a friend of Houdon, Christian von Manlich, a German artist at the French Academy in Rome, kept a journal, in which he described how it came into existence.[12] In 1766 Houdon obtained an impressive commission for an artist who was still technically a student. André Le Masson, the French prior of the Carthusian church, Santa Maria degli Angeli in Rome, selected him to create two monumental sculptures, one of Saint Bruno, patron saint of the Carthusians, and the other of Saint John the Baptist.[13] Charles Natoire, director of the Academy, wrote on July 16, 1766, to the Marquis de Marigny, Protector of the Academies of Painting, Sculpture, and Architecture, and *Directeur-Général des Bâtiments* for the French Crown. In his letter Natoire described Houdon's commission

Fig. 57

PEASANT GIRL

Figs. 62–3
Plate 2

ROMAN YOUTH
Fig. 64, Plate 3

Fig. 65

Fig. 86
L'ÉCORCHÉ
Fig. 58,
Plates 4–5

Figs. 59–60

with obvious pride: 'I very much approved of his idea, assuring him of the merit of the subject he had chosen: so that the young sculptor has started to work and has made a very good model, which he is now enlarging.' Thus these two sculptures were well under way in the middle of 1766. In the same year Christian von Manlich described in his journal how he went with Houdon to the hospital of Saint-Louis des Français, where the surgeon Séguir, instructed them in anatomy from the corpses. Houdon, according to von Manlich, devoted his time to the modeling of an anatomical figure as a study for his *Saint John*. The work was highly praised by Séguir as well as by other artists and *amateurs*. The latter, declaring it to be the finest anatomical model ever made, persuaded the sculptor to cast it in plaster and to make several copies. This was the origin of *L'Écorché*, which certainly did become the outstanding and most admired anatomical model in the history of sculpture.

On February 11, 1767, Natoire wrote again to Marigny, praising the figure, referring to its relationship to the *Saint John the Baptist*, and requesting permission to buy a cast for the Academy at Rome, so that Houdon might derive a little profit from his experiment. Marigny duly granted this permission. Houdon's anatomical figure is so generally known in all languages under its French name, *L'Écorché*, that it seems reasonable to continue to use it. The figure and the circumstances of its creation as an intensive preliminary study for the *Saint John the Baptist* are the first indications of the artist's almost fanatical devotion to qualities of precise realism. In his portraits we know that it was his habit wherever possible to take life-masks and to make exact measurements. For the posthumous busts of Jean-Jacques Rousseau and Mirabeau he made death-masks. Thus, *L'Écorché*, quite literally based

Fig. 58   on muscle-by-muscle detail studies of dissected corpses, would seem to represent the opposite pole to the generalized, idealized *Vestal* taken from the classical model. But it is not its fidelity to nature that makes it a work of art. The figure is depicted striding slowly, the left arm hanging loosely by its side, the right arm outstretched in a gesture of blessing—or of command. The total pose including the outstretched arm is carried into the surviving version

ST. JOHN   of *Saint John the Baptist*, a figure of immense authority and repose. *Saint John* has all those
Fig. 59, Plate 6   attributes of strength and withdrawal associated with Greek art of the fifth century B.C. It has been related to the *Christ* of Michelangelo, and it is perfectly possible that Houdon was influenced by the *Christ*, which he must have seen and studied in Rome, and of which Michel-Ange Slodtz made a copy. A better prototype is the Roman statue of *Augustus Imperator*, or even such a work as the *Doryphoros* of Polykleitos, Roman copies of which were available. *L'Écorché* anticipates and defines the classical pose of the *Saint John*, but its precisely realistic anatomical depiction as a flayed figure adds a dimension of tragedy. One is reminded of

Fig. 1   Ligier Richier's statue on the tomb of René de Châlons.

L'Écorché and the *Vestal*, while representing in one sense extreme contrasts in the talents of the young sculptor, both illustrate the controlling force of classical art. This is what one might expect of an artist, working in Rome, whose training had so largely been dedicated to the ideal of antiquity. The fact still needs emphasis, since Houdon is not traditionally thought of as an artist exemplifying this ideal. Yet it can be demonstrated to permeate much of his sculpture, yielding at times and in specific projects to rococo flourish or to realist precision. Houdon's classicism, growing out of the Renaissance as well as deriving directly from antiquity, evinces a quality more subtle than most late eighteenth-century historical neo-classicism, a quality at times surprisingly close to the spirit of classical idealism.

The *Saint John the Baptist* was never carved in marble, perhaps because the sculptor's four years at the Academy in Rome were over before he could complete it, and he seems to have been eager to return to Paris.[14] The plaster was installed in a niche in Santa Maria degli Angeli, where it remained until it was accidentally broken and destroyed in 1894. This original plaster, approximately the same size as the *Saint Bruno* (*c.* 10 feet high), was one of the most monumental figures created by Houdon. Fortunately we have a good idea of its

Fig. 59   appearance and quality from a reduced but still life-size plaster, now in the Villa Borghese in Rome, and from a drawing by the artist Saint-Aubin in the catalogue of the 1769 Paris Salon. The destroyed *Saint John* and the reduced plaster displayed in the 1769 Salon differed from the first version of the *Écorché* and from the Villa Borghese plaster of *Saint John* in that the right arm, rather than being stretched outward and forward, curves up over the head. A bronze version of *L'Écorché* created in 1792, now in the École des Beaux-Arts in Paris, repeats this gesture. There is also an over life-size plaster head of *Saint John* in the museum at Gotha, which suggests the dimensions of the original.

Plate 4a

The *Saint Bruno* in the church of Santa Maria degli Angeli is Houdon's most impressive and monumental surviving religious sculpture, and one of the finest religious works of the eighteenth century.[15] Michel-Ange Slodtz had created a *Saint Bruno* for Saint Peter's Basilica in 1744, and a comparison of the two works reveals the particular quality of the younger sculptor's achievement. Slodtz' sculpture, one of his masterpieces, is in the Baroque tradition of Bernini. The saint, founder of the Carthusian Order, is seen at the moment when he refuses the bishopric which Pope Urban II wished to confer on him, in order that he may devote himself to his Order and to a life of contemplation. He shrinks dramatically away from the mitre and crozier offered him by the putto-angel, one hand in a gesture of refusal, the other indicating the skull, the *memento mori* symbolizing the contemplative life. The event is dramatized with twisting diagonals and swirling draperies in the Baroque manner still very much alive in Rome in the mid-eighteenth century. Houdon dispenses with accessories and dramatic movement or moment, and emphasizes the generalized quality of contemplation, the saint's robe falling in simplified, vertical folds, his expressive hands folded quietly over his chest, his head bent, his eyes downcast. Whereas there is a family resemblance in the shaven heads and the gaunt, ascetic features of both figures, the saint of Slodtz is delicate, almost feminine, that of Houdon is ascetic and masculine. In fact, a comparison of the head of Houdon's *Saint Bruno* with that of *L'Écorché* reveals how closely he followed the head structure and features of the flayed man. Houdon's *Saint Bruno* may again be said to exemplify qualities of classic withdrawal, but there is here an intensity appropriate to the portrayal of revealed religion. An analogy to his interpretation might be found in some of Zurbarán's paintings of monks, although it might also be related, without predicating any direct influence, to early Gothic French cathedral sculptures.

ST. BRUNO
Fig. 60, Plate 7

Fig. 29

The other statue probably executed in Rome is the *Priest of the Lupercalia*. This small work some three feet high, survives in a plaster at Gotha. In a list *c.* 1784 Houdon also refers to a version of the *Priest* presented as his *morceau d'agréé* for the Academy which was [later] cast in bronze.[16] The subject would suggest that it is a copy after an antique model, but the exact source has not been identified. In any event it is undoubtedly a very free interpretation, and again contrasts with Houdon's other Roman sculptures.

PRIEST
Fig. 61, Plate 8

On the feast day of the god, Lupercus (Pan), his priests would race through the streets about the Palatine hill, wielding bloody whips cut from the skins of goats sacrificed at his altar. It was believed that women struck with the whips could be rendered fertile. Houdon's *Priest* is a study in violent motion suggestive of the frenzy imbued by the ritual. His expression is one of drugged, ecstatic joy. The pose can be related to ancient works such as the Borghese warrior, but it is closer to the *Apollo* in Bernini's group of *Apollo and Daphne*. Rome in the eighteenth century was still dominated by the sculptural tradition of Bernini and, despite the wide divergence in their styles, there can be no doubt that Houdon studied the works of his great predecessor. Perhaps closest of all as a prototype is Nicolas Coustou's *Apollo*, dated 1713–14, from his and his brother Guillaume's group of *Apollo and Daphne*, now in the Louvre. This group, which Houdon could have known before he went to Rome, also derives from that of Bernini.

Thus in the few works that survive from Houdon's years of study in Rome can be seen not only complete control of his medium, but a wide range of experiment, ranging through precise realism, classic idealism, and Baroque expression. The only curious fact is that there are no portraits recorded, unless the *Peasant Girl of Frascati* can be so considered. It may seem strange that this master of portrait sculpture should have recorded no portraits before 1769, when he was twenty-eight years old. The explanation, however, is not difficult to find. Most of his subjects would have been prescribed by the curriculum at the French Academy in Rome. Also, when Houdon returned to Paris in 1768, he was still hoping to make his reputation as a sculptor of grand themes taken from history, religion, or classical mythology. These were the themes designated by the academic system as the noblest pursuits of the artist, the themes thought to lead most directly to recognition by posterity, not to mention that they were the most profitable for the artist. Subjects in painting and sculpture were severely categorized by the Academy, with the portrait down the list somewhere with the still life. Houdon became a portrait sculptor in part because of the shrinking opportunities for large-scale subject sculpture during the eighteenth century. We know that he was continually seeking large-scale commissions and, throughout his life, whenever he referred to his own sculptural achievements, it was usually the few statues, such as the *Diana* or *L'Écorché* or *Saint Bruno* that he singled out.

THE SALON OF 1769

HOUDON returned to Paris in November 1768, as soon as his mandatory four years at the Academy in Rome were completed. Many young French academicians, caught in the spell of Rome and antiquity, asked for extensions of their terms, and some, following the examples of Poussin and Claude Lorrain, lived out their lives in Rome. But Houdon seemed anxious to get back to France as soon as possible, perhaps concerned with the necessity of beginning his independent career after his years as a scholarship student. The sculptor, it must be remembered, had no independent means, and may already have been faced with the problem of contributing to the support of his parents and sisters.

In order to be eligible to exhibit at the Academy's biennial Salons he had to apply for and be accorded the status of *agréé* of the Academy. This was vital, since these Salons were almost the only means a young artist had of placing his works before the public and, most important, the controllers of royal patronage. Houdon was accepted without difficulty on July 23, 1769, and made his first submissions to the Salon that opened on August 25, 1769.[17]

In 1769, when Houdon became an *agréé*, Jean Baptiste II Lemoyne was director of the Academy of Painting and Sculpture, having succeeded François Boucher in 1768. Allegrain and Pajou were professors, Caffieri, *adjoint à professeur*. Huès, Mouchy, and Dumont (largely forgotten today) were Academicians; Berruer, Gois, Lecomte, and Monnot were *agréés*. There were of course other senior sculptors who did not exhibit that year, such as Pigalle, busy with his mausoleum of the Maréchal de Saxe, and Falconer, in Russia working on his statue of Peter the Great. Among painters, Boucher, former director, led the list with seven works. Joseph-Marie Vien was professor, Jean-Baptiste-Siméon Chardin was counsellor and treasurer of the Academy; Georges de la Tour was counsellor. Among recognizable Academicians were Perronneau, Drouais, le Prince, Guérin, and, decidedly, Hubert Robert, friend of Houdon from Rome, who presented thirteen identified paintings, principally classical landscapes, and two groups of 'plusieurs autres Tableaux d'Architecture, & Monumens antiques de Rome . . .' and 'plusieurs Dessins coloriés faits en Italie'. Hubert Robert brought significance to landscape because his subject was the noble theme of classical ruins. Chardin, most highly regarded today, had a solid reputation during his lifetime, despite his preference for the lowly forms of still life and genre. But it was another *agréé*, Jean-Baptiste Greuze (1725–1805), extolled by Diderot during his years as critic of the Salon, whose sentimental narratives of virtue rewarded, or corrupted, caught the imagination of the generation to come.

Houdon's entries were not listed in the official *livret* (catalogue) of the Salon of 1769, undoubtedly because he had become eligible too close to the deadline, but they are documented by Saint-Aubin's drawings in his copy of the *livret* as well as by contemporary journals reviewing the show. From these sources we know that he exhibited reductions, perhaps original plaster models, of his *Saint Bruno* and his *Saint John*; a separate head of *Saint John*; as well as the *Priest of the Lupercalia*, the *Peasant Girl of Frascati*, and a bust of an infant in white marble. This last is lost or not identified, but the others, discussed above, constituted the core of the Roman works, and are, with the exception of the statue of *Saint John*, fortunately preserved in the Schlossmuseum at Gotha.[18]

The *livrets* are invaluable but frustrating documents of the Salons and of the course of painting, sculpture, and graphic arts in the eighteenth century. As catalogues they are extremely summary and unreliable.[19] The Academy officials responsible for the editing of the *livrets* as well as the reception of the works of art, seem to have depended largely on the artists for their own entries; with the result that these vary greatly in terms of the care with which they were presented. Houdon, not the most literate of artists, was frequently careless and inaccurate. Names of portrait subjects are often mis-spelt, particularly when they are foreign; materials are sometimes given, sometimes not; as his production increased he would frequently list *Plusieurs portraits en marbre*, *Plusieurs animaux*, or *Plusieurs médaillons*, etc. under a single catalogue number. Nevertheless, when so many of the works have disappeared, the listings are often our only records of his activities. Since he exhibited regularly in almost all Salons between 1769 and 1814, the lists of his entries form a chronological account of his commissions and other works and tell us a great deal about his struggles for patronage, his manner of working, and the development of his style. This is particularly important since he was not consistent in his manner of dating, signing, or otherwise identifying his sculptures. As noted above for the marble variants of the *Peasant Girl of Frascati*, he frequently dated a replica at the time he made it rather than give it the original date. In the case of plasters made from an old model, the original date was sometimes repeated. Later in his career he frequently signed but did not date new works. Plasters were often identified by a seal of the atelier, rather than a signature and date. Thus the entry in the Salon *livret* sometimes assumes a unique significance. It has also been used on occasion to give an attractive label to an unidentified sculpture or even to a forgery.

After his election as an *agréé* of the Academy and his participation in the Salons of 1769 and 1771, the next known fact is that between October 12 and December 20, 1771, he visited the court of Saxe-Gotha in Germany. The purpose of the trip was to settle details and study the location for a projected tomb chapel for Louisa-Dorothea, late Duchess of Saxe-Gotha, a project never executed. To make the trip it was necessary for Houdon, as an *agréé* of the Academy and officially a member of the family of Court artists, to receive permission from the *Directeur des Bâtiments*, still the Marquis de Marigny.[20] His note of permission survives as early evidence of patronage from these minor German princes, the first important official support recorded for the artist.

HOUDON'S most significant portrait bust in the Salon of 1771 was that of Denis Diderot, the great encyclopedist, *philosophe*, a leader of the French Enlightenment, and the most perceptive French critic of art during the eighteenth century.[21] Diderot's *Salons*, the account of his reviews of these exhibitions between 1759 and 1781, are classics in the history of modern art criticism. Although he modestly did not discuss his own portrait, merely noting that it was an excellent resemblance, obviously he liked it and, through posing for it, he became acquainted with the sculptor. A close friend of Diderot was Baron Friedrich Melchior Grimm, whose monument is the *Correspondance littéraire*, a private news letter, whose selective subscription included members of the German nobility and a few others, notably

Catherine the Great of Russia.[22] It seems certain that Houdon was introduced to the German princes and to Catherine through Grimm and Diderot. These noble Germans, from Frederick the Great downwards, were completely French in their culture, loved to visit Paris and, when they could not do so, to stay in touch with all the news and scandal through Grimm's letters and other news sheets. Houdon made portraits of some of them over the next several years, and sold them copies of his portraits of the French *philosophes*, Diderot, Rousseau, Voltaire, d'Alembert, and Buffon. As noted above, the Dukes of Saxe-Gotha also bought plasters of most of the important early works. Catherine shortly became Houdon's first great royal patron. Thus, his initiative at the beginning of his career in doing a portrait bust of Diderot, unquestionably solicited by the artist and executed gratis, paid excellent dividends.

In contrast with the Salon of 1769, where four of the six known entries by Houdon were religious or mythological sculptures, and the two portraits are generalized or unidentified, the Salon of 1771 included four identified portrait busts among eight submissions.[23] Three of the others were reliefs *à l'antique*. There was a single statue, but an important one, the life-size plaster of a sleeping *Morpheus*, now at Gotha.[24]

MORPHEUS
Fig. 65, Plates 9–10

In 1777 the *Morpheus* in a marble version of reduced scale became Houdon's reception piece, his *morceau de réception* for full membership in the Academy of Painting and Sculpture. In its broken outlines and delicate movement of surfaces it belongs with and elaborates the rococo classicism of the *Priest of the Lupercalia*, as contrasted with the severe, abstract classicism of the *Saint Bruno*. Although related to ancient types of the *Sleeping Eros* or *Hermaphrodite*, there is none of the feminine quality associated even with male nudes in the rococo tradition. The body of *Morpheus*, classic in a Praxitelean sense, is that of a well trained athlete. The head with its tightly modeled cap of curls is generalized, although Houdon's close study of a specific model is evident in the somewhat anachronistic side whiskers. The figure spirals effectively on the rock where he sleeps, in the traditional spatial arrangement of Hellenistic or Baroque; the effect, with the arms framing the head in a Michelangelesque reminiscence, the easy flowing motion of the legs, is one of complete unity between figure and rock pedestal.

Houdon's manner of modeling the hair, mentioned above, deserves closer attention at this point. *Morpheus*' mass of curls is given the soft texture and life of actual hair. In this treatment Houdon was actually an innovator in the history of sculpture. The greatest masters before him, Donatello, Michelangelo, Bernini, treated hair like carved stone, even when they were modeling flesh as actual flesh. This was true in Roman sculpture and, as far as can be determined from surviving originals, in most Greek sculpture. The point here is not whether Houdon's method is superior to that of his predecessors or his contemporaries; it is simply a technical signature obvious in most of his sculptures. It is rarely if ever seen in the works of his contemporaries; more frequently among a few of his followers who were deliberately imitating him. But one can almost date the end of Houdon's era and the triumph of the neo-classicism of Canova when one observes the homely feature that hair ceases once more to be hair in sculpture.[25]

Although the *Morpheus*, Houdon's most ambitious new Salon sculpture to this date, was on the whole favorably received by the critics (whose quick and often interdependent reviews are strangely reminiscent of their twentieth-century counterparts), Diderot had some critical remarks: 'It is a figure unfortunately too academic . . .' The word 'academic' already had an occasionally pejorative sense in the eighteenth century. His principal criticism was iconographic, perhaps deriving from his delight in showing off his own 'encyclopedic' knowledge of antiquity. He justifiably complained that the artist was confusing Morpheus, god of dreams, with his father, Hypnos, god of sleep.[26] In this context there is in the Louvre an interesting small terra cotta sketch, attributed to Houdon and in essentially the same pose as the *Morpheus*, in which the god is shown as an aged, bearded figure.[27]

18

Of the other entries in the Salon of 1771, all but the *Diderot* have disappeared. The *livret* lists portraits of *M. Bignon, prévôt des marchands* [provost or supervisor of the merchant guilds], and his wife; *Mme de Mailly*, wife of the painter in enamel; a medallion *Head of Alexander*, with the note that it is larger than life and intended as pendant to a similar but ancient *Head of Minerva*; and two heads of young men in high relief and life-size; one crowned with myrtle, the other encircled with a riband.[28]

The problem of lost works by Houdon is a tantalizing one. Since he worked predominantly on a relatively small scale, creating portrait busts and *sculptures d'appartement*, as well as many reductions of his popular large statues such as the *Seated Voltaire* and the *Diana*, and even miniature versions of the most famous busts, it is to be expected that many of these would have disappeared. They are easily transported and changing fashions have made them liable to be moved about. One eminent French *amateur* has linked the decline of the portrait bust with the disappearance of the mantelpiece in modern architecture. Plasters are easily broken or made almost unrecognizable by nineteenth-century overpainting. But it is curious that works made from more durable materials such as marble or bronze should have dematerialized in such quantities. Fortunately, when we use this word the work in question is often sitting quietly in someone's country house waiting to be rediscovered by the persistent sleuths of auction houses and art dealers. As noted in the preliminary remarks, there is also ever present the temptation to 'rediscover' some works listed in the *livrets* of the Salons in modern forgeries; or to enhance the value of a genuine Houdon portrait of an unknown lady by attaching her to the listing in a Salon *livret*.

Although I do not propose to speculate about most of the lost sculptures, these first examples deserve some comment in terms of Houdon's progress. The *Alexander* and the heads of the two young men were conceivably adaptations of classical themes executed in Rome or shortly after Houdon's return to Paris, evidencing his continuing experiments with the antique.[29] The three portraits that have disappeared are only of interest as evidence of the sculptor's increasing concentration on portraiture and show that he had not yet found patrons among the nobility. Monsieur Bignon in his capacity of provost of guilds was an important functionary who could have been of use to Houdon; and the portrait of Madame de Mailly, wife of the painter in enamel, was probably a courtesy extended without charge to a colleague.

The surviving portrait bust from the Salon of 1771, that of Denis Diderot, establishes at the very beginning of Houdon's career the qualities that make his portraits outstanding in his time and in many ways unique in the history of portrait sculpture. It deserves, thus, to be examined at some length. Diderot was not only a great thinker, enormously influential in the history of ideas, the personification of the Enlightenment—if not always the age of reason—he was a brilliant wit, a hypnotizing conversationalist or monologuist, a man of mercurial moods and inexhaustible vitality. Throughout his life he was continually a storm center and, despite his frequent complaints, his moments of panic, his battles with both enemies and friends, he seems by and large to have enjoyed being at the heart of controversy; even when his liberty was endangered in the process. His portrait was painted, drawn, sculpted, and engraved, time and again; by the painters, Greuze, Michel van Loo, Fragonard, among others. Portrait busts were made not only by Houdon, but by Anne-Marie Collot, the young woman whose intricate career encompassed episodes as the mistress, 'protégée' and sculptural assistant of Falconet, the wife of his son, and finally in a happy or at least comfortable resolution, Falconet's nurse-companion during his old age. The best portrait bust of Diderot other than that by Houdon was made in 1777 by Jean-Baptiste Pigalle. Statues of Diderot were made by L.-A.-J. Le Cointe, an excellent portrayal of the wild disarray of dress characteristic of the *philosophe*; and in 1885 for Diderot's native city of Langres, by Frédéric-Auguste Bartholdi, author of the *Statue of Liberty* in New York Harbor. Bartholdi's posthumous commemoration has all the animation of an American Civil War

DIDEROT
Fig. 70
Plates 12–13

Fig. 43

monument and illustrates the sad decay into which the academic tradition had sunk by the later nineteenth century.

Houdon, like most of Diderot's portraitists, chose to portray him without a wig (in the eighteenth-century phrase, 'not wearing his hat'). This may have been on the insistence of Diderot, whose notorious hatred of wigs manifested itself in his wearing them continously askew. It also enabled the artist to follow the formula of a Roman portrait of a philosopher or a man of letters, presenting Diderot with abbreviated, undraped torso (to the collar bone), *à l'antique*. The twist of the head, angled from the torso, the slightly parted lips, and the wide, penetrating eyes, give to the work a marvellous quality of alertness and immediacy.

Certain technical characteristics may be noted which become further personal signatures of the sculptor. Diderot's somewhat disheveled hair is modeled in what was to be Houdon's characteristic manner, lightly and freely, to suggest the life and texture of the actual hair. Obviously textural differences can be sensed between the versions in terra cotta, plaster, marble, and bronze, depending on the characteristics of the materials themselves. Thus the effect in a terra cotta or a bronze might be somewhat harder and sharper than in a marble; but in all of them the illusion is remarkable that the hair might yield to the touch. Other textural distinctions are apparent between versions in different materials. In the plasters and terra cottas the artist typically enhances the textural variation to create the feeling that it comes directly from his hand rather than mechanically from the mould. The chisel marks defining the eyebrows or the wrinkles on the forehead or neck or around the eyes are done summarily and directly as chisel marks. In his bronzes also it was his custom, although not invariably, to texture the surface with a scraping tool rather than to seek the highly polished smoothness found in later copies. Bronzes unquestionably from Houdon's hand, such as the *Diderot*, the Louvre *Diana*, and the second version of *L'Écorché*, normally have a rather roughly scratched surface quality very different from the mechanical precision evident in bronzes of the later nineteenth century. In the marbles, on the other hand, not only the hair but the flesh parts are marvels of subtle modeling, in which an imperceptible softening creates the illusion of life and mobility.

Except in a few instances, including the deliberately classic works, the eyes in Houdon's portraits are deeply undercut, giving such an impression that Grimm, writing of his *Voltaire*, could say: 'M. Houdon is perhaps the first sculptor who has known how to model eyes. The eyes are full of life due to a light effect so ingeniously managed that Greuze himself, seeing the bust for the first time, imagined that the eyes were made of enamel or some other material.'[30] Houdon had many different techniques for rendering the eyes. Sometimes he bored a deep hole in the center of the pupil; sometimes, often in children's portraits, he bored a circle of small holes to create a star-like effect for the iris. Most frequently he cut out the entire iris, bored a deeper hole for the pupil and, by allowing a small fragment of the material to overhang the iris, established an illusionistic effect of light and shadow that made the eye actually appear to move. While there were isolated examples before him, Houdon was one of the few sculptors, since Greek and Roman sculptors had used painted or inlaid eyes, to realize the tremendous importance in the rendering of the eyes for the creation of a sense of life and personality in the sculptured portrait.

Another quality of the eyes in Houdon's portraits, if not unique with him, still merits mention. Rather than have the eyes of the sitter stare straight at the spectator when the bust is frontalized, Houdon was frequently in the habit of angling them so that they seemed to look slightly past the spectator. Thus in the case of the *Diderot*, as in many subsequent works, the head is sharply angled to the right of the torso, and then the eyes look slightly further to the right. The fact that *Diderot* and many of his sculptural descendants do not stare directly at us creates an invisible barrier between us and the sitter. As a result there is in these portraits by Houdon, despite the enormous animation of examples like *Diderot*,

Voltaire, or *Buffon*, a curious quality of containment, of withdrawal or reserve, which may make us seek more intensely for the inner nature of the image.

Without insisting too strongly on the rendering of the eyes—although it is crucial to the effects Houdon established in his portraits—we may ask, since it is seen perfected at the very beginning of his career, where it came from. It is not contended here that it was his invention but that he recognized its significance as apparently no sculptor had done before him; and throughout his life he made it central to his techniques for character portrayal. Portraitists from Coysevox to Pigalle, Pajou, or Caffieri render the eyes by a light circle or shallow indentation on the eyeball. The same technique is generally used in Italian Renaissance and Baroque sculpture, with the notable exception of Bernini; and Bernini would be Houdon's most obvious source.[31]

In general, as far as technique is concerned, it should be noted that Houdon was primarily a modeler rather than a carver, even though the marbles demonstrate extraordinary abilities in fashioning the surfaces of the stone. He worked first in clay, from which he made a plaster mould. The mould, the clay model, fired to preserve it, and perhaps an initial plaster cast were kept in the studio as matrices and models for subsequent replicas in plaster, terra cotta, bronze, and marble. The eighteenth century did not have the obsession for uniqueness evident in twentieth-century art. When Houdon did the portrait of a distinguished individual such as Diderot or Voltaire, he expected to duplicate it as long as there was a market. Choice of materials was largely a matter of cost. Obviously plaster was far less expensive than marble, bronze, or terra cotta; it is for this reason that his first patrons, minor German princes, not too affluent, ordered principally plasters, and that Catherine II of Russia would be satisfied only, with rare exceptions, with marbles or bronzes.

Since the plaster version was the first to be executed from the mould, it was normally this or the terra cotta model that was exhibited first at the Salon; to be followed a Salon or two later by a marble. This was not an exclusive pattern; many portraits were commissions in marble not duplicated in other materials. In his portraits of the great men of the eighteenth and early nineteenth centuries, however, the artist would expect to be able to make an indefinite number of replicas. In the case of Diderot, although the material is not specified in the *livret*, we may assume that the bust exhibited in 1771 was the original terra cotta or a plaster, perhaps painted to resemble terra cotta.[32]

Although no attempt is made in the present study to describe more than a narrow selection of surviving replicas, which on the basis of their impeccable history or their high quality seem to have come directly from the sculptor's hand, it may be useful to go into somewhat greater detail for *Diderot*. The most probably authentic surviving plaster is that in the Schlossmuseum at Gotha. This, dating from the days of Houdon's early patron, the Duke of Saxe-Gotha, retains much of its sharp detail although unfortunately some may have been lost through subsequent painting of the surface. The problem is not serious here, but it is a distressing fact that with the rise of neo-classicism it became the custom of museums during the nineteenth century to cover their plasters with a heavy white paint, presumably whenever they became dirty. The result is that many eighteenth- and nineteenth-century plasters have been virtually ruined by layer after layer of paint blurring all details. Several examples of Houdon plaster busts in American and European museums with clear histories extending back to the artist's lifetime are only shadows of their original selves. Since these old plasters are usually soft and brittle it is almost impossible to remove the paint without destroying the original surface.

Other plasters of Diderot survive in Berlin, Langres, Paris, and Stockholm. A cast in a clay agglomerate exists in New Haven, Connecticut, as well as the terra cotta in the Louvre. The last is of excellent quality and whether or not it was the 'original', deserves to be starred as one of those certainly straight from the hand of Houdon. There are also four known marbles surviving, one in the Louvre, one at Versailles, one in the Hermitage in Leningrad—

Plate 12a

from the collection of the Empress Catherine [32a]—and one in the Wrightsman Collection, New York, formerly in the Stroganov Collection. A bronze of reduced proportions exists in the Museum at Besançon, and a reduced marble is listed in the *livret* for the Salon of 1789. Houdon frequently made small versions of his busts of famous men as well as of his most admired statues, such as *L'Écorché*, the *Diana*, and *La Frileuse*. These were designed for the private collections, *les cabinets des amateurs*, of those who wished to have examples on a manageable scale of renowned contemporary sculptures. This was a substantial market, which the artist, a persistent if not always a sharp businessman, did not neglect. Unfortunately their small scale has resulted in the disappearance of most of those listed in the *livrets*, by the artist, and in nineteenth-century sales. In the case of the most sentimentally attractive pieces, *Diana*, the *Seated Voltaire*, *La Frileuse*, and his matchless portraits of children, these small versions have been reproduced in countless later copies and forgeries.[33]

Many other replicas of the *Diderot* are listed in sales and some of them undoubtedly still exist, but enough have been mentioned to indicate the proliferation of these immensely popular portraits of great men, both during the artist's lifetime and, regrettably, after his death during the nineteenth century and even well into the twentieth century. One last, pristine example must be discussed, however. This is the magnificent bronze cast presented by Diderot in 1781 to the municipality of Langres, his birthplace. Before discussing this, some other characteristics should be noted of the various *Diderot* busts in different materials, characteristics that sometimes predict those of subsequent portrait busts. One fact, rather unusual, is that all the known Houdon busts of Diderot are of the same type, with natural hair without perruque, upper torso sharply abbreviated, without shoulders, undraped, *à l'antique*. This was Houdon's typical classical rendition for a distinguished man of letters or science and, on occasion, even a literary lady. But when he made many replicas, as in the case of Jean-Jacques Rousseau or Voltaire, it became customary for him to vary the formula, presenting the savant at times draped *à l'antique*, sometimes in modern dress with perruque. Voltaire appears in every conceivable manifestation. This distinction in the *Diderot* bust is not particularly significant; perhaps it only indicates that as Houdon developed his presentations of great men, he found that different interpretations appealed to different viewers.

If the discussion is limited to the superior versions of the *Diderot*, it may be noted that the Gotha plaster has neither signature nor seal of the atelier (*cachet d'atelier*). With the terra cotta version in the Louvre Houdon initiated the formula of identification whereby plasters and sometimes terra cottas were stamped with a wax seal reading: ACADEM. ROYALE DE PEINTURE ET SCULPT. HOUDON SC. The marbles and bronzes were usually but not inevitably signed, and frequently but not always dated. It is necessary to reiterate how erratic the artist was in the matter of signature and dating, although perhaps not more so than most of his contemporaries. Even authentic plasters do not invariably have the seal; some are signed, some have both signature and seal. Nevertheless, as will be noted, a very general pattern may be traced in the signatures. Three of the marbles are not only carefully signed but contain inscriptions. Those made for Catherine (see note 32a) and Count Stroganov are
Plate 143a
inscribed around the edge of the bust: *Mr. Diderot, fait en 1773 par houdon*. The front of the base contains the couplet:

> il eut de grands Amis et, quelques bas jaloux.
> le Soleil plaît a l'aigle, et blesse des hiboux.

Obviously Houdon took particular care with the marble for Catherine, who promised to become his greatest patron; and that ordered by Count Stroganov, a noted Russian collector and Maecenas, was an exact replica of Catherine's. The inscriptions give an excellent example of Houdon's signature, so often forged. The date, 1773, rather than 1771, is also of interest as documenting Houdon's frequent habit of dating a replica in the year it was actually

Fig. 56. *A Vestal.* Plaster, about 1768. Gotha, Schlossmuseum

Fig. 55. *A Vestal.* Terra cotta, about 1768. New York, Wildenstein & Co.

Fig. 57. *A Vestal.* Marble, 1788. Paris, Louvre

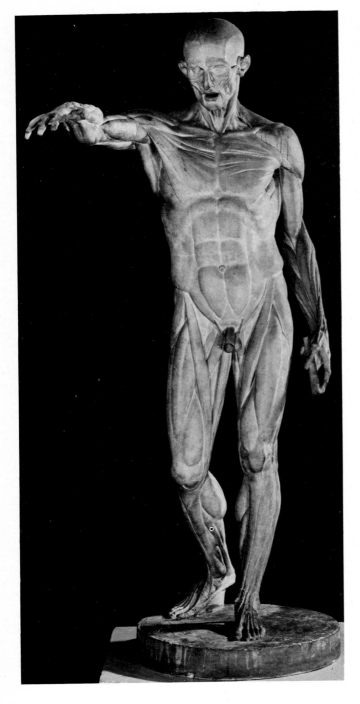 

Fig. 58. *L'Ecorché* (*Flayed Man*). Plaster, 1766–7. Paris, Ecole des Beaux-Arts

Fig. 59. *St. John the Baptist*. Plaster, 1766–7. Rome, Villa Borghese

Fig. 60. *St. Bruno*. Marble, 1766–7. Rome, Santa Maria degli Angeli

Fig. 61. *A Priest of the Lupercalia*. Plaster, about 1768. Gotha, Schlossmuseum

Fig. 62. *A Peasant Girl of Frascati*. Plaster, about 1768. Gotha, Schlossmuseum

Fig. 63. *An Unknown Girl* (*Peasant Girl of Frascati*). Marble, 1774. Paris, Musée Cognacq-Jay

Fig. 64. *A Roman Youth*. Marble, 1775. New York, Dr. Peter Guggenheim

Fig. 65. *Morpheus*. Plaster, about 1769. Gotha, Schlossmuseum

Fig. 66. *Madame de Charrière*. Plaster, 1771.
Neuchâtel, Musée d'Art et d'Histoire

Fig. 67. *Fredericka Louisa(?) of Saxe-Gotha*. Plaster,
about 1773. Gotha, Schlossmuseum

Fig. 68. *Ernest-Louis II,
Duke of Saxe-Gotha.*
Plaster medallion, 1773.
Gotha, Schlossmuseum

Fig. 69. *Frederick III,
Duke of Saxe-Gotha.*
Plaster medallion, 1773.
Gotha, Schlossmuseum

Fig. 70. *Denis Diderot*. Marble, 1773.
New York, Wrightsman Collection

Fig. 71. *Belisarius*. Plaster, about 1773. Toulouse,
Musée des Augustins

Fig. 72. *Empress Catherine II of Russia*. Marble, 1773.
Leningrad, Hermitage

Fig. 73. *Drawing for a Tomb of Monsieur Guillard*. 1774. Providence, Rhode Island School of Design,
Museum of Art

Fig. 74. *Tomb of Prince Alexis Dmitrievitch Galitzin*. Marble, 1774. Moscow, Donskoy Monastery

Fig. 75. *Tomb of Mikhail Mikhailovitch Galitzin*. Marble, 1774. Moscow, Donskoy Monastery

Fig. 76. *Madame His*. Plaster, about 1774.
Williamstown, Mass.,
Sterling and Francine Clark Art Institute

Fig. 77. *La petite Lise*. Marble, 1775.
Leningrad, Hermitage

Fig. 78. *Christoph Willibald von Gluck*. Plaster, 1775.
Weimar, Landesbibliothek

Fig. 79. *Sophie Arnould as Iphigenia*. Marble, 1775.
Paris, Louvre

Fig. 80. 'Baroness de la Houze'. Marble, 1777.
San Marino, Calif., Henry E. Huntington Library
and Art Gallery

Fig. 81. Armand-Thomas Hue, Marquis de Miromesnil. Marble, 1777.
New York, Frick Collection

Fig. 82. An Unknown Lady. Plaster, about 1775.
Schwerin, Staatliches Museum

Fig. 83. Anne-Robert-Jacques Turgot, Baron de l'Aulne. Terra cotta, 1778.
Boston, Museum of Fine Arts

Fig. 84. *Elisabeth-Suzanne de Jaucourt, Comtesse du Cayla.* Marble, 1777. New York, Frick Collection

Fig. 85. *Monsieur, le Comte de Provence (later Louis XVIII).* Plaster, 1776. Stockholm, National Museum

Fig. 86. *Le baiser donné.* Marble, 1778. New York, Wildenstein & Co.

Fig. 87. *Madame Adélaïde, aunt of Louis XVI.*
Marble, 1777. Paris, Louvre

Fig. 88. *Madame Victoire, aunt of Louis XVI.*
Marble, 1777. London, Wallace Collection

Fig. 89. *Comtesse de Jaucourt.* Marble, 1777.
Paris, Louvre

Fig. 90. *Marie Adélaïde Servat.* Marble, 1776. New York,
Wildenstein & Co.

Fig. 91. *Baron de Vietinghoff.* Marble, 1791. East Berlin, Staatliche Museen

Fig. 92. *A Naiad.* Drawing, by Saint-Aubin, of a lost plaster of 1777.

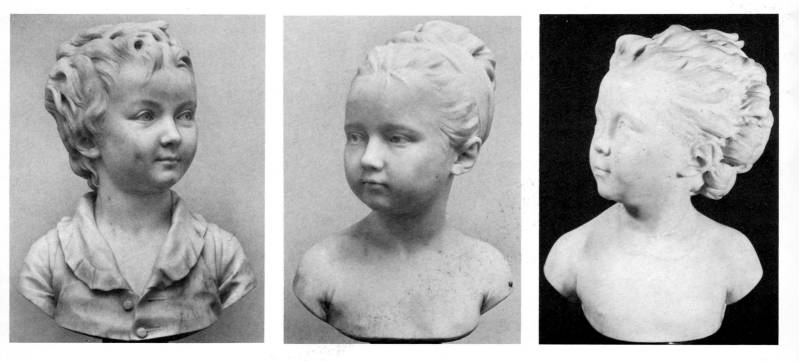

Figs. 93–94. *Alexandre and Louise Brongniart.* Marble, 1777. Washington, D.C., National Gallery of Art, Widener Collection

Fig. 95. '*La petite Robert.*' Marble, 1777. Barnard Castle, Bowes Museum

Fig. 96. *Sketch for the Tomb of Prince Alexander Mikhailovitch Galitzin.* Terra cotta, 1777. Paris, Louvre

Fig. 97. *The Dead Thrush.* Marble, about 1777. Private collection

Fig. 98. *Eagle attacking a Deer.* Plaster. Private collection

Fig. 99. *Diana*. Plaster, 1776. Gotha, Schlossmuseum

Fig. 100. *Diana*. Bronze, 1782. San Marino, Calif., Henry E. Huntington Library and Art Gallery

Fig. 102. *Minerva*. Plaster medallion, about 1777. Formerly Gotha, Schlossmuseum

Fig. 101. *Diana*. Marble, 1780. Lisbon, Calouste Gulbenkian Foundation, Museum

Fig. 103. *Diana*. Marble, 1778. Washington, D.C., National Gallery of Art

Fig. 104. *Aymard-Jean de Nicolay*. Marble, 1779. Coll. Comte de Contades

Fig. 105. *Antoine-Louis-François Le Fèvre de Caumartin*. Marble, 1779. Paris, Musée Jacquemart-André

Fig. 106. *Molière*. Plaster, 1778. Princeton, N.J., University Library

made, rather than in the year of the original model. Also the many veins in the marble of the Stroganov (now Wrightsman) bust should be noted. These are characteristic of many of Houdon's finest marbles. Since marble usually had to be brought from the Italian quarries of Carrara or Seravezza and was normally doled out to the Academicians by the *Direction des Bâtiments*, each sculptor often had to work with what he could get; with the result that even important monuments may contain serious marble flaws. The eighteenth-century sculptor—although some complaints are recorded—did not seem to have minded this so terribly, and frequently the veining lends a warmth that enhances the vitality of the work. One of the characteristics of neo-classic sculpture was the insistence on pure, unflawed marble, something that exaggerated its mechanical appearance.

The marble of Diderot at Versailles is dedicated: A M. Robineau de Bougon. Houdon sculpsit. 1775., indicating the later date of this work. A fourth marble which should be noted is that in the Louvre, signed on the back edge: Houdon Sculpsit 1775.

The bronze portrait of Diderot presented by him to his native city of Langres in 1781 is of extraordinary importance, not only for its superb quality but for its associations and its impeccable history. The citizens of this provincial city, where Diderot grew up, had watched his career with fascination and at times with horror. He was certainly their most distinguished son but at the same time he was notorious for the radicalism of his ideas. At one time or another he had attacked every institution and every idea that this conservative little community revered. However, by 1780 most of the scandals had abated and his reputation was so secure that the city fathers decided to request his portrait to be placed in the town hall. The request was forwarded on August 29, 1780, and on April 30, 1781, it was announced that Diderot had sent a bronze of the portrait by Houdon.[34] This bronze is to be seen today in the Hôtel de Ville of Langres. Madame de Vandeul, Diderot's daughter, recounts in her memoirs that the town, presumably in the persons of the mayor and four aldermen, had offered to pay Houdon something; and he in his turn had sent each of them a plaster of the *Diderot* (a record of five more plasters).[35]

During the 1770s, at a date not exactly determined, Houdon began to learn the techniques of bronze casting, which for some time had been neglected by most French sculptors. His first bronze recorded in a Salon was that of the *Vestal* in 1777. In the same Salon were listed several portraits in wax, probably models for bronzes; and bronzes of Voltaire and Rousseau are dated 1778. It was after this time that the bronze of Diderot was made from a new wax model, based on the original from 1771. Madame de Vandeul says that Diderot sent 'his bust in bronze' to Langres, indicating that it was already in his possession. It is identical—given the difference in materials—to the versions based on that of 1771, and could not have involved a new sitting toward the end of the 1770s. Diderot was born in 1713; in 1771, when he probably sat for Houdon, he was fifty-eight years old. In 1777, when he was sixty-four, his portrait was done by the sculptor, Jean-Baptiste Pigalle. This is a fine representation showing that Diderot had aged appreciably, grown heavier and somewhat less animated. It would have been a miracle of rejuvenation had Houdon in a new sitting about 1780 been able to recapture so dramatically the appearance and spirit of 1771.[36]

The type of Houdon's surviving Diderot busts, torso truncated to approximately the collar bones, no arms or shoulders, undraped, *à l'antique*, would perhaps be more correctly described as a portrait head rather than a portrait bust; since the term 'bust' is defined as the representation of head and shoulders. This kind, which is extremely rare before Houdon (and Defernex) unless we go all the way back to antiquity, places all the emphasis on the head and specifically on the face, with only as much of the neck as might serve as a base, In seventeenth-century busts much more attention was paid to the torso, which at times extended to the waist, heavily clothed, draped, or encased in armor. In fact, although the faces in Baroque busts are frequently majestic, sometimes they are almost lost between swirling masses of draperies below and magnificent perruques above. The more informal

Plate 12b

Fig. 43

seventeenth-century presentations, as noted above, are usually found in portraits of artists or literary men, friends of the sculptor; and these characteristically are shown with the shirt informally open at the collar. A superb example of this type is Antoine Coysevox's portrait of the architect, Robert de Cotte. Houdon also used this informal version as he was to use every tradition from the most Baroque to the most severely classic. But the *Diderot*, stripped of all accessories, all embellishments, with everything concentrated on the structure and turn of the head, on the immediately caught expression of the face, introduced a new epoch in the history of portrait sculpture.

A final technical detail: all the known busts of Diderot, whatever the material, have one other characteristic in common; they are open and relatively unfinished at the back. In other words the artist did not attempt to fill out and complete the back of the torso as he did the front. Even the marbles are undercut to emphasize the post fastening them to the base, and this area is left comparatively rough. This is also true of the terra cottas, the plasters, and the bronze. This technique, arising partly because all versions were based on the same model, and partly because such busts were usually placed against a wall, to be viewed largely from the front, is common in less formal portraits at least from the time of the Renaissance. More elaborate works in marble, portraits of kings or other high dignitaries, were often finished at the back as well. Bronzes on the other hand, whatever the subject, were left open from the Middle Ages to the end of the eighteenth century. Houdon, who probably exploited his plasters as independent works of art more than any of his predecessors had done, used every conceivable treatment for the backs of his marbles and terra cottas, as he progressed. Plasters (except when they were cast after marbles) and bronzes, as far as can be determined, he always left open. In some plasters the back has been filled in at a later date; and the only bronzes in which the back is filled in are problem pieces.

Fig. 66
Plate 11

Another work by Houdon from the year 1771, which was not included in the Salon of that year, is the portrait of Madame de Charrière, born Isabelle de Tuyll de Zuylen, a Dutch lady of letters who lived much of her life in Switzerland. She visited Paris in 1771, on her honeymoon, when Houdon made her portrait. The terra cotta is recorded in his inventory, *c.* 1784: 'No. 5. Buste en terre de Mad. Charlier [de Charrière] en Suisse.' A bust in plaster, painted terra cotta and bearing the seal of the atelier, is in the museum of Neuchâtel, Switzerland. Here Belle de Zuylen, as she was popularly known, is depicted very much as the woman of letters, *à l'antique*, undraped, with abbreviated torso, without shoulders, and with the blank eyes of the classical tradition.

In March 1772 Houdon was installed in one of the old ateliers of Paris on the Fauburg du Roule, reserved for academicians.[37] The year 1773 saw another trip to Germany between April 23 and July 1.[38] The Salon of 1773 featured four portraits of members of the house of Saxe-Gotha: Ernest Louis II, reigning duke, his wife, Maria-Charlotte of Saxe-Meiningen, his sister, Fredericka-Louisa, and his deceased father, Frederick III. The portrait of Fredericka-Louisa[38a] is a plaster bust, those of Ernest Louis and Frederick are medallions. The portrait of Maria-Charlotte has disappeared. After their exhibition at the Salon at least three of them returned to Gotha, where they have remained safely ever since. Although they may not be considered outstanding examples of Houdon's art, they are important documents.

It is evident in the three surviving portraits that Houdon was attempting to transform these German nobles into noble Romans, a not completely successful endeavor. The quite specific classicizing undoubtedly arose not only because the sculptor was still close to Rome, but more because the duke and his family were caught up in that German enthusiasm for antiquity fired by the publication in 1764 of Winckelmann's *Geschichte der Kunst des Altertums*. This enthusiasm was then a common phenomenon. The duke submitted Houdon's design for a memorial chapel of the Duchess Louisa-Dorothea to Reiffenstein, Winckelmann's successor in Rome. As a result of Reiffenstein's criticisms—conceivably because the design was not literally classical—the commission was never executed.

The portrait of Fredericka-Louisa, who is made to resemble a bluestocking steeped in the classics, shows her clad in a loose gown draped over the shoulders to suggest Roman dress. The face is austere and rather grim, the hair tightly pulled back under what looks like a coronet, the iris barely sketched on the surface of the eyeballs. The aura of chastity is certainly not that of Diana. There is, however, an interesting family resemblance to Houdon's *Peasant Girl of Frascati*, purchased by the duke, in the treatment of eyes and hair, and in the generalization of the face. In the tight mouth and solid jaw of the lady one senses, however, that specific characterization that the sculptor could rarely avoid.

The two medallions are more successful essays in the Roman portrait. The bas-relief profiles of both dukes are depicted with only the slightest indication of the undraped torso below the neck. The short hair, rendered with precision, is combed forward and in both cases bound with a riband. The young duke has handsome, unlined features; his deceased father, who had rather run to weight, gives a good approximation of the decadent or Nero type of Roman emperor. Both portraits are surrounded by beautifully lettered Latin inscriptions; the father's is signed at the bottom in Houdon's characteristic cursive: *houdon f.* [fecit], the son's: *houdon ft. 1773*. Frederick, the older, although a posthumous portrait based on a painting or, as a profile view, more likely on a drawing or engraving, is the more interesting, as a mature and rather belligerent-looking individual. One small detail of passing interest is his somewhat battered ear. Houdon was given to generalizing or idealizing the ear, modeling it with a loving sense of its peculiar beauty. But his microscopic hand and eye could not refrain from recording exactly a detail such as this.

In the other two busts exhibited in the Salon of 1773 Houdon was also—as in the case of the late duke—separated from his models, in one case by time and in the other by distance. These were the *tête d'expression* or *de fantaisie*, of *Belisarius*; and the portrait of *Catherine the Great* of Russia. Belisarius, the general of Justinian of Byzantium, had been disgraced and blinded as a result of the emperor's suspicion and jealousy. Jean-François Marmontel had published in 1767 a widely popular moral tale recounting the tragedy of Belisarius. Since Marmontel had contributed to the *Encyclopédie* and thus was known to Diderot, it could have been the latter who recommended the subject to Houdon.[39] The bust, both in technique and subject, represents something quite different from anything the sculptor had previously attempted. It is one of the freest and most dramatic sculptures of his career, the beard and hair modeled roughly and sketchily, the head with its blind, staring eyes straining upwards as Belisarius seems to rage defiantly at his oppressors. Houdon, like so many of his contemporaries, was strongly drawn to the stage, particularly the classic but emotional drama of Corneille and Racine. This enthusiasm erupts sporadically in remarkable portrayals of the dramatic singer, Sophie Arnould, the actor, Larive, and the charlatan, Cagliostro. It is to this tradition, the drama or novel of emotion or sentiment, that the *Belisarius* belongs, rather than to any narrow documentation of antiquity. The theme is also an early instance of the moral tales drawn from the ancient world that were to characterize so much of neo-classic art. In his first Salon, 1781, Jacques-Louis David was to exhibit a painting of *Belisarius Receiving Alms* (Lille Museum), which, despite its Baroque reminiscences, heralded the severity and clarity of his 1785 *Oath of the Horatii*.

Houdon's bust of Catherine was commissioned by Count Stroganov in Paris, and the artist, who never visited Russia, was forced to rely on paintings, drawings, or engravings. Many of these by French artists were available in Paris. We know that de Mailly, the painter in enamel, whose wife's portrait Houdon had exhibited in the Salon of 1771, painted several miniatures of Catherine. However, none of Houdon's secondary sources seems to have been very stimulating, and Catherine's resemblance to a middle-aged, bourgeois matron could

Fig. 67

Figs. 68-9

Plate 14

BELISARIUS

Fig. 71

EMPRESS
CATHERINE
Fig. 72

not have lent much inspiration. But as Diderot and Grimm may have already been recommending the artist to the empress, she loomed as a likely and major patron, one not to be offended.

It has been a cliché of Houdon scholarship, used to explain some less satisfactory works—particularly a number created late in his career—that he could not function effectively without the stimulus of the living model. The superb images of Rousseau and Mirabeau could be explained by the fact that in each case he was able to make a death-mask. This does not explain the *Molière* and the *La Fontaine*, dead a hundred years, yet marvellously alive in Houdon's interpretation. It is perhaps more to the point that Houdon had difficulty being inspired by uninspiring subjects, such as King Louis XVI. In terms of her character and her achievements Catherine should have been a fascinating subject, but the sad fact is that, as most portraits of her bear witness, she did not look very fascinating. Houdon did the best he could, and produced an impressive official portrait.

He went back for inspiration to the royal and noble sculpture of the seventeenth century such as Coysevox's portrait of *Louis XIV*. In a comparable manner *Catherine* is given majesty by the heavily indented draperies surrounding the figure and integrating it with the pedestal. In contrast with the *Diderot*, *Catherine* is conceived in terms of the mass and elabo-

Plate 16 ration of the torso. Her lace bodice and imperial chain of office are magnificently rendered; the curls of her hair falling down over her shoulders, become integral with the total design.

Plate 15 Her face seems to be, when compared with other portraits of her at this time, an excellent likeness, somewhat bland and idealized, with her characteristically complacent, self-satisfied look. In the context of technique it should not be forgotten that this marble appears at the very beginning of Houdon's professional career, when it was doubtful that he had much aid from assistants. The hair is treated in his already familiar manner. The signature on the right of the base: *houdon ft. 1773.*, is a perfect example of his cursive lettering. Only the treatment of the eyes, in which the iris and the pupil are undercut rather shallowly, is relatively uncharacteristic. Since the history and provenance of this bust are impeccable, the unusual treatment of the eyes may be explained by experiment, by the example of seventeenth-century prototypes, or by the simple fact that Catherine was slightly pop-eyed.[40] One is left with the impression that, despite her intellectual enthusiasm for the new spirit of the Enlightenment, she does not look like a very appealing individual. Despite what may be a slight softening and idealization in the total effect, Houdon with his ruthless eye does not seem to have flattered her very much. The tendency of some scholars to denigrate this work may arise from the fact that they have never seen the actual sculpture, now splendidly displayed in the Hermitage in Leningrad.

The other two works by Houdon in the Salon of 1773 are of extraordinary importance as two of the rare surviving examples of his tomb sculpture. These are the monuments commissioned by Prince Dmitri Alekseyevitch Galitzin, who was Russian Ambassador to

GALITZIN TOMBS France from 1765 to 1773. Four of these tombs are recorded, but only those of the Field
Figs. 74–5 Marshal Mikhail Mikhailovitch Galitzin and the Senator Alexis Dmitrievitch Galitzin were carried to completion. These two were listed in the Salon *livret* as on exhibit in the artist's studio, Faubourg du Roule. The other two, not carried beyond the sketch stage, are listed in the *livret* for the Salon of 1777.

For an eighteenth-century sculptor seeking monumental commissions in a period when royal patronage was diminishing, one of the most promising fields was that of tomb sculpture for the nobility, great churchmen, or military leaders. The tomb in fact has offered some of the best opportunities for grandiose sculpture ever since the pyramids of Egypt.[41] Michelangelo labored much of his life over the tombs of Pope Julius II and the two Medici dukes. The Italian Renaissance tradition of tomb sculptors was brought to France in the sixteenth century; and the influence of Bernini's tomb sculpture was assimilated to the long line of

French Gothic and Franco-Italian Renaissance tombs in examples such as Girardon's
tomb of Cardinal Richelieu and Coysevox's tomb of Mazarin. It was with the French tombs
of the eighteenth century that Italian Baroque actually established itself in France. In their
elaboration and emotionalism, Michel-Ange Slodtz's tomb of Languet de Gergy and Pigalle's
tomb of the Maréchal de Saxe represented the norm for French tomb sculpture at the
moment when Houdon presented his modest and severely classic monuments to the
Galitzin.[42]

In the relief of Prince Alexis' monument a mourning figure of *Justice* leans on the tablet,
on which appears a long eulogy to the prince, in Latin and in Russian. *Justice* is adapted
from an ancient representation of a Muse, probably Polyhymnia, Muse of Oratory and
Sacred Music, seen in an example in the Louvre in a similar pose leaning on a column.
The *pleureuse* was, of course, a common attribute of seventeenth- and eighteenth-century
tombs. She appears in a form similar to that by Houdon in Slodtz's *Capponi Monument* in
Rome, of the early 1740s. A particularly fine example of *La Douleur* in the Louvre, designed
c. 1765 by L. C. Vassé for the tomb of the Comte de Caylus, is also close to the pose of
Houdon's *Justice*. The quality of Houdon's figure of *Justice* does not rest in its priority or
its uniqueness but in its restraint and its beauty of conception and execution.

Aside from the inscribed tablet and the figure silhouetted in high relief against a neutral,
rectangular marble slab, the only other accessories are the cinerary urn grouped with a
branch of cypress at the foot of the tablet, and the two horizontal *fasces*, symbols of law,
worked into the base. Prince Alexis, a senator, is presented as a lawmaker, as Prince Mikhail,
a general, is presented as a warrior. The *fasces*, incidentally, are later used in a similar symbolism on Houdon's statue of George Washington.

The winged military genius on the monument to Prince Mikhail stands before an obelisk Plate 18
with the Latin inscription lettered on the upper part. He leans on an urn, which in turn is
placed on a block, on which appears the Russian inscription. On both tombs the Russian
inscriptions are crudely lettered, in comparison with the Latin versions, and were probably
added later in Russia. The genius, accompanied by arms and other symbols of the prince's
victories, is a youthful figure and, despite his elegant helmet, suggests an Eros rather than a
Mars, or perhaps a Mercury such as the *morceau de réception* by Pigalle (terra cotta, 1742),
which had proved so popular.

Another possible relationship is to be seen with the figure of *Conjugal Love* on the *Monument to the Dauphin* in Sens Cathedral, designed by Guillaume II Coustou, completed and Fig. 31
dated in 1777, and exhibited in his studio for the Salon of that year. The winged *Conjugal
Love*, obviously an Eros, faces the spectator, but is otherwise similar in proportions, fall of
drapery, and even the extinguished torch he bears in his right hand—which perhaps makes
more sense for an Eros mourning the death of a loving couple than it does for a military
genius. He wears no helmet, his pose is dramatic, his face is contorted in grief; whereas
Houdon's *Genius* is quiet, his face shadowed by the helmet, contemplative in grief. Although
Coustou's free-standing monument is an important prototype of neo-classicism in its absence of excessive Baroque imagery, particularly the exclusion of gruesome representations
of Death and the dying, it is in all a cluttered and rather mediocre work. Houdon could
certainly have seen Coustou's monument during the years it was in process, and have
adapted the figure of *Conjugal Love*, as well as been inspired by the classic restraint of the
total design; but then Coustou (or his assistant, Julien, who may have been responsible for
the *Conjugal Love*) certainly saw Houdon's monuments when they were exhibited in 1773.
In any event both figures have a common source in traditional representations of Eros;
and, as noted, any distinction Houdon may have within a classical tradition does not rest on
the priority of his concepts.

As far as the iconography is concerned, Diderot, who liked advising artists, could have
been involved in both Coustou's and Houdon's monuments. The obelisk of Prince Mikhail's

tomb was a commonplace of eighteenth-century monuments; and the green, painted cypress trees flanking it are not unique.

The two completed monuments of the Galitzin, little known because of their remoteness in the old Donskoy Monastery outside Moscow, remain early and remarkable examples of neo-classicism; or perhaps they reveal the strength of a continuing classical tradition in Houdon's sculptures. Remembering that up to this date the only large-scale sculpture he had been able to carry out in marble was the *Saint Bruno* in Rome, these tombs are impressive for their quality and for their departure from the Baroque vein in tomb sculpture. Since Houdon's most markedly classic sculptures, the monuments of the Galitzin and later that of the Comte d'Ennery, were soon removed from Paris to isolated destinations, they could have had little or no influence, and so are important essentially for their quality and for evaluation of the ingredients of his style.[43] This style was to develop into a continual dialogue between rococo and classic, rooted in his intense observation of nature.

The signatures on the Galitzin monuments illustrate his two basic manners: that on the **Fig. 143b** tomb of Prince Alexis is in his cursive: *houdon. Parisiis Sculpsit. 1774*; that of Prince Mikhail is in roman: *A. Houdon. Sculpteur du Roi. Fait a Paris. 1774.* Since the works in progress were shown in marble at the artist's studio, Faubourg du Roule, on the occasion of the Salon of 1773, the signatures were added later, probably when the monuments were about to be shipped to Russia.[44]

IN 1775 Houdon's father was retired with a small pension from his position as concierge for the *hôtel* formerly occupied by the *École des élèves protégés*, now the residence of the first painter to the king.[45] A letter of 1776 from the Marquis d'Angiviller, who had succeeded Monsieur de Marigny as *Directeur des Bâtiments*, indicates that Houdon senior had maintained a tobacco concession at the door of the *hôtel*, which he gave up when he retired. This letter is principally interesting as evidence for the manner in which major royal functionaries watched over minor details.[46] Also in 1776, Houdon was elected an honorary associate of the Academy at Toulouse and as his reception piece submitted the *Belisarius*.[47] In 1777 he and his brother, Jacques-Philippe, who was now the architect in charge of royal fêtes and entertainments, tried, by pleading the illness of their parents, to obtain a life annuity for them; apparently without much success.[48] During the 1770s a series of letters indicates that the artist was busy placing casts of *L'Écorché* in as many art schools as possible. One letter, probably inspired by Houdon, was written by Diderot in 1773 to Catherine of Russia, strongly recommending the acquisition of an *Écorché* to be cast in bronze for the Academy of Fine Arts in Saint Petersburg.[49]

While the documents illustrate little of significance occurring in the career of the artist, the works he submitted to the Salon of 1775 reveal some sensational developments in his art of portraiture.[50] From his surviving works it is clear that he was an accomplished and mature sculptor before he left Rome, both in the technical and in the conceptual sense. With the 1771 portraits of Diderot his idea of a particular kind of likeness, that of the man of letters, the scientist, the *philosophe*, was fully realized; and in most cases he merely played variations on it, sharply keyed to the specific individual, for the rest of his career. This, it is hardly necessary **Fig. 72** to emphasize, was no small accomplishment. With the portrait of Catherine of Russia, the official portrait type of royalty or nobility, it is evident that his solution was still somewhat tentative. Taken at second hand and perhaps involving some apprehension, it fell somewhere **Figs. 67–9** between literal image and royal symbol. The portraits of the Saxe-Gotha family were minor, though interesting classical exercises done while the artist was working on his plans for the mortuary chapel intended for the memory of the Duchess Louisa-Dorothea. But the busts documented by the *livret* of 1775, and others dated 1774 or 1775, are evidence of some important facts. First, Houdon had now realized that the individual portrait rather than the sculptural monument was to be his most regular commission. Second, his quality as a portraitist had become so apparent that important commissions were coming in from high French government dignitaries and noble ladies; he was no longer dependent on foreign patronage. Thirdly and most significant, the range and accomplishment of his abilities were displayed in a dazzling variety of portrait sculptures. And the pace that he set in 1775 was to be maintained until the French Revolution began in 1789. Although he was now working with assistants, who did much of the preliminary work in preparing the moulds or roughing out the marble blocks, the sheer quantity displayed in 1775 and in subsequent Salons is awe-inspiring. The *livret* of 1775 lists eleven works, as well as one entry (No. 261) of 'Plusieurs têtes ou portraits en marbre, sous le même numéro'. These were sculptures submitted too late to be distinguished in this hastily assembled catalogue. Most of the works were new portraits created during the previous year or two.

A head of *Medusa, imitée de l'antique,* and two figure sculptures exhibited in 1775 are lost. The *Medusa* was a conventional subject and even though taken from the antique was perhaps suggested by a well-known work of Bernini. *Une femme sortant du bain* was an early experiment with the subject of the eighteenth-century *Bather* or *Nymph.* Falconet and Clodion were recognized masters of the rococo genre, and Allegrain in 1767 had created for Madame du Barry a much admired version of a *Venus* emerging from the bath. The other figure sculpture which has disappeared was a model for the ill-fated chapel in memory of Louisa-Dorothea of Saxe-Gotha, on which Houdon had been working since at least 1771. As was the custom with elaborate projects, this was described in some detail: 'At the rear of the Chapel is the door of the Temple of Death who, emerging in the figure of a skeleton, raises the curtains in which he is partially veiled and seizes the Duchess. The Duchess, her hair dishevelled, is covered with a shroud. She expresses her affection for all her kindred and for the People.' Although this description does not give us much idea what the chapel looked like, we know that it was conceived earlier than those of the Galitzin, and it sounds like a much more pretentious and traditional project, close to the Baroque formula in its *mélange* of noble and macabre emotion. It may have been influenced by Slodtz' Tomb of Languet de Gergy in Saint-Sulpice; and Bachaumont's *Mémoires secrets* stresses its dependence on Pigalle's already famous tomb of the Maréchal de Saxe at Strasbourg.[51] The sketch presented in 1775 was followed by at least two subsequent designs as the terms of the contract changed, and finally, as a result of the criticisms by the classicist, Reiffenstein, Houdon lost the commission. This may have been as well since Melchior Grimm, who had been sponsoring Houdon, suggested to the reigning duke, Ernest II, that he should compensate the artist by ordering a statue for his gardens; and this was the origin of one of Houdon's masterpieces, the marble *Diana.*[52]

The fact that Houdon's original designs for the chapel of Louisa-Dorothea go back to 1771 should be restated. This is, then, his first essay in tomb sculpture, and it is not unreasonable that he should look for inspiration to the great tradition of Baroque tomb sculpture and specifically to the well-known projects of Slodtz and Pigalle. We must also not forget the desires of the patrons and the possibility that Diderot offered some advice on iconography. In any event the concept antedated the much more restrained, classic relief monuments of the Galitzin, listed in the Salon of 1773. The surviving maquette for a third Galitzin monument, in the Salon of 1777 (Louvre), also a relief, suggests what might have been a successful assimilation of Baroque emotion to classic form. With the tomb of the Comte d'Ennery (1781, see p. 62) classic restraint triumphed both in form and in emotion.

Fig. 96

The unrealized chapel of Louisa-Dorothea is important to an understanding of the development of Houdon's tomb sculpture, which in turn is important within the broader aspect of his style. It is fortunate that it is so well described in the Salon *livret.* Another document of his tomb sculpture is a drawing by him, signed and dated: *Houdon inv. 1774.* This is a

Fig. 73

Fig. 63
Plate 2

Fig. 77

Plates 20–1

project for another unrealized tomb, of a Monsieur Guillard, a councillor of the *Parlement* in Paris. It is puzzling that there are virtually no surviving drawings by Houdon. This is almost the only one that can be accepted with a degree of assurance.

The drawing (Rhode Island School of Design, Providence, Rhode Island) shows Sorrow, consoled by Justice (the *Parlement* in the eighteenth century was the Courts of Justice), who points to the symbols of Fame. It suggests an elaborate, classical-Baroque scheme, with free-standing figures and accessories such as coffin, column, medallions etc., set in a massive frame of arches. The macabre elements of Death or the dying have been eliminated in favor of more abstract symbols, but the three figures, garbed *à l'antique* and arranged in a meticulous right-angle triangle, evince a good deal of emotion and fluttering drapery.

Although not specifically listed in the *livret* for the Salon of 1775, three marble heads, discussed above (p. 13), belong here: the *Young Girl*, 1774 (Cognacq-Jay Museum, Paris) and the *Young Girl*, 1775 (Hermitage, Leningrad)—both adapted from the Roman period *Peasant Girl of Frascati*—and the *Roman Youth*, 1775 (Dr Peter Guggenheim, New York, and Heim Gallery, London), the original model of which is also probably from the Roman period or shortly thereafter.[53]

A fourth bust, which belongs with these as evidence of Houdon's continuing classicizing mode, introduces an element of eighteenth-century *sensibilité*. This is *La petite Lise*, whose charming story is well known.[54] In 1774 the City of Paris, instead of giving a fête in honor of the marriage of the Comte d'Artois, decided to pay for the weddings of young girls scheduled for that day. A Mademoiselle Lise presented herself, and when asked the name of her fiancé, replied that she had none—she assumed that the city provided everything. The story of her naiveté was widely circulated, and Houdon, quick to capitalize on a popular event, did her portrait. It is not known, and is not significant, whether this is an actual portrait or, as seems likely, a generalized rendition of a girl personifying innocence. In fact when he sent a copy of the bust to the Society of Fine Arts at Montpellier, of which he had become a member, it was listed in the catalogue as: *La petite Lise sous l'emblème de l'innocence*. This bust, marbles of which exist in the Hermitage, signed and dated: HOUDON. F. 1775., as well as in a private collection, signed and dated: Houdon Sculpsit 1774., is in scale and design almost an exact counterpart of the *Peasant Girl* and her offshoots. Her hair, in this case tied with a broad riband, whose bow at the back is beautifully rendered, is pulled back severely in the manner of the *Peasant Girl*. But unlike the latter, Lise is an adolescent with immature features, eyes cast down in confusion or a semblance of it. Aside from its charming subject, its stylistic interest, and its technical quality, the bust of Lise should be remarked as one of Houdon's rare excursions into the realm of overt sentimentality. This was the heyday of the sentimental, moral tale exemplified in the novels of Richardson and the paintings of Greuze. *Lise* may remind us of such paintings by Greuze as *The Broken Pitcher*, but conveys none of the double entendre of Greuze's deflowered virgins.[55] Although Houdon explored aspects of excessive emotion in some of his theatrical sitters, his portraits of children—in which category the adolescent Lise should probably be placed—are with this single exception delightful because they are presented without sentimentality. This 'symbol of innocence' is obviously a departure, in its own terms an effective one, arising from the particular event.

The seven identified portrait busts in the Salon of 1775 represent an enormous expansion of Houdon's powers as a portraitist.[56] The individuals portrayed demonstrate the increased number of the artist's patrons among the French nobility and in the world of the arts. These seven are of such importance that it might be well to identify the subjects before discussing the works in detail. Armand-Thomas Hue, Marquis de Miromesnil (1723–96), was *Garde des Sceaux* (Minister of Justice), highest dignitary in the magistrature of France, under Louis XVI. He succeeded to this eminent position in 1774 on the death of Louis XV, and it is proudly recorded on the back of the marble in the Victoria and Albert Museum,

London: A. T. HUE MARQUIS DE MIROMENIL GARDE DES SCEAUX. Houdon F. 1775. The marble version in the Frick Collection, New York, is inscribed: A. T. HUE   DE MIROMENIL. FAIT PAR HOUDON EN 1777. A point of some curiosity is the blank space in this latter inscription after HUE, where the marble has been scraped as though the word MARQUIS had been erased. Conceivably this occurred during the French Revolution.[57]

Anne-Robert-Jacques Turgot, Baron de l'Aulne (1727–81), one of the most distinguished French economists of the eighteenth century, controller general or minister of finance under Louis XVI, sought, largely in vain, for major reforms in the precarious finances of France. Opposed by the privileged classes, he was finally driven from office. During his brief tenure, however, he was one of the most popular ministers of the king, both among intellectuals and among the masses. He was a cultivated and a sympathetic man, a *philosophe*, a patron of the arts and letters.[58]

The third portrait of distinguished men differs from the other two both in subject and concept. This was Christoph Willibald von Gluck (1714–87), one of the founders of modern opera. Gluck had made his principal reputation in Vienna, and therefore, when he visited Paris in 1773–4 to present his opera *Iphigenia in Aulis*, he enjoyed the patronage of the Austrian dauphine, Marie-Antoinette. The opera was an enormous success both for the composer and for the singer Sophie Arnould in the title role. Houdon, with his rapidly developing talent for seeking out celebrities, commemorated both.[59]

The Salon of 1775 contained, in addition to the remarkable histrionic portrait of Sophie Arnould (1744–1802), three portraits of ladies of the old regime who in different ways typify the qualities of elegance and charm associated with *le Siècle des Femmes*. Madame His (1707–86) was the wife of a banker. She and her husband lived not far from Houdon's studio in the du Roule quarter, and they seem to have become good friends of the sculptor and later of his wife. The Baroness de la Houze was the wife of a diplomat, successively ambassador to the courts of Parma and of Denmark. The Comtesse du Cayla (1755–1816), Élisabeth-Suzanne de Jaucourt, had married her first cousin, Hercule de Baschi, Comte du Cayla, who served in the army of the Prince de Condé and followed him into exile during the Revolution. With the portrait of the countess Houdon had passed in the hierarchy of French society from the wealthy bourgeoisie to the aristocracy of the sword, as with de Miromesnil and with Turgot he had succeeded to the aristocracy of the robe.[60]

Of the seven portraits named, one was designated as plaster, two as marble, and four with the material not specified. From other mentions, as well as from the 1775 date of the London marble of Miromesnil, we may assume this to have been the work shown. *Turgot, Gluck, Madame du Cayla*, and possibly *Madame de la Houze* appeared in the Salon of 1777 as marbles, following Houdon's customary procedure, so it is probable that the 1775 versions were plasters.

The Marquis of Miromesnil is shown in his magisterial robe and wig, which lend him the amplitude of Baroque portrayal, but whose sobriety creates an effect entirely different. The Baroque official portrait image, carried well into the eighteenth century by Jean-Louis Lemoyne, is excellently illustrated in his portrait of the architect, J.-H. Mansart, mentioned above. In the bust of *Mansart*, if anything more imperial than Coysevox's *Louis XIV*, all elements—head, perruque, lace, medals, and cloak—are in suggested movement. Houdon had still followed this tradition in his portrait of Catherine. The eighteenth-century official portrait bust, exemplified in the work of the principal practitioners, J.-B. Lemoyne II, Pajou. Pigalle, Caffieri, and others, tended to be diminished in the scale and undercutting of accessories (as the perruque was diminished under Louis XV) as well as in the accentuation of movement, but to maintain the pose, the dramatic moment, and the swinging rhythm of the rocaille. All these characteristics of the age—although rocaille decoration had already begun to change to the Pompeian classicism of Louis XVI—appear in a number of Houdon's portraits, particularly those of court ladies. But Monsieur de Miromesnil has a quite distinct

MIROMESNIL
Fig. 81

Fig. 17

aura. While his robe has all the amplitude of a Baroque representation, the sculptor accentuates its sobriety by modelling it severely and simply. The considerable mass of the torso, extending almost to the waist, with upper arms represented, is given a static, rectangular frontality rather than a twisting diagonal movement. Only the head turns slightly to his left; and the heavy, judicial wig carries forward the theme established by the austere gown. Houdon has played subtle variations in the modelling of face, gown, and wig, to suggest different textures. The perruque, which is palpably a 'hat of office', has a somewhat unreal look suitable to its nature; the gown is highly finished and the face less so, with a slightly crystalline quality that lends warmth (and, it is to be hoped, does not derive from over-cleaning). The deliberately rectangular organization of the bust is emphasized by the rectangular rather than cylindrical post at the back, and the square base. But in the last analysis all accessories in a portrait bust are only devices to create a harmony and to reinforce the quality of the man or woman portrayed. And here the marquis does not disappoint us. His face is wonderfully mobile, intelligent, caught in a transitory expression with a half-controlled smile, which is in process of change before our eyes. Here can be seen Houdon's ability to catch a passing mood and to record it in a manner that implies what has gone before and what is to follow.

Plate 22

While all the details of finish in the Frick marble of Miromesnil are remarkable, the subtleties in the modeling of the face bear particular examination. The drooping eyelids, the slight shadow under the eyes, the line of the cheekbone, and the creases around the mouth framing the barely caught smile, are not merely illustrations of technical virtuosity and truth to nature. They are the means whereby the artist has penetrated surface appearance to identify a particular individual.

One of the notable characteristics of Houdon's marble sculpture is the manner in which he was able to work the surface of the marble to create effects beautiful in themselves and suggestive of underlying anatomical and formal structure as well as of the intangibles of mind and personality.[61] His developing technique with its stylistic implications can be traced from the *Saint Bruno*, in which the face is schematized, the surface throughout uniform, to the *Diderot*, in which the flesh areas of face and neck are imperceptibly softened, to the *Miromesnil* and other marbles of 1775, in which there are apparent if extremely subtle variations in the surface modeling and texture of flesh, hair, and garments. This process continues in the marbles of the 1770s and 1780s. The later, more neo-classic portraits tend to a greater smoothness and uniformity of surface.

TURGOT
Fig. 83
Plate 23

Terra cottas, plasters, and bronzes posed different problems. Within the medium of terra cotta the manner in which Houdon worked the surface was dependent on whether the particular piece was hand-formed clay or a terra cotta cast. The bust of *Turgot* in the Museum of Fine Arts in Boston is a fine terra cotta perhaps cast from a marble, a fact that is suggested in the precision of details and the way in which the back is carefully closed and finished. The degree of finish for the back of this bust is unusual even in marbles to this point in the artist's career, although it became more common thereafter, particularly in official and commissioned busts. As already noted, the bust of *Turgot* in the 1775 Salon was plaster, probably open at the back, and that exhibited in 1777 was marble.[62] The only surviving marble is in the collection of the Marquis de Naurois-Turgot in the Château de Lantheul (Calvados). This, signed and dated: *par houdon 1778*, has always been in the Turgot family. In 1810 Pierre Samuel du Pont de Nemours, who had been a friend of Turgot and had served under him, 'wrote to his [Turgot's] nephew with the request that he permit a mould to be taken from the marble bust in his possession in order that various friends of Turgot might obtain casts. The mould retained by the artist, Jean-Antoine Houdon, has been broken. In 1812 Mr. du Pont presented to the Society [the American Philosophical Society in Philadelphia] the edition of Turgot's work which he had edited and in 1816 he added to this a cast of the bust.'[63] The plaster cast is still in the Society's headquarters. The date, 1778, probably added when Turgot took possession of the marble, is another instance of Houdon's tendency to delay signing a commissioned work until he actually delivered it.

The account of the American Philosophical Society's plaster is of interest not only in giving a specific history to this piece, something all too often lacking, but also in documenting a serious problem of Houdon research. Here is a clear instance of the casual habit of reproducing Houdon's portrait busts both within the lifetime of the artist and after his death. In this case, since Houdon was alive and active in 1810 and since du Pont de Nemours must have been in touch with him to know that the mould was broken, it is safe to assume that the sculptor made this and presumably other plasters. However, in the case of many reproductions undoubtedly made in his studio during the last years of his life when he was old, inactive, and somewhat senile, it is doubtful that he ever saw them. In the letter addressed to Bachelier, dated October 11, 1794, Houdon complained bitterly at the proliferation of forgeries: '. . . despite the laws of the Old Regime, my works were constantly recast, forged with my name put on them, while others, even less honest, simply copied them adding their own names; and now despite the decrees of the Convention to protect the arts and ownership, they continue to be sold, to be exhibited, to be paraded publicly, and to rob me of my labors . . .'[64] It is perhaps fortunate that he could not foresee the extent to which his sculptures have been copied and forged in the hundred and fifty years since his death.

The terra cotta bust of *Turgot* is a fine example of Houdon's developed style applied to a great man who was also an aristocrat, an important political figure, an intellectual, a scholar, a *philosophe*. Turgot spent the last years of his life in retirement, writing not only on economics but also on science and philosophy, as well as composing commendable poetry. He was a massive man and the bust, showing the full upper torso and the arms half way to the elbow, emphasizes qualities of mass and dignity. In contrast with the *de Miromesnil*, the effect here is of roundness not only in the face but in the manner in which the curving planes of the front torso are carried around the fully modeled and completed back. The hair at the back swings to the left in counterpoise to the turn of the head to his right. The smooth and heavy face, coupled with the intense gaze, suggests great seriousness of purpose. If one dared press character analysis one could see this as the face of an idealist, and a somewhat impatient idealist, in contrast with Monsieur de Miromesnil, who exudes a sardonic wit coupled with a degree of complacency, or with Diderot, who emanates restless energy and insatiable curiosity. It is not difficult to read individual traits in a painting or sculpture when the personality and achievements of the sitter are already known, but the salient fact in the comparison of these three portraits of distinguished eighteenth-century men is how clearly and emphatically they are separated as individuals. There is no formula here, a fact that becomes more striking with each member of Houdon's vast gallery of the men and women of the eighteenth and nineteenth centuries.

Turgot is shown in contemporary court dress presumably of velvets, silks, and laces. As in other court portraits, particularly of ladies, the artist seems to be seeking to demonstrate his ability to render meticulous details in the accessories.[65] The patterned coat, the brocaded vest and the lace at the throat are all depicted with scrupulous precision and obvious delight in the total, decorative pattern achieved. The contrast with the sobriety of Monsieur de Miromesnil's dress is striking. The long hair (which, unusually, seems to be the sitter's own), dressed with elaborate informality, with locks casually arranged around the shoulders and flowing down the back, is more scrupulously rendered than is generally the case with Houdon. Nevertheless the tool marks in the terra cotta are sharply emphasized.

The power of this portrait is such that despite its unusual precision of detail we are not distracted from the face, the central impression of a profound and forceful personality. Rather, we should not be, since du Pont de Nemours, on first seeing the bust in the Salon of 1777, was shocked by what he considered its insipid and even feminine character, but

Fig. 83

apparently changed his mind by 1810, and decided to acquire copies for a number of Turgot's friends.[66]

Yet another instance of Houdon's concern for making the portrait bust a unity, for relating the design of the torso and accessories of dress to the individual portrayed, is to be seen in the *Gluck* presented in the Salon of 1775. Gluck was an artist, a great musician, and therefore must be given the attributes of genius. His face was deeply pockmarked, and the sculptor used this fact to establish his theme. He clothed him in a heavy coat, whose texture is an overall pattern of slashed grooves, free and direct in their expressive impact. Here there was no attempt to simulate the appearance of the actual material, but rather, in a manner almost Rodinesque, to bring out the quality of the clay. The open shirt, the unbuttoned vest, the short, dishevelled hair, and the alert, tilted pose of the head all emphasize the impact of genius. Surviving examples of the bust exist in two versions, one with truncated shoulders, one with full shoulders and indications of the upper arms.[67]

A discussion of Houdon's attempts at formal differentiations in the portrait busts of his early maturity is essential to an understanding of his contribution to the genre. While, in looking at these portraits, we may be primarily concerned with whatever he brought to the understanding and interpretation of a wide diversity of remarkable individuals, it must not be forgotten that the portrait bust represents a difficult artistic form. When a sculptor has isolated and characterized the face, textured the hair and appropriately angled the head, he is faced with the problem of what to do with the segment of torso, which he must add as a sort of base, support, or frame for the head. Obviously even for the greatest sculptors the easiest solution is to establish a more or less uniform fomula, to indicate enough of the body to suggest that it exists and then to swing a fold of drapery establishing a transition to the base or pedestal. This is what most sculptors did even in the eighteenth century, one of the greatest ages of the portrait bust. In a sense these sculptors are fortunate in that their viewers are accustomed to the concept of the truncated figure and give little thought to what a peculiar image the portrait bust actually is. Houdon, with his concern for identification and characterization of all the diverse individuals he portrayed, seems to have been one of the very few eighteenth-century sculptors who gave serious thought to the secondary elements of the figure and how these might serve to bring out the primary nature of the person he was attempting to understand and to interpret.

It must be admitted that Houdon's efforts were limited by the demands of his patrons and by the increasingly prosaic nature of men's clothes towards the end of the eighteenth century and in the early years of the nineteenth. During the latter seventies and eighties he was beginning to secure as patrons dignitaries of the court of Versailles, noblemen who wanted a standard official portrait, medals and all, and ladies of fashion who demanded they be portrayed as such. With the men of letters and science he had no difficulty. There was always the effective portrait *à l'antique*, shoulders draped or undraped; and with universally popular figures such as Voltaire, Rousseau, and Benjamin Franklin, he could happily play every variation. The ever increasing tide of neo-classicism towards the end of the century made the presentation of the modern *philosophe* as ancient philosopher most appropriate. The problems with women's portraits began to appear in the Salon of 1775—if they had not already done so in 1773 with the bust of *Catherine the Great*—and also, where the

opportunity presented itself, his triumphant solution. Of Madame His there is little to say beyond recalling her friendship with the Houdon family. The portrait reflects the elaborate piled up hair-do in imitation of the young Queen Marie Antoinette; and the lady has a greater liveliness and suggestion of intelligence than the queen, at least as the latter appears in the leaden busts of Lecomte and J.-B. Lemoyne. The simple *décolleté* and the band over the left shoulder would suggest an assimilation to the type of Diana so popular with ladies of fashion at this time.[68] Another portrait of a lady, a particularly charming one, may be mentioned here in relation to the lady of fashion theme. This is the plaster of an unknown lady in the Staatliches Museum, Schwerin, bearing the *cachet d'atelier*. It is dated by the museum as *c.* 1770 but seems to belong more properly with *Madame His* and the '*Baroness de la Houze*' *c.* 1775. The hair is done like that of *Madame His*, similarly in the Marie-Antoinette mode, with a long curl falling over the shoulder; the gown is simple and casually draped over the breasts, a large fold of drapery acts similarly as a transition to the base.[69] The marble of '*Baroness de la Houze*' in the Huntington Library is the most monumental in scale of Houdon's busts of women and one of the finest in quality. Although he may not have been able to draw fine distinctions between his ladies of fashion, about whom he probably knew little, the sculptor did obviously warm to the challenge when the lady was also lovely. There was no question that the 'Baroness' was this, and he brought her to life with all the elegance, grace, and even sensuousness that we associate with but do not always find in the old regime of France. Although the formula is the same as in the two preceding busts, the elements are now composed with a flair and sweep that take us back to some of the great portraits of the seventeenth century. The dress with its delicate lace edge is pulled tightly to emphasize the breasts, twisted with the diagonal turn of the torso. The drapery is modeled with the resonance of the Baroque, deeply indented, with strong diagonal lines in front and encompassing curves at the back, which take in the pedestal as well as the figure. This is one of Houdon's finest bravura performances. The 'Baroness's' coiffure, less elaborate and by that token more naturally attractive than the Marie-Antoinette style, falls in soft curls over both shoulders; the head sharply turned to her right, she seems on the point of greeting someone, her eyes wide, her lips parted.[70]

Mademoiselle Sophie Arnould in the title role of Gluck's *Iphigenia in Aulis* is a very different but equally spectacular achievement in this year of 1775. The famous actress-singer, born in 1744, was at the height of her powers. Only four years later she was forced into retirement as a result of her scandalous love affairs. She was the first of Houdon's small but remarkable gallery of theatrical sitters, certainly the most melodramatic in the interpretation of the role of Iphigenia. Iphigenia, daughter of Agamemnon and Clytemnestra in the plays of Sophocles and Euripides on which Gluck's operas were based, condemned to be sacrificed to Artemis-Diana, was reprieved by the goddess and dedicated to her cult at Tauris. She is shown as consecrated to Artemis, and hence the wide sash she wears is ornamented with crescent moon and stars. Houdon's master, Michel-Ange Slodtz, had also made a marble bust of Iphigenia, although in a quite different context; it was highly praised by Diderot when shown in the Salon of 1759.[71] There is little relationship between the figure by Slodtz and that by Houdon beyond the fact that each wears a wide sash decorated with a crescent moon. The former is more pensively tragic, her head turned far to her right, her eyes half closed; her hair is decorated with the laurel leaves sacred to Artemis. The interpretation is in general more quietly classic, closer to Houdon's *Vestal* than to his *Mademoiselle Arnould*; who, in fact, is one of his most rococo concepts, theatrical in pose and expression, at once delicately feminine and chastely erotic, elegant and abandoned. It is obvious that the sculptor, though his theme is classical, is here in no sense concerned with the imitation of antiquity. What he gives us is antiquity as interpreted in the classical French drama (or in this case opera), in which there was no concern for anachronisms in costume; and the more violently an emotion was torn asunder the better pleased were both audiences and actors. Iphigenia appears to us here as she undoubtedly did on the stage, her hair and dress in careful disarray, one charming breast exposed, face turned up to the heavens and exaggerated eyes rolling even higher as she prays for the mercy of the goddess. Although Houdon's bust is deliberately theatrical in the stage sense, it does remind us of several works by Bernini in which the emotion expressed is both more violent and more authentic. Proserpina in the group of *Pluto and Proserpina* and Daphne in that of *Apollo and Daphne* express their panic with wide staring eyes and screaming mouth. The ecstasy of Saint Theresa is apparent not only in the gasping mouth, but in the eyes, which seem to have rolled up

THE SALON OF 1775

Fig. 82
Plate 26

MME DE
LA HOUZE
Fig. 80, Plate 27

MLLE ARNOULD
Fig. 79
Plate 25

under the upper eyelid until the pupils have disappeared. The formula appears time and again in saints and angels by Bernini, to express the ultimate of passion. A notable relationship can be seen in Bernini's bust of the *Anima Beata*, in which the expression of the saved soul with deeply undercut, upturned eyes and parted lips—and even the roses in her hair—recall Mademoiselle Arnould. Although Slodtz, in general a much closer follower of Bernini than was Houdon, did not follow Bernini in his interpretation of Iphigenia, his companion bust of the priest of Apollo, Chryses, is Berninesque in the emotionality of the aged, upturned face and rolling eyes, and at the same time reminiscent of ancient portraits of the blind Homer.[72]

A fascinating sidelight on the Sophie Arnould portrait is the existence of the contract between the singer and the artist, a document of unparalleled value.[73] In this, which is dated April 5, 1775, Houdon agreed to deliver the marble the following August. Further, he agreed to make for her *thirty* copies in plaster repaired [in the sense of 'finished'] by himself; and to deliver to her the terra cotta which had served as a model. He promised to make no further busts in any material for anyone else, but to furnish her with additional plasters as she might need them, at a small additional fee. This is clear proof of the incredible proliferation of duplicates authorized and supervised by the artist. It is also remarkable that almost all traces of the plasters, not to mention the unique terra cotta, have disappeared. While it was somewhat unusual for an individual to order so many replicas (Mademoiselle Arnould had a wide circle of friends and lovers), and in most instances the sitter wished to restrict rather than to multiply the copies; in the case of models who were great public figures, such as Voltaire, Rousseau, or Franklin, we know that the artist himself reproduced his portrait busts almost indefinitely; and, of course, these have continued to be copied or forged down to the present day.

The last identifiable portrait of a woman in the Salon of 1775 is that of the *Comtesse du Cayla*, one of the most delightful likenesses in Houdon's repertoire. As has been pointed out, his ruthless eye did not permit him to flatter a sitter, even a lady of noble birth; but when he was faced with a sitter as obviously lovely as the countess, with all the charm and freshness of youth, he was clearly inspired to extra effort. Thus, as is inevitable with great portraiture, the subject cannot be divorced from the work of art. At the same time, even when faced with so inspiring a subject as the Comtesse du Cayla, it is the task of the most realist sculptor to call into being a new and parallel reality.

The youthful loveliness of the countess is self-evident in the bust and needs no further description or analysis. The marble in the Frick Collection, New York, is sufficient evidence. It was the plaster that was shown in the Salon of 1775, the marble in that of 1777. In contrast with *Mademoiselle Arnould*, only one plaster and one marble are recorded and, as far as is known, only the marble survives. The countess was twenty years old when portrayed by Houdon in the guise of a bacchante, a personification that may have been suggested by the count as a play on his family name of Baschi. The god, Bacchus, appeared on his coat of arms. In any event it is a most chaste and slightly amused bacchante, not one of the company of noble ladies who chose to appear as Venus or Diana as a means of revealing their unadorned charms. The theme of bacchante did suggest to the artist a composition in motion, the first he had attempted since the *Priest of the Lupercalia* from his student days in Rome. The countess is shown with her hair and light draperies blown back, the figure acutely angled as though she is running. Even the manner in which the marble is cut under the arms emphasizes the angularity of the off-balance position. Although each work is highly individual, there are many relationships between the *Comtesse du Cayla*, *Mademoiselle Arnould*, and the '*Baroness de la Houze*'. The sharp precision in the modeling of the draperies the particular fineness of the hair texture, the clinging, revealing dresses, even details like the roses in the hair of the countess and Sophie Arnould; all these and other elements, such as the linear feeling and the emphasis on broken contours, reveal Houdon at his most rococo.[74]

This rococo quality was unquestionably in large degree a consequence of the fact that his models were ladies of high fashion who belonged, or who aspired to belong, in the world of Versailles. Even the style of their dress and coiffure put them in a different, more rarefied and more traditional world than the artist had yet encountered among his patrons. Just at the time when he was at his most rococo, exploring a mode already well past its peak in the 1770s except, curiously, at Court, Houdon continued to experiment with his own approach to classicism. The idea of sculpting the *Comtesse du Cayla* in motion may reflect the fact that he was already working on a design for a running *Diana*. The plaster of the statue is dated 1776 and the marble bust of *Diana* appeared in the Salon of 1777. There are also the classic variants on the *Peasant Girl of Frascati* dated 1774 and 1775, and the *Roman Youth*, 1775.

The origin of Houdon's *Le Baiser donné*, *The Given Kiss*, probably goes back to about 1774 although the best surviving marble is signed and dated: HOUDON 1778. (Wildenstein Gallery, New York). This is a group, in the form of busts, in which the handsome lover leans tenderly over his beloved, who abandons herself to the ecstasy of the kiss. The subject derives from La Fontaine's *Fables* and was a popular subject for both painters and sculptors of the eighteenth century. Houdon's version is his most conscious exercise in the rococo vein of Falconet and Clodion. It has even been attributed to Clodion. Although not exhibited in any Salon there are many contemporary references to it as well as to a companion piece, *Le Baiser rendu*, which has not been identified.[74a]

Houdon made many copies of this popular subject, which in its rococo quality belongs with the *Comtesse du Cayla* and *Sophie Arnould*. Like the former the beloved is conceived as a bacchante, though by no means so chaste a follower of Bacchus; rather her abandonment to passion and her bared breast suggest *Mademoiselle Arnould*. The wreaths of roses binding the lovers together remind us of those that decorate the hair of the countess and Sophie. The young lover could be the same model who posed for the *Morpheus* with the same cap of soft curls and even the same suggestion of side-whiskers. That the sculptor had estimated the market shrewdly for so erotic a work as *Le Baiser donné* is evidenced by the innumerable later copies in terra cotta, Sèvres porcelain and bronze.

THE Salons of 1775, 1777, and 1779 witness the period of greatest activity in Houdon's career, in the quantity and quality of portrait busts produced. 1777 included a substantial number of the marbles for which the plasters were introduced in 1775. The principal personal event of this period was the artist's admission as a full member of the Academy, July 26, 1777, with a reduced marble version of his *Morpheus* as his *morceau de réception*.[75] He could now sign himself Academician. His established reputation as a portraitist was documented by the number and the nature of his commissions; but he still had received no royal or official commission for major sculptures in France. Although some discrimination against him has been inferred on the part of the artistic establishment, it should also be recalled that with the death of the Marquise de Pompadour in 1764 royal patronage had declined drastically. Under Louis XVI this decline continued as a result of perennial budget problems; and there were few informed and influential patrons in the immediate circle of the Court. The French Royal Academy of Painting and Sculpture under the old regime was, as has been pointed out, an extremely small, inbred, and stratified organization; and both seniority and politics played a large part in the assignment of major commissions. In 1777 Guillaume II Coustou, the Rector of the Academy, had just died. Pigalle, a favorite of Madame de Pompadour, devoted his latter career to a series of great monuments, of which the tomb of the Maréchal de Saxe is the most notable. In fact he seems largely to have controlled the available commissions, with the result that he did not exhibit in the Salons during these years.[76] Augustin Pajou (1730–1809), favorite sculptor of Madame du Barry, became the official sculptor of the king, Louis XVI, assuming thus a preferred position in the matter of commissions. In 1777 only ten sculptors exhibited, of whom nine were academicians (Houdon, the most recent appointee, was at the bottom of the list) and one was *agréé*. Although the total number of exhibitors had increased substantially in 1789, the last Salon of the old regime, there were still eight academicians senior to Houdon. This was, after all, a life appointment.[77] The problem as far as royal commissions were concerned seems not to have been discrimination against Houdon but the scarcity of such commissions during his maturity, and the fact that, as will be seen with the commissions of the Great Men, these were largely assigned in order of seniority. So the sculptor continued to cultivate his patrons outside France and to work obsessively on his portrait commissions. He was also resuming his experiments with mythological themes, in some cases commissioned by private patrons, in others carried out on his own. And he was soon to be launched on his own enormously successful series of Great Men.

Houdon contributed to the Salon of 1777 a marble bust of *Diana*, his marble *Morpheus*, a life-size *Naiad*, a marble medallion of *Minerva*, and the bronze of his *Vestal*; as well as fifteen busts of contemporaries, a miscellany of medallions, study heads, animals, and portraits in wax, two sketches for further tombs of the Galitzin, and a posthumous bust of *Charles IX* for the Collège Royal.

Of the fifteen portrait busts, the *Comtesse du Cayla*, *Turgot*, and *Gluck* were marble versions of the plasters of 1775. There was also the superb marble bust of *Madame de ****, traditionally identified as the Baroness de La Houze, discussed above.[78] *Madame* (la Comtesse de Provence) has disappeared, as have *Mademoiselle Bocquet*, and *Charles IX*; also the study heads in terra cotta, the marble of *Gluck*, the unidentified medallions and now it seems even the marble medallion of *Minerva*; the life-size *Naiad*, the wax portraits, and one of the sketches for the Galitzin tombs. Nevertheless much remains.

This was the year when the artist finally gained access to the royal family, though not to the king himself. The first four portraits listed, all in marble, are those of *Monsieur*, the Comte de Provence, brother of Louis XVI, to be Louis XVIII under the Restoration; *Madame*, his wife; *Madame Adélaïde*, and *Madame Victoire*, aunts of the king. The letter from Houdon, dated January 29, 1789, cited in note 81, describes the circumstances of these commissions, as well as summarizing his problems of receiving payment:

> *Sir*:
>
> I have the honor to make reply that, having gone to make the bust of Madame Victoire, agreeably to the order rec'd from that Princess, through Monsieur le Comte d'Altay, now some 9 or 10 years since, she persuaded Madame Adélaïde to have hers made also; that in the same way at the solicitation of these ladies Monsieur and Madame determined to confide to me the execution of their own, and that at the last sitting, having thought it appropriate to ask the Prince and Princess whether it was their desire to have the busts executed in marble, they said they so wished it. These are the orders I received from their own lips, and I am reminded that having presented myself for admittance at Monsieur's I was asked by what authority? To which I replied that the Prince had bidden me call at that hour, and that immediately the door was opened to me.
>
> When after several years I addressed myself to each house for payment, Madame Adélaïde sent me word to apply to Monsieur le Comte d'Anguilliers [Angiviller, *Directeur des Bâtiments*].
>
> The letters and appeals on this subject addressed to Monsieur Pierre and the *Directeur* mention the period at which these works were executed. Neither Monsieur Pierre nor the Comte has honored with their replies my various statements—which I would

not have expected, after sending the history of the matter to Monsieur Pierre, at his own request, for presentation to the *Directeur*.

I am, Sir, with gratitude,

Your very humble and obedient servant,

Houdon

At Paris, this 29th January, 1789. [Translation, Hart and Biddle, *Houdon*, pp. 22–3.]

A plaster of *Monsieur* survives in the National Museum, Stockholm, signed and dated 1775, with MONSIEUR COMTE DE PROVENCE lettered on the front of the base. This comes from the collection of Gustaf III of Sweden (1746-92). *Monsieur* (1755-1824) is depicted as a heavy, rather handsome young man in richly engraved armor, wearing all his decorations. Head and torso are compactly organized and much attention is paid to accessories. It is in effect an official portrait, a junior version of the later *Louis XVI*, and equally uninspired in the subject. One detail in the organization of the torso bears mention, one that already had appeared in the *Gluck*. This is a bust extending below the chest with shoulders and upper arms indicated. The stump of the right arm is extended from the body as though indicating an invisible gesture. An innovation is the signature appearing on the end of the stump, a device Houdon was to use increasingly in his larger, more formal portraits of men.[79]

COMTE DE PROVENCE

Fig. 85

Plate 30

If the *Comte de Provence* lacks individuality this cannot be said of his two elderly maiden aunts, daughters of Louis XV.[80] Beautifully rendered in marble with exquisite detailing of dress, skin, and hair, they are again superb examples of the artist's decorative style. There is no flattery in either of the characterizations. *Madame Adélaïde*, with her squirrel-like teeth, has a certain eager, inquisitive quality, while *Madame Victoire*, who has run to the embonpoint to which members of the royal house tended, exudes complacency in her royal status. Not that there is anything particularly royal about either of the ladies. They have, in fact, something of the aggressively bourgeois quality to be found in the American portraits of John Singleton Copley. Although these first royal portraits undoubtedly helped to consolidate Houdon's reputation, we can see that his financial dealings with royalty were not so happy. In 1785, when he was about to depart for the United States to undertake the statue of George Washington, he was still attempting to secure payment for the bust of *Madame Adélaïde*. The princess contended that she had never ordered the bust, and attempted to pass the bill to d'Angiviller, *Directeur des Bâtiments*. The latter, after vainly trying to find out what had happened, although recognizing that the artist must be paid, finally went in desperation to the king, who authorized him to pay. That was in 1785, but from the letter quoted, Houdon still does not seem to have been paid in 1789. This long exchange of letters is typical of many surviving documents about Houdon's life.[81] Since he was not a literary artist (unlike Falconet, who wrote perceptively on sculpture) nor even a literate man, the records from which his biography must be pieced together are all too often of the most mundane nature.

MME ADÉLAÏDE
MME VICTOIRE

Figs. 87–8

Plates 31–2

As the number of the sculptor's portraits multiply, so do problems of attribution. An instance is the marble bust of the *Comtesse de Jaucourt* (1735-74), mother of the Comtesse du Cayla. *Madame la Comtesse de Jaucourt* is No. 240 in the *livret* of the 1777 Salon.[82] This work seems to have an impeccable history, to have descended in the de Jaucourt family until 1912. It was presented to the Louvre by the great collector, David-Weill, in 1937. The marble is signed on the back of the base: A. HOUDON FECIT. 1777, in a manner and style completely characteristic of this period. The Louvre handbook of sculpture states that the model was made in 1773, a date corroborated by the late Louis XV coiffure. The marble was thus a posthumous bust, dated at the time of exhibition or delivery. The carving of the figure and details such as the lace over the breasts, and the cloak tying together figure and base, are fine and typical of the portraits of the time. The small head suspended on the long, graceful neck, the close curls of the hair, as well as the alert turn of the head, suggest that the artist

COMTESSE DE JAUCOURT

Fig. 89

Plates 34–5

may have posed the countess *à la Diane*, an hypothesis supported by her elegant, somewhat aquiline features and the band arranged diagonally between her breasts—Diana's quiver strap. Since the marble bust of the late Comtesse de Jaucourt must have been presented in the Salon of 1777 as a commemorative companion to the marble of her daughter, the Comtesse du Cayla, and since the latter was depicted as a bacchante, it was not inappropriate although a trifle odd iconographically, that her mother should appear as Diana.

We know that at this time Houdon was much involved with the theme of Diana; and his use of the quiver strap has been mentioned. The general concept of this portrait seems to combine elements of the classic with the rococo, again very likely at this point. Yet with all these arguments in its favor, there is something disturbing about the marble. The head in particular has a certain coldness, a mechanical quality such as is found in accomplished copies. The fact that the nose has been broken and not perfectly repaired may add to the impression, but probably the most uncharacteristic feature is the treatment of the hair, which is completely dead and mechanical. Yet as a whole the bust has great beauty and finesse and it is certainly not adapted from any known sculpture by Houdon or by anyone else. In fact, given the basic appearance of the subject, this is an interpretation, combining as it does the classic and rococo aspects of the artist's style—as he was to combine them even more dramatically in the *Diana*—that one would almost expect of him in the mid-1770s. We have, then, three alternatives: first, this is a studio piece or a later copy; second, given Houdon's presumed dislike of posthumous busts, his inspiration flagged and he left much of the execution to assistants (though apparently the model was made from life); third, the sculpture is unfinished. Having studied the bust at length at several different times, the third theory is the one to which I lean. The existing qualities both in conception and technique are too remarkable and individual to belong to anyone else at this period but Houdon. The main flaw is in the carving of the hair; and here the impression I have is not that of another sculptor or of Houdon on a bad day, but rather that the main effect has been blocked out and the refinements never completed. Towards the apex of the coiffure at the left is a circular form, meaningless in its present state, that looks like nothing so much as an uncompleted rose. It should be compared with the roses in the hair of the *Comtesse du Cayla* or of *Mademoiselle Arnould*.

If this theory is accepted, there are still questions. Why was the sculpture never finished? Why would Houdon sign it in this unfinished state? Why would the family of the countess accept it? I do not have the final answers to these questions, but until these are found I am happy to see *Madame de Jaucourt* on exhibition in the Houdon room in the Louvre with *Madame Adélaïde* and *Mademoiselle Arnould*. I only regret that, owing to restrictive lending policies of various museums, it will never be possible to see them joined, even briefly, by the *Comtesse du Cayla*, *Madame Victoire*, the purported '*Baroness de la Houze*' and, to complete this wonderful company, the bust of *Diana*.

To the assemblage of noble and/or lovely ladies who graced the Salon of 1777 should MME SERVAT
Fig. 90
Plate 143d be added the marble portrait of *Madame Servat*,[83] inscribed: MARIE ADELAYDE GIRAUT SERVAT A. HOUDON, F. AN. 1776. Madame Servat, the wife of an *amateur des arts* whose distinguished collection of paintings and prints marked him as an obvious man of substance, was portrayed by the artist with the elaborate elegance of this background. Her hair is swept up and back in the coiffure *à la mode*, which even the elderly Madame Adélaïde affected. Her *décolleté* is low and revealing, her rounded breasts delicately outlined in exquisitely rendered lace; her torso enveloped in an intricately draped wrap, whose bravura carving transcends even those of *Mesdames*, and rivals that of the '*Baroness de la Houze*'. In these Salons and that of 1787—but in the latter for men—Houdon is at his most Baroque in his use of the enveloping drapery as a base for the portrait and as transition to the pedestal.

Throughout, *Madame Servat* is a technical achievement in the carving of the marble. This was obviously a commission in which Houdon was told to spare no expense and, since there was not a great deal he could do with the rather bland face, he lavished his talents on the accessories. One is reminded in some degree of the portrait of Catherine the Great, a recollection emphasized by the fact that the eyes are treated in the same uncharacteristic, shallowly modeled manner.

Three other busts exhibited in 1777 deserve particular mention. The Baron de Vietinghoff was another of those Russian noblemen who, impressed by the patronage of Catherine, or introduced by the Russian ambassador, Prince Galitzin, were always dropping in at Houdon's studio, and rarely left Paris without being recorded by him for posterity. A distinguished patron of theatre and music, the baron, whose estates were in Livonia, was German by birth and French by culture. Although the plaster of his portrait is recorded in the 1777 Salon, the terra cotta in Houdon's list of his sculpture, *c.* 1784: 'No. 16. Buste en terre de *M. le Barron de Fitinioff*' [Houdon's spelling], and the marble in the Berlin Museum until 1944, this claim to immortality was almost frustrated. The terra cotta, as might be expected, disappeared; the plaster was destroyed in 1905 in a fire; and the marble was damaged, thought to be destroyed, in the 1944 bombing of Berlin.[84] Despite its present damaged state it is possible to report that this is one of Houdon's superior portraits of an imperious gentleman whose features and bearing suggest a considerable degree of intelligence. Although he is shown in modern dress, simple but elegant, and wearing the short, compact wig of the period, the truncated torso in the manner of *Diderot, d'Alembert, Buffon*, and others, suggests that the artist was placing his sitter among the intellectuals, the *philosophes*, rather than the aristocracy.

The marble of *Baron de Vietinghoff* has another interesting feature; it is signed and dated in Houdon's cursive script: *houdon f. 1791*. Since the plaster was exhibited in 1777 and in Houdon's *c.* 1784 list the terra cotta is grouped with the works made before 1777, the question arises whether the marble represents a different bust, made at a later sitting. As later replicas in Russia of the 1777 plaster, although of inferior quality, are clearly the same as the marble, it must be concluded that the marble was not ordered or delivered until thirteen or fourteen years after the plaster was made, and that Houdon, with his own peculiar logic, dated it as of the time of delivery.[85]

The other two portrait busts to be discussed from the Salon of 1777 may be said to have suffered an almost entirely opposite fate to that of the *Baron de Vietinghoff*: that of being destroyed by their very popularity. These are the portraits of *Alexandre* and *Louise Brongniart*. The father of these delightful children, a distinguished architect, was a friend of Houdon; so the sculptor had the opportunity to reveal himself as a master in the portraiture of children.[86] Aside from representations of the Christ child and putti—infant Angel or Eros, none precisely a portrait—there are few satisfactory sculptures of children before the eighteenth century. But this century found a new image of children as it had found of women. Houdon's children's portraits are particularly engaging. When the terra cottas of *Alexandre* and *Louise Brongniart* were acquired by the Louvre in 1898, André Michel was inspired to an ecstatic description: 'I do not think that the master has modeled anything more simple and more delicate, ever caressed the human form in its flower with a hand more knowing and more tender.'[87] Houdon revealed in these busts and subsequently in others, including those of his own three daughters, a marvelous capacity for conveying the freshness and innocence of childhood without sentimentality. His children are definite personalities with their own thoughts and their own integrity. The boy, Alexandre, who was born in 1770 and was to become a noted geologist and director of the Sèvres porcelain factories, looks into the distance, wide-eyed, seemingly lost in a reverie. The girl, Louise, lifts her head alertly and gazes past the spectator, as though listening intently.

As might be expected, these portrayals of children were among the most popular of all Houdon's busts and were reproduced in innumerable versions and all conceivable materials. Houdon himself made a variant of the *Louise Brongniart* showing her with a little shawl over her shoulders and her hair done up in a sort of turban.[88]

Plate 38

Another child equally meriting Monsieur Michel's paean may join the *Brongniart* children in this year of 1777, even though she does not appear in the Salon. Here we have another instance where the problem is not the authenticity of the bust but the identity of the sitter. In the Musée des Arts Décoratifs, Paris, there is an unsigned plaster of a little girl with wind-blown hair. A marble exists in the Courty Collection, signed *houdon* under the left shoulder, but not dated. In an article in *The Connoisseur* in October, 1950, Réau identified her as Adèle, the third daughter of the painter, Hubert Robert. The Salon of 1783 includes:

'LA PETITE
ROBERT'

'No. 244. *Mademoiselle Robert*, fille de M. Robert, peintre du Roi [Marble]'; and the inventory, *c.* 1784, lists, under 1783, 'No. 107. Buste en marbre de la petite Robert.' Since the birth date of Adèle is not known, Réau conjectured that she could have been four or five years old in 1783, approximately the age that the little girl portrayed appears to be. He presented his identification as an hypothesis and, on the basis of Houdon's apparent old friendship with Robert, dating back to their days in Rome, it was attractive and had been generally accepted.

Fig. 95

Plate 143e

Another marble of the same child, in the Bowes Museum, Barnard Castle, County Durham, England, was recently brought to my attention by Bryan Crossling, Keeper of Art. This includes across the back the signature and date: A. HOUDON, F. AN. 1777, in a form so characteristic of the artist at this period as to be unquestionably authentic. There was never any question about Houdon's authorship but, unfortunately, the child would have been too old in 1783 to be *La Petite Robert*.

The Salon of 1777, one of Houdon's banner Salons in quantity and quality of works exhibited, saw a wide variety of other subjects aside from this impressive group of portrait busts—only the unquestionable surviving examples of which have been discussed. The

NAIAD

Vestal and the *Morpheus* have been described above. The life-size plaster of a *Naiad*, exhibited, as was frequently the case with large and fragile objects, at the Bibliothèque du Roi, has disappeared; but Saint-Aubin made a detailed drawing of it separate from his

Fig. 92

livret sketches. The drawing, of two views, reveals this as an elaborate fountain design, the figure of the nymph pouring water from an urn to the shell basin surmounting a decorative pedestal. Figure and pedestal are in the tradition of rococo fountain sculpture, a point of some interest since the artist at this very moment was working on his much more austere and classic *Diana*. The marble of the *Naiad*, intended for the gardens of Monsieur Boutin, treasurer-general of the navy, was apparently never carried out; so Saint-Aubin's drawing remains the sole visual record.[89]

The terra cotta sketches for the other Galitzin tombs—never to be realized in final form—were also shown. That for Prince Pjotr Mikhailovitch Galitzin, who was killed in a duel (according to rumors assassinated at the instigation of Potemkin, the most notable of Catherine's minister-lovers), has also disappeared. The other sketch survives, a gift to the Louvre by Albert de Vandeul, a descendant of Diderot. It is again a relief, more intricate in composition and subject than the two earlier marble tombs. Prince Alexander

Fig. 96

Mikhailovitch Galitzin, vice-chancellor of Russia, rests on his sarcophagus, consoled by *Virtue* while *Friendship* mourns him. The phantoms of Life, *Envy* on one side and *Abundance* on the other, fade into the background. Saddled with the elaborate literary symbolism, the artist managed to achieve a work of considerable distinction, avoiding the overblown theatre of eighteenth-century Baroque tombs. The miniature figures of the small sketch are beautifully modeled, grouped with restraint, idealized—with the exception of *Envy*, where he allows himself some appropriate violence. The use of very low relief for the background figures contrasts with the emphasis normally placed in Baroque tomb sculpture on the macabre death symbols.[90]

Houdon's occasional excursions into animal sculpture are represented in this Salon by one entry: No. 252. Several animals in marble. Of these, one sketched by Saint-Aubin (who

Fig. 97

documented the Salon of 1777 in particular detail) survives: *La Grive morte* (The Dead Thrush), a high relief marble, exquisitely rendered, signed in the cursive script: *houdon f.*[91]

Two specifically classical subjects remain to be examined: the little known marble medallion of *Minerva* (No. 251), and the most important marble bust of *Diana* (No. 248). The medallion of *Minerva*,[92] of which there was formerly a plaster in the Gotha Museum, was modeled in low, relatively uniform relief, the drapery stylized, the flesh parts, face, neck, and arms, flattened. The profile has the aggressively classic nose, small mouth and heavy chin of the Hellenistic tradition.[93] The effect is that of a Hellenistic coin of good quality, and this might conceivably have been its model. If the plaster actually represents Houdon's *Minerva*, the interpretation is different from the heads of the *Vestal* and the *Diana*, both exhibited in the same Salon of 1777.[94]

Saint-Aubin drew the bust of *Diana* in the Salon of 1777 with particular precision. From the shoulder strap passing diagonally between her breasts and over her right shoulder, this would seem to be the bust now in the National Gallery of Art, Washington, D.C., dated 1778.[95] The band to hold her quiver appears in the marble statue in Lisbon but neither quiver nor band appears in the plaster, bronze, or terra cotta statues.[96] Houdon had been experimenting for several years with the idea of a *Diana* parting for the chase. In 1775, when the Duke of Saxe-Gotha had finally rejected the designs for the tomb of his mother, the late duchess, Grimm had suggested that the duke should compensate the artist for his years of work, and for the damage done to his reputation, by ordering a statue for his gardens.[97] He proposed a *Diana* which Houdon had made the previous year, 1774, and which he described as a seated figure, curved in an academic [classic?] posture. Grimm was somewhat vague about the figure he had in mind and may have been confusing the *Diana* with another statue in Houdon's studio; in any event it was not the *Diana* that finally evolved. The duke accepted the proposal for a *Diana* and Houdon produced the plaster of his statue, which is signed and dated: Houdon. F. 1776. This was shown in his studio while the marble bust was exhibited at the Salon proper.[98]

Fig. 99

The theme of *Diana the Huntress* derives from antiquity; and there is a continuous tradition in painting and sculpture from the Renaissance to the eighteenth century and beyond. It was particularly popular in France from the sixteenth to the eighteenth century, transplanted from Italy with Primaticcio and the School of Fontainebleau. One of the Renaissance interpretations close to that of Houdon is the painting in the Louvre attributed to Luca Penni and inspired by Diane de Poitiers, mistress of Henri II, in which the striding goddess is shown virtually nude. Usually *Diana Huntress* was garbed in a short tunic, following Hellenistic representations such as the *Diana with Hart* at Versailles. It was this version that Coysevox adapted in his portrayal of Marie-Adélaïde of Savoy, as did Coustou, J.-L. Lemoyne and others in their *Companions of Diana* for the gardens of the Château of Marly. The sculptor L.-C. Vassé designed a *Diana Huntress* for Frederick the Great in 1770, a work that Houdon saw in the studio before it was sent to Berlin. Despite its academic coldness it could have sparked the concept of a *Diana Huntress* of his own.[99]

Fig. 15

Houdon's statue embodied two elements which, if not unique, were at least unusual in the tradition of *Diana Huntress*, those of rapid movement and complete nudity. The suggestion of motion exists in previous versions but not the running stance achieved by balancing the goddess on the ball of one foot. Motion of all degrees permeates both painting and sculpture of the Baroque and its extension to the rococo. Poses even more daring than that of Houdon may be seen in late Renaissance bronzes such as Giovanni da Bologna's *Mercury* and Pierre Biard's statue of *Fame* (Louvre). The nude *Diana* was depicted from the sixteenth to the eighteenth century, but normally as a reclining figure, for instance Cellini's *Nymph of Fontainebleau* and the *Diana with Stag*, in the Louvre; or in the common theme of *Diana at her Bath*, *surprised by Actaeon*. Allegrain exhibited his marble *Diana at her Bath* in 1777. It was shown in his studio while Houdon exhibited his life-size plaster *Diana* at his studio the same year.

Allegrain's *Diana*, which the Salon commentators inevitably compared with that of

Houdon, is a charming figure, intended as a companion to his *Venus at her Bath* executed in 1766 and listed as a *Baigneuse* in the *livret* of 1767. This *Diana* continues the rococo tradition of soft and erotic femininity. As Bachaumont describes her: 'But much as she hides them [her charms] on one side, so does she expose them on the other.'[100] The exhibition of Allegrain's *Diana* at his studio was explained by the size and fragility of the piece and, although the fact is not stated explicitly, the same reason might account for Houdon's plaster *Diana* not appearing in the Salon proper. Another possible reason of some interest was the stricter censorship that had been in force since Louis XVI ascended the throne in 1774.

Houdon's *Diana* shocked some of the bureaucrats, if not the general public of the time, by her stark nudity and the explicit rendition of the vulva. Whether Houdon was compelled to be explicit by his passion for veracity, or deliberately set out to draw attention to his work through the element of shock, is not known. The dominant impression in the *Diana*, despite the sensuous handling of surfaces, particularly in the marble, is one of chaste, classic elegance; so the latter hypothesis seems unlikely. Nevertheless, the plaster for the Salon of 1777 which, unlike a marble could have been transported easily and safely, was exhibited in the artist's studio rather than at the Salon; and the bronze listed in the Salon of 1783 was exhibited at the home of the owner, Monsieur Girardot de Marigny.[101]

Fig. 101
Plate 40a

The marble *Diana* was intended for the Duke of Saxe-Gotha, as Grimm's letter of January 24, 1775, and a contract of sale dated January 10, 1782, clearly document.[102] The price in this contract, it should be noted, was 10,000 livres, with the cost of the marble borne by the duke. Thus the marble at this point (1782) belonged to the duke. Baron Grimm, as the duke's minister to France, acted for him. Then, on February 7, 1783, Grimm, who was also acting as agent for Catherine the Great in the purchase of works of art, wrote to tell her that the statue of Voltaire she had ordered was ready to be shipped, and offering her the same marble *Diana* at a price of *20,000* livres. His explanation was that the *Diana*, ordered by the duke, had been delayed in Paris because of the war and, as the moment of its departure approached, the artist was becoming increasingly apprehensive that it might be damaged in transit to Germany, since it would have to travel much of the way by land. On the other hand it could go all the way to Saint Petersburg by water, a much safer trip. Grimm assured Catherine that he could persuade the duke to take a bronze in its place. Catherine was at first somewhat reluctant, for fear of offending the duke, and also does not seem to have had much enthusiasm for the piece—her taste ran rather to fine furniture and portraits of the great French *philosophes*. Finally she agreed and the marble went to Russia where it remained until it was sold by the Soviet government to Calouste Gulbenkian in 1930. It is now part of his collection in the museum endowed by him in Lisbon.[103]

There has been much speculation on the actual reason for the change in destination of the marble *Diana*. It may be that the existing documents tell the entire story. The doubling of the price makes one wonder if Grimm and Houdon were conniving at a little chicanery, but nothing we know about either of them would suggest such a thing. So it is perhaps best to accept the facts at their face value. Whatever happened, the duke received the plaster

Fig. 99

cast dated 1776 (now in the Gotha Museum) and, since there is no evidence that he ever received a bronze, he must have decided to settle for the plaster.[104]

Fig. 101

The marble, signed in capital letters, and dated 1780, shows certain technical modifications from the plaster, terra cotta, and bronzes. In this material it was necessary to provide additional support for the goddess, and hence the artist set her against a bush of reeds, to which she is attached at various points of the left leg, thigh, the bow held diagonally in her left hand, and the quiver slung behind her suspended by the shoulder strap. Her right hand holds an arrow. Large, free-standing marble statues, such as the *Hermes* of Praxiteles, from Greek and Roman times down through the Renaissance and Baroque, have been supported in a comparable manner, usually by the stump of a tree. The reed bush provided a more open and less obtrusive support. Bernini and his followers solved the problem by enveloping figures in draperies or surrounding them with clouds of glory. Houdon himself in earlier plasters, such as *L'Écorché* at Gotha, the plaster of *Saint John the Baptist* in the Borghese Gallery, and the *Priest of the Lupercalia* at Gotha, had used the tree trunk support, perhaps because he envisaged translating them into marble. In later plaster casts of *L'Écorché* he abandoned the tree trunk support.

THE SALON OF 1777

Two casts in bronze of the *Diana* were made by Houdon and one was made in 1839 after his death. The first, listed in the Salon of 1783, is signed, dated, and inscribed to the patron who had ordered it: HOUDON F. 1782. POUR JN. GIRARDOT DE MARIGNY. It was actually exhibited at the home of Monsieur de Marigny. This is the bronze now in the Huntington Collection, San Marino, California. The second bronze, signed and dated 1790, is in the Louvre; the posthumous cast in the museum at Tours. The terra cotta, executed c. 1778, is in the Frick Collection, New York.[105]

Fig. 100
Plates 40b, 42, 143j

Plate 41

Seen from various angles the statue combines in an extraordinary degree qualities associated with both the rococo and neo-classicism. Viewed directly from the front Diana is most delicately feminine, in the manner of Clodion, Falconet, and Allegrain. In the three-quarter or profile view we are aware of the elongation and controlled outline that relate her to antiquity and to sixteenth-century Mannerism. Although Houdon does not make use of the spiraling organization of figures by Giovanni da Bologna, the *Diana* is fully conceived in space, intended to be seen from all sides; but the three-quarter and side views are in many ways the most successful. In the assimilation of realistic, sensuous detail to pictorial modeling, to controlled outline, to specifically classic rendering of the head, she is in fact one of the most notable examples of the Louis XVI style in sculpture. This style, classical at base, retains much of the linear elegance of the rocaille; and resists the increasing pressure of archaeological neo-classicism until the advent of the Directory. The face of Diana, perhaps best studied in the marble bust, is an abstract, classical mask between the soft, flowing texture of the hair and the sensuous reality of the torso. The sharp turn of the head accentuates the spatial flow of the figure, a movement principally realized in contours. The statue must be studied in detail to understand all the elements that went into its realization: the personal interpretation of the spirit of the antique that Houdon had brought back from Rome, his innate passion for reality, the decorative detail he had absorbed after returning to Paris, and the beginnings of a new and more authentic classicism. Out of these seemingly disparate elements he created in the *Diana* a new synthesis, an individual concept of the classic ideal.[106]

Plate 39

WITH the Salon of 1779 Houdon entered fully upon that field of his achievement with which he is most frequently associated: the unsurpassed recording of the great men of the eighteenth century. Previously most of his portrait subjects had been noblemen, the wealthy bourgeois, foreign princes, and some members of the French royal family. Of individuals who made notable contributions to the thought or the arts of the eighteenth century there had been three—Diderot, Turgot, and Gluck, and in a sense that remarkable monarch Catherine of Russia. From 1779, however, until Houdon's last Salon of 1814, almost every Salon included portraits of the great figures of the late eighteenth and early nineteenth centuries, portraits that in many cases have established our permanent visual images of these individuals.

THE SALON OF 1779

On the basis of the scientific and philosophical achievements of the seventeenth century, of Newton, Descartes, Bacon, Pascal, and many others, the eighteenth century, the age of the Enlightenment, or the age of Reason, developed a confidence in human reason and in its applicability to all aspects of man and society. The approach of the leading thinkers to political, social, religious, or economic questions was rational and scientific. The French *philosophes*, Voltaire, Diderot, d'Alembert, Rousseau, Buffon, Condorcet and others, sought through their individual publications, or through the *Encyclopédie*, to popularize their convictions, to spread them to the more or less educated masses. The word, *philosophe*, has the particular connotation of the intellectual concerned not only with ideas but with the dissemination of those ideas. The ideas of the *philosophes* were international, affected by and themselves affecting those of David Hume, Lessing, Kant, Franklin, Jefferson, and others throughout Europe and America. Opposed by the French Crown, and by much of the nobility and the clergy, they were supported, up to a point, by the enlightened monarchs, Catherine of Russia and Frederick of Prussia. It was the *philosophes* who were principally responsible for the designation of these 'philosopher rulers' as 'the Great'. And the ideas of the Enlightenment contributed substantially to the background of both the American and French Revolutions.[107]

The first two portraits listed by Houdon in the *livret* of 1779 had little to do with the Enlightenment, but represented rather solid men of the establishment on whom he had to depend for his basic patronage. Both busts are excellent examples of what might be termed his official portraits, not in the grandiose sense of Coysevox in the seventeenth century or Jean-Louis Lemoyne in the early eighteenth. Monsieur de Nicolay, *premier président de la Chambre des comptes*, and Monsieur de Caumartin, *prévôt des marchands*, typified the increasingly powerful wealthy bourgeoisie, the bureaucracy, the nobility of the robe. It must be emphasized that the world portrayed by Houdon was not simply divided between nobles and bourgeoisie, a confrontation of aristocracy with democracy and liberal thought. In the latter eighteenth century many nobles were on the side of the *philosophes*. Turgot, Buffon, Condorcet, Malesherbes, not to mention Lafayette, were men of family who sought to improve the existing order. Many others, like de Nicolay or de Caumartin, served in important administrative positions. Not only an intellectual élite but a professional, judicial, scientific, or financial class became more prominent; and members might be drawn from the middle classes or from the aristocracy. Whereas a successful architect or entrepreneur in the reign of Louis XIV might have wanted to be depicted like a great noble, the Marquis de Miromesnil and de Nicolay, Marquis de Goussainville, preferred to appear in professional robes, as stamp of their personal achievement. This was, of course, a gradual process. The traditional Court portrait persisted until the Revolution and was quickly revived in a different form under Napoleon. But the number of 'professional' portraits and men's portraits in simple everyday dress, whatever the original status of the sitter, indicates changes within the structure of society well before the Revolution.

NICOLAY
Fig. 104
Plate 44

The marble bust of *de Nicolay* is similar in its judicial dress, and in quality quite comparable, to the marbles of *de Miromesnil*. It is signed and dated: F. P. Houdon en 1779 and inscribed: Messire Aymard-Jean Nicolay Premier President. This is a full bust extending to the waist, with the arms under the sleeves indicated to the elbows. Although the robe of office is severely simple in comparison, for instance, with Lemoyne's *Mansart*, Houdon makes up for this simplicity with the subtlety in the carving of details; the robe carelessly caught back over the bow of the sash, buttons absently left unbuttoned. Monsieur de Nicolay, a massive, full-faced gentleman, wears his own, long, delicately rendered hair, and is given a wide-eyed, questioning gaze, the quizzical, momentary nature of his expression accentuated by the slightly parted lips, the raised eyebrows, and the wrinkled forehead.[108]

CAUMARTIN
Fig. 105

Antoine-Louis-François Le Fèvre de Caumartin (1725–1803) assumed his influential position of *prévôt des marchands*, supervising the guilds of Paris, in 1778, and Houdon had his portrait in marble ready for the Salon of 1779. It is probably no coincidence that the artist also portrayed de Caumartin's predecessor, Monsieur de Bignon, in 1771, and his successor, Monsieur Le Peletier de Morfontaine, in 1785. In his highly competitive business Houdon had to keep his eye out not only for men and women of position and rank already on the scene, but also for newly appointed officials and visiting dignitaries. By 1779, of course, many of these were coming to him. The marble portrait of *Caumartin*, in the Jacquemart-André Museum, Paris, signed and dated: Fait par Houdon, 1779, shows him in court dress, wearing the Order of Saint Louis, his perruque carefully curled, a contented smile on his face. The total effect is nevertheless simple and straightforward, perhaps because the torso is finished abruptly just below the chest, and there is no elaborate undercutting, no large, curving swags of drapery such as the artist uses for the nobility of the sword as well as for ladies of fashion. Despite the obvious elegance of the dress, the presentation points to the more prosaic civilian clothes worn at the turn of the century.[109]

De Caumartin's portrait is also of some interest as one of the few in which Houdon permitted the sitter a quite specific expression, in this case a warm smile (your friendly *prévôt des marchands*?) Other instances are the theatrical portraits, *Sophie Arnould* and *Larive*, where the actor is playing a particular part; the busts of *Malesherbes* and *Lenoir*, discussed below, feature a comparable smile, as do some versions of the *Voltaire*. But in most portraits, even most of the *Voltaires*, the expression is usually somewhat ambiguous. Much of the quality of the portraits arises from a sense of implied change in the expression. The sitter, rather than looking the spectator directly in the eye, normally looks past him as though he were pursuing his own thoughts. It is these ambiguous and guarded qualities in the portraits that makes verbal analysis of them so fascinating and so dangerous.

If Messieurs de Nicolay and de Caumartin are known to posterity largely because Houdon portrayed them, this is not the sole claim to fame of other sitters represented in the Salon of 1779. These included Molière, Rousseau, Benjamin Franklin, and Voltaire in terra cotta and, since nothing is indicated to the contrary, presumably in modern dress: Voltaire, the prize for the occasion, also in a marble bust, '*drapé à la manière des Romains*'. There was finally a statue of Voltaire represented seated, in gilt bronze. This was actually a statuette, a miniature version of the still unfinished marble of the Comédie Française and the Hermitage. The *livret* notes that the bust *drapé à l'antique* and the bronze statuette are in the *cabinet* of the Empress of Russia.

The bust of *Molière*, father of the Comédie Française, had been ordered by the *Comédiens* in 1776.[110] It is one of the most brilliant of Houdon's characterizations and fully disproves the cliché that Houdon's inspiration flagged when he had to make a posthumous portrait. It remains true that he had an obsession for the meticulous study of nature and normally made life-masks or, for Rousseau, Mirabeau, and one or two other recently deceased notables, death-masks. He measured the heads of his subjects; for George Washington he took all the dimensions.

Molière had been dead for a century, and Houdon, not having access to the portrait by Mignard (then in private hands), had to work from an inferior copy. He only saw the Mignard painting after he had completed his bust, and expressed relief when he saw how like was his representation. In this case exact resemblance was not the major point since Houdon was more concerned with presenting Molière as the symbol of French theatre than as an archaeological reconstruction. The head, framed in long, freely flowing hair, is sharply turned in a pose which suggests with extraordinary vividness an immediate action or movement. The hair swings back as the head turns. The eyes are sharp and alive, the mouth opens slightly as though in speech. Molière is informally dressed as befits a poet, with a large scarf loosely knotted around his neck.

A comparison of this portrait with Mignard's *Molière as Caesar in 'The Death of Pompey'*, (now in the Comédie Française) is suggestive. Although the resemblance is close enough to have satisfied the sculptor, Houdon has transformed the effect. Mignard shows Molière as the actor in a part, his seventeenth-century wig contrasting somewhat ludicrously with his Roman armor. Houdon presents him not as the romantic actor, although there is a strong theatrical touch in the interpretation, but as the romantic poet and hero.

The bust was exhibited at the artist's studio, Bibliothèque du Roi, and the critics were enthusiastic. Grimm repeated the comment on the *Voltaire*: 'His gaze (M. Houdon is perhaps the first sculptor who has known how to represent eyes) pierces the heart.'[111]

A sour note was struck by Houdon's principal rival in the art of the portrait bust, Jean-Jacques Caffieri. Considerably senior to Houdon in the hierarchy of the Academy, Caffieri was something of a specialist in posthumous busts, and as a result of his many commissions considered the Comédie Française his private domain. His rage when Houdon was given the Molière commission was accentuated when his rival's bust of Voltaire replaced his own of Quinault in the foyer of the Comédie. As a consequence he wrote an anonymous letter to d'Angiviller, *Directeur des Bâtiments*, accusing Houdon of having represented Molière as '. . . un homme stupide, sans aucune passion dans la physionomie . . .'.[112] Caffieri was even more enraged when, having preceded Houdon in portraying Benjamin Franklin, the latter secured the commission for the statue of Washington.[113] His hostility was perhaps extreme, but in the small, closed hierarchy of the Royal Academy of Painting and Sculpture, and of Architecture, particularly at a moment when declining royal and ecclesiastical patronage led to intense competition, it is not to be wondered at. Pajou, who had been sculptor to the king during the reign of Louis XVI, returned to Paris after fleeing the Terror of the French Revolution and accused Houdon of attempting to take over his functions as curator of sculpture at the Louvre.[114] Madame Houdon, that strong-minded lady, in 1796 accused the painter Jacques-Louis David of having displayed extremist tendencies in 1793.[115]

ROUSSEAU
Figs. 107–8
Plates 48–9

Jean-Jacques Rousseau died suddenly on July 2, 1778, at the estate of the Marquis de Girardin at Ermenonville near Paris. Houdon was summoned and on July 3 he made a death-mask of the writer.[116] On this was based the terra cotta bust which appeared in the Salon of 1779 as No. 220: '*J. J. Rousseau*, Appartenant à M. le Marquis de Gerardin' [Girardin].

Houdon's interpretation, particularly when we consider that it was based on a death-mask and that the sculptor apparently had not known his subject personally, is remarkable and, in terms of what is known of Rousseau's personality, rather startling. Rousseau was one of the great intuitive minds of the eighteenth century. His *Contrat social*, published in 1762, had important implications not only for the extremists of the French Revolution but also for modern philosophies of state control. The concept of education in *Émile* (1762) was unorthodox but widely influential. The inconsistencies, emotionalism and even naïveté of many of his ideas were disguised by the brilliance of his writing. He was the great romantic of the eighteenth century, and like many romantics a man of intense feeling but little humor.

This is certainly the impression which comes down to us from his writings and from what we know of his wildly disorganized life. In the light of these facts, Houdon's interpretation is a brilliant but baffling one. It is one of his most vital portrayals, with an intense presence. The Rousseau who looks out from deeply set eyes is a man of strong, searching intelligence, a man with even a suggestion of sardonic humor. It is possible that Houdon may here, as in the case of the posthumous *Molière*, have given us an ideal, somewhat abstract impression of a great thinker. It is also possible, of course, that there were aspects of Rousseau's personality which even the intense self-searching of the *Confessions* has never revealed. The portrait of Rousseau was probably the most popular of Houdon's portraits after that of Voltaire. It was produced in several variants both of material and dress, many of which still survive. In these the philosopher is shown in modern dress, draped and undraped *à l'antique*, in marble, terra cotta, plaster, and bronze. The version in modern dress shows Rousseau simply clad and wearing a perruque; the bust is of the larger type, including the shoulders and upper arms. The version undraped *à l'antique* is truncated to the shoulder blades like the *Diderot*, and the short hair is combed forward. That draped *à l'antique* is similarly abbreviated but the torso, instead of ending in a curve, is squared off in a block-like effect. There is also a band encircling the hair, which accentuates the image as Roman philosopher.

The hair circlet appears as well in the seated statue of Voltaire; and the herm-torso is used for busts derived from the statue. This block version of the upper torso represents a new departure adapted from certain ancient busts, and was to become characteristic of the neo-classical portrait bust. An unusual number of bronze busts of both Rousseau and Voltaire exist, since this was the period when Houdon was becoming deeply involved in bronze casting. Needless to say there are also many later bronze replicas of these subjects.

Another *philosophe* belongs chronologically in this company although no portrait of him by Houdon was exhibited until 1802 (Year X of the Republic). This was Jean Le Rond d'Alembert, one of the outstanding mathematicians of the eighteenth century, author of the famous *Prologue* and Diderot's principal collaborator in the inception of the *Encyclo-pédie*. In contrast with Rousseau or Voltaire there are only two known surviving busts of d'Alembert by Houdon, a plaster in the Staatliches Museum at Schwerin and a marble in the Yale University Art Gallery at New Haven. The plaster shows him in modern dress with perruque, truncated torso. It is signed and dated: *houdon. 1778*. The marble is undraped, *à l'antique*, torso also without shoulders, but squared off rather than rounded at the bottom, signed and dated: *houdon.f. 1779*. [117]

Although d'Alembert, one of the profound minds of his time as mathematician, physicist and social scientist, was reticent, somewhat awkward and withdrawn, he was both brilliant and emotionally ambivalent. Whether, without knowing something about his personality, one could deduce these characteristics from his portrait it is impossible to say. It is, however, a portrayal of great subtlety, the eyes veiled, the smile slightly forced, the picture of a man who seems to be on guard.

More than any other writer it is Voltaire (François Marie Arouet de Voltaire, 1694–1778) who symbolizes the spirit of the French Enlightenment. As philosopher, dramatist, poet, historian, social scientist and fantastic propagandist, he stayed in touch with every progressive trend in Europe and with those who supported new ideas or who were against repression in any form. For the last twenty years of his life he poured forth his stupendous correspondence from his estate Ferney, on the Swiss border, where he lived in semi-exile, but still venerated by the enlightened monarchs, Catherine, and (at least until Voltaire had visited him) Frederick the Great, as well as by most liberal thinkers. Despite his authority opinions were not always unanimous even among the *philosophes*. Diderot was frequently highly critical, and Rousseau gradually became hostile to everyone. But they were all fighting the same battle.

In February 1778 Voltaire returned to Paris in triumph. Since Houdon had never visited Ferney, he was most anxious to take advantage of Voltaire's visit to add him to his collection of great men, and on March 6 a bust of the aged philosopher by Houdon was crowned with laurel on the stage of the Comédie Française, on the occasion of the sixth performance of his *Irène*.[118] Sittings had been arranged by the Marquis de Villevielle,[119] and the statue now in the Comédie Française was commissioned by Voltaire's niece, Madame Denis.[120] Houdon took a life-mask and seems to have worked with incredible speed even for him, turning out an assortment of busts in different materials and presentations. As soon as it was known that he was modeling Voltaire's likeness he was probably inundated with orders. Judging by the number of surviving busts deriving directly from Houdon or from his studio, Voltaire was by far the most popular subject he ever attempted. It was fortunate that he arranged his sittings so quickly since Voltaire, sick, old, and exhausted after his triumphal return, died in May, immediately after the last sitting for the statue.

Houdon's statue of *Voltaire* is unquestionably one of the most famous if not the most famous portrait sculpture in history. Almost as many myths have grown up around it as around the *Mona Lisa*. Since most of these cannot be verified, one will suffice as an illustration. The Marquis de Villevielle, justifiably proud of the part he had played in arranging sittings with the artist, liked to explain how he also was responsible for the expression of diabolical wit, intellectual penetration, or what have you, attributed to Houdon's *Voltaire*. The marquis arranged with the sculptor at the last moment of the last sitting to slip on Voltaire's head the crown he had received at the Comédie; so that Houdon could record the illumination of Voltaire's expression. The plot went off as arranged; and then in a scene of *sensibilité* worthy of Greuze or Richardson, Voltaire demanded: ' "What are you doing, young man?" ... "Throw that on my tomb, which is opening." Rising forthwith and turning to the artist: "Adieu, Phidias." And seizing me by the arm: "My friend, I go to die." "Oh! Master," I cried, falling at his knees, kissing once more the hand that had written *Zaïre*! Then his tears flowed and mingled with mine. His suffering became unbearable. We departed, and a few days later he was no more.'[121] A story which, in the phrase, if it is not true, is at least *ben trovato*.

Voltaire had been portrayed innumerable times before, but the most remarkable or rather most 'curious' sculpture of him had, in the process of creating a scandal, established a favorable environment for the reception of Houdon's portrait. In 1770, at a convivial dinner at Madame Necker's (whose husband, the noted financier and statesman, Houdon portrayed later), attended by some of the leading *philosophes* and also by the sculptor, Pigalle, it was decided that a subscription should be raised for a statue of Voltaire. Pigalle, unquestionably one of the outstanding French sculptors of the time, was the obvious choice to carry out the commission. Those leading the subscription drive included Diderot, d'Alembert, Helvétius, and Grimm; and Frederick the Great among many other notables duly sent his contribution. Pigalle posted to Ferney to make his sketches and take a life-mask and on his return had the incredible idea of presenting the aged Voltaire as a nude philosopher, using as a model for the body an equally aged and decrepit veteran of the Seven Years War. When the word got around that, as Voltaire put it, Pigalle intended to 'portray him as a monkey' he was understandably horrified and did his best to dissuade the sculptor, even addressing him (also as Phidias) to this effect in verse. Pigalle was adamant; Voltaire duly appeared

Fig. 39 'en singe' to the wild derision of the critics. The King of Sweden, Gustaf III, then in Paris, announced that he would happily have contributed for a cloak to the sculpture.[122]

Pigalle's statue is another instance both of this artist's devotion to precise realism of detail and of the ever increasing tendency to archaeological classicism—the latter manifesting itself earlier in eighteenth-century art than is frequently realized, and sometimes in odd forms. Taking into account the general emphasis on subject-matter in eighteenth-century art criticism and the fact that this was a particularly eccentric depiction of a man universally known, widely admired, but also widely hated, it is no wonder that the commentators should have had a field day. But viewed objectively, without all the immediate emotional associations, Pigalle's *Voltaire* is a strange and wonderful work, a masterpiece of expressive sculpture that belongs more in the milieu of Rodin than of the eighteenth century.

While it is doubtful that it would ever have occurred to Houdon to represent the aged Voltaire in the nude, the scandal of Pigalle's experiment was still sufficiently fresh—the work itself was on view in the Royal Academy—to force him to ponder seriously exactly how he should present the modern Socrates or Seneca. He seems to have had little hesitation in deciding on a portrait *à l'antique* rather than in modern dress. Later he wanted very much to portray George Washington in classical robes as the modern Cincinnatus. On this idea Washington put his foot down quietly but firmly (see p. 76 below).

Fig. 111
Plates 54, 55 In the case of Voltaire we may assume that Houdon was overwhelmed with good advice from Diderot and others. The result was a particularly happy one, in spite of Diderot's criticisms. Voltaire, seated in an armchair adapted from the antique, is swathed in an ample robe ('un manteau de chambre' actually based on the heavy robe worn by the aged writer to receive visitors and to keep out the cold), which gives the effect of Roman dress without attempting to be explicit. The robe falls in massive folds over the shoulders and knees, describing the underlying figure but lending it an effect of monumentality. A discreet head of natural hair—not a perruque—is given to the totally bald ancient, thinning perhaps a trifle at the top but falling softly and amply around ears and neck, and the riband encircling the hair mirrors that crown of glory presented at the Comédie Française. Thus the accessories evoke the image of the poet-philosopher who belonged both to the modern world and to that of antiquity. It is, of course, in the face that the unique power of the portrayal resides. The skin is stretched tightly over the almost fleshless bones of the old man. The structure of the head recalls Houdon's early, emaciated head of Saint Bruno, which in turn is so closely based on that of *L'Écorché*, the flayed man. But the difference lies in the burning vitality, the indestructible spirit that shines forth from Voltaire. Houdon's genius for suggesting living personality through the transitory expression is here exemplified. Although a thousand attempts have been made to define Voltaire's expression, it is probably beyond definition. It seems as though something has just caught his attention, he has suddenly seized on the flaw in an argument, and with wit, penetration and even malice, he poises himself to spring upon and destroy his hapless opponent. This is one attempt at verbal paraphrase; many others are possible. The point is that as we look at the old man we cannot exactly define his expression. He is not exactly smiling, frowning, scowling, grimacing, posing for his portrait. He is caught at a moment of transition, and it is this that imbues not only the face but the entire figure with the intense sense of an inner life.

THE SALON OF 1779

Plates 52–4, 56
Plates 5, 7

The head of Pigalle's *Voltaire*, if it is isolated, is unquestionably a fine and accurate and dignified portrait of the man. His aged figure is conceived in strongly sculptural terms. But Houdon's *Voltaire* is the personification of a century, the image of the age of Enlightenment.

As might be expected, Houdon reproduced his statue of *Voltaire* in miniature for the *cabinets des amateurs*. Surviving examples exist in plaster, usually painted terra cotta color, as well as in bronze, terra cotta, and marble. These are of varying quality but almost all differ in certain respects from the large versions. As instances of good quality, the versions in the Houdon Museum at Versailles and the Walters Gallery, Baltimore, signed on the left of the base and dated 1778, are more complicated in the folds of the drapery than the statue. The left hand, instead of gripping the end of the chair arm, rests loosely on the upper thigh. The toes of both shoes are exposed as though Voltaire is sitting flatly and firmly in his chair. He wears a wig. His face is relaxed and he stares into the distance as though lost in thought. These have very much the quality as well as the freshness and immediacy of a first sketch (comparable to the little terra cotta sketch for the tomb of Prince Galitzin), as opposed to a reduced copy after the large plaster or marble. If we may assume that they actually are preliminary sketches after the sitter, the changes the artist made in order to establish his final concept are revealing. Changing the perruque to the natural hair identifies Voltaire as the ancient philosopher. The hands gripping the arms of his chair, his legs and feet poised as though he is on the point of rising, and above all the focus and intensity of his gaze, transform the total image from one that is passive and contemplative to one that is sparked with life.

Figs. 112, 113

Of the large seated statue there exist two marbles with impeccable histories—that in the Comédie Française and another made for Catherine, now in the Hermitage, Leningrad— as well as a beautiful plaster in the Bibliothèque Nationale, Paris, described as the original plaster.[123] Voltaire's niece, Madame Denis, later Madame Mignot-Duvivier, had intended that the first marble be installed in the French Academy; and Caffieri wrote his customary letter of denunciation. It is doubtful that he was mollified when Madame Denis changed her mind and presented the work to the Comédie. She had become infuriated with the academicians when, on her remarriage after a widowhood of thirty-six years, they had, she felt, insulted her by abandoning her salon.[124]

Plates 54–7
Fig. 111

As has been noted, the portrait busts of *Voltaire*, including those produced by Houdon himself and in his studio under his supervision, far exceed in number those of any other subject. Voltaire became even more popular, if that were possible, after the French Revolution than he had been earlier. Every large or small theatre, academy, library, or other learned society and educational institution throughout France and many throughout the rest of Europe and America wanted a bust of him. Houdon himself presented a plaster one to all forty members of the French Academy. The busts emerged from his studio until the end of his life and have continued to be copied thereafter.[125]

There are at least five different types of the *Voltaire* bust, with many different variations within the type. These are:

1. The classical-realist formula without shoulders, truncated, undraped torso fragment; here given a quality of aggressive nudity by the stark presentation of the almost totally hairless head. Examples of excellent quality are: the plaster in the Gotha Museum (although heavily repainted); the terra cotta in the collection of the Duc de Mouchy, Paris; the bronzes

Plate 52b
Figs. 114, 115
Plate 53a

in the Pushkin Museum, Moscow, in the Walters Art Gallery, Baltimore, and the collection of Mrs Vincent Astor, New York; and the marble in the Metropolitan Museum, New York. This last, signed and dated: HOUDON. 1778, was ordered by Count Stroganov, who had also ordered the marble of Diderot now in the Wrightsman Collection, New York, and had commissioned the portrait of Catherine. It may serve as the exemplar for this form of bust. In general Voltaire's expression in these portraits *à l'antique* seems to be somewhat more contemplative than in the statue, old and even tired; perhaps closer to the living model as he actually appeared to the sculptor.[126]

2. The second type is that in modern dress with perruque. Superior examples in marble

Plate 51

are to be found in the Louvre, Versailles, and the National Gallery, Washington; a terra cotta, signed and dated: HOUDON. F. 1782, is in the possession of the author. The wig, as contrasted with that on the seated statuette, is long, heavy, and old-fashioned, belonging to an earlier generation. In the different busts in modern dress Houdon frequently plays some slight variation in the dress, such as changing the shape of the cravat.[127]

3. The third type, essentially a variant on the second, is of historical importance since it is the one that Houdon prepared in time to be presented on the stage of the Comédie Française, on Monday, March 6, 1778, at the ceremony at which Voltaire received the laurel wreath from the *Comédiens*. Here the writer is in modern dress with perruque, but now adorned with cloak or swag of drapery swinging over the right shoulder and down across the base. The

Fig. 117
Plate 53b

marble in the Comédie is inscribed across the front of the base: François Marie Arouet de VOLTAIRE. né à Paris en 1694 et mort en 1778. On the right side of the base it is signed: *Fait par Houdon Sculpteur. 1778*. Houdon in this instance was not too proud to take something from his rival, Caffieri, who had the useful habit of inscribing his portrait busts in such detail. It was probably the terra cotta or a first plaster that was presented on the stage of the Comédie with the inscribed marble substituted later. Frederick the Great ordered a second copy of the Comédie Française marble for the Berlin Academy of Science. There is also a plaster of this type, painted terra cotta, with the seal of the atelier in the Schwerin Museum.[128]

Fig. 116
Plate 52a
Plate 143f

4. A fourth type is described in the 1779 Salon, the bust draped *à l'antique*, ordered by Catherine and now in the Hermitage. This marble, of superb quality, is also elaborately inscribed: Ordonné Par S. M. J. L'Impératrice de Toutes Les Russies. *Fait Par Houdon, en 1778*. Conceived with full torso, shoulders and upper arms, the bust is the most specifically Roman of all Houdon's portraits of the great men up to this moment; probably as a particular homage to Voltaire rather than to a new neo-classicism. Such deliberate classical revivals were occurring, particularly in history painting, with increasing frequency during the 1770s. Jacques-Louis David made his Salon début in 1781 with an impressively varied group (highly praised by Diderot), of which his *Belisarius Receiving Alms* forecast a new era. Houdon's *Voltaire* of 1778, presented as a Roman senator, his head innocent of hair, his aged face weary but flickering with an undying light, is significant as an early document of that era but more so as a personification of the age of the Enlightenment.[129]

5. The fifth type of *Voltaire* bust is that adapted from the seated statue. In this Houdon gives Voltaire his stint of hair encompassed by a riband; the torso fragment is of the abbreviated, squared-off herm type with a suggestion of drapery. Two such marbles, one in the Victoria and Albert Museum, London, and the other in the De Young Museum, San Francisco, have an added feature, masks of Comedy and Tragedy on the front of the base. Others without this feature, of varying proportions, repeat the upper part of the seated statue's draperies. Many of these are of inferior quality and are probably later casts from the statue.[130]

Aside from his reception as an Academician in 1777, the other recorded event of the latter 1770s in Houdon's personal life seems to have been his affiliation with the Masonic lodge of the Nine Sisters.[131] It took its name from the Muses, identifying this as a lodge particularly frequented by artists and men of letters. Voltaire was a member, as was the Russian patron of the arts, Count Stroganov, and the Americans Benjamin Franklin and John Paul Jones. Freemasonry flourished in the eighteenth century both in Europe and in the United States, frequently as a gathering-ground for liberal intellectuals. Leaders of the American Revolution including George Washington were Masons. In France, as in many absolute states, Masonic organizations were regarded with suspicion as potential centres of sedition. For Houdon, his affiliation had a particular significance in that it led to his portraits of Franklin and Jones, and through Franklin to his acquaintance with Thomas Jefferson, which in turn led to the commission for the statue of George Washington.

Benjamin Franklin (1705–90) had visited France in 1766 and 1769. He came back in 1776 FRANKLIN to negotiate a treaty of alliance between France and the United States and remained as Minister to France until he returned to America with Houdon in 1785. During this period he became to French intellectuals of the liberal wing a symbol of America, the New-Found Land, of the democratic ideal and of the American Enlightenment. His homely wit and simple manners, perhaps somewhat played up for the French Court, his Quaker dress and his delight in the company of lovely ladies, made him immensely popular in the salons of Paris.

Houdon's portrait of Franklin has become so much a part of the iconography of America that it is difficult to analyze it objectively. It has appeared for generations on American currency, stamps, national memorials of every description; as a symbol of thrift and economic wisdom for banks and other financial institutions. Lamentably, it has also been frequently used to advertise less commendable examples of American industry and ingenuity.

The basic type of *Franklin* bust by Houdon shows him in plain, modern dress, without shoulders and, as is customary with the abbreviated type, rounded at the bottom. The fine Fig. 118 marble in the Metropolitan Museum, New York, signed and dated: *houdon f. 1778.*, has a Plate 58 sufficiently interesting history to merit mention here. When Houdon returned from the United States in November, 1785, after having visited George Washington at Mount Vernon, he left behind in Philadelphia a number of sculptures in the care of Robert Edge Pine, the painter, hoping that they might be sold. Pine died in 1788 and others took up the task of disposing of them. On January 20, 1802, Pierre Samuel du Pont de Nemours, who was friendly with Houdon and his wife, wrote to Thomas Jefferson, soliciting his interest in selling to the Virginia Congress the bust of *Franklin*, now in du Pont de Nemours' possession. But there was little money available and not enough interest in buying works of art so soon after the Revolutionary wars. Du Pont de Nemours' son finally sold the bust to John Church Cruger about 1836. From Cruger it passed to his daughter and son-in-law, Dr Samuel Bard, and then to their son, John Bard, who presented it to the Metropolitan Museum in 1872. Whereas this marble has an unbroken, well-documented history, many of Houdon's portrait busts have changed hands with even greater frequency and, unfortunately, records of the transactions have not survived or, for some question of taxes or ownership, have been concealed.[132]

The marble bust of *Franklin* in contemporary dress, simple and puritanical, has a somewhat rigid frontality suggesting his qualities of forthrightness. The eyes look up into the distance. He wears his own hair, thin on top and flowing down over his ears and shoulders. The wrinkles at the corners of the eyes are emphasized, the lips are slightly parted in what might be the beginning of a smile. The entire expression is one of benevolence, wisdom, and humor, as appropriately it should be. Curiously, viewed from certain angles, these characteristics are replaced by an expression that can only be described as somewhat weary and apprehensive. However, long experience in photographing portraits by Houdon makes one acutely aware of the fact that, with different angles and lighting, they can be made to assume a wide variety of expressions. The bust exists in innumerable examples of varying quality. There are fine plasters at Gotha, in the Saint Louis and Toledo Museums, as well as an excellent terra cotta in the Louvre. The only bronze I know that could be an original is that in the Middendorf collection, Washington. As might be expected, the *Franklin* has been reproduced almost indefinitely.

Fig. 119
Plate 59

Although there is no evidence that Houdon ever attempted to present Franklin *dénudé*, the subject, by far the most popular of his American portraits, interested him sufficiently that he later made a variant, *en philosophe, drapé à l'antique*. This is possibly the *Franklin* listed in the *livret* for the Salon of 1791, one plaster of which is in the Boston Athenaeum and another in the Musée des Beaux-Arts at Angers, both of good quality but neither signed nor dated. That at Angers came to the museum from the sculptor, David d'Angers, a disciple of Houdon, in the mid-nineteenth century. This is a larger bust than that in contemporary dress, showing Franklin draped in a senatorial robe. It might be described as a modified version *à l'antique*, since he wears the robe or cloak over his normal dress. In fact, Houdon seems simply to have adapted the earlier bust to an image in which a larger torso including shoulders and upper arms, draped in a robe, gives Franklin more the dignity of an ancient philosopher. This presentation becomes more frequent as Houdon adapts his portraits to the increasing neo-classicism of the end of the century. The Boston plaster has been cleaned in recent years and sprayed with a plastic paint which, as ever, tends to blur the fine detail.[133]

The history of this plaster of *Franklin* also merits some discussion here as an instance of the problems of history and provenance. The Boston Athenaeum owns three plaster busts by Houdon, this *Franklin*, and portraits of *Washington* and *Lafayette*. It originally owned four, the fourth being a bust of *John Paul Jones*, perhaps that now in the Boston Museum of Fine Arts. There is also another bust of *Franklin*, in modern dress, on loan to the Athenaeum from the American Academy of Arts and Sciences, which conceivably was at one time the property of the Athenaeum. The *Washington, Lafayette, John Paul Jones*, and a *Franklin* came originally from the collection of Thomas Jefferson. They were willed to Jefferson's grand-daughter, the wife of Joseph Coolidge Jr of Boston, and were deposited by Mr Coolidge in the Athenaeum in 1828. The Trustees' records at the Athenaeum for March 11, 1828, note that it had been voted that the busts of *Jones, Franklin*, and *General Washington* belonging to Joseph Coolidge Jr be received as a deposit. The treasurer's journal for October 1828 states that Mr Coolidge had been paid $100.00 for the bust of *Lafayette*. In 1912 the Coolidge heirs formally presented the other Jefferson Houdons to the Athenaeum.

There is some question as to which of the two *Franklins* came from Jefferson, but the probability is that it was the earlier version in modern dress. In scale and format that *Franklin* is comparable to the other three busts and all four are supposed to have been on display in the dining room of Jefferson's home, Monticello. The draped *Franklin* is very probably that given to the American Philosophical Society in Philadelphia in 1800 by Colonel Jonathan Winters. In 1803 the Society, having other busts of Franklin in its possession, presented it to the American Academy of Arts and Sciences in Boston. The American Academy occupied quarters with the Boston Athenaeum between 1817 and 1899. When it moved to its own quarters, the bust of *Franklin* was left behind. In 1911 the Athenaeum

54

Fig. 107. *Jean-Jacques Rousseau.* Plaster, 1778. Schwerin,
Staatliches Museum

Fig. 108. *Jean-Jacques Rousseau.* Bronze, 1778.
Paris, Louvre

Fig. 109. *Jean Le Rond d'Alembert.* Plaster, 1778.
Schwerin, Staatliches Museum

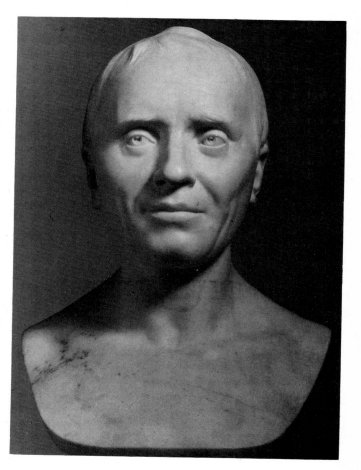

Fig. 110. *Jean Le Rond d'Alembert.* Marble, 1779.
New Haven, Conn., Yale University Art Gallery

Fig. 111. *Voltaire*. Plaster, 1780. Paris, Bibliothèque Nationale

Fig. 112. *Voltaire*. Terra cotta, 1778. Versailles, Musée Lambinet

Fig. 113. *Voltaire*. Plaster, about 1779. Baltimore, Walters Art Gallery

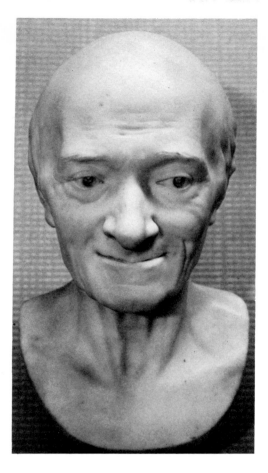

Fig. 114. *Voltaire*. Marble, 1778. New York, Metropolitan Museum of Art

Fig. 115. *Voltaire*. Bronze, 1778. New York, Mrs. Vincent Astor

Fig. 116. *Voltaire*. Marble, 1778. Leningrad, Hermitage

Fig. 117. *Voltaire*. Marble, 1778. Paris, Comédie Française

Fig. 118. *Benjamin Franklin*. Marble, 1778. New York, Metropolitan Museum of Art

Fig. 119. *Benjamin Franklin*. Plaster, 1786–91(?). Boston, Athenaeum

Fig. 120. *César-Gabriel, Duc de Choiseul-Praslin*. Plaster, 1780. Paris, Louvre

Fig. 121. *Comte de Valbelle*. Terra cotta, 1779. New York, Wildenstein & •

Fig. 122. *Tomb of the Comte de Valbelle*, now destroyed, in the Chartreuse de Montrieux. Drawing by Vallon. Aix-en-Provence, Musée Paul Arbaud

Fig. 123. *Charles Palissot de Montenoy*. Terra cotta, 1779. Paris, Institut de France, Bibliothèque, Mazarine

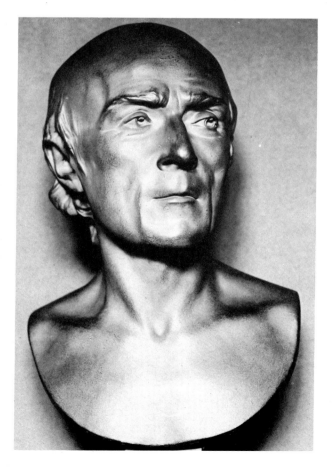

Fig. 124. *Pierre-Jean-Baptiste Gerbier de la Masselaye*. Plaster, 1781. Paris, Bibliothèque des Avocats

Fig. 125. *Dr. Théodore Tronchin*. Marble, 1781. Geneva, Musée d'Art et d'Histoire

Fig. 126. *John Paul Jones*. Marble, 1781. Annapolis, Maryland, U.S. Naval Academy

Fig. 127. *Madame de Sérilly*. Marble, 1782. London, Wallace Collection

Fig. 128. *Anne Audéoud*. Plaster, 1780. New York, Metropolitan Museum of Art

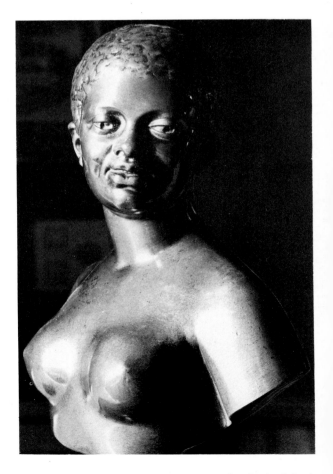

Fig. 129. *A Negress*. Bronze, about 1781. Paris, Musée des Arts Décoratifs

Fig. 130. *Maréchal de Tourville*. Marble, 1781. Versailles, Château

Fig. 131. *Ceres*. Plaster, about 1781. Maisons-Laffitte, Château

Fig. 132. *Tomb of Victor Charpentier Comte d'Ennery*. Marble, 1781. Paris, Louvre

Fig. 133. *General Ivan Petrovitch Soltykov*. Marble, 1783.
Leningrad, Hermitage

Fig. 134. *Antoine Louis*. Marble, 1782. Paris, Ecole de Médecine

Fig. 136. *Joseph and Etienne Montgolfier*. Plaster medallion, about 1783. Paris, Musée Carnavalet

Fig. 135. *Georges-Louis-Leclerc, Comte de Buffon*. Plaster, 1781. Glasgow, Art Gallery and Museum

Fig. 137. *Alexander the Great*. Marble, 1784. Warsaw, National Museum

Fig. 138. *Jean Mauduit, called de Larive*. Marble, 1784. Paris, Comédie Française

Fig. 139. *Jean de La Fontaine*. Marble, 1783. Philadelphia, Museum of Art

Fig. 140. *Prince Friedrich Franz I of Mecklenburg-Schwerin.*
Terra cotta, 1782. Schwerin, Staatliches Museum

Fig. 141. *Princess Louise of Mecklenburg-Schwerin.*
Terra cotta, 1782. Schwerin, Staatliches Museum

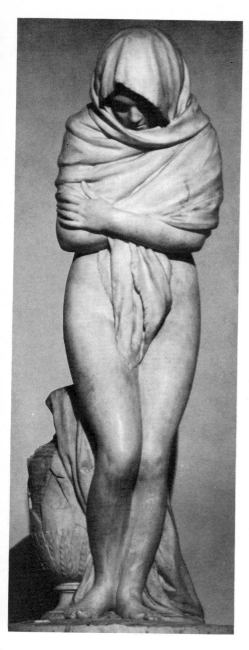

Fig. 142. *La Frileuse (Winter)*. Marble, 1783.
Montpellier, Musée Fabre

Fig. 143. *Summer*. Marble, about 1785.
Montpellier, Musée Fabre

Fig. 144. *A Bather*. Marble, 1782. New York,
Metropolitan Museum of Art

Fig. 145. *Prince Henry of Prussia, brother of Frederick the Great.* Plaster, 1784. Weimar, Landesbibliothek

Fig. 146. *Prince Henry of Prussia.* Bronze, 1789. Potsdam-Sanssouci, Staatliche Schlösser

Fig. 147. *A Magistrate.* Marble, 1788. Montpellier, Musée Fabre

Fig. 148. '*Charles François Fontaine, Marquis de Biré.*' Marble, 1786. Boston, Museum of Fine Arts

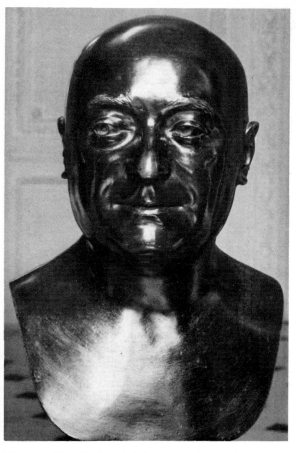

Fig. 149. '*J.-Ch. Lenoir.*' Bronze, 1786. Paris,
Pierre David-Weill

Fig. 150. '*Chrétien-Guillaume de Lamoignon de Malesherbes.*'
Marble, 1784. Paris, Louvre

g. 151. *Marie-Jean-Antoine-Nicolas Caritat, Marquis de
ndorcet.* Plaster, about 1785. Paris, Louvre

Fig. 152. *Françoise-Eléonore de Manville, Comtesse de Sabran.*
Plaster, about 1785. Eisenach, Thuringian Museum

Fig. 153. *George Washington*. Marble, 1786–95(?), signed 1788. Richmond, Virginia, Capitol

Fig. 154. *George Washington*. Plaster, about 1786. Boston, Athenaeum

Fig. 155. *George Washington*. Plaster, about 1786. Washington, D.C., Hon. W. J. Middendorf

Fig. 156. *George Washington*. Marble, about 1786. New York, Mrs. Sarah Hunter Kelly

Fig. 157. *George Washington*. Marble, 1801. Versailles, Château

Fig. 158. *Pierre-André de Suffren*. Marble, 1787. The Hague, Mauritshuis

Fig. 159. *King Louis XVI*. Marble, 1790. Versailles, Château

Fig. 160. *François-Claude Marquis de Bouillé*. Marble, about 1785. Coll. Marquis de Bouillé

gave the Academy the smaller *Franklin* bust, and this was returned to the Athenaeum in 1955 on indefinite loan when the Academy sold its house. Although labels may have been mixed up during the nineteenth century, there is no question about the authorship and virtually none about the provenance and history of these *Franklin* busts; and the gentlemen who administer these venerable scholarly organizations seem to feel that, as long as the sculptures are well cared for and properly displayed, it does not much matter who has title to them.

An addendum to this involved story has much the same conclusion. The plaster of *John Paul Jones* that belonged originally with this group of Jefferson Houdons disappeared at some time during the nineteenth century. Presumably it was rather casually loaned to the 'Boston Museum' (which at that time was actually a theatre, not a museum; it being considered more respectable for nineteenth-century Bostonian gentlemen to spend the evening at a museum rather than a theatre). The bust was borrowed as a stage prop in a play, forgotten by all concerned, and never returned. The 'Boston Museum' was torn down about 1900 and its contents were sold. Charles W. Taylor, one of the editors of the *Boston Globe*, bought the bust of *Jones* at the sale and later presented it to the Museum of Fine Arts. Again, the trustees of the Athenaeum, while realizing that this is in all likelihood their sculpture, feel that it is in good hands so there is no point in making a fuss about it.[134]

These accounts of the wanderings of certain Houdon portrait busts are introduced here rather than in the notes, where they properly belong, not only because they are pleasant anecdotes but because they illustrate again the problems of judging these busts by their histories or provenances. A large number were scattered during the French Revolution and passed through many hands during the last two centuries. Even when a bust has stayed in one collection or in one museum, such as that at Gotha, since the artist's lifetime, particularly when it is a small museum without adequate records, identification can become confused. When I finally examined the Houdon sculptures in the Pushkin Museum in Moscow, most of which have long histories, a marble bust of *Franklin* labelled as from the hand of Houdon proved to be by Houdon's rival, Caffieri. Houdon's statue of *General Joubert*, exhibited in the Salon of 1812, one of the most important full-length portrait sculptures from the artist's last period, was long shown at the Palace of Versailles as the work of a minor sculptor, Jean-Baptiste Stouf.[135]

Caffieri's *Franklin*, exhibited in the Salon of 1777 and surviving in many versions, was executed before that by Houdon, and provides an interesting comparison. It is an effective interpretation, more stylized in its effect, but for that reason imparting a sense of almost abstract sculptural power. It does not present Franklin in our familiar image of him, perhaps because that image has been so largely created by Houdon's portrait. In the context of this portrait Caffieri once more felt that Houdon had infringed on his rightful territory. When he heard of the proposed *Washington* statue, in 1784, he wrote to Franklin, reminding him of his own seniority as a sculptor, his portrait of *Franklin*, and his design for the tomb of General Montgomery. On learning that the commission had been awarded to Houdon, he wrote again, in 1785, to Franklin's grandson (who acted as his secretary), repeating his claims, and reminding him that he had made Franklin's portrait gratis. Franklin *petit-fils* answered him rather summarily that Houdon also had made his grandfather's portrait gratis, had presented four casts without charge, and had asked no special consideration in consequence. Finally, Franklin himself wrote, also somewhat shortly, that the decision on the *Washington* had been made by the Congress of the State of Virginia.[136]

IN the Salon of 1781 Houdon exhibited the marble statue of *Voltaire*, with a note under the *livret* entry indicating the change in destination from the Academy to the Comédie

Française.[137] Also featured was another major work, the life-size statue of the *Maréchal de Tourville*, Houdon's contribution to the series of the Great Men of France, favorite project of d'Angiviller, *Directeur des Bâtiments*. These two were among the artist's chief labors during the previous two years but they were by no means the only ones. He had still found time to complete ten new portrait busts for the Salon, a *buste d'expression* of a Negress, and a medallion representing the Sun.

There was always a steady output of replicas of earlier portraits and, notably during this biennial, important commissions for architectural, religious, funerary, and garden sculpture that did not appear in the Salons. In 1776, for example, the sculptor signed a contract for a group of reliefs to decorate the entrance to the church of Sainte-Geneviève in Paris. In 1781 he was commissioned to make a statue of Saint Paula as part of the new decoration of the Hôtel des Invalides.[138] This seems to have been changed to a statue of Saint Monica, which, like almost all of Houdon's religious sculptures, disappeared or was destroyed during the Revolution. He was working on a tomb for the Comte de Valbelle, which was placed in the chapel of the Chartreuse de Montrieux in 1782, and was subsequently dispersed and partially destroyed.[139]

A superb tomb for the Comte d'Ennery, described below, was finished in 1781. During 1779 long negotiations in regard to a monument to the Empress Maria-Theresa to be raised in Brussels were finally abandoned.[140] The bust of the Negress in the Salon of 1781 was related to a project for a fountain to be installed in the garden of the Duc de Chartres (later the Duc d'Orléans and Philippe-Égalité) at Monceau near Paris. Although the black attendant of this fountain, cast in lead, was destroyed during the Revolution, the beautiful *Bather* has survived. (See below, p. 68.) About 1780 Houdon executed a statue of Henry IV for the garden of the Duc de Chartres' Palais Royal. Presumably this, too, was destroyed during the Revolution.[141]

The account of projects Houdon was now engaged in while at the height of his career is sufficiently impressive even if only judged by those that have survived. While he may seem to have been unusually unfortunate in the number of his monumental sculptures that have disappeared, his case is not unique among French artists of the Revolutionary period. The number of works of art destroyed by vandalism, pillage, and decree during the Revolution is incalculable. That so many survived, particularly religious works and statues of royalty, was largely owing to the efforts of a number of dedicated citizens of the Republic who devised various ingenious schemes for concealing suspect works of art, or in some manner making them respectable.[142]

Of the portrait busts exhibited in the Salon of 1781, those of the *Princess Dachkov* and of *Monsieur Quesnay* have disappeared. The latter was either the distinguished surgeon and economist, François Quesnay—it would then have been a posthumous portrait—or his son, Blaise-Guillaume. The Princess Catherine Dachkov, whose Russian name is spelt or misspelt in many different French transcriptions, was deeply involved in the plots and perhaps the murder of Catherine's husband, Paul III, which led to Catherine's accession to the throne. A cultivated lady, the princess, after a period of disgrace and exile, was forgiven and appointed honorary president of the Russian Academy of Science. In this capacity she traveled widely, meeting with many of the leading intellectuals of France and England.

CHOISEUL-PRASLIN

César-Gabriel, Duc de Choiseul-Praslin (1712–85), a diplomat and cabinet minister who belonged to one of the old families of France, lived the last years of his life in retirement at his château of Vaux-Villars, where he amassed an important collection of paintings by contemporaries and older masters. His portrait, of which the plaster, painted terra cotta, signed and dated: *houdon f. 1780*, and the marble are in the collection of the Louvre, is austere in the dress and short, compact perruque, lively and intelligent in the sensitive, handsome face. The head is tilted up, the eyes are wide but concentrated, the lips slightly parted as at the moment of speech, an illusion enhanced by the manner that they are caught at one or

Fig. 120
Plates 60–1, 143h

two points to suggest their moisture. Houdon had already used this device in the portrait of *Molière* for the same effect to imply the moment when the poet is about to speak.[143]

The *Comte de Valbelle*, a posthumous portrait designed for the tomb completed by the sculptor in 1782, shows the count as a rather heavy, though alert gentleman. Houdon, as in the bust of *Turgot*, pays close attention to the braiding on the coat. The count (1729–78) was a noted patron of the arts who left a generous bequest to the Royal Academy, the income to be disbursed to a notable man of letters. As recognition, a bust was ordered from Houdon by the Academy, and unveiled on April 25, 1779, at a ceremony with d'Alembert giving the eulogy. The terra cotta in New York is signed and dated *houdon f. 1779*. Valbelle's lively characterization, like that of Turgot, transcends the elegance of his dress, despite the fact that this may be a posthumous portrait.[144]

Fig. 121

Charles Palissot de Montenoy (1730–1814), a man of letters, is perhaps best remembered as a rabid opponent of the Encyclopedists, whom he attacked in his play, *Comédie des philosophes*, 1760, and in a poem imitated from Alexander Pope, *La Dunciade ou la guerre des sots*, 1764. During the Revolution he became director of the Bibliothèque Mazarine at the Institute of France, where his bust in terra cotta is preserved. It is a simply but effectively presented portrait, the man of letters in casual, open-neck shirt, abbreviated torso without shoulders. Palissot's natural hair is thinning at the front but curled up over the ears in the manner of a perruque; his head is turned sharply to the right, his expression nervous, the eyes not so much looking past as avoiding the gaze of the spectator.

Seemingly much more sure of himself is the famous orator, Pierre-Jean-Baptiste Gerbier de la Masselaye (1725–88)—L'Avocat Gerbier—one of the most sensational trial lawyers of his day. His public appearances occasioned mob scenes of spectators avid to see and hear the 'Modern Cicero', the 'French Demosthenes'. His bust, in plaster painted terra cotta, is in the Palace of Justice in Paris, close to another bust of him in terra cotta, by J.-B. Lemoyne II, dated 1767. Houdon's plaster has been overpainted, and has lost some of the detail, but it preserves the general impression sought by the artist. Gerbier is presented, torso truncated, without shoulders, like Palissot, but undraped *à l'antique*, as befits the modern Cicero. As in the comparable version of Voltaire's bust, the aggressively bald head contributes to the total effect of stark nudity. The head is lifted, the heavy brows contract over the penetrating gaze, to suggest the spell-binding orator in action. In this presentation Gerbier joins Houdon's distinguished company of Diderot, Voltaire, d'Alembert, Rousseau, Buffon, and others yet to follow.[145]

The other two portraits of men in the Salon of 1781 round out this gallery of intellectuals with a noted man of medicine, Dr Théodore Tronchin of Geneva (1709–81), and a hero of the American Revolution, John Paul Jones. The portrait of Dr Tronchin is a straightforward presentation of a distinguished professional man. The marble in the Geneva Museum and the plaster at Châalis show him (with shoulders) soberly dressed, wearing a heavy, professional wig, brows knotted, lips pursed as though deep in the examination of a patient. This is the face of a strong, serious, and perhaps somewhat impatient individual. We know him from contemporary records as a brilliant diagnostician at a time when not many doctors could claim the distinction; and notably a pioneer in the use of smallpox inoculation.[146]

The naval hero, John Paul Jones (1747–92), whose plaster portrait, painted terra cotta, was exhibited in the Salon of 1781, was Houdon's second American sitter, following Benjamin Franklin. After harassing the coast of England and Scotland in April and May 1778, Jones was given command of a French merchantman, which he rebuilt and rechristened *Le Bon Homme Richard* in honor of Franklin, author of *Poor Richard's Almanack*. It was in his historic battle with the British frigate *Serapis* that Jones, his ship badly damaged, was asked by the British captain if he would surrender. His answer was the famous, 'Sir, I have not yet begun to fight.' When he returned to Paris after his notable victory, he was lionized by the Court and the capital. A bust was ordered from Houdon by the Masonic Lodge of the Nine Sisters. According to Grimm in the *Correspondance littéraire*: 'The Lodge of the Nine Sisters, of which he is a member, engaged M. Houdon to make his bust. The portrait is another masterpiece worthy of the chisel which seems destined to consecrate to immortality illustrious men in every walk of life.'[147]

When he returned to Paris in 1786 Jones ordered at least eight plasters of his portrait, and probably several more, as gifts for distinguished friends and military colleagues, including Washington, Jefferson, Franklin, Lafayette, and others. In some cases the gift may have been intended as a reminder of his achievements during a period when these tended to be forgotten in the United States. The result is the existence today of an unusual number of original plasters in American collections. Notable for its quality is that in the Boston Museum of Fine Arts, referred to above, which very likely came from the collection of Thomas Jefferson. As was also the case with *Franklin* and *Washington*, some of these plasters of *John Paul Jones* have been cast in bronze during the nineteenth and twentieth centuries, and these bronzes appear on the market from time to time as original works by Houdon.[148]

Fig. 126 The fine marble in the Naval Academy at Annapolis, signed and dated 1781, came from the collection of the Duc de Nemours, to whom it had descended from his ancestor, the Duc d'Orléans, its original owner. It shows Jones in his uniform decorated with the cross received from Louis XVI. Jones was a small man, slightly built, immaculate in dress and extremely courteous in manner. Although in the salons of Paris he obviously subordinated the qualities which made him a notable commander, they shine forth from the portrait by Houdon: this is a strong, resolute face, suggestive of intelligence and the ability to act quickly and decisively. The face also illustrates the sense of structure which reflects Houdon's passion for anatomy and his control of sculptural form.[149]

A somewhat macabre postscript to the story of this bust testifies to the precision which Houdon achieved in his portraits. Jones died in Paris in 1792 and was buried in the Saint Louis cemetery for foreigners. His grave was long forgotten and when it was rediscovered in 1905, the head measurements of Houdon's bust were used for comparison in the identification of the body and were found to conform exactly.[150] Jones's remains were then transferred to the Naval Academy at Annapolis.

MME DE SERILLY
Fig. 127
Plate 66 The plaster painted terra cotta of *Madame de Sérilly* was shown in the Salon of 1781, the marble in the Salon of 1783. The latter may be assumed to be that in the Wallace Collection, London, signed and dated: HOUDON F. 1782, another outstanding example of Houdon's ability to commemorate the exquisite ladies of eighteenth-century France. Little is known of Madame de Sérilly's personality except what might be guessed from the portrait. She was lady-in-waiting to Marie-Antoinette, her husband and brother were guillotined under the Terror, and subsequently she was remarried twice, the last time to Général de Montesquieu. Her face is one of great charm and mobility. The large, hooded eyes look out with an expression of rapt, even sensuous attention. The long, soft hair is modelled with particularly loving care; the upper arms and shoulders are wrapped in a flowing cloak, which encompasses the figure, acts as a base and extends in finished detail across the back. This is the consummate type of the late Baroque and rococo portrait of a noblewoman, presented with the decorative grace of an earlier time. She is almost an anachronism among the soberly dressed (or undressed in the instance of Gerbier) gentlemen who accompany her in the Salon of 1781. As she belongs to an age of elegance rapidly drawing to a close, so most of them seem to predict a more democratic, bourgeois, and perhaps less picturesque century.[151]

The marble statue of *Voltaire* listed in the *livret* for the Salon of 1781 has been discussed under the Salon of 1779 together with the portrait busts of him. Before turning to the statue of *Tourville* and the tomb of of the Comte d'Ennery, two other busts and a medallion exhibited in 1781 remain to be mentioned briefly. All three are in one way or another problem pieces.

Mademoiselle Odéoud is Houdon's spelling for Anne Audéoud, daughter of a Swiss banker. The problem here is that there exists one of Houdon's charming portraits of a child, in many different casts and variants, which is possibly but not certainly Mademoiselle Audéoud. A plaster in the Schwerin Museum, signed and dated: *houdon 1780* and bearing the *cachet d'atelier*, is listed in the museum as *Unknown Little Girl*. A signed plaster variant in the Musée Nissim de Camondo, Paris, in which she wears a shawl over her head, is catalogued as *Portrait Presumably of Sabine Houdon* (which she certainly is not). There is also another variant, in which the shawl is draped over her shoulders. The little girl, whether or not she is Mademoiselle Audéoud, is a delight, comparable to Louise Brongniart and, somewhat later, to Houdon's three daughters. This is an instance where there seems no serious reason for doubting the identification. The date of the Schwerin bust and the age of Mademoiselle Audéoud, born in 1776, seem about right, and there are no competitors. The number of surviving casts is evidence of her continuing popularity.[152]

The bust of a *Negress* in plaster imitating antique bronze may be associated with the *Fountain* described in the *livret* of 1783. It must be a separate bust of the maidservant who, in the fountain group, pours water over the shoulders of her mistress. Only the head of the *Negress* survives, in the Soissons Museum, the rest of the bust having been destroyed during World War I. In 1794, during the Revolution, Houdon added to the base a topical inscription commemorating the freeing of the slaves in the French colonies. This is a gay and lively and, for Houdon, a somewhat exotic bust. Its original form, nude to below the breasts, may be seen in a reduced bronze, probably a studio piece, in the Musée des Arts Décoratifs in Paris, in old photographs of the original, and in a bronze replica in the Camondo Museum.[153]

The medallion relief in plaster representing the head of the *Sun*, which has disappeared, is of interest as a variant on the medallion of Apollo mentioned in Houdon's inventory, *c.* 1784, under the year 1780, and drawn, his hair 'blown in the wind', by Saint-Aubin in the *livret* of 1777, although not specifically listed in that *livret*. Despite a coincidence in dates, the designation here as the *Sun* would suggest a full-face representation, possibly surrounded by rays of light.[154]

Houdon's only royal commission under the old regime was the statue of the *Maréchal de Tourville*, one of the series of portrait statues dedicated to the great men of France. The concept of the 'great man' was central to the French Enlightenment, taken from the model of antiquity and given particular application in the belief that man could control his own fate. The passion for Plutarch's *Parallel Lives* of the great men of Greece and Rome was shared by Rousseau, Diderot, and other *philosophes*; and it was perhaps their example that made the commemoration of the great men of France a favorite project of d'Angiviller. Under his *Direction des Bâtiments* this became one of the last important royal commissions of the old regime, and was carried beyond the Revolution in the concept of the Panthéon.[155]

Beginning with the Salon of 1777 d'Angiviller projected four statues of great men to appear at each Salon. Since these were specifically the great men of France, the criteria for selection included patriotism, examples of incorruptibility and other national virtues, as well as achievement in arts and letters, science and philosophy, war and statesmanship. Thus the Salon of 1777 included *René Descartes*, by Pajou, the *Chancellor Michel de l'Hôpital*, by Gois, the *Duc de Sully*, French statesman under Henri IV, by Mouchy, and *Archbishop Fénelon*, theologian and educator, by Lecomte. For the *Chancellor de l'Hôpital* the *livret* contains the explanation that 'the Chancellor, exiled in his château, learning from his servants that his enemies are coming to assassinate him, far from becoming alarmed, commands them to open all the doors. The artist has shown the qualities of firmness and determination in his attitude and expression.'

In 1779 appeared the *Chancellor d'Aguesseau*, statesman and orator, by Berruer, *Charles Louis de Montesquieu*, the political philosopher, by Clodion, *Bishop Bossuet*, again by Pajou, and *Pierre Corneille* by Caffieri.

Fig. 40

On October 5, 1779, d'Angiviller wrote to the painter, Pierre, Director of the Academy of Painting and Sculpture:

> As the interval of approximately two years is not too much for the execution of a marble figure such as those which have been made for the King and exhibited at the last two Salons, I do not wish to lose time in arranging for the subjects of the four new figures for the Salon of 1781 as well as the artists to execute them.
>
> I have already presented to His Majesty the following subjects, namely *Pascal*, the *Duc de Montausier* [governor of the royal children under Louis XIV], the *Maréchal de Tourville*, and the *Maréchal de Catinat*, that is to say, a philosopher who has enlightened the nation and humanity by his writings, a man of the court who has given an example of austere virtue in the midst of corruption, an admiral noted for his victories, and a general no less to be recommended for his military talents as for his impartiality, his humanity and his philosophic spirit.
>
> His Majesty having agreed to these subjects, I have chosen to execute them MM. Pajou, Mouchy, Houdon, and Dejoux. You will do me the favor of informing them as soon as possible. As to the work which each of them should execute, my intention is that M. Pajou should choose first, then M. Mouchy, then M. Houdon, and when the choices are made you will be good enough to inform me.[156]

Much has been made of the fact that Houdon received so few royal commissions. Questions have been raised as to whether, in the light of his obvious talents and rapidly mounting reputation, senior sculptors might have formed a cabal against him; or whether d'Angiviller discriminated against him, either because he was something of an outsider in the face of the great families of sculptors who surrounded him, or because the *Directeur des Bâtiments* was shocked by the 'indecency' of the *Diana* and later of *La Frileuse*. On the occasion of the Salon of 1779, Bachaumont, the commentator, published a letter protesting against the selection of Clodion over Houdon in the commission for the *Montesquieu* (a letter that could have been inspired by Houdon), pointing to Houdon's brilliant achievements and the fact that he was senior to Clodion in the Academy. A number of letters exist from Houdon to d'Angiviller inviting him to his studio to view the *Diana* or the *Voltaire*, and the polite but formal answers in which the latter regrets that other business prevents him from coming at that moment, but assures the artist that he will come as soon as possible. We do not know whether he went but we have no reason to doubt that he did.[157]

There does not seem to be clear evidence that Houdon suffered from official discrimination. It is inevitable that in an institution as small and as inbred as the French Academy in the eighteenth century there would be jealousies, factions, and a degree of discrimination. It is surprising to us that sculptors such as Mouchy, Lecomte, Dejoux, and Gois, largely forgotten today and, on the evidence of surviving works, inferior to Houdon, should have been preferred to him. But they were senior to him within the system and, despite one or two aberrations, d'Angiviller seems to have attempted to follow the rule of seniority as closely as possible. Why Clodion, then an *agréé*, should have been chosen over Houdon, an academician, in 1779, will probably remain a mystery unless some further document appears, but it should be noted that he was also chosen in preference to Boizot and Julien, academicians, and Monnot, senior to him as an *agréé*. Obviously Clodion was a highly talented sculptor although not primarily a portraitist (his *Montesquieu*, nevertheless, is one of the most successful of the series). D'Angiviller could have been privately one of the *amateurs des arts* seduced by his delightfully erotic terra cotta groups. Or perhaps it was in this instance simply family influence. Clodion, after all, was a nephew of L.-S. Adam of the distinguished family of sculptors, and the son-in-law of Pajou, who as senior sculptor to the king received the largest number of commissions in the Great Men series. Houdon, on the other hand, uneducated, the son of a servant, with few important connections, *was* something of an outsider.

Having finally been commissioned, Houdon chose the Maréchal de Tourville as his subject. He would probably have preferred Pascal, but Pajou, having first choice, not surprisingly claimed him, and Mouchy selected Montausier. The surviving documents relevant to the Tourville statue are not of particular interest in themselves, but they are the kind of record which has a habit of outlasting all others: they have principally to do with Houdon's problems in obtaining the marble for the statue and being paid for the work.[158]

The statues of the Great Men were originally designed for the Grande Galerie du Louvre. They are now divided between the Institute of France and the Louvre on the one hand, where the men of letters and science are housed, and Versailles, on the other, which provides a home for the heroes of France. *Tourville* at Versailles, signed and dated Fait par Houdon. 1781, has been criticized by Réau and earlier students of the artist. Anne Hilarion de Contentin, Comte de Tourville (1642–1701) commanded the French navy in the War of the Grand Alliance, winning several notable victories over the English. Although he was defeated by superior forces in the battle of La Hogue, 1692, it was the 'significant moment' before this battle that Houdon's statue commemorated as the supreme occasion of the admiral's career. As the *livret* of 1781 describes it, 'The Admiral is represented at the moment when he shows to the Council of War the letter from the King commanding him to give the signal for the battle of 1692.' Knowing that he is outnumbered and doomed to defeat, he proceeds to the battle—an example of heroic obedience to his sovereign.

The posthumous sculpture is certainly a costume piece. Houdon seems to have been anxious to display his virtuosity in the carving of every button, every detail of lace and velvet, ribands and medals, plumes and wind-swept hair. The admiral's knit brows, glaring eyes, flaring nostrils, and grimly set jaw, at his supreme moment of decision are effective Baroque theatre. In a way he reminds us of *Sophie Arnould as Iphigenia* and of *Larive as Brutus*, which appeared in the Salon of 1783. Although *Tourville* is more controlled than some of Bernini's saints and angels, he does illustrate Houdon's most Baroque phase, not only in the emotionalism of the concept but in the swing and counterpoise of the organization. Committed to the theme of a seventeenth-century hero, the sculptor was obviously doing his best to be historically correct in matters of dress and also in his interpretation of the forms and spirit of the time.

Fig. 130
Plate 67

As I have suggested, the statue of Tourville, Houdon's only royal commission under the old regime, has generally been neglected. I must admit that in 1956, when I saw it for the first time, I was not greatly impressed. It was then, and still is, exhibited in a corridor at Versailles not open to the public, one of a long row of sculptures, dimly lighted and relatively indistinguishable. When I first photographed it I was rather surprised to find that in the prints it looked much better than I had expected. For this reason I rephotographed the *Tourville* in 1973. In the process of restudying it in relation to all of its companions in this isolated and neglected gallery at Versailles, I came to realize that this is in actuality a remarkable work. As one looks down the long row of sculptures, the Houdon *Tourville* stands out dramatically from its companions. This is certainly the artist's most virtuoso experiment in Baroque theatre: an enormously effective recapitulation in the latter part of the eighteenth century of Bernini's Roman Baroque.

Most of the Great Men in the series, before the Revolution, with the exception of Montesquieu, belonged to the seventeenth century or earlier. It was only in 1808 that so complete a man of the eighteenth century as d'Alembert was included, in the portrait by Lecomte. But the interpretations of Pascal, Descartes, Bossuet, and Corneille, by Pajou, Lecomte, and Caffieri, are very much in the spirit of the eighteenth century. Houdon's *Tourville*, for whatever reason, seems to belong to the time of the subject rather than to the

TOMB OF
D'ENNERY

time of the artist. On the other hand his statue of *Voltaire*, which also appeared in the Salon of 1781, is the very embodiment of the eighteenth century.

The contrast between the statues of *Tourville* and *Voltaire*, both finished within a year of each other, is sufficiently dramatic; but even more intriguing is the fact that in 1781 Houdon completed the tomb of the Comte d'Ennery, the climax of his exploration of classicism. The monument commemorates Victor Charpentier d'Ennery (1732–76), a soldier and colonial administrator, and was designed to be placed in his family church of Saint-Aubin d'Ennery near Pontoise. The d'Ennery monument was also the climax of Houdon's efforts in the realm of tomb sculpture. The sepulchral chapel in memory of Louisa-Dorothea, Duchess of Saxe-Gotha, was his first recorded tomb sculpture, although the model was not exhibited until the Salon of 1775. This was never carried out and the model has disappeared, so we are dependent on the description in the *livret* for an idea of its appearance.[159] From this it is apparent that it was an elaborate Baroque scheme in the tradition extending from Bernini to Pigalle's tomb of the Maréchal de Saxe. The two completed Galitzin tombs in Moscow on the other hand were remarkable instances of classical simplicity and restraint, both in their iconography and in their formal structure. These marbles, in process in the artist's studio during the Salon of 1773 before being shipped to Russia, are obvious prototypes for the d'Ennery tomb in specific details as well as in their total conception. All three are simple relief sculptures with the figures in high relief against a neutral

Plate 17a–b ground. The most striking analogy is between the mourning figure of *Justice* on the tomb of Prince Alexis Galitzin and the *Comtesse de Blot* on that of the Comte d'Ennery, both freely derived from an antique *Muse*, possibly a *Polyhymnia* in the Louvre, but both familiar types of eighteenth-century *Pleureuse*. We may also note the inscribed altar, the decorative branches, the attributes of arms. The cinerary urns in the Galitzin tombs are replaced by a cinerary casket on top of the altar in that of d'Ennery. But the common quality in all three tombs is their classic clarity, their affinity to Greek grave stelae of the fifth or fourth centuries B.C.[160]

The other two Galitzin tombs were never carried out and only one of the two sketches exhibited in the Salon of 1777 is known to survive. This small terra cotta maquette for the

Fig. 96 monument to Prince Alexander Galitzin indicates a more elaborate design than the two earlier tombs or even than the later d'Ennery tomb, with something of the intricate symbolism and emotionalism of the Baroque tradition. As noted, however, these aspects are comparatively subordinated, and the organization of the relief figures against the blank background is that of an impeccable classic triangle.

Fig. 132 The tomb of the Comte d'Ennery returns in a total sense to the ideal of classic structure.
Plate 68 Three figures are grouped on either side of an altar or plaque, on the face of which is a beautifully lettered inscription commemorating the count. His portrait, in the form of a
Plate 70 medallion, appears at the base. Figures and altar are in high relief against a rectangular, dark grey marble wall—a recent replacement. On one side the widowed countess, draped in heavy robes like an ancient vestal or a medieval saint, presents her small daughter, who is also heavily robed but with undraped hair tied with a riband, suggesting an infant votary.
Plate 17b On the other side the count's sister, Marie-Cécile-Pauline Charpentier, Comtesse de Blot, rests her arms on the altar, her head resting on her left hand, in a pose of deep grief. The
Plates 69, 108 *Comtesse d'Ennery* belongs in the line of Houdon's *Vestals*, particularly the large marble of 1787, with her head similarly covered. Like the Galitzin tombs, the classicism here does not rest primarily in motifs taken from antiquity but in the austere and restrained organization, the qualities of apartness yet communion of the protagonists, the asymmetrical balance of the elements. There are somewhat melodramatic, Baroque reminiscences, such as the pose of the Comtesse de Blot and the marble tear that stains the cheek of the Comtesse d'Ennery; but these fade within the total effect of unity.

Although this tomb was set up outside Paris, and thus could not have exercised any direct influence on the emerging tradition of neo-classicism, it was a remarkable work to have been produced in France in 1781. It precedes by three years David's painting of the *Oath of the Horatii* (1784), generally considered the painting that marked the first maturity of neo-classicism in France. Antonio Canova (1757–1822), nine years younger than Houdon, was only settling in Rome and discovering Roman antiquity in 1779. His outstanding sculpture to that date, the *Daedalus and Icarus*, 1778–9, is a mannered and somewhat niggling treatment of an antique theme in a detailed, realistic copy of his posed models. His first classic subject in Rome, the *Apollo Crowning Himself*, 1781, an antique partial figure, is similarly a detailed, realistic copy, but this time after a Roman statue. Despite his literal use of antiquity, it should also be recalled that Canova, even in late works such as the *Three Graces*, 1813–16, maintained rococo qualities of sensuous elegance.

The particular quality of Houdon's classicism perhaps needs to be emphasized again. Despite his direct exposure to antiquity through his years at Rome, through the French royal collections and copies of ancient art, through the expanding knowledge of the times deriving from excavations, research, and books of travel, his classicism, like that of most of his colleagues until the last quarter of the eighteenth century, was still primarily that of the Renaissance filtered through two hundred years of Baroque and rococo variations.

Houdon was unquestionably an eclectic sculptor, though in no pejorative sense of the term. His most specifically classic works are paralleled even chronologically by his most rococo or, in other instances, by his most narrowly realistic. The *Maréchal de Tourville*, *Seated Voltaire*, and the tomb of the Comte d'Ennery, all completed in 1781, have been mentioned. In 1781 Houdon was also working on the fountain which was installed in the garden of the Château de Monceau by 1783, one of his most rococo compositions. He belonged to the age of Louis XVI, a time of rapidly changing trends in the arts. But when all this is said, a work such as the tomb of the Comte d'Ennery demonstrates a remarkable sensitivity to the idea of classical antiquity. Another statue of a classical subject which belongs at this point is the *Ceres* in the Château of Maisons-Laffitte. This was one of four statues ordered *c.* 1781 by the Comte d'Artois, brother of Louis XVI, for the redecoration of the dining room. They represented the Seasons by the appropriate goddess: Houdon, *Ceres*; Clodion, *Erigone*; Foucou, *Flora*; and Boizot, *Pomona*. Although intended to be finished in stone, they have remained in plaster. The *Ceres*, which did not appear in any Salon, is mentioned by Houdon in his letter of 1794 to Bachelier: 'Cérès en pierre, à Maisons, château qui appartenait à d'Artois'. It is a heavily draped, rather massive figure of the Greek Demeter or Latin Ceres type, goddess of earth, raising her veil of mourning—for her daughter Persephone—over her head. The face is literally classical in the tradition of the original small *Vestal*, but appropriately more mature. The arrangement and mass of the draperies are close to those of the *Comtesse de Blot* on the d'Ennery tomb. Although conceived as a figure within a decorative ensemble, the *Ceres* demonstrates close study of Roman prototypes and, in its dignity and serenity, is an important link in the chain of Houdon's classical themes. It should also be compared with Houdon's *Themis* for the Palais Bourbon.[160a]

Fig. 131

THE Salon of 1783 was as rich as that of 1781 in terms of new portrait busts by Houdon, but several of these have disappeared. All trace has been lost of the marble portrait of the *General Nicholas Ivanovitch Soltykov*, although that of his father, *General Ivan Petrovitch Soltykov* (1730–1805), is preserved in the Hermitage. The bronze of the *Princess Dachkov* is lost, but fortunately not the marble of *Madame de Sérilly*, already discussed. If we accept the date of 1777 on the Bowes Castle Museum marble of the presumed daughter of the painter Hubert Robert, we must assume that *la petite Robert* is missing, and we are faced with another delightful portrait of a child in search of an identity. (See p. 42.) In a sense it is a pity, since her wind-swept hair accords well with that of the *Brothers Montgolfier* in Houdon's bronze medallion dated 1783. However, this feature also occurs in what looks like an *Apollo* sketched by Saint-Aubin in the *livret* of 1777.

The other portraits in the Salon constitute a wonderful miscellany: *Monsieur Louis*, the noted surgeon; the posthumous portrait of *La Fontaine*, designed as a companion for the *Molière* of 1779; *Larive* of the Comédie Française in the role of Brutus; *Buffon* for Catherine of Russia; and the *Prince and Princess of Mecklenburg-Schwerin*. The statues listed in the *livret* are even more impressive, although none was actually exhibited within the walls of the Salon. They included the bronze *Diana*; the marble *Frileuse*; and the Monceau fountain for the Duc de Chartres. A marble bust of *Alexander the Great* for the King of Poland completes the roster.

The two generals Soltykov visited Paris in 1782 in the train of the Grand Duke Paul, son and later successor to Catherine. The marble bust of *Ivan Petrovitch*, signed and dated 1783, shows him in a bemedalled court dress that cannot detract from his intelligent and sensuous face. The eyes are half closed, the lips full. Although somewhat heavy, it is a handsome and imperious face, filled with delicate nuances in the shaping of the marble. The bust illustrates again Houdon's ability to combine clarity of detail with an almost imperceptible generalization of surface.[161]

Antoine Louis (1723–92), the surgeon, wrote extensively on problems of military surgery, contributed articles on medicine to the *Encyclopédie*, and compiled a dictionary of surgery. He also had the distinction of being the actual inventor of the guillotine, conceived by him

Fig. 134
Plate 72

as a humane instrument of execution. Houdon's portrait in marble, signed and dated: HOUDON F. 1782, is another in that distinguished line of professional men that includes de Miromesnil, de Nicolay, de Caumartin, Tronchin, Necker, and Fulton. His bust, like those of de Nicolay and de Miromesnil, is full to the waist; the ample academic robes as well as the sedate professional perruque lend him an aura of dignity, authority, and professional competence. Houdon seems to have had a particular fondness for and sensitivity to this type of occupational portrait, and to have lavished on the marble all his technical virtuosity. In a sense these were his response to the official portraits of the seventeenth century. For the Baroque flamboyance of portraits by Coysevox or Girardon, Houdon in these professional portraits substitutes sobriety, integrity, and the authority of reason and knowledge. Dr Louis not only symbolizes the dignity of his station and his professional achievements, but his face with its wrinkled forehead, quizzical eyes, and pursed lips, suggests, like that of Dr Tronchin, the competent analyst in action.[162]

Catherine the Great, having acquired a marble bust of *Diderot*, two of *Voltaire*, with and without perruque, two small gilt-bronze versions of the *Seated Voltaire*, and having ordered through Grimm the second marble of the large *Seated Voltaire*, sent, July 6, 1781, another urgent request to Grimm: 'One thing I beg of you is to have made for me a bust in white marble of Monsieur de Buffon and give it, if you please, to be made by Houdon. Besides that I would have you know that Monsieur de Buffon holds a most distinguished place in my mind and that I regard him as the first mind of the century in his field.' Four days later she added, 'I repeat my request to have the bust of this distinguished man made for me.'[163]

Georges-Louis-Leclerc Comte de Buffon (1707–88), the great naturalist, became director of the Jardin du Roi (now the Jardin des Plantes) in 1739. His monumental *Histoire naturelle*, which appeared between 1749 and 1804 in forty-four volumes, classified all the plants in the Jardin du Roi. In his respect for evidence obtained through careful observation and experimentation, he was a pioneer of modern scientific method. He anticipated in broad outline the theories of Darwin in terms of the evolution of plant forms. Catherine became a passionate devotee of Buffon after reading *Les époques de la nature*, which appeared in 1779. On finishing it she wrote to Grimm in ecstasy: '. . . here is an hypothesis which is to this point the *ne plus ultra* of the spirit or rather of the human genius. Newton made a giant step:

here is the second.' In her enthusiasm she sent Buffon a case of gold medals as well as furs from Siberia.

Houdon's marble of *Buffon* in the Salon of 1783 was destined for Catherine (it is now in the Hermitage) as the *livret* states. As might be expected, the initial version is undraped without shoulders, truncated torso, *à l'antique*, the basic type of the ancient philosopher. There are several other examples of this version in different materials; and a painted plaster at Schwerin, signed and dated: *houdon. 1781*, shows Buffon wearing an open-neck shirt. In all examples he seems to be wearing his own plentiful hair, curled in the fashion of the short perruque of the period and tied in a queue. At the time of the portrait he was seventy-four years old but his strong face and powerful neck make him seem much younger. The presentation of one of the great minds of the century is remarkably sharp, both in the total characterization and in the shaping of hair, eyes, and eyebrows. It is an intense portrayal of a searching, analytical personality, brought to life by all those subtle details which suggest momentary, transitory action. The sharp turn and lift of the head, the slightly parted lips, as though they are about to shape a phrase, the heavy, compressed brows, and the wide, searching eyes all reflect and dramatize a forceful personality.

Buffon had been painted and sculpted many times before. Pajou had made his statue for the Jardin du Roi and from it derived three types of bust between 1773 and 1776, in contemporary dress, draped, and undraped *à l'antique*. (It is interesting that Catherine should not simply have asked for a copy of Pajou's bust.) This is a powerful representation and, although made eight years before Houdon's, shows a more aged and heavily lined face. Since no one could ever accuse Houdon of hiding a wrinkle, Pajou must have been deliberately seeking to emphasize the heavy lines for dramatic effect. The statue was conceived as a symbolic image, the features a mask of force. The eyes are depicted, in Pajou's characteristic manner, as a thin circle and shallow central hole. Whereas this sometimes gives to Pajou's sitters an unflattering, somewhat pop-eyed look, in the case of Buffon the treatment of the eyes is effective within the harsh, masklike quality of the face. Pajou succeeds admirably in giving the *idea* of the great scientist; Houdon succeeds comparably in giving the impression of the man.[164]

The portrait of the actor, Jean Mauduit, called Larive (1747–1827), is one of Houdon's superlative theatrical portraits, in its way even more effective than his portrait of *Sophie Arnould* in its interpretation of eighteenth-century high drama.[165] Caffieri exhibited his magnificent bust of the seventeenth-century actor-dramatist, Jean de Rotrou (for the Comédie Française) in the same Salon of 1783. The two busts merit comparison although it is probable that Caffieri was attempting to outdo Houdon's *Molière*, whose entry into the Comédie in 1779 he had so bitterly resented. *Rotrou* like *Molière* is conceived in a romantic Baroque form; the torso similarly is full, the period costume with informally open-neck shirt is a marvel of virtuoso carving. The handsome head is lifted in a moment of dramatic declamation. Whereas Houdon, in the *Molière*, had suggested speech by parting the lips slightly, Caffieri goes one better by placing Rotrou's tongue visibly between his lips. Caffieri was a specialist in the posthumous portrait, and this is his masterpiece.[166]

The art of acting ranked among the major arts in the eighteenth century—as it properly should—and Diderot among other critics placed great actors with great painters or poets. The eighteenth-century tradition of tragic acting was one of passionate declamation and gesture. Larive, whose portrait is also at the Comédie Française, is shown in the role of Brutus in Voltaire's *The Death of Caesar*, caught in a supreme theatrical moment of defiant passion. Despite the patronage of the actress Clairon, whose last lover he was, there were strong differences of opinion about his talent. Nevertheless he had a long and distinguished career at the Comédie, gaining particular note for roles demanding nobility and fiery anger of expression. It was thus that Houdon portrayed him. Larive is shown in a toga caught up at the right shoulder with a fibula, his eyes almost starting out of his handsome head,

Fig. 135
Plate 73

Fig. 46

LARIVE
Fig. 138
Plates 75, 143k
Fig. 44

which is turned sharply to the right as though 'giving his best profile'. The hair is a cap of tight curls, suggestive of those of the *Morpheus* but cut even closer in the Roman manner. The general effect recalls the well-known ancient portrait of Caracalla, which Houdon undoubtedly knew in Rome or through replicas; as well as Michelangelo's *Brutus* (itself adapted from the *Caracalla*), which the artist could have seen in Florence or known through engravings. Although there is no record that Houdon visited Florence, he could hardly have avoided it on his way to or from Rome, if only for its sculptures by Michelangelo.

Aside from its superb quality and its theatrical reminiscences, *Larive* is of interest for its demonstration of Houdon's use of classical sources. Some of these may have been in the nature of stage properties. For instance, Larive's toga with its fibula is essentially the same as that used for the *Belisarius* of 1773 and for the bronze, armored version of the *Prince Henry of Prussia*, of 1789. The most intriguing comparison is the *Alexander*, the marble of which was shown in the Salon of 1783, where the plaster of *Larive* appeared.

The King of Poland, Stanislas-Auguste Poniatowski, ordered from Houdon a marble bust of *Alexander the Great*, which shows Alexander helmeted and draped *à l'antique*. The bust, youthful, idealized, yet with specific characterization, may derive from the lost medallion of Alexander in the Salon of 1771, which in turn may have been made in Houdon's Roman period. It also resembles a bust of Alexander by Girardon, constructed from an ancient Roman porphyry head, with which had been combined armor cast in bronze.[167]

Fig. 137

Houdon's *Alexander*, now in Warsaw, is helmeted and armored with his cloak fastened by a fibula at the right shoulder. His face has the traditional, handsome, classic profile, small mouth, full lips, and heavy chin, all surrounded by long, wavy hair falling over his shoulders. He is the perfect type of the ancient Greek hero, except for his long hair and that his eyes, rather than being shown blank, are deeply undercut, full of life though focused on the distance. Here, as in the *Napoleon* and the *Washington*, Houdon seems to give his military leader a quality of introspection.

Another work not specifically classic but with classic overtones is the medallion, not shown in the Salon, of the aeronauts, the *Brothers Montgolfier*. The gilt-bronze version in the Musée de l'Air, Paris, is signed and dated: *houdon fecit 1783*. Joseph (1740–1818) and Étienne (1745–99) Montgolfier invented and demonstrated one of the first operative balloons, an event that caused vast excitement in France, and was commemorated in countless prints, paintings, and medals. Many of these were based on Houdon's medallion since he, as usual, was on the scene early to record so astounding an event. He made many medallion reliefs, either portraits or mythological-classical subjects, but most of these have disappeared. Thus the *Montgolfier* medallion is important as a record, aside from its fine quality. The profile heads, superimposed as on a cameo, are idealized resemblances deriving from that lost medallion of *Apollo* with wind-blown hair, sketched by Saint-Aubin in the *livret* for the Salon of 1777.

The bust of the poet, *Jean de la Fontaine* (1621–95), author of the *Fables*, was commissioned by Monsieur Haudry, an art collector of the city of Orléans, as a companion piece to a portrait of Molière, and the marble was shown in the Salon of 1783. This is a worthy companion piece to *Molière*, filled with affection for the fabulist, one of the glories of seventeenth-century France. The portrait, after a painting by Rigaud, is proportioned to match the *Molière*, the torso full to lower chest and including shoulders. La Fontaine is informally clad in an open coat, with a large scarf, like that of Molière, knotted around his neck. His long hair, again resembling that of Molière, more natural than a seventeenth-century wig, falls softly over his shoulders. His face is older than that of his companion, more reflective, but similarly is admirably structured. This is a beautiful evocation of poetic genius, a warmly realized tribute to one of the greatest French writers, another effective reply to the myth that Houdon had no talent for posthumous portraiture. Caffieri, that specialist in the posthumous portrait, also did La Fontaine in 1778 for the Comédie Française, after a painting by Mignard; but here he was far less successful than with Rotrou. While treated in a similar manner to Houdon's *Molière* and *La Fontaine*, even to the knotted scarf, his *La Fontaine* is a dull and blocky work with an expression of peevishness rather than of poetic fire.[168]

The young Prince Friedrich Franz I of Mecklenburg-Schwerin (1756–1837) and his wife, Louise, visited Paris in 1782, where they had their portraits done by Houdon, and, perhaps inspired by their cousins of Saxe-Gotha, acquired excellent plasters of *Molière*, *La Fontaine*, *Gluck*, *Rousseau*, *Voltaire*, *Buffon*, *d'Alembert*, the *Empress Catherine*, and others. This collection, preserved in the Schwerin Museum is, like that at Gotha, of the greatest importance both for the quality of the pieces and for their impeccable history. Friedrich Franz was only twenty-seven years old when Houdon portrayed him in terra cotta, and looked even younger than his years. Though somewhat immature, this is a sensitive, even poetic face, a simple and homely contrast to the worldly Count Soltykov. His wife, Louisa, although presumably about the same age, has a comfortable, housewifely appearance, perhaps because she is already somewhat overweight; but her face is not unhandsome nor unintelligent. Whether it means anything or not, the artist has let her share her husband's reflective expression. We are reminded that Catherine was similarly a minor German princess before she ascended the throne of Russia; and the two ladies share a solid, bourgeois air, although Louise has nothing of Catherine's aura of sublime self-satisfaction.

The technique of the two terra cottas, which preserve their original sharpness of detail, is of some interest. Neither is signed but both have the *cachet de l'atelier*. The bust of the prince is left completely open at the back in a manner more usual for plasters; while that of the princess is closed as though the artist envisaged this as the model for a marble. In fact the treatment of the back, complete but somewhat simplified, is very similar to the marble of *Madame de Sérilly* exhibited at the same Salon. Whatever his intention, Houdon was probably fortunate to be able to persuade the couple to acquire terra cottas; since German princes, not overly rich, were usually satisfied to settle for plasters. The selection of works by Houdon made by Friedrich Franz would suggest that his interest lay more in the great men of the French Enlightenment than in forming a representative collection of Houdon's sculptures. In this he was typical of those 'enlightened rulers'—including Catherine, whose portrait he placed with those of the *philosophes*—who were fascinated by the ideas of Voltaire, Rousseau, or Diderot, until the French Revolution caused a rude awakening.[169]

The *livret* of the 1783 Salon included three major life-size sculptures: the first bronze of the *Diana*, displayed at the home of its owner, Monsieur Girardot de Marigny, rue Vivienne; the marble of the statue of *La Frileuse* (*Winter*, the cold or shivering girl) at the studio of the sculptor, Bibliothèque du Roi; and a *Fountain* 'of two figures, life-size, the one in white marble and the other imitating a negress, executed and placed in the garden of Monseigneur le duc de Chartres, at Monceau, near Paris'.[170]

According to the list of his works compiled *c.* 1784 Houdon had made models for a *Frileuse* in 1781[171] The life-size marble statue of the *Winter* (*La Frileuse*) was executed by 1783, the *Summer* by 1785; both are now in the Musée Fabre in Montpellier.[172] In the marble of *La Frileuse* a large vase, partly draped and cracked as though the water in it had frozen, supports the figure. Reduced marble versions of the two statues were completed by 1785 and were submitted to the Salon of that year. In a letter to d'Angiviller, the painter Pierre wrote concerning these: 'Tomorrow the jury will consider the entries for the forthcoming Salon. Among the entries are two half-life-size figures by Monsieur Houdon: one of these which is clothed [*Summer*], is nothing extraordinary, whereas the other [*La Frileuse*] could easily be excluded from the exhibition on account of its state of false modesty . . . I think I should observe in its defence that this figure is the better of the two, and that it could be shown in a corner.' He concluded speculating why 'the so-called Callipygian Venus fails to offend against decency, while the present figure, which exposes the same areas, looks exaggerated and indecent'. D'Angiviller replied: 'With regard to the two half-life-size figures of

Monsieur Houdon, I shall act in conformity with the decision of the Academy. The solution may indeed lie in placing the partly-clothed figure in a corner, thereby screening the areas that should not be exposed.'[173]

For whatever reason, either rejection by the jurors of the Academy or perhaps indignation on the part of the artist, neither statue appeared in the Salon of 1785. Having already shown the life-size marble of *La Frileuse* in his studio during the 1783 Salon, he may well have felt that it was not important to show it again. *La Frileuse* rapidly became one of his most popular figure sculptures, with the result that he turned out many replicas on a reduced scale in bronze and marble. There are even life-size papier-maché versions.[174] A small sketch now in the Louvre, very freely rendered in terra cotta and bronze, has the figure completely nude; both in the pose and the expressive handling of the surfaces it is remarkably like the *Eve* of Rodin, who was an admirer of Houdon.[175]

Fig. 142
Plates 80b, 81a, 82–4

The marble *Frileuse* at Montpellier and the life-size bronze in the Metropolitan Museum, New York, in which the cracked vase is eliminated, are the definitive versions.

The bronze *Frileuse*, signed and dated on the base: HOUDON F. 1787, together with the bronze *Dianas*, the *Apollo*, and the second version of *L'Écorché*, represent some of the sculptor's major efforts in bronze casting.[176]

Houdon's personification of *Winter* as a lovely, semi-nude, shivering girl is unusual if not unique. Sculptures and paintings representing the Seasons had existed in ancient and medieval times, had been popular since the Renaissance, and had proliferated during the eighteenth century. The standard form showed *Winter* as an aged woman and later as an aged man, contrasted with a young peasant girl symbolizing *Summer*. Falconet, in a sculpture of *Winter* in the Hermitage, *c.* 1763–71, depicted her as a charming maiden seated on a square, ornamented pedestal, becomingly draped in a long robe, with whose edge she is covering a bouquet of flowers. Houdon's *Frileuse*, even more of a departure, leans forward, her arms clasped across her breast, compactly holding the shawl, which covers her head and shoulders, in a pose both expressive and beautifully integrated. The arrangement of the shawl fortunately leaves exposed the delightful rear view, which offended Pierre. In this matter of censorship, incidentally, it should in all fairness be said that the tone of the correspondence between Pierre and d'Angiviller seems more tolerantly amused than shocked.

Houdon's statues of *La Frileuse* and *Diana* again summarize the range of his formal means. As the *Diana* represents his Louis XVI classicism, so *La Frileuse* together with the charming

Plate 85b
THE BATHER
Fig. 144
Plates 86–7

—if somewhat denigrated by Pierre—marble *Summer*, have him looking back nostalgically to the rococo tradition. The marble *Bather*, all that remains of the Monceau fountain, while closer than the *Diana* to the rococo image of Venus, Diana, Bather, or Nymph, nevertheless is close to Houdon's *Diana* in its elegant, mannerist elongation. In the original composition of the fountain the group was placed in a marble basin; a black attendant stood behind the *Bather*, holding in one hand a piece of marble drapery and in the other a gilt-bronze ewer, from which she poured water over her mistress.

The attendant, cast in dark lead, was vandalized during the Revolution. Her head was broken off and finally the entire figure disappeared. The left leg of the *Bather* and the right hand resting on that knee were also broken off and have been replaced. Considering how long she was exposed to the elements, not to mention the water with which her attendant deluged her, it is remarkable that the *Bather* should have survived as well as she has. She remains one of Houdon's most lovely sculptures; the figure, seated on a rock form, over which is arranged a large drapery, turns gracefully in space, the head and torso bent forward and pivoting gently to the left. The hair is loosely and softly arranged, almost as though it were actually wet. The face, with its delicate nose, and its soft, rounded cheeks, in which there is the suggestion of a dimple, is much more of a particular portrait than is the abstract-classic head of the *Diana*. Still, the figure of the *Bather* has much the same sense of elongation and accent on linear contours as the profile and angle views of the *Diana*.[177]

68

THE Salon of 1785 contained the shortest list of identified entries by Houdon since 1769. We do not know how many works were included under the entry, No. 231: 'Several portraits under the same number.' Aside from these, which may have been replicas of earlier works, there were three busts in marble and three in plaster. Some other important portraits, not listed in the *livret* of the Salon, are dated between 1784 and 1786, and will be discussed together with those exhibited. Of those in the Salon, *Gustave III, King of Sweden* has been lost or is not identified, as has the plaster of *Le Peletier de Morfontaine*, successor to Monsieur Caumartin as *Prévot des marchands*.[178] *Larive*, whose marble faithfully followed his plaster of 1783, has been discussed.

Prince Henry of Prussia (1726–1802), brother of Frederick the Great, was another of those Francophile German princes who could have imagined no greater joy than to have been able to spend their lives in Paris. On trips to Paris in 1784 and 1788 he was treated by the king and court with all the ceremony due to the representative of Frederick. Houdon's plaster, bearing the *cachet d'atelier*, shows the prince in the abbreviated version without arms or shoulders, in severe and simple contemporary dress. Henry was not a particularly impressive or prepossessing individual, but he seems to have been a cultivated man of the German *Aufklärung*; and the sculptor caught qualities of sensitivity and reflection, qualities, incidentally, not shared by his brother. A marble, ordered by Louis XVI as a tribute to Henry —and his brother—appeared in the Salon of 1787, and a bronze in the Salon of 1789. In these the portrait was expanded into the representation of a classical military hero, with Henry in full armor, over which is a military cape fastened at the right shoulder with a fibula. Although he still has his withdrawn expression and wears his perruque (the head seems to have been transferred directly from the plaster in modern dress) rather than a helmet, the image is suspiciously close to that of the *Alexander the Great* in Warsaw. Although the prince looks a little embarrassed in his stage armor, the bronze, cast by Houdon's great disciple, Thomire, fully confirms his claims concerning the art of bronze casting. It is signed by Thomire on the edge of the right shoulder: *Fondu et ciselé par Thomire d'après le modèle de M. Houdon. 1789*.[179]

Although not exhibited in the Salon of 1783 or 1785, the marble bust of the *Comtesse de Moustier* (1758–85), signed and dated: HOUDON F. 1784, should here be mentioned. It has always remained in the possession of the de Moustier family and there is even preserved an account book with the note: Année 1784. A. M. Oudon [*sic*] pour le buste de Mme de Moustier 1200 livres. The bust is unusual in its presentation of the countess without shoulders, undraped, abbreviated torso, *à l'antique*, the formula usually reserved for men or women of letters.[179a]

The small number of entries in this Salon was the consequence of Houdon's trip to the United States to make the studies from life for his portrait of George Washington, an historic occasion in the career of the sculptor and one that needs to be discussed at length. The two busts supposed to represent de Biré and Lenoir are extraordinary pieces of the highest quality, but both involve problems of identification as far as the sitters are concerned. From the *livret* we know that Houdon exhibited a marble bust of de Biré. The Marquis Charles-François Fontaine de Biré was a financial administrator during the reign of Louis XVI, and from 1788–91 was administrator of the Public Treasury. In the Boston Museum of Fine Arts there is a superb marble bust, from the Forsyth Wickes Collection, Newport, Rhode Island, purporting to be that of Monsieur de Biré, signed on the back: *houdon f. 1786* in cursive script. Can this marble be identified as a portrait of Monsieur de Biré? In the first place it is a reduced bust, approximately half life-size, whereas there is no indication of this fact in the *livret* of 1785. Houdon, like other French sculptors of the eighteenth century frequently made reduced versions of portrait busts and statues in marble, terra cotta, and bronze. Smaller sculptures were also manufactured in Sèvres porcelain. Examples of the *Diana*, *La Frileuse*, and *Tourville* among others have been mentioned. The Salon of

PRINCE HENRY
OF PRUSSIA

Fig. 145
Plate 88

Fig. 146

COMTESSE
DE MOUSTIER

DE BIRÉ

Fig. 148
Plate 89

1789 lists marbles of *Rousseau*, *Buffon*, and *Diderot* 'petite proportion' and small versions of the *Vestal* and *L'Écorché* also exist. As has been pointed out, such reductions were much in demand for the *cabinets des amateurs* during the eighteenth century. Although the accuracy of the *livret* listings can never be guaranteed, they usually stated the fact that a sculpture exhibited was 'petite proportion', either by this phrase, or another (une petite *Frileuse*) or by giving the dimensions (statue de *Diane*. Hauteur 18 à 20 pouces). Still, the fact that the *de Biré* is not so described does not completely exclude its identification with the marble. More significant is the lack of any positive evidence relating the particular bust to the name. So it must be concluded that we do not know whether the gentleman portrayed actually is the Marquis de Biré. We may have here a case where an unquestionably authentic bust of an unknown man has been given the most probable identification in terms of those listed in a Salon of appropriate date. But what is important is that the portrait, whoever the sitter, demonstrates again Houdon's ability to suggest, within the framework of a total characterization, a momentary but marvelously caught mood. Even if it is de Biré, we know very little about the personality of the gentleman, but Houdon presents to us a man of obvious intelligence and warm humor. The half-smile is fully caught in the eyes and has just begun to reach the mouth. The face vibrates with surface movement extending from the summarily indicated hair through the wrinkles around the eyes to the furrows of the mouth and chin. The flesh around the mouth and chin hangs somewhat loosely from a firmly rendered bone structure. In every way this is a characterization formulated and presented with a mastery comparable to that of the *Voltaire* or the *Franklin*. The sitter appears with the torso indicated to below the chest, soberly but elegantly dressed in a manner appropriate to an administrator of the end of the century. The hair seems to be his own, dressed in the form of a short wig of the period, a queue at the back tied with a riband. The finish of the marble demonstrates again the artist's ability to charge the surface with a sense of movement.[180]

LENOIR

With the portrait of Monsieur J.-Ch. Lenoir there is a comparable problem of identification. In his inventory *c.* 1784 Houdon lists a bust in terra cotta of 'M. Le Noire, lieutenant général de police'. In the *livret* for the Salon of 1785 Lenoir is described as 'Conseiller d'État, Bibliothécaire du Roi'. This is not an improbable combination in eighteenth-century France and, judging from the eulogies of Monsieur Lenoir by the commentators of the Salon, he seems to have been a man of parts.[181]

Fig. 149, Plate 91
Plate 143k

The surviving bust purporting to be that of Monsieur Lenoir is a fine bronze signed and dated on the back in cursive script: *houdon f. 1786*. There is no evidence that it really represents Monsieur Lenoir, even though it has gone under this label at least since 1865. The collector, David-Weill, who owned it, tended to doubt the identification. According to Réau, Monsieur David-Weill wrote to him raising the question whether the sitter might not be the architect, Dumont, called the Roman. Commentators on the Salon of 1785, while united in their praise of the portrait of Lenoir, seem, to judge from their descriptions, to be referring to a different work.[182] The question has not been resolved, and the bronze now in the collection of Pierre David-Weill in Paris may be the bust of an unknown man. Whoever he was, his portrait was executed by Houdon in 1786 and is a superlative example of the sculptor's technique in bronze; and the man is as fascinating as anyone in Houdon's gallery. The bronze, abbreviated, without shoulders, undraped *à l'antique*, is open at the back of the torso, the chest simply a narrow sheet fastened to the base with a clamp. The surface is meticulously chased, and the dark patina, although slightly worn over the nose, is of fine quality, warm and mellow in texture.

Lenoir—to maintain his traditional identification—was not a handsome man. He was completely bald, the ears are gnarled and somewhat distorted, the face heavy and round, the nose short and thick, the chin pugnacious. But his is a face filled with humor, and creased in a perhaps malicious but jovial and contagious smile. The complete absence of hair accentuates how important to Houdon (as to Rodin) was the total structure of the head in the characterization. This bronze, like the bronze *Diderot* at Langres, may serve as the canon against which all the bronze replicas of Houdon portrait busts should be tested.

The problem of the *Lenoir* bust is compounded by the existence in the Louvre of a marble bust by Houdon said to be of Chrétien-Guillaume de Lamoignon de Malesherbes (1921–94) and signed and dated under the right arm: HOUDON, F. 1784. It was owing to the sympathy and tolerance of Malesherbes, who could act as censor in his capacity as director of book publishing in France, that the *Encyclopédie* and many of the other writings of Diderot and the *philosophes* could be published. On one occasion when Diderot learned that his rooms, filled with seditious manuscripts, were about to be searched by the police, he turned to Malesherbes in panic. Malesherbes said simply: 'Bring the manuscripts to my house; they won't think of looking there.' Member of a great family, son of a Chancellor of France, he was not only a man of wide tolerance for new ideas, but was so loyal a defender of the king that he finally died on the guillotine. Despite his noble family, he was without pretensions, carelessly dressed, his clothes sprinkled with snuff, clumsy and bumbling but filled with humor and understanding. It is such a man that Houdon portrayed in the Louvre marble of 1784 and, despite the fact that the bronze of 'Lenoir' dated 1786 shows the sitter without perruque or dress, there is no question that the purported '*Lenoir*' is the same sitter as the purported '*Malesherbes*'. Which probably shows what a wig and a cravat can do for a man.[182]

The marble bust of the *Marquis de Condorcet*, which is signed and dated: *houdon fecit, 1785*, was never exhibited in a Salon. A bust of *Condorcet* without designation of material was mentioned in the inventory *c.* 1784 under the supplement. There is no other reference in the documents, and the marble was unknown to European scholars until it was published by Florence Ingersoll-Smouse in 1914.[183] A plaster bearing the *cachet d'atelier* entered the Louvre as a portrait of Lavoisier early in the twentieth century, although the identification has long been corrected.

Fig. 151
Plate 93

Plate 92

There can be no doubt that the marble in the American Philosophical Society, Philadelphia, and the plaster in the Louvre represent the same man and that the man is Condorcet. He is shown in modern dress with perruque, the sober dress of scholars or professional men at the end of the eighteenth century. Marie Jean-Antoine-Nicolas Caritat, Marquis de Condorcet (1743–94), mathematician, philosopher, and political leader, belonged with the liberal wing of the *Encyclopédistes*. He was elected to the Academy of Science in 1769 and to the French Academy in 1782. His friend d'Alembert, then permanent secretary of the Academy, who died in 1783, had designated Condorcet his successor. On the side of the Revolution, Condorcet was elected a deputy from Paris, but he opposed the excesses of the Jacobins under the Terror and was condemned to death. He remained in hiding for eight months during 1794, and at the time wrote his *Esquisses d'un tableau historique des progrès de l'esprit humain*, a work in which he still saw the Revolution as the gateway to a utopian society. Emerging from hiding to protect his helpers, he was captured, imprisoned, and according to tradition, committed suicide.[184]

The history of the marble in the American Philosophical Society, Philadelphia, is impeccable. It has been in the Philosophical Society continuously since it was deposited there in 1819, by William Short, earlier Thomas Jefferson's secretary. Short's letter to Thomas Jefferson dated from Philadelphia October 21, 1819, recounting the circumstances of his acquiring the *Condorcet* bust, is published in the catalogue of the Philosophical Society:[185]

Apropos of philosophers; you recollect without doubt the marble bust of Condorcet, which stood on a marble table in the Salon of the Hôtel de la Rochefoucauld. When it was determined no longer to receive him in the house [for his revolutionary leanings], it was thought *inconvenient* to keep the bust there. The grandchildren, who never liked him, availed themselves of this to have the bust transported to the *garde meuble* without consulting the old lady, whose leave was generally asked on every occasion. She passed over this in silence, however, & never made a remark or enquiry as to the disappearance of the bust. It had cost her a great effort to signify to the original that his presence had become disagreeable; she had really a parental affection for him, & had given a remarkable proof of this at the time of his marriage. On her death I asked this bust of the granddaughter, who gave it to me with great pleasure. It has been on its way here ever since I left France, & has passed through as many cases & *discrimina rerum* as Eneas himself (or perhaps it was Ulysses) on its way. It has finally arrived & is at present placed in the Philosophical hall in the most suitable company, the busts of Franklin, yourself, Turgot.

Houdon's portrait, created in 1785, shows the marquis with his head sharply turned to his left, his eyes fixed on the distance. The expression is aloof, withdrawn, seeming almost disdainful, despite the fact that he was a noted champion of human rights against tyranny. The bust bears comparison with that of the so-termed Marquis de Biré, 1786. Although this is full size whereas *de Biré* is 'petite proportion', half life-size, the two marbles are almost identical in their presentation, even in the details of the contemporary dress. Condorcet is wearing a perruque, whereas de Biré seems to be wearing his own hair, dressed like a wig. The *Condorcet* marble seems to be somewhat more uniform and colder in texture, perhaps because it needs to be cleaned. The plaster in the Louvre, open at the back, but otherwise essentially identical with the marble, is of particularly fine quality, despite a few old surface scratches. A comparison of plaster and marble illustrates effectively Houdon's method of imperceptibly generalizing and softening in his marbles the sharp details of the plaster or terra cotta.

COMTESSE
DE SABRAN
Fig. 152
Plate 94

Another portrait which belongs to this period but did not appear in either the Salon of 1783 or that of 1785 is the charming *Comtesse de Sabran*, one of Houdon's last commemorations of a lovely lady of the old regime. Françoise-Éléonore de Manville (1749–1827) married at a young age the aged Comte de Sabran, fifty years her senior. Left a widow at the age of twenty-five, she became the mistress of the Chevalier de Boufflers, whom she eventually married in 1797, after the Revolution. Prince Henry of Prussia paid court to her during his visits to Paris in 1784 and 1788, and gave her shelter at his castle of Rheinsberg during the Revolution. Madame de Sabran wrote novels, composed poetry, and was an excellent musician. Her letters to her second husband, the Chevalier, are among the most delightful produced in this age of great letter-writers. Madame Vigée-Lebrun, who was her friend and who painted her portrait in 1786, described her in her *Souvenirs*: 'She was then very pretty; her blue eyes expressed her sensitivity and her kindness. She loved arts and letters, composed charming verse, which she recited marvelously, and all without displaying the slightest pretensions. Her naïve and gay spirit had a completely gracious simplicity which made everyone love her and court her. Yet her great success in the world affected her in no way.'[186] This is the lady depicted by Houdon in the portrait apparently commissioned by Prince Henry *c.* 1785. She belongs, with the Comtesse du Cayla and Madame de Sérilly, in Houdon's gallery of the women who created *le siècle de femme*.

HOUDON'S TRIP
TO AMERICA
AND THE
STATUE OF
GEORGE
WASHINGTON

THE story of Houdon's trip to the United States to make preparatory studies for a statue of George Washington has particular significance for Americans, but it also deserves to be retold at some length as marking a milestone in the career of the artist. The principal figure in obtaining the commission for Houdon was Thomas Jefferson, American Minister to France, following Franklin, from 1785 to 1789.[187] On June 24, 1784, the Assembly of the State of Virginia had voted the commission of a marble statue of General Washington. It was assumed that the statue must be made in Europe, since there was then no sculptor in the United States capable of carrying out the commission. On July 22, 1784, Benjamin Harrison, Governor of Virginia, wrote to Jefferson: 'The intention of the Assembly is that the statue should be the work of a most masterly hand. I shall therefore leave it to you to find out the best in any of the European States.'

Jefferson wrote Washington from Paris, December 10, 1784:

I find that a Monsieur Houdon of this place, possesses the reputation of being the finest statuary of the world.

I sent for him and had some conversation with him on the subject. He thinks it cannot be perfectly done from a picture and is so enthusiastically fond of being the executor of this work that he offers to go to America for the purpose of forming your bust from the life, leaving all his business here in the meantime.

He thinks that being there three weeks with you would suffice to make his model in plaster with which he will return here and the work will employ him three years.

M. Houdon is at present engaged in making a statue of the king of France. A bust of *Voltaire* executed by him is said to be the finest in the world.

On January 12, 1785, Jefferson replied to Harrison:

There could be no question raised as to the sculptor who should be employed, the reputation of Mons. Houdon, of this city, being unrivaled in Europe. He is resorted to for the statues of most of the sovereigns in Europe.

Of course, no statue of Gen. Washington which might be a true evidence of his figure to posterity could be made from his picture. . . . M. Houdon offered to abandon his business here, to leave the statues of kings unfinished and to go to America to take the true figure by actual inspection and mensuration.

We are agreed that the size shall be precisely that of life.

Houdon had already established relations with Americans through his portraits of *Franklin* and *John Paul Jones*, and we may assume that it was Franklin who first recommended him to Jefferson. Caffieri, on hearing of the proposed commission, had attempted to secure the good offices of Franklin in his own behalf, without success.[188]

The original idea was to have the statue made in Europe after a painting executed for the purpose by Charles Willson Peale. Although Peale made the painting, even including a view of Yorktown in the background, to assist the sculptor in decorative details for the pedestal, Houdon insisted on working from the living model, both because of his reluctance to work from replicas and also, as became evident, because he had a secret desire to use this commission as the means of obtaining a much more ambitious commission for an equestrian portrait of Washington. This was evidently a passionate dream of the sculptor, for a sculptural monument that could be his crowning achievement. The fame of Falconet's great equestrian statue of Peter the Great, in Leningrad, completed in 1778, undoubtedly inspired him.[189]

The references to Houdon's innumerable monuments to the crowned heads of Europe, none of which actually existed, represented a certain amount of salesmanship, which may or may not have taken in Jefferson, but which he nevertheless passed on.

On July 15, 1785, Jefferson wrote to Patrick Henry, now Governor of Virginia, discussing the terms of the contract: 25,000 livres for statue and pedestal, plus expenses, and 10,000 livres insurance if Houdon should die on the voyage. Franklin and Jefferson were disposed to add another 250 livres, half of Houdon's original demand, pointing out the sculptor's heavy family expenses and adding: 'and he himself is one of the best men in the world', but they respected the State of Virginia's depleted finances. Franklin was on the point of leaving and Houdon, whose departure had been delayed by a serious ailment, was to follow him in a few days and join him on board ship.

In a letter to Nathaniel Macon, dated January 22, 1816, apropos of another project for a statue of Washington, Jefferson reviewed the terms of Houdon's contract, indicating that the sculptor had finally been paid the agreed 25,000 livres (1,000 guineas) and in addition had been given 500 guineas for his own expenses and 100 guineas for those of an assistant. In the same letter, Jefferson expresses some regret concerning the costume: 'As to the style or costume, I am sure that the artist and every person of taste in Europe would be for the *Roman*. Our boots and regimentals have a very puny effect.'

The impending departure of Franklin and Houdon in the latter part of July 1785 kept Jefferson busy with correspondence. In a letter to Washington, July 10, he extols the sculptor again as an artist and as a man:

> . . . He is without rivalship . . . being employed in all parts of Europe in whatever capital. He has had difficulty to withdraw himself from an order of the empress of Russia, a difficulty however which arose from a desire to show her respect, but which never gave him a moment of hesitation about his present voyage, which he considers as promising the brightest chapter of his history.
>
> I have spoken of him as an artist only; but I can assure you also that, as a man, he is disinterested, generous, candid and panting after glory, in every circumstance meriting your good opinion.
>
> He brings with him a subordinate workman or two, who of course will associate with their class only.

The description of Houdon's character is of particular interest, coming as it does from Thomas Jefferson; as is also the slight note of class distinction in the remark about Houdon's assistant. Actually Houdon took three assistants with him, as is documented by Washington's Diaries and the artist's expense account, submitted on October 20, 1788.

Having been informed by Houdon of his hope for an equestrian commission, Jefferson took up his cause. In a letter to the Assembly of Virginia, July 12, 1785, he recommended their consideration and reiterated the sculptor's qualifications. In a memorandum to Jefferson of 1786, Houdon stipulated a price of 600,000 livres for the bronze equestrian monument, and ten years to complete it. Jefferson again recommended the project, this time to the Congress of the United States, on July 8, 1786, again without success. In the light of the generally depleted economies of the American States after the Revolution, this price probably killed the project, although Houdon did not lose hope. As late as 1804, he was still pleading his cause to Robert R. Livingston, then Minister to France, pointing out how advantageous his terms were compared with those of Falconet for the statue of Peter the Great. Unfortunately this must be added to the list of monumental sculptures never realized.

Houdon arrived safely in Philadelphia about September 14, but he had been forced to sail without his luggage and that of his assistants, as well as all his equipment, as it had not arrived in Le Havre in time for his departure. Thus his arrival at Mount Vernon, home of George Washington, was delayed until he could re-equip. On hearing from Franklin about the artist's mishap, Washington wrote him a polite letter of welcome, September 26, 1785:

> By a letter which I have lately had the honor to receive from Dr. Franklin at Philadelphia, I am informed of your arrival at that place.
>
> I wish the object of your mission had been more worthy of the masterly genius of the first statuary in Europe: for thus you are represented to me.
>
> It will give me pleasure, Sir, to welcome you to the seat of my retirement, and whatever I have and can procure that is necessary for your purposes or convenient to your wishes, you must freely command.

We are fortunate in that the extensive and well preserved correspondences of Jefferson and Franklin, two men very much of the eighteenth century in their ability to write at length and with elegance concerning every detail of their activities, have given us so complete a record of the transactions for the Washington statue. The remarks of Jefferson about Houdon as an individual are also in the highest degree illuminating. We probably know more about this particular commission than any other of the artist. It is only unfortunate that Washington, a man of far fewer words, should have been so terse in recording Houdon's visit to Mount Vernon. His Diaries contain only a few references:

October 2. After we were in bed (about eleven o'clock), Mr. Houdon, sent from Paris by Dr. Franklin and Mr. Jefferson to take my bust, in behalf of the State of Virginia, with three young men assistants, introduced by a Mr. Perrin, a French gentleman of Alexandria, arrived here by water from the later place.

Friday 7th. Sat to day as I had done yesterday, for Mr. Houdon to form my Bust.

Sunday, 9th. Accompanied by Mr. Houdon and the two Mr. Bassetts, attended the Funeral of Mrs. Manley at the Plantation of Mr. Willm. Triplett, and returned to Dinner.

Monday, 10th. Observed the process for preparing the Plaister of Paris, and mixing of it, according to Mr. Houdon. The Oven being made hotter than it is usually heated for Bread, the Plaister which had previously been broken into lumps, that which was hard, to about the size of a pullets egg; and that which was soft, and could be broken with the hands, larger; was put in about Noon and remained until Night; when, upon examination, it was further continued until the Morning without any renewal of the heat in the oven, which was close stopped. Having been sufficiently calcined by this operation it was pulverized (in an iron Mortar) and sifted through a fine lawn sieve, and kept from wet.

When used, it is put into a Bason, or other vessel with water; sifted through the fingers, till the Water is made as thick as Loblolly, or very thick cream. As soon as the plaister is thus put into the Water, it is beat with an Iron spoon (almost flat) until it is well mixed, and must be immediately applied to the purpose for which it is intended with a Brush, or whatever else best answers, as it begins to turn hard in four or five minutes, and in seven or ten cannot be used, and is fit for no purpose afterwards, as it will not bear wetting a second time. For this reason no more must be mixed at a time than can be used within the space just mentioned.

The brush (common painters) must be put into Water as soon as it is used, and the plaister well squeezed out, or this also becomes very hard. In this case to clean it, it must be beaten until the plaister is reduced to a powder, and then washed.

Wednesday, 19th. Mr. Houdon having finished the business which brot him hither, went up on Monday with his People, work, and impliments in my Barge, to Alexandria, to take a Passage in the Stage for Philadelphia the next Morning.

While we could have wished for more detail, Washington's particular interest in the process of plaster casting is of some interest. From other sources we know that Houdon made a terra cotta model of a bust which he left at Mount Vernon and which is still there, signed and dated: HOUDON F. 1785.[190] From this he must have made a plaster mould and at least one plaster cast (and probably two or more) which were seen and admired in Philadelphia by Francis Hopkinson. William Temple Franklin persuaded Houdon to show the bust he had given Franklin, to the Congress of the United States, in order that he might gain preference in the matter of the equestrian statue.

On January 4, 1786, Jefferson wrote to Washington from Paris:

Sir, I have been honored with your letter of September 26, which was delivered me by Mr. Houdon, who is safely returned. He has brought with him a mould of the face only, having left the other part of his work with his workmen to come by some other conveiance. Doctor Franklin, who was joined with me in the superintendance of this just monument, having left us before what is called the costume of the statue was decided on, I cannot so well satisfy myself and am persuaded I should not so well satisfy the world, as by consulting your own wishes or inclination as to this article. Permit me therefore, to ask you whether there is any particular dress or any particular attitude which you would rather wish to be adopted? I shall take a singular pleasure in having your own idea executed if you will be so good as to make it known to me . . .

In a letter to the Governor of Virginia, January 24, 1786, Jefferson refers to '. . . mr. Houdon, who is returned with the necessary mould & measures for General Washington's statue . . .'

Thus we know that Houdon, as was his practice, took a mould of Washington's face and measurements of his dimensions. In the matter of dress, Washington indicated his preference in his reply to Jefferson:

Mount Vernon, 1 August, 1786. Dear sir, The letters you did me the favor to write me, on 4th and 7th of January, have been duly received. In answer to your obliging inquiries respecting the dress, attitude, &c., which I would wish to have given to the statue in question, I have only to observe, that, not having sufficient knowledge in the art of sculpture to oppose my judgment to the taste of connoisseurs, I do not desire to dictate on the matter. On the contrary, I shall be perfectly satisfied with whatever may be judged decent and proper. I should even have scarcely ventured to suggest, that perhaps a servile adherence to the garb of antiquity might not be altogether so expedient, as some little deviation in favor of the modern costume, if I had not learnt from Colonel Humphreys, that this was a circumstance hinted in conversation by Mr. West [Benjamin West] to Mr. Houdon. This taste, which has been introduced in painting by West I understand is received with applause, and prevails extensively.

Despite his seeming diffidence, Washington made it quite clear that his preference lay with modern dress, so modern dress it was. Jefferson, a noted classicist, seems to have leaned to the antique, as did also Houdon, who visualized Washington retired on his acres as the modern Cincinnatus, protector of agriculture; but the general's wishes obviously prevailed.

Houdon returned to Paris on Christmas day, 1785, and a bust of *Washington*, presumably a plaster, which had been shipped separately, arrived in May 1786. The rest of the documentation of the Washington statue pertains to matters of shipping, payment, the inscription, and reliefs planned for the base. Houdon objected to the length of the inscription, but when it was eventually carved upon the pedestal in 1814, it followed the elaborate original text written by James Madison. Reliefs of the siege of Yorktown, planned for the pedestal, were never carried out, perhaps because the artist felt that he had not been adequately paid for the statue. In 1789, Gouverneur Morris, later Minister to France, noted in his diary: '5 June 1789. Go to Mr. Houdon's. I stand for his statue of general Washington, being the humble employment of a manikin. Promise Mr. Houdon to have my bust taken, [also disappeared] which he desired to please himself.' The statue was shipped to the United States in January 1796, but it was not until June 1803, that James Monroe, then a special envoy to France, made the final payment. The first five Presidents of the United States were involved in the project.[191]

Fig. 153
Plates 98–101
Despite Jefferson's regret that Washington did not appear *à l'antique*, the marble statue, in the Capitol at Richmond, Virginia, is a noble work, perhaps the finest portrait of Washington in existence. He is shown, tall and dignified, his head lifted somewhat, dressed in his regimentals, the vest casually unbuttoned at the top, his slight embonpoint not concealed.

The right hand rests on a cane and the left on *fasces* with a plowshare, a reminiscence of Houdon's concept of the modern Cincinnatus, protector of agriculture, leading his people in peace as he had in war. His sword hangs symbolically on the *fasces*. Despite the modern dress the statue has a profound quality of classical restraint, particularly when contrasted with the *Tourville* of 1781.

As might be expected, the sculptor made many busts of Washington, in terra cotta, plaster, marble, and probably in bronze. All of these that are known to survive, with the exception of later copies made from the statue, are, perhaps *en revanche*, either draped or undraped *à l'antique*. The terra cotta model, as noted, is at Mount Vernon, signed and dated: HOUDON F. 1785, undraped *à l'antique*. Another fine terra cotta cast in the Louvre, draped *à l'antique*, is not signed; while the marble of the same type, in the collection of Mrs Sarah Hunter Kelly in New York, is signed: *houdon*, but not dated. The simple cursive signature with or without date, appears frequently in late busts. A plaster of the same type, also signed in cursive, *houdon f.* and with *cachet d'atelier*, but not dated, is in the Middendorf Collection, Washington, D.C. The plaster in the Boston Athenaeum, undraped, *à l'antique*, although not signed, is the one that came originally from the collection of Thomas Jefferson. It has been heavily painted in the nineteenth century. Similar to this although somewhat squared off at the lower edge of the chest—whereas the Boston plaster is rounded—is the marble acquired by the National Museum in Stockholm. In the three undraped versions, terra cotta, plaster, and marble, the hair at the back is gathered in an added lock of hair, a queue, tied with a riband and hanging down the back. In the draped versions, terra cotta, marble, and plaster, this is absent and the hair is cut loosely at the back.

The surviving busts made after the original model at Mount Vernon reveal Washington in a reflective mood, more the thinker than the man of action, a personification which may not accord with our traditional impression of him, but which actually adds a dimension to that impression. When Houdon portrayed Napoleon in 1806 in the beautiful terra cotta now at Dijon, it was also as a visionary rather than as a man of action. Whereas in the undraped versions *à l'antique*, Washington joins Houdon's great company of eighteenth-century *philosophes*, from Diderot through Voltaire, Rousseau, d'Alembert, and Buffon, all portrayed in this manner; with the version draped *à l'antique*, in its somewhat more generalized effect, he seems to draw closer to the neo-classical ideal. This becomes explicit in a later marble bust of him, signed and dated: *houdon an 9* [1801] made for the Gallery of Consuls of the Tuileries palace and now at Versailles, in which Houdon conforms deliberately to the now dominant style of neo-classicism. Washington here is also draped *à l'antique*, the broad riband across his right shoulder elaborately decorated with sword, *fasces* and his initials set in wreaths. The torso is squared off as a herm to form its own heavy base. The hair follows the style of the earlier draped version. The interpretation is much more that of Washington the hero, the great leader, the Roman imperator, than the philosopher-ruler.[192]

Plate 97b
Plate 97a

Plate 95, Fig. 156

Fig. 155
Fig. 154, Plate 96

Fig. 201
Plate 136–7

Fig. 157
Plate 144c

After Houdon's return from the United States at the end of 1785, some important events are recorded in the sparse documentation of his private life. On July 1, 1786, he was married to Marie-Ange-Cécile Langlois, described as the younger daughter of Jean Langlois, an employee in the affairs of the king. Houdon was forty-five at the time, his wife twenty. On July 26 his father died at the age of eighty-one. An attempt on the part of his mother to have her husband's pension continued for herself and her two unmarried daughters met with no success. Houdon's first daughter, Sabine-Marguerite-Josèphe was born February 25, 1787; his second, Anne-Ange, October 15, 1788; and his third, Antoinette-Claude (called Claudine), October 29, 1790. Madame Houdon and their three daughters were to be the subjects of some of the artist's most charming portraits. Houdon's wife was far more literate than he, apparently a strong-minded lady, yet despite some indications of diffi-

HOUDON'S
MARRIAGE

HOUDON'S MARRIAGE

culties the marriage seems to have been successful. She was certainly most helpful to him in matters of correspondence and even in arrangements for contracts and commissions.[193]

A footnote to the marriage ceremony indicates how the details of Houdon's life must be pieced together from fragmentary documents. We know that he worked with assistants, in some cases technicians such as the bronze founders whom he trained, the most notable of whom was Thomire. Most of the assistants were apprentices, young sculptors learning their craft from him as he had learned from Michel-Ange Slodtz. However, no sculptors of any distinction seem to have emerged from Houdon's studio or to have claimed him as their master. The two witnesses at the marriage were Jean-François Beaudoin (Baudoin), Sculptor, and Vincent Mazetti, Sculptor. Mazetti assisted on the work for the Tourville statue, and we may assume that both he and Beaudoin assisted on other works, but neither seems to have gone on to much greater achievements. We have seen that three technicians accompanied Houdon to America; and Louis Boilly's painting of his studio (Cherbourg Museum) shows two young students drawing diligently from the life model. While we may speculate why Houdon trained no outstanding followers, some of the greatest artists have not been teachers. The immediate influence of towering personalities such as Michelangelo, Leonardo da Vinci, or Picasso, may even have been destructive to their followers and imitators. In Houdon's case, from what we can gather of his personality and his habits of work we would not expect him to have been a dedicated or enlightened teacher. He was probably too busy and not particularly interested. Although as an academician he had to have students working with him periodically, what he wanted to help him with his immense output were technicians, stone carvers, foundrymen, and professional modelers. In his latter years, particularly after he had been appointed Professor in the Schools of the Institute of France, successor to the Royal Academy, he seems to have been diligent in his teaching duties. But this was probably in the sense of a visiting critic to the studio classes rather than as a master sculptor training assistants.

Fig. 206

THE SALON OF 1787

THE *livret* for the Salon of 1787 demonstrates Houdon's rapid resumption of his schedule. Although the only major new figurative sculpture listed was the *Vestal*, the large marble version with covered head, the Salon does include several new portrait busts of importance. The marble bust of *Prince Henry of Prussia*, 'pour le roi', has been mentioned; and a plaster bust of *Washington* is described, 'General Washington, made by the artist in the General's land of Virginia. Plaster.'

LOUIS XVI

With the marble bust of *Louis XVI*, Houdon had finally attained the commission sought by all portrait Academicians as the hallmark of their professional stature. Houdon entered the august company of royal portraitists somewhat belatedly and through the back door, since the commission did not come directly from the king nor from d'Angiviller, but from the *Compagnie des agents de change*, or Stockbrokers, to be placed in the Paris *Bourse* or Stock Exchange. The project was announced in 1778 when the *Compagnie* requested from d'Angiviller marble from the royal depot for the bust and pedestal. The next we hear is in 1784 when Houdon wrote to d'Angiviller explaining that he had not been able to complete the bust since he had been waiting three years for an audience with the king.[194] Apparently he finally obtained it, although probably not until his return from America.

Fig. 159

The marble of the 1787 Salon is presumed to be that now at Versailles, signed and dated: HOUDON F. 1790; but the late date may well indicate that it is a second version.[195] Although Louis XVI was not a notable patron of the arts, a substantial number of portraits of him are recorded, many of them destroyed during the Revolution. Of the sculptors, Pajou, as might be expected, did the first portrait of Louis as king, in 1775, Boizot made busts in 1777 and 1785, Houdon *c.* 1787, and Deseine in 1790. Louis was more interested in hunting, food, and wine than in art, and was not a noble subject for the artist. The revolutionary, Barère de

Vieuzac, described the king as short and fat, of sallow complexion, with dull blue eyes lacking expression, a loud, idiotic laugh, and the general demeanor of a clumsy, gauche, badly brought-up farm boy.[196] While this description may well be prejudiced, all the evidence is that to make the king kingly would tax the powers of any artist. Deseine's version is so flattering that one might question the identification of the sitter, Houdon's is the best compromise between the king's station and his appearance.

For the royal portrait Houdon returned to the Baroque image, with the king represented to the waist, swathed in a cloak encompassing much of the figure and base. The sculpture is finished at the back with the perruque extended in a particularly long, beribboned queue. The artist has exercised his technical skill and ingenuity mainly on the carving of the dress and decorations. The broad riband across the chest is a demonstration of virtuosity in its simulation of watered silk. On top of all this, the head is something of an anticlimax. Although lifted imperiously, the face is dull, uniform, and without character. The two aunts of the king, Mesdames Adélaïde and Victoire, had been equally undistinguished in appearance, yet Houdon created marvels of perceptive characterization. But the old ladies were at least interesting personalities, whereas the king was sadly dull. The face of his bust at Versailles is not improved by a series of pointing marks indicating that someone has been making replicas carelessly.

Plates 31–2
Plate 102

To appreciate the limitations of the bust of *Louis XVI* it should be compared with another marble bust, also exhibited in the Salon of 1787, that has many points of similarity as well as differences. This is the so-termed *Bailli de Suffren*, which was noted in the *livret*: 'Pour MM. les directeurs de la noble Compagnie des Indes hollandaises du département de Zélande'. Pierre-André de Suffren, Commander of the Order of Malta (1726–88), was a French naval hero who won notable victories against the British in the East Indies on behalf of the Netherlands. Among the honors heaped on him by the Dutch was that of commissioning his portrait from Houdon. The sculptor was perhaps selected on the recommendation of Prince Dmitri Alexéiévitch Galitzin, who served as Russian ambassador to the Netherlands after leaving his post in Paris.

SUFFREN

De Suffren's magnificent portrait, in the Mauritshuis, The Hague, is on a splendid black marble pedestal with an oval white plaque bearing the inscription (in Dutch): 'Pierre-André de Suffren, Grand Cross of St John, General of Malta, Chevalier de Saint-Esprit, Vice-Admiral of France, Defender of the Colonies of Holland in the East Indies. 1787'. The Admiral, known as the 'Bailiff' for his forthright, belligerent manner, was even fatter than Louis XVI, but he is, in comparison, an immense and tangible presence. His full torso is draped in a manner very similar to that of Louis; on the chest are the riband and cross of the Order of Saint-Esprit conferred on him by the king in 1784. The dress and specifically the riband are carved, if anything, with even greater meticulousness than those of the king. But here there is nothing vapid about the face. De Suffren was an impatient, truculent man, and to look on him is to make no doubt of this. The face, round as a globe, is beautifully and subtly carved, filled with nuances of expression, the eyes scowling, the mouth contemptuous. He died shortly after this likeness was taken, presumably and believably of apoplexy.[197]

Fig. 158
Plate 103

The Salon of 1787 seems to have been dedicated by Houdon to the nobility of the sword, including as it did two other noblemen presented in much the same manner as the king and the Bailli de Suffren. François-Claude Marquis de Bouillé (1739–1800) was Governor of Martinique. During the Revolution he, together with the Comte de Fersen, planned the flight of Louis XVI, fought with the Prince de Condé, served in the army of Gustave III of Sweden, and then moved to England, where he died in 1800. He was cousin to the Marquis de Lafayette, whose marble bust appeared in the same Salon, but did not approve of his revolutionary tendencies. The bust of *de Bouillé*, confiscated during the Revolution, was later recovered and remains in the possession of the de Bouillé family. It is another superb portrait, presented in essentially the same manner as the king and de Suffren, with cloak

DE BOUILLÉ

Fig. 160
Plate 105

encompassing the figure and the base, wearing the ribbon of the Order of Saint-Esprit also bestowed on him in 1784. The characterization is entirely different from either of the previous ones. The head turns sharply to the right, the expression is sensitive, thoughtful and intelligent, the features delicately shaped. De Bouillé, an administrator and a soldier, seems to have been both an intellectual and a man of action, and his *Mémoires*, written in 1797 and published in 1821, reveal the eighteenth-century man of many talents as suggested by Houdon's portrayal. The bust, although not dated, was completed in 1786, as the receipts, still in the possession of the de Bouillé family, confirm.

LAFAYETTE

The next in this gallery of the nobility of the sword is as well known in the United States as he is in France. This is Marie-Joseph-Paul-Yves-Roch-Gilbert du Motier, Marquis de Lafayette (1757–1834), the 'Man of Two Worlds', whose incredible career encompassed both the American and French Revolutions and continued well into the nineteenth century. Houdon's marble bust in the Salon of 1787 bore the designation: 'M. le Marquis de la Fayette, pour les Etats de la Virginie.' Another bust appeared in the Salon of 1791, with the material not specified.

Fig. 162
Plate 106

The marble in the Salon of 1787 is that which had been voted by the Virginia Assembly and which is now in the rotunda of the Capitol at Richmond, facing Houdon's statue of George Washington. Lafayette is shown in his uniform of Major General in the American army of the Revolution, with a large cloak draped over his shoulders and, as in the other royal and noble portraits of this Salon, flowing down over the pedestal.

In December 1781 the Virginia Assembly had voted to commission the bust in Paris and present it to the marquis. He was sent a copy of the resolution but the project then lagged until, always willing to be commemorated, he complained to Washington. Washington brought the matter to the attention of Benjamin Harrison, Governor of Virginia, who, after approval by the Council, instructed Thomas Barclay, American Consul at Nantes, to see to the execution of the commission. Harrison's action took place on April 5, 1784, and on December 1, 1784, the Virginia Assembly changed its resolution to the effect that the bust 'be presented in the name of the Commonwealth, to the City of Paris, with a request that the same be accepted and preserved in some public place of the said city'. The Assembly also resolved that a second bust should be obtained to be placed with the proposed statue of George Washington voted by the Assembly. In the meantime, Barclay had chosen Houdon as the appropriate sculptor to proceed with the bust after his return from the United States. Houdon actually made his model before sailing for Philadelphia, since the marquis was about to leave for Germany and might not be available on Houdon's return. The first marble, that to be presented to the City of Paris, was completed early in 1786 and the marble for Virginia a short time later. Jefferson undertook the new and complicated arrangements for the presentation of the bust in Paris, obtaining first the permission of the king. The bust was duly installed in the great hall of the Hôtel de Ville in an elaborate ceremony. It was destroyed during the French Revolution.

Fig. 161
Plate 104

An earlier plaster bust, in the Boston Athenaeum, shows the marquis simply in his uniform without the elaboration of drapery, the torso somewhat more abbreviated than in the marble. This is probably a version of the original model, made from life in 1785. Whereas the Virginia marble is now almost unique, there are a number of the plaster types in different American collections; and many modern bronze copies have been made from one or another of them.

The Boston Athenaeum *Lafayette*, although neither signed nor dated, is one of the four busts which came from the collection of Thomas Jefferson at Monticello, the others being the *Franklin*, the *Washington*, and the *John Paul Jones*. Although Houdon did his best to cast Lafayette in an heroic role, he was working under severe difficulties due to the marquis's actual appearance. While Lafayette poses with chin lifted, head turned, shoulders back and chest out, eyes fixed on the horizon, in as soldierly a fashion as possible, the net effect is rather that of a pose than an authentic symbol. The face is unlined and rather callow (Lafayette was only twenty-nine years old in 1785).

The marble in Richmond succeeds better because the Baroque treatment of the cloak lends majesty to the figure; the face, although identical to that in the plaster, is somehow given a greater dignity and authority through the accessories. The marble is also beautifully worked, comparable in every way to the *de Suffren* and the *de Bouillé*. Even though the *Louis XVI* is less satisfactory than the others, these four marbles constitute a remarkable group, illustrating Houdon at his most heroically Baroque. It is ironic that these portraits, so specifically commemorative of the old regime, should appear together at the moment of its collapse.[198]

In another version, presumably that exhibited in the Salon of 1791, Lafayette is shown in the uniform of the Garde Nationale. This is a bust with the torso and upper arms rendered and changes in the dress: he is shown without medals; buttonholes are strongly accentuated in both outer coat and jacket. He now wears a new wig, of a type that partially covers the long, sloping forehead so accurately recorded in the earlier busts. A marble at Versailles of this bewigged type is signed and dated: *houdon an. 1790*, crudely scratched over another signature: *houdon fecit*, with no attempt to conceal the earlier one. In general, the Versailles marble of the 1790 bust, like that of *Louis XVI*, also dated 1790, is cold and dead when compared with the earlier, Richmond marble. Whereas there is no reason to doubt that it is the type of the bust that appeared in the Salon of 1791, there remain unanswered questions about the particular marble and its offshoots.[199]

To this gallery of the nobility of the sword, portrayed almost nostalgically in all their magnificence on the eve of the French Revolution, there must be added another gentleman who seems to personify qualities of the old regime. His portrait, not included in the Salon of 1787, was executed *c.* 1787, and belongs stylistically and conceptually with the group just discussed. This is Louis-Jules Mancini, Duc de Nivernais (1716–98), great-nephew of Cardinal Mazarin, who originally acquired the duchy of Nivernais. The Duc de Nivernais might have been considered something of a newcomer by the old families of France, but his career, his achievements, and his demeanour as portrayed by Houdon, all seem to make him a personification of his class. Barred from a military career by his delicate health, he achieved distinction in the diplomatic world, serving at various times as ambassador from the courts of Louis XV and Louis XVI to Rome, Berlin, and London; returning to Paris in 1787 to be appointed a Minister of State. A poet in the tradition of La Fontaine and of sufficient distinction to be elected to the French Academy, Monsieur de Nivernais was closely associated with the *philosophes* and the French Enlightenment. In his portrait by Houdon he is presented, like his companions in this group, in court dress wearing the Order of Saint-Esprit, the swag of drapery encompassing torso and base. But his quality rests in his small, fragile, sensitive, almost feminine head, the eyes luminous in their intelligent awareness.[200]

Two more portrait busts, not listed in the *livret* for the Salon of 1787, but executed in 1786, complete this particular roster of remarkable or unusual men commemorated by Houdon in the mid-eighties. The Marquis de Méjanes (1729–86) did not appear on the national or international scene, but made a lasting contribution to his own city of Aix-en-Provence. A provincial gentleman, he was a passionate bibliophile and founded the library at Aix. He died in Paris and, at the request of the Archbishop of Aix, the sculptor made a death-mask and the marble portrait now in the Aix library. In contrast with the noblemen of the court who dominated Houdon's 1787 Salon, the Marquis de Méjanes is represented informally, his shirt open at the throat, a plain coat or cloak draped over the torso. This is a full bust, with shoulders and upper arms, of the form Houdon used increasingly in commissioned portraits of the eighties; but Monsieur de Méjanes is conceived very much as a poet, an intellectual, a man of the Enlightenment. His head, on a long, strong neck, is lifted, the lips are slightly parted, the eyes look into the distance. This is not one of Houdon's well-known

THE SALON
OF 1787

Fig. 162
Plate 106

Fig. 163

DUC DE
NIVERNAIS

Fig. 164
Plate 107

MÉJANES

Fig. 165

portraits, but it is a sensitive interpretation, a work of high quality, and refutes yet again the myth that the sculptor's inspiration flagged when he made posthumous portraits.[201]

The last man among those portrayed by Houdon about 1786–7 is something of a contrast to the others although he is by no means the least interesting. This is Giuseppe Balsamo, better known under his alias, Alessandro, Conte Cagliostro (1743–95), a Sicilian adventurer who, together with Casanova, ranked as a leading charlatan of the eighteenth century. After various adventures in Italy and extensive travels in the Near East, Cagliostro embarked on a full-scale European career as alchemist, physician, mesmerist, astrologer, and necromancer. In France between 1780 and 1786, he had a great success at the Court of Versailles until finally banished. Returning to Rome in 1789 he was condemned by the Inquisition for heresy and sorcery, and died in prison.

Cagliostro was a Freemason and used his actual or pretended knowledge of Oriental mysteries of Freemasonry as a cover for other activities. It was probably through Houdon's membership in the Lodge of the Nine Sisters that he met Cagliostro, then at the height of his fame in Paris, and did his portrait. The marble bust is a masterpiece of interpretation.

Fig. 166

Although Cagliostro habitually wore a strange, intricately arranged perruque, and was extravagantly—in all senses of the word—dressed, covered with large diamonds which he contended he had made himself through his control of the philosopher's stone, the sculptor

Plate 110

chose to subordinate the accessories. Cagliostro is shown informally dressed, his frilled shirt open, his waistcoat partly unbuttoned, with no wig covering his balding head. The charlatan, not yet revealed as such, is presented as the poet, the man of imagination. As in Houdon's great portraits of the *philosophes*, the men of the Enlightenment, he concentrates on the face and head in an effect that can only be described as hypnotic. Cagliostro's head is turned sharply to his left and lifted high as though he were seated and had turned to look at someone who had approached him from the side. All who had met the magician in Paris seem to have commented on the power and intensity of his gaze, and it is on this that Houdon focuses. The face is fat and undistinguished, the slightly open mouth rather unpleasantly sensual. The eyes are large and somewhat protuberant, fixed exactly on some specific object or person; and the artist has managed to convey a sense of absolute concentration. It is a strange and disturbing characterization. Cagliostro gives the impression of being not just a clever trickster, but a sinister and possibly dangerous individual. In looking for comparable studies among Houdon's portraits, one is reminded perhaps of the actor Larive. There is the same sharp turn of the head, the same wide and staring eyes. But while Cagliostro is also obviously an actor, he is acting his part much more convincingly than Larive.[202]

THE *livret* of the 1787 Salon lists, as No. 257, *Une Vestale*, with no further description. Although no material is indicated, one of the Salon commentators refers to it as a marble; and it is grouped with the five busts already discussed, under a general heading, *Bustes en marbre*.

The recurrence of the *Vestal* theme, which had originated in Rome, *c.* 1766–8, is sufficiently intriguing to deserve some recapitulation. First it might be useful to list the actual mentions of the various versions of the *Vestal* to determine exactly what is known of its history (see also pp. 11–13, and notes 8–10).[203] The chronology, which is carried as far as 1828 and is not necessarily complete for private sales, nevertheless tells most of what surviving documents have to say about the different versions. These documents show that most of the versions were replicas, with some variations, of an original made in Rome after a statue in Rome popularly known as *Pandora*. Houdon's first *Vestal*, approximately 22 inches high, existed in many copies (some of which have survived) in plaster, terra cotta, marble, and bronze; some with an altar, some without. The artist also, as was his habit, made separate busts from this statue.[204] We have already discussed two life-size busts of a *Vestal*, with head covered: a plaster probably from the Roman period and a marble replica dated 1788.[205] The first mention of a large *Vestal* is in Houdon's inventory of his works, *c.* 1784, where he lists, under the year 1779, 'a large *Vestal* executed for the staircase of M. le duc d'Aumont'. In his 1794 letter to Bachelier he mentions a life-size *Vestal* in marble, in his possession. In the 1795 list of the sale from his studio are two of the small *Vestals* and, No. 72, 'A *Vestal* standing, bearing the sacred flame; she is draped in the antique mode, the head partially covered with a veil, and posed on a pedestal. Height of the figure: 6 feet; that of the pedestal: 3 feet 4 inches.'[206] This *Vestal* is listed under Figures and Busts in Marble.

Fig. 167
Plates 108, 143m

The life-size marble *Vestal* is certainly that in the Wildenstein Gallery, New York, which is signed and dated on the base: *houdon f. 1787*; and it is also believed to be the *Vestal* described so succinctly in the 1787 *livret* as *Une Vestale*, with no other identification. This assumption is supported by the various comments on the *Vestal* in the 1787 Salon. Although no commentator mentions the actual scale of the figure, it is described as a marble, and the number of notices indicates that it must have been an important piece. One refers to it as 'a pretty little *Vestal*, imitated from the antique, but a little short'. Others: 'but this figure is so short, the feet are so heavy . . .'; 'the feet nevertheless appear to us a trifle large . . .'; 'the pretty little face of the Vestal . . .'; 'this marble *Vestal* is only a reminiscence of an antique figure. Moreover, the head lacks the severe style that it should have, the draperies are round and soft, the folds are too parallel and do not allow one to see the form . . .'; 'I recognize here the chisel of a great artist; the well arranged draperies show how much he has learned from the ancients . . .'; 'I don't know if I am mistaken; but I don't find it big enough. I would like to see the physiognomy of this priestess, who carries the flame, somewhat more august, which would tell me that she is suffused with her sublime functions. For, after all, strip her of her veil and her attributes, suppose her dressed in the habit of a shepherdess: the expression of her countenance [physionomie] would serve as well . . .'.[207]

The best that can be said is that this sculpture received a mixed press; probably more bad than good reviews. The general inanity of the comments gives one pause, but added together they leave no doubt that the marble referred to is that now in New York. The face of this *Vestal*, which is actually one of the most delightful of all Houdon's statues, is charming in an eighteenth-century sense rather than austerely classic, much more rococo than is the small *Vestal*, the bust with covered head, or the *Diana*. The draperies are heavy, round and full, somewhat in a High Gothic manner, and do conceal the figure. The *Vestal* is actually 62 inches high, but placed as she is on a pedestal over 3 feet high, she appears, partially as a result of the heavy draperies and the small face, shorter than she is. Also, the high pedestal, which is the original one, does make the feet somewhat too obtrusive. And if she were stripped of her heavy robes and lightly clad like Houdon's statue of *Summer*, she would make a charming little shepherdess.

But there still remain some problems. There is the large *Vestal* listed in the inventory, *c.* 1784, under the year 1779, which the Duc d'Aumont apparently never received. In the sale list of 1795 the *Vestal* (5 feet 2 inches tall) is described as 6 feet tall. No satisfactory explanation has appeared for these discrepancies, but there is no doubt that the *Vestal* of the 1787 Salon is that now in New York. If the plaster had been designed in 1779, but not delivered to the Duc d'Aumont, and a marble made and dated in 1787, this would explain the rococo quality unusual for a late work. In 1779 Houdon was still involved with such rococo pieces as the *Naiad* of 1777 and the Monceau fountain of 1781. Finally there is the striking analogy of the *Comtesse d'Ennery* on the tomb of the Comte d'Ennery, dated 1781. Here, as pointed out, the countess is draped in heavy robes covering her head as well as concealing her figure, the appropriate type of the mourning Roman matron. Her face is probably an idealized portrait, with features more mature than those of the large *Vestal*,

Plate 109

Fig. 57

but not too different from them. Even the eyes are carved in the same manner, indicated but not deeply undercut.

It is a point of some interest that the reviewers writing in 1787 should have expressed their disapproval of the large marble *Vestal* as not sufficiently classic. This is further evidence of the trend of the times towards historical or archaeological neo-classicism. And the next year, as though in reply to his critics, Houdon produced the marble replica of his earlier *Head of a Vestal*, signed and dated: *houdon f. 1788*, which is now in the Louvre.[208] This *Vestal*, with draped head, more specifically classic than almost any other work by him, is a remarkable piece, generalized and idealized in an approximation to Greek antiquity. In fact, it makes the head of Canova's *Venus Italica*, modelled *c.* 1812 after the Hellenistic *Venus de Medici*, appear sentimental and over-refined.

PORTRAITS OF HOUDON'S FAMILY

Fig. 172
Plate 111

Fig. 174

Fig. 177

IN the Salon of 1787 there appeared one portrait bust of a woman: No. 258. Head of a Young Girl, in plaster. Although the *livret* does not identify the young lady, what might be termed a rave review permits her identification with the plaster, now in the Louvre, of his newly acquired wife. 'The head of a young girl by Monsieur Houdon rivals the most graceful portraits of antiquity. The contours are soft and charming, the resilience of the flesh, the sparkling countenance, fill the connoisseurs with admiration and astonish even the ignorant. Dazzling purity, grace, sensuousness, the ease of the muscles, these are what one notes in the neck and in the head.' The reviewer only regrets that, the artist 'had placed the nipples of the breast a trifle too low' (in other words, not shown). Since this portrait is that of Madame Houdon (perhaps made before their wedding in July 1786), we can understand why, even though he presents her informally, with nude shoulders, he would not care to go as far as the reviewer desired. In any event the plaster in the Louvre is one of the most engaging of all Houdon's portraits of women, her hair informally dressed and falling down over her shoulders, her laughing, dimpled face filled with animation, her partially closed eyes caught in the expression of voluptuousness the reviewer so rightly noted.[209]

Houdon also depicted his three daughters at various ages and, although their portraits extend into the Post-Revolutionary period, they are perhaps best grouped with that of their mother. Together his children's portraits constitute, with those of Louise and Alexandre Brongniart, 'the little Audéoud', and the 'daughter of Hubert Robert', the sculptor's consummate achievements in the portrayal of children. The little daughter of the Comtesse d'Ennery, shown at full length on the tomb of the count, may be added to this group, as may one other child's portrait, that of a very young baby. The baby is known through a painted plaster in the Staatliches Museum, Schwerin, formerly with the *cachet d'atelier*, and not signed or dated, but unquestionably by Houdon. Wearing a shawl half covering his still hairless head, he is a wonderful interpretation of an infant newly entered into the world but sharply aware of his environment.[210]

Aside from these portraits and those of his own children, there are a number of other busts of children attributed to Houdon, none that I have seen of significant interest. Even the likenesses of his daughters, Sabine, Anne-Ange, and Claudine, have been reproduced, copied, and imitated so often that the greatest care must be taken in selecting those particular busts which best show the sculptor's own hand.

The earliest portrait of one of his children is the marble of Sabine as a baby, formerly in the Harkness Collection, now in the Metropolitan Museum, New York. This is inscribed and dated: *sabinet houdon. 1788*, and may be the bust of a child listed in the Salon of 1789: No. 246. Head of an infant at the age of ten months. It is a marvelous portrait of a baby, somewhat older than that discussed above, now advanced from a state of emerging awareness to become a definite individual, serious, intent, and reflective.[211]

84

The portrait of Sabine at the age of four, executed in 1791, is by far the most popular of the series and, as a result, has been copied many times by other hands and in different materials.[212] The plaster in the Louvre and the marble in the Henry E. Huntington Library, San Marino, California, the latter signed in cursive: *houdon f.*, may be regarded as the exemplars for this portrait. The Huntington marble is particularly fine. Whereas most of the later copies are done in impeccable and rather deadly white marble, this one shows on the face those dark flaws so frequent in the blocks of marble drawn from the eighteenth-century royal depot by the sculptors of the king. The carving is as fresh and direct as is normal to Houdon's finest marbles, the little girl is a vision of delight.

Sabine appeared in a Supplement to the Salon of 1791: No. 227. *Mademoiselle Sabine Houdon,* belonging to Monsieur Girardot; as did Anne-Ange: No. 234. *Mademoiselle Ange Houdon at fifteen months.* The plaster of Anne-Ange in the Louvre bears the *cachet d'atelier,* and the terra cotta in the Museum of Fine Arts in Houston, Texas, is signed *houdon* under the right shoulder, but not dated. Anne-Ange at the age of fifteen months, in age somewhere between the two portraits of Sabine as a child that are illustrated, is already a very different kind of personality. Compared with Sabine at the age of four, she is apparently more of an extrovert, at this stage more the little boy that Houdon seems to have been hoping for.[213]

Antoinette-Claude, called Claudine, born October 29, 1790, is perhaps number 123 of the Salon of 1793: *Un buste d'enfant en plâtre.* A number of plasters of Claudine are recorded in French and American collections, but the only known marble is that in the Worcester Art Museum, Worcester, Massachusetts, signed on the back: *houdon f.* This is again of superb quality, showing the little Claudine as a small baby, less than a year old. She lifts her head with a wonderful eagerness, almost a trance-like quality of rapt attention, providing a delightful contrast with Sabine, almost the same age in her first portrait, but a very different, equally well identified personality. In all his portraits of children it is fascinating how precisely Houdon is able to describe and differentiate them, presenting them always with dignity, never with sentimentality, while letting them preserve their wonderful childlike freshness.[214]

THE Salon of 1789 was the last under the old regime, the last confined exclusively to members of the Royal Academy of Painting, Sculpture, and Graphic Arts. By the time it opened in August, the events leading to the French Revolution were well under way, although the Republic was not officially decreed until 1792. In retrospect, all the major political, economic, and religious events of eighteenth-century France seemed to be leading inevitably to revolution. The French Enlightenment was a fundamental struggle of intellectuals for equal rights and freedom of expression. French support of the American Revolution, while motivated in large part by the Anglophobia of the ruling classes, had the unintended by-product of implanting in the minds of the masses, specifically of the middle class, the realization that successful revolution was not impossible. Events were brought to a head by the financial collapse of the kingdom, and the States General were convened on May 5, 1789, for the first time since 1614. On June 17, the Third Estate, the Commons, declared themselves the National Assembly; and on June 20, when their meeting place was closed, they adjourned to an indoor tennis court and there took the Oath not to separate until they had made a constitution. On July 14 the prison of the Bastille was stormed. Thus, though the title-page of the *livret* follows the customary form of the Royal Academy and d'Angiviller is presented with all his titles, the events shaking the nation were also changing the entire system of the Royal Academies and their Salons.

Jacques-Louis David presented to the Salon of 1789 a large painting with the note that this was for the king, and would not appear until towards the end of the exhibition. It had

PORTRAITS
OF HOUDON'S
FAMILY
———————
Fig. 178
Plates 112–13

Fig. 175
Plate 114

Fig. 176
Plate 115

THE SALON
OF 1789

the long descriptive title: 'J. Brutus, first Consul, on his return to his home, after having condemned his two sons, who had joined the Tarquins and conspired against the liberty of Rome, the Lictors bring back their bodies for burial.' David (1748–1825), after his years of study in Rome, had been appointed *agréé* in 1781, and had submitted to the Salon of that year, among others, three important paintings varying in style. The *Saint Roch interceding with the Virgin* continues the Baroque, Rubenist tradition, from which he had been emerging during his studies in Rome. The equestrian portrait of *Count Potocki* is a masterpiece of official portraiture and naturalistic drawing. *Belisarius receiving Alms* realizes already the classic austerity and moral fervor with which he is to create his personal revolution. These paintings arrived too late to be included in the *livret*, but Diderot gave them an ecstatic review in this, his last *Salon*. It is undoubtedly pure coincidence that the heavily draped Roman matron who gives alms to Belisarius should resemble so remarkably in dress and pose the Comtesse d'Ennery on Houdon's tomb of the Comte d'Ennery completed the same year.

In 1785 David, now an Academician, submitted *The Oath of the Horatii, from the Hands of their Father*; and in 1787 one painting, more modest in scale: *Socrates at the Moment of Taking the Hemlock*. These paintings, in their austerity, their frontalized, sculptural space, their precise archaeological approach to antiquity, marked the moment—if any specific moment can be stated—when neo-classicism assumed its dominance in French painting—and shortly thereafter in French sculpture. It had already established a firm hold on architecture.

David's paintings were an immediate popular success, evidenced by the fact that his 1789 *Lictors Bringing the Bodies of the Sons of the Consul Brutus* had been commissioned by the king. What neither the king nor the average spectator recognized was that these works marked a revolution not only in their plastic form but even more so in their subject-matter, with its emphasis on the stoic virtues of Republican Rome, or on Socrates as the hero of liberty and martyr of tyranny. Certainly Houdon, although concerned about the turmoil in the streets around him, was unaware of the revolutions actually taking place, not only political and economic, but those that would soon threaten the world of Royal Academies, in which he had lived his life. His entries for the 1789 Salon were rather modest, not so much because of outside events as because he had recently become deeply involved in problems of bronze casting.[215]

Of his portrait busts in this Salon four were marbles in miniature: three—*Rousseau, Buffon*, and *Diderot*—replicas of earlier works; and the fourth the head of an infant at the age of ten months. These have all disappeared, unless the child was Sabine, as have the portraits in plaster of the *Chevalier de Boufflers*, beloved of Madame de Sabran, and the aeronaut, *Jean-Francois Pilâtre de Rozier*. Various busts have been associated with the plaster of the actress, *Mademoiselle Olivier, pensionnaire du Roi*, none convincingly. Thus, aside from the presumed *Sabine*, the only works of any significance to survive are the bronze of *Prince Henry of Prussia*, already discussed, a plaster of *Monsieur le président du Paty*, and one other plaster whose garbled listing in the *livret* deserves repeating. This is 'No. 241. M. Sesserson, Envoyé des Etats de Virginie'. This portrait of Thomas Jefferson, to become third president of the United States, is a work of prime importance, a superb representation.[216]

Despite the close association between Houdon and Jefferson over the years of negotiation in relation to the statue of George Washington, there are few records concerning the execution of the bust of Jefferson himself. In comparison with the *Voltaire, Franklin, Washington*, or *Rousseau*, among others, very few of the busts of Jefferson have survived.[217] The marble in the Boston Museum of Fine Arts is perhaps the best example, signed and dated: *houdon f 1789*. Jefferson is presented in simple, modern dress, very much the republican—or perhaps more appropriately democrat—hero, his face tilted upward and angled slightly to his left. The hair is dressed in a manner similar to that of Washington, worn rather full at the sides,

Fig. 168
Plates 116–17

Fig. 161. *Marie-Joseph-Paul-Yves-Roch-Gilbert du Motier, Marquis de Lafayette*. Plaster, about 1785. Boston, Athenaeum

Fig. 162. *Marquis de Lafayette*. Marble, 1787. Richmond, Virginia, Capitol

Fig. 163. *Marquis de Lafayette*. Marble, 1790. Versailles, Château

Fig. 164. *Louis-Jules Mancini, Duc de Nivernais*. Plaster, about 1787. Schwerin, Staatliches Museum

Fig. 165. *Marquis de Méjanes*. Marble, about 1786.
Aix-en-Provence, Bibliothèque

Fig. 166. *Giuseppe Balsamo, known as Conte Cagliostro*. Marble,
1786. Washington, D.C., National Gallery of Art, Kress Collection

Fig. 167. *A Vestal*. Marble, 1787. New York, Wildenstein & Co.

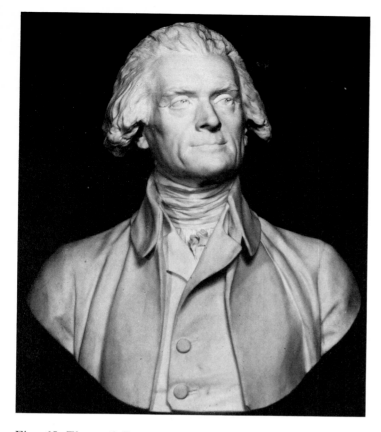

Fig. 168. *Thomas Jefferson*. Marble, 1789. Boston, Museum of Fine Arts

Fig. 169. *Jacques-Antoine-Hippolyte, Comte de Guibert*. Marble, 1791. New York, Private Collection

Fig. 170. *Jacques Necker*. Marble, 1790. Geneva, Musée d'Art et d'Histoire

Fig. 171. *Jean-Sylvain Bailly*. Terra cotta, about 1790. Altenburg, Lindenau Museum

Fig. 172. *Madame Houdon, the artist's wife.* Plaster, about 1787. Paris, Louvre

Fig. 173. *Madame Houdon and Sabine Houdon.* Detail of a terra cotta medallion, 1798. Paris, Petit Palais

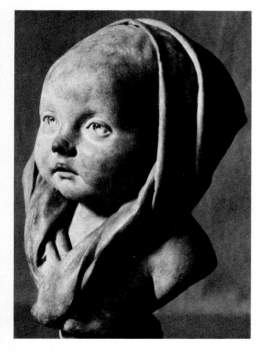

Fig. 174. *A Baby.* Plaster, about 1789. Schwerin, Staatliches Museum

Fig. 175. *Anne-Ange Houdon, the artist's second daughter, at the age of three.* Plaster, about 1791. Paris, Louvre

Fig. 176. *Claudine Houdon, the artist's youngest daughter, at the age of one.* Marble, about 1791. Worcester, Mass., Worcester Art Museum

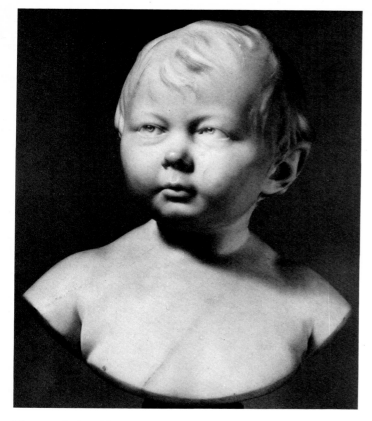

Fig. 177. *Sabine Houdon, the artist's eldest daughter*. Marble, 1788.
New York, Metropolitan Museum of Art

Fig. 178. *Sabine Houdon at the age of four*. Marble,
about 1791. San Marino, Calif.,
Henry E. Huntington Library and Art Gallery

Fig. 179. *Sabine Houdon at the age of fifteen*. Plaster, about 1802.
Formerly Paris, Perrin Houdon Collection

Fig. 180. '*Sabine Houdon at the age of twenty*.' Marble, 1807.
New York, Wildenstein & Co.

Fig. 181–182. *Honoré-Gabriel-Victor Riquetti, Comte de Mirabeau.* Terra cotta, 1791. Paris, Louvre

Fig. 183. *Comte de Mirabeau.* Plaster, 1791. Angers, Musée des Beaux-Arts

Fig. 184. *Comte de Mirabeau.* Marble, 1800. Versailles, Château

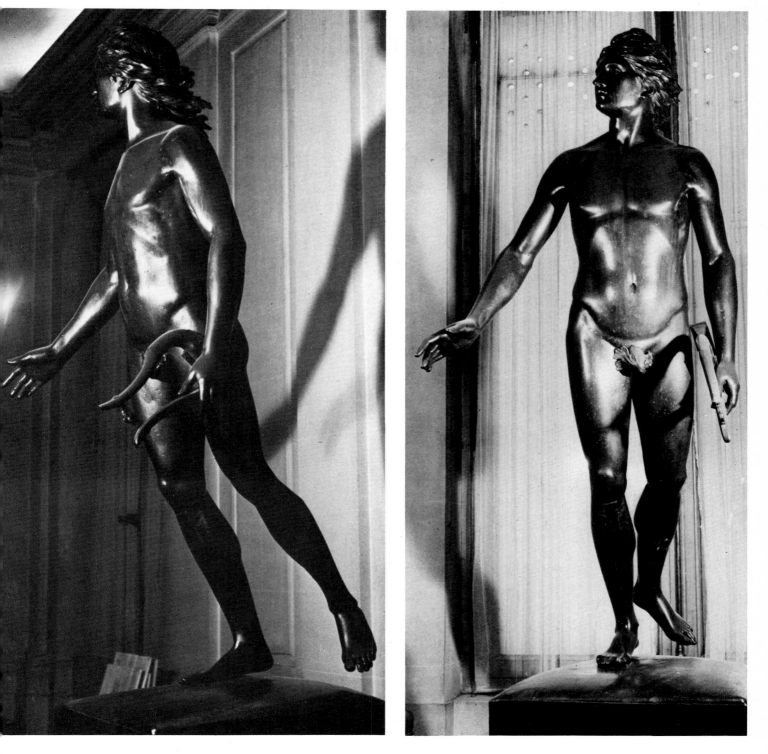

ig. 185. *Apollo*. Bronze, 1790. Lisbon, Calouste Gulbenkian Foundation, Museum

Fig. 186. *The Abbé Jean-Jacques Barthélemy*. Marble, about 1802. Paris, Bibliothèque Nationale

Fig. 187. *General Charles-François Dumouriez*. Terra cotta, about 1792. Angers, Musée des Beaux-Arts

Fig. 188. *Constance-Marie de Theis, Princesse de Salm-Dyck*. Plaster, about 1800. Chatillon-sur-Bagneux, Courty Collection

Fig. 189. *Joseph-Jérôme Le François de Lalande*. Plaster, about 1801. Paris, Observatoire

Fig. 190. *Madame Duquesnoy*. Marble, about 1800.
San Francisco, M.H. De Young Museum

Fig. 191. *Adrien-Cyprien Duquesnoy*. Marble, about 1800.
Paris, Louvre

Fig. 192. *Dorothea von Rodde-Schlözer*. Marble, 1802. Berlin-Dahlem,
Staatliche Museen

Fig. 193. *Pierre-Simon Laplace*. Plaster, about 1803.
Paris, Musée des Arts Décoratifs

Fig. 194. *Joel Barlow*. Marble, about 1804. Washington, D.C., The White House

Fig. 195. *Robert Fulton*. Marble, 1804. Detroit, Institute of Arts

Fig. 196. *Marquise de Créqui*. Plaster, 1803. Le Mans, Musée de Tessé

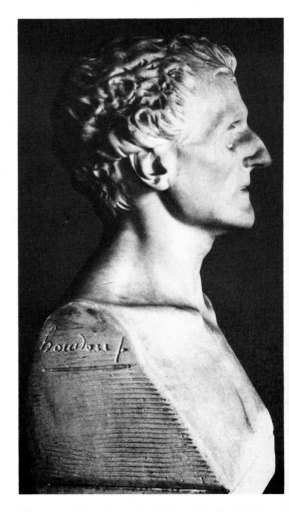

Fig. 197. *Jean-François Collin d'Harleville*. Plaster replica, about 1806. Versailles, Musée Lambinet

Fig. 198. *Cicero*. Plaster, 1804. Paris, Bibliothèque Nationale

Fig. 199. *The Empress Joséphine*. Marble, 1808. Versailles

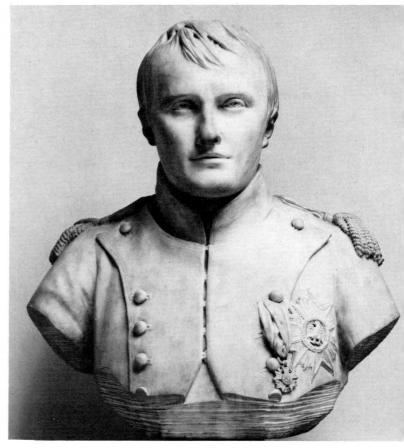

Fig. 200. *The Emperor Napoleon*. Marble, 1808. Versailles

Fig. 201. *The Emperor Napoleon*. Terra cotta, 1806.
Dijon, Musée des Beaux-Arts

Fig. 202. *Félix-Julien-Jean Bigot, Comte de Préameneu.*
Marble, 1809. Paris, Comte Boulay de la Meurthe

Fig. 203. *General Barthélemy-Cathérine Joubert*. Marble, about 1812. Versailles

Fig. 204. *Voltaire*. Marble, about 1812. Paris, Panthéon

Fig. 205. *Houdon in his studio, working on the portrait bust of Laplace* (cf. Fig. 193), *watched by his wife and daughters*. Painting by Louis Léopold Boilly, 1803. Paris, Musée des Arts Décoratifs

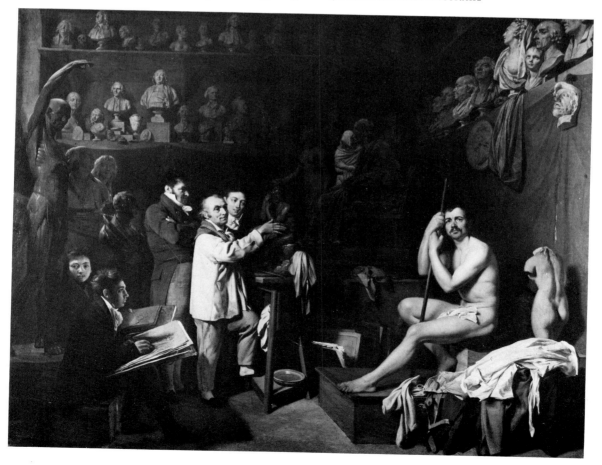

Fig. 206. *Houdon in his studio, correcting a study of a nude made by a pupil.*
Painting by Louis Léopold Boilly, 1804. Cherbourg, Musée Thomas Henry

Fig. 207. *Houdon.* Detail of a sketch by Louis Léopold Boilly for Fig. 205.
Lille, Palais des Beaux-Arts

Fig. 208. *Houdon working on the portrait bust of Laplace.* Detail of a sketch by Louis Léopold Boilly for Fig. 205.
Lille, Palais des Beaux-Arts

gathered in a long queue tied with a riband at the back. The eyes are large and cut unusually deep, shadowed under heavy brows to give them an exceptionally penetrating quality. The lean, symmetrical face, with its sharp, straight nose, compressed lips and jutting chin, suggests the intellectual man of affairs that we know Jefferson to have been. It is at once a face of decision, of sensitivity, and the face of an aristocrat. Jefferson did have the advantage of being a handsome man.

The marble is beautifully cut; within all the precise detail there is still the control, balance, and even generalization of the classic tradition. Jefferson's appearance is so familiar in Houdon's portrayal (at least to Americans through its repetition on currency, stamps, and coins—how many millions of the profile have appeared on the American five cent piece?) that it is impossible to know when describing it whether one is discussing a work of art, a man, or a symbol. Nevertheless, with continued exposure to this and other historic portraits one begins to wonder whether Houdon and other great portraitists could suggest national as well as individual traits. Could the *Jefferson*, the *Franklin*, the *John Paul Jones* be distinguished as American; the *Diderot*, the *Voltaire*, the *Rousseau* as French? But this is merely pleasant speculation, as it is pleasant to speculate whether, aside from matters of dress and coiffure, Houdon's eighteenth-century ladies, e.g., the *Comtesse du Cayla*, could be identified as eighteenth-century, when compared with Carpeaux's nineteenth-century ladies, e.g., *Mademoiselle Fiocre*. Considering the number of late nineteenth-century portrait busts attributed to Houdon this latter speculation is not without relevance.

DURING 1790 and 1791 events in the French Academies of Art were moving as rapidly as in the political sphere, and Jacques-Louis David was in the forefront. He remained an academician—in 1792 he even accepted election to the post of adjunct-professor—but he carried on his battle against the officers and against the methods of teaching. In July 1790, calling himself the President of the Academy, in the sense of being the leader of the academicians against the officers, he submitted to the National Assembly a demand for reforms. Then, deciding that more drastic action was necessary, he formed a broadly based Commune of Artists which, in September 1790, demanded the dissolution of the Academy. The first victory of the new group was that the Salons were opened to all artists, with the immediate result that the Salon of 1791 had two hundred and fifty-eight entrants as against eighty for 1789. In both cases most artists submitted several entries. The *livret* announced the exhibition, 'by the order of the National Assembly, the month of September, 1791, The Year Three of Liberty'.[218]

The introduction of the *livret* noted that, 'The Arts have received a great benefit; the empire of Liberty is finally extended to all; she has broken their chains; genius is no longer condemned to obscurity.' The decree of August 21, 1791, was reprinted, with Article 1: 'All Artists French or Foreign, Members or Non-Members of the Academy of Painting & of Sculpture, will be equally permitted to exhibit their Works in the part of the Louvre reserved for this purpose.' The Salon was delayed until September as a result of the obvious complications, and the *livret* was no longer arranged in a hierarchy of academicians, but according to the disposition of the exhibits within the galleries. Academicians were still noted with the abbreviation, *Ac.*, after their names. From Houdon's entries it would seem that he was working energetically through this period of crisis. His works were listed under three entries: No. 484. Eleven sculptures in marble, terra cotta, plaster and bronze; of which *Lafayette*, *Voltaire*, *Franklin*, *Bailly*, *Necker*, and *Mirabeau* were identified. No. 492 simply listed busts of women in plaster, and No. 788, a figure in bronze representing a *Frileuse*. Although there is no specific designation, the *Lafayette* may be the bust in his revolutionary role; the *Franklin* may be the enlarged version (Boston and Angers). (Franklin had died in

87

1790.)[219] The others have disappeared or have not been identified. Thus, there are three new, identifiable portrait subjects, *Necker*, *Bailly*, and *Mirabeau*. Aside from the bronze *Frileuse*, Houdon completed the life-size *Apollo* in 1790 and the large bronze variant on *L'Écorché* in 1792 (École des Beaux-Arts, Paris).[220]

Before discussing the new portraits in the Salon of 1791 there is a marble, something of a transition between the old regime and the Revolution, which merits examination: the *Comte de Guibert*, signed and dated in cursive under the right shoulder: *houdon f. 1791* (private collection, New York). Jacques-Antoine-Hippolyte Comte de Guibert (1743–1890)

GUIBERT

was a professional soldier who became a marshal of the French army in 1788 and was notable as a writer and theoretician on military tactics. His *Essai général de tactique* and his *Défense du système de guerre moderne* were instrumental in reforming the French army on the eve of the Revolution, were highly admired by George Washington, and influenced the young Napoleon. Aside from his military distinction, Guibert was the author of many literary works and was made a member of the French Academy in 1786.

Fig. 169
Plate 118

Houdon's interpretation is a romantic one, showing the count informally in an open-necked shirt, his handsome head lifted, eyes and mouth suggesting the shadow of a smile. Curiously, the turn of the head as well as the informal costume with the open, frilled shirt is closely modeled after that of the *Cagliostro* of 1786. Since there is no demonstrable affinity between the two individuals, Houdon was obviously using a formula to suggest a visionary. Both busts are prototypes of the romantic tradition to be exemplified in the portraits of François Rude in the second quarter of the nineteenth century. Houdon's receipt for the marble of *Guibert* survives and merits quoting: 'I have received from Madame de Guibert the sum of two thousand eight hundred livres for a marble, a terra cotta and four plasters of the bust of Monsieur de Guibert. Paris, November 2, 1791. houdon.'

NECKER

The three new portraits in the Salon of 1791, *Necker*, *Bailly*, and *Mirabeau*, are all of figures involved in the French Revolution or in the events leading up to it. Jacques Necker (1732–1804), the financier and statesman, was born in Geneva, but spent much of his active life in France. As an economist he opposed the single tax and free trade doctrines of Turgot and the Physiocrats; notably in his influential *Essai sur la législation et le commerce des grains*, 1775. In 1779 he was made director-general of government finances. His attempts at radical reforms forced his resignation in 1783, but he was recalled in 1788. He recommended that the States General be called to meet the growing crisis, was dismissed again despite his popularity with the people; the Bastille was stormed, he was recalled once more, and resigned for the last time in 1790, retiring to his estate in Switzerland. During the years in Paris Madame Necker kept a famous salon, subsequently surpassed by those of their daughter, Madame de Staël.

Necker was apparently a man of strong opinions and his personality excited both enthusiasm and hostility. The Comte Axel de Fersen, favorite of Marie-Antoinette, compared him to the charlatan, Cagliostro, but a Cagliostro 'stiff, inflexible, and disagreeable'. Beyond this topically interesting comparison, Fersen's opinion may not count for much; but it is recorded that Napoleon—who, of course, could have been prejudiced in other contexts—called him 'a stupid, pompous schoolmaster'. Despite his record of honesty and his conscientious efforts to bring order and economy into a chaotic financial situation, his motives were also attacked during the Revolution. Considering the fate of other distinguished individuals who sat for Houdon during this period, Necker probably demonstrated sound, practical sense by retiring to Switzerland when he did.

Fig. 170
Plate 119

Necker's bust was voted by the Commune of Paris in 1789 after the fall of the Bastille, when his reputation was at a high point among the populace. Installed in the Hôtel de Ville, it was destroyed in 1792 by order of the Assembly. There survives a marble in the Geneva Museum of Art, signed and dated 1790, which came from the Necker family. It is a splendid portrait, showing him with short, Louis XVI perruque, in modern dress covered in part with the flowing, Baroque cloak to place him (at this moment somewhat anachronistically) in the company of the king and the gentlemen of the old regime who had been given Houdon's almost last hurrah in the Salon of 1787. The face is arrogant and belligerent, with prognathous, pugnacious jaw, the face of a man with few doubts about the righteousness of his opinions or about his ability to put them into effect. Recognizing his virtues and his wide popularity, one can understand from this characterization how he might have made enemies.[221]

The second portrait from the Salon of 1791 carries us several stages further into the events of the Revolution; it also poses some interesting questions concerning the influence of Houdon on other sculptors. This is the terra cotta of *Jean-Sylvain Bailly* (1736–93), a noted astronomer who became one of the leaders in the initial phase of the French Revolution. Author in 1775 of a history of ancient and modern astronomy, Bailly went on to become a member of the Academy of Science, the Academy of Inscriptions, and the French Academy. He was a deputy from Paris to the States General in 1789 and then first president of the Constituent Assembly. Elected mayor of Paris, he was attacked by the Jacobin party for his moderate views, condemned to death and guillotined in 1793. During his brief period of power Bailly was painted and sculpted by several artists, including the sculptors Houdon, Pajou, and Louis-Pierre Deseine (1749–1822).

Houdon's marble bust was commissioned, like that of Necker, by the Commune of Paris in 1789 and was placed in the Hôtel de Ville, where it remained together with the sculptor's portraits of *Louis XVI*, *Lafayette*, and *Necker* until all four were destroyed in 1792. The terra cotta of Bailly at Altenburg is signed *houdon* under the stump of the right arm and bears the *cachet d'atelier* on the back. The plaster by Deseine is in the Carnavalet Museum, Paris, a gift from Bailly's grand-daughter. It is signed and dated under the right shoulder: *Deseine Sc. Regis fecit 1789*. At first glance the busts are almost identical. Both are fine presentations of Bailly's long, melancholy, lantern-jawed face, his sober, republican dress, with cravat tied loosely around his neck, the perfect type of the Citizen Bailly, who at this moment of history is superseding the gentlemen of the old regime and creating one of the most influential, political, social, economic, and cultural revolutions of all time. The face is thoughtful, the expression drawn inward—the face of one of those moderate revolutionaries who sought to achieve reform from centuries of misrule without destroying all the existing institutions—only to be destroyed himself in the process. A comparison of the portraits reveals slight differences in detail; principally that Deseine shows more of the elaborately frilled shirt under the scarf, whereas the coat, vest, scarf, and wig are essentially the same. More careful scrutiny shows technical differences as well as relationships. Deseine undercuts the eyes in the manner associated with Houdon; in fact the eyes of his *Bailly* are even more deeply undercut than those of Houdon's. The head of Houdon's figure sinks slightly on the chest and is turned to the left; that of Deseine's is lifted and turned to the right. Deseine's *Bailly* is characterized throughout by greater sharpness of technique; the coat is deeply creased, the face is marked by definite hollows and ridges. The wig and eyebrows are treated in a manner that emphasizes the sharp edges so that they appear less as hair and more as clay cut with a tool. Throughout, Houdon's *Bailly* is more generalized, both in the modeling of costume, wig, and features, and also in the mood of contemplation. The coat is softly and broadly modeled; the wig is more of a mass of hair than sculptured clay. Houdon continues to draw that distinction between natural hair and the slightly artificial appearance of a perruque. A difference can even be seen in the treatment of Bailly's particularly heavy eyebrows. The lids of Houdon's *Bailly* droop slightly as he stares past the spectator into the distance; the eyes of Deseine's *Bailly* are wide open and fixed on some specific object. Comparisons and contrasts might be multiplied, but it would be difficult to choose between the two busts in terms of quality. Although Deseine's total achievement is far less than Houdon's, he did, in this sculpture, arrive at something comparable. He was more

Fig. 171

concerned with details and externals, but his image of Bailly is both effective and impressive. He was certainly influenced by Houdon although they were almost exact contemporaries. Like many younger portrait sculptors of the Revolutionary and Napoleonic periods he used technical devices learned from Houdon to extremely good effect. On the other hand Houdon, like his younger contemporaries, was inevitably affected by the neo-classicism that was becoming the official style of Revolution, Directory, and Empire. The portraits of Bailly by Deseine and Houdon illustrate problems that recur during the last twenty years of Houdon's active career. But the comparison here is particularly valuable in pointing up how, in Houdon's portraits, the quality of generalization was essential to the total effect. By imperceptibly softening and generalizing details he was able in fact to heighten the impact of living reality.[222]

MIRABEAU

The third in this group of those who participated in the first stages of the French Revolution is neither attractive-looking nor was he, by all accounts, an attractive man. Honoré-Gabriel-Victor Riquetti, Comte de Mirabeau (1749–91), son of the Physiocrat economist, the Marquis de Mirabeau, was a man of violent passions and led a dissolute and profligate life until about 1786, continually ridden by debt and involved in quarrels with his family and incidents with the law. As a result of his attacks on abuses of the old regime he was elected a delegate for Aix-en-Provence to the States General, and soon became a figure of great influence in the Constituent Assembly, in large part through his brilliant oratory and overpowering presence.

Despite his powers as a rabble-rouser, Mirabeau secretly supported the concept of a constitutional monarchy. Driven by personal ambition, he even advised Louis XVI while pretending to oppose him. In 1790 he drew closer to the royalists and continued surreptitiously in the pay of the Court. Although rumors of his clandestine activities had lost him some popularity among the people, on his death in 1791 he was buried in the Panthéon. Houdon was summoned to make a death-mask, from which he made his busts. When proof of Mirabeau's double-dealings was discovered in 1793 his body was removed from the Panthéon, to be replaced by that of Marat.

Almost immediately after Houdon had made the death-mask the Abbé d'Espagnac, who had made the arrangements, reported the fact to the Société des Amis de la Constitution of which Mirabeau had been a member, and proposed the commission of a bust. Perhaps as a gesture against the former official control of the Academy, Houdon was not given the commission but a competition was proposed. Houdon did not participate but independently modeled his bust for the Salon of 1791. In a letter to the president of the Society accompanying a plaster bust of Mirabeau, he pleaded his case for the commission but, in a stormy session in which his letter was read, his plea was rejected. '. . . M. Dufourny.—There can be no distinction among artists except on the basis of merit. That of Monsieur Houdon is too great that he should have any reason to avoid a competition. He has not entered it; I demand that his plaster should not be admitted.

'Monsieur David affirmed that before coming to the meeting he had had a conversation with Monsieur Houdon in which the latter had attempted to justify his reasons. But Monsieur David had not found them adequate and, far from promising to support him he had warned him that he would blame him for this conduct and that he would be against him.'

The meeting broke up in confusion and the bust was not admitted to the *concours*. Shortly thereafter Houdon requested that it be returned to him so that he might make a marble version.[223]

Figs. 181–2
Plates 120–1

Houdon's bust of *Mirabeau* presents him, like Bailly, as *Citizen Mirabeau*. His heavy, pockmarked face, with hooded eyes and the tight, rather small mouth, is not a pleasant one, although it is of great power. Based on the death-mask, it is still a work of tremendous presence, projecting the aura of a forceful and complicated personality. The three types of the *Mirabeau* bust are the terra cotta in the Louvre, without shoulders, open at the back;

the marble in the family of Charles Delagrave, with shoulders and upper arms; and
the later marble at Versailles, commissioned in 1800, like the late version of the *Washington*, for the *Galerie des Consuls*. All three are in modern dress with the heavy perruque that
replaced the lighter, more elegant style at the end of the old regime. In the Delagrave marble
the head is lifted energetically, the stump of the left arm against the torso, that of the right
arm lifted as though the invisible arm were gesturing. The marble is signed under the right
stump in cursive script: *houdon f. 10 avril 1791*. As noted above, this type of bust, in which
the torso is full almost to the waist and the arms alternate in a twisting movement, recurs
frequently during the later phase of the artist's career. A plaster of the same type as the
marble is in the Museum at Angers, signed and dated: *houdon f. 1791*, a gift of the sculptor,
David d'Angers. The later marble, at Versailles, probably a studio work, is based on the
Louvre type, without shoulders, but is more massive in presentation, the torso squared off
to form the base, in the neo-classic formula. The name, MIRABEAU, is lettered across the
front of the base, as required in all busts commissioned for the *Galerie des Consuls*. A number
of replicas of the first *Mirabeau* exist, in some of which the pock marks have been smoothed
out to give him a less oppressive appearance. Others are obviously copies by other hands
after the original by Houdon.

David d'Angers presented another bust of a remarkable man of the Revolution to the
Museum at Angers: the terra cotta of General Charles François Dumouriez (1739–1823).
Most probably dating from 1792, this is an excellent study of a military man, in the tradition
of *John Paul Jones*. A surviving description of Dumouriez illustrates the fidelity of Houdon's
interpretation: 'Small, hardy, and wiry; face plain, almost ugly, eyes small but lively and
stern, mouth large. The sound of his voice, low but clear and strong, his manner brusque
without being rude.'[223a]

General Dumouriez distinguished himself in the French Revolutionary Wars, was made
Minister of War in June 1792 and took Lafayette's place as Army Commander in August
of that year. There is evidence that the portrait was commissioned after his great victory
over the Austrians at Jemappes in November 1792. After a defeat at Neerwinden he
negotiated, and then in April 1793 he deserted to the Austrians. The latter part of his life
was spent in exile in England.

A comparison of the busts of Lafayette (1790), Guibert (1791) and Dumouriez (*c*. 1792)—
three soldiers, before, during or after the Revolution—suggests how faithfully Houdon's
portraits mirror the times and their attitudes. Lafayette and Guibert, aristocrats, are still
cast in a heroic mould, heads lifted nobly, the modeling generalized, the characterization
idealized or romanticized insofar as the sculptor would permit it. Dumouriez, on the other
hand, a soldier of the Revolution, is shown in sober, civilian dress (in marked contrast to
Napoleon's magnificent marshals), the features modeled with a ruthless precision.

A word should be added on the place of the Marquis de Lafayette in this company of
men of the Revolution. A member of the States General in 1789, he was given command of
the National Guard in 1790, and it is in this uniform as well as with the new, heavy style
of perruque that Houdon portrayed him in 1790 (see p. 80). Lafayette attempted to use his
influence and prestige to arbitrate among the contending factions, without success; he
became less popular when on July 17, 1791, he ordered the Guard to fire into a crowd
gathered to petition the dethronement of the king; and in 1792 fought in the Revolutionary
Wars against Austria. Captured by the Austrians, he was imprisoned until liberated by
Napoleon in 1797. After living in retirement during the First Empire, he was a liberal member
of the Chamber of Deputies during the Restoration and took part in the July 1830 Revolt as
a leader of the moderates. His incredible career thus spanned the years from 1777 when, at the
age of twenty, he arrived in Philadelphia to join George Washington until his death in 1834;
and encompassed two continents and three revolutions.

BRONZES THE late 1780s and early 1790s saw Houdon's greatest activity in bronze casting. The life-size statue of the *Apollo*, dated 1790, appeared in the Salon of 1791. A second cast of the *Diana*, now in the Louvre, is also dated 1790, and the large, bronze *Écorché* in the École des Beaux-Arts, Paris, was cast in 1792. The bronze *Frileuse* in the Metropolitan Museum, New York, dated 1787, is possibly that which was also in the 1791 Salon.

Since 1772 the sculptor had occupied one of the ateliers of the City of Paris at No. 24 Rue du Faubourg du Roule. He had also established a foundry at No. 195 Rue du Faubourg Saint-Honoré, and had yet another studio at the back of the Bibliothèque du Roi (Bibliothèque Nationale), Rue de Richelieu, for work in terra cotta, plaster, and marble.[224]

In the letter addressed to the painter Bachelier, written in October 1794, Houdon described his work in bronze casting:

> . . . Resuming the account of my work, I should say that I have devoted myself essentially to two studies, which have occupied my entire life, to which I have devoted everything I have earned, and which would have been most useful to my country if I had had any support and if I had had the means; *anatomy* and *bronze casting of sculpture*.
>
> Long housed in the ateliers of the City, I profited by this position by being at the same time *sculptor* and *metal founder* (in modern times the two professions were always exercised by different individuals), and by reviving in my country this useful art, which could have been lost, since all the founders were dead when I began to concern myself with it. I constructed furnaces, I trained workmen, and after many fruitless and costly attempts, I succeeded in casting two statues: the *Diana*, of which one cast still belongs to me, and my *Frileuse*. In 1787 I was evicted from these ateliers by Breteuil, and within three weeks I had bought a house across the street and constructed new furnaces, and there I cast my *Apollo*.
>
> Since the Revolution, not having any work [major sculpture commissions] (never having worked except for private collectors or foreigners, except for the *Tourville*), I wanted to support my atelier, and keep in my country the valuable workmen who would have taken their talents to neighboring countries. I spent a small fortune on bronze casting in order to continue my work in this medium: I cast busts of the great men: Molière, Buffon, Voltaire, Rousseau, etc. . . ., always carried along by the love of my art, by the desire to leave a lasting monument to posterity and a subject for young artists to study.
>
> Despite my obligations as the father of a family, I cast my great *Écorché* in 1792. When the statue on the dome of the Panthéon was cast [the *Renommé* (*Fame*), by Dejoux], it was necessary to seek a founder in my atelier: an excellent man but one who had only worked with me, one who owed everything to me alone, to my perseverance, my money, and my guidance, my knowledge of this art. He was trained as a foundryman with me.
>
> There, Citizen, is the report you have requested of me.
>
> As a result I may be considered in the double role of *sculptor* and *founder*. In the first I am a creator; in the second, I can execute the creations of others in a permanent form, far less expensively than anybody else. Never having had any money to carry on this work except my own savings, I have been careful to keep expenses down and to eliminate anything extraneous.[225]

This letter, of special importance in view of the meagre documentation that exists concerning Houdon's life, gives a graphic account of the artist's activities in the realm of bronze casting during the last years of the old regime and the first of the Revolutionary period. It also documents Houdon's feeling of discrimination in the matter of royal or official commissions. Despite the lack of large-scale or even of many private portrait commissions during the first Revolutionary years, he was, with a new studio-foundry and with well-trained workmen, in an excellent position to carry on bronze casting on an expanded scale, and apparently he plunged into it.

The bronze statue of *Apollo*, now in the Gulbenkian Collection in Lisbon, is signed and dated: HOUDON F. 1790. Pour Jn. de Marigny a Paris. It was commissioned as a companion piece to Marigny's bronze *Diana*, and is the only known version of the *Apollo* extant. In private hands during the nineteenth and much of the twentieth century and, as far as is known, not reproduced in life-size or reduced form by Houdon, it is much less well-known and less admired than the *Diana*.[225a] The statue is a free version of the *Apollo Belvedere*, modified to make it an appropriate companion to the *Diana*. *Apollo* repeats the pose of *Diana* almost exactly except that he is balanced on the right rather than the left foot. His head is turned to his right in the same direction as that of *Diana*, his right arm swings forward to balance the backward movement of his left leg, his left hand holds a lyre. His hair is blown back in a manner reminiscent of Houdon's medallion of *Apollo* and that of the *Brothers Montgolfier*.[226]

The second bronze version of *L'Écorché* is to all intents a new sculpture. The figure is somewhat more elongated and emaciated; the right arm, rather than being extended forward in a gesture of command, salute, or blessing, is lifted over the head, fingers curved, forefinger and thumb touching delicately. The head is completely restudied. The gesture of the right arm restores that of the *Saint John the Baptist* as it appeared in the destroyed original in Santa Maria degli Angeli in Rome and the model sketched by Saint-Aubin in the Salon of 1769. Whereas the mouths of the surviving *Écorchés* from the Roman period are open as though they are speaking, the mouth now is firmly closed. The blank eyes of the first version are now undercut and defined. The impact is macabre, that of Death. The bronze is heavily scored with tool marks and technically has a certain primitive quality. The small bronze of *L'Écorché* in the Courty Collection with the right arm curled closely over the head, signed by Thomire and dated 1776, is a transition between the two large versions. This is more of a muscle man than a cadaver, more dramatically posed, the head with blank eyes but closed mouth; the technique of the bronze, perhaps because of its small scale, seemingly more polished and sophisticated than the later version.[227]

Fig. 185
Plates 122-3

Plates 4a, 5

Plates 4b, c

FROM the Salon of 1793 until that of 1814, the last in which he participated, Houdon's entries were relatively modest compared with the peak years of the seventies and eighties, and many of his contributions were replicas of earlier works. That so many of his sculptures have disappeared is in part a consequence of the disruption, organized destruction and vandalism that occurred during the Revolution, when portraits of kings, nobles, and even revolutionary leaders as well as religious sculptures were for a time in extreme danger. With the fall of Napoleon many of the monuments erected to him were destroyed. There were some anxious periods for the sculptor and his family. The enmity of Jacques-Louis David, who became a virtual commissar of the arts under the Revolutionary and Napoleonic regimes, undoubtedly resulted in the loss of possible commissions; but much more important were the great social and artistic changes arising with the Revolution. The system of the Academy was disrupted and the royal and noble patronage of the old regime disappeared. When Napoleon re-established a form of patronage after 1800, the emphasis was on the new, neo-classic styles, which had come to dominate the arts of Europe. In 1802 Canova visited Paris to make his first portrait of Napoleon as Consul, and from that time forward he remained the favored sculptor of Bonaparte and his Court. Neo-classicism became the official art of the Revolution and the Napoleonic period, not only because it was reaching maturity after its gradual but inevitable emergence during the second half of the eighteenth century, but also because a new art was needed to celebrate first the virtues of republicanism and then the glories of imperialism. This had to be an art as remote as possible from that of the old regime, and it seems almost fated that an art deriving literally from ancient Rome should have been already at hand.[228]

Houdon was an eclectic artist, as Diderot, Voltaire, and in fact most of the *philosophes* were eclectic philosophers. Yet the classicism of his Roman apprenticeship recurred constantly, to become explicit in works such as the *Vestal*, *Saint Bruno*, *Diana*, *Apollo*, the tomb of the Comte d'Ennery, and others, and to lend a particular quality to many of his portraits. Without pressing the point it can be argued that his *Diana*, with all her rococo elegance, is more authentically within the classic frame of antiquity than the mannered or melodramatic historicism of Canova or Thorvaldsen. But at the end of the eighteenth century it was the sculpture of Canova and his school that created the criteria by which classical authenticity was judged. After 1790 Houdon did make concessions to the new style by adopting the rectangular herm base for some of his portraits, by simplifying surfaces and emphasizing contours. He could not, however, adapt sufficiently or with enough enthusiasm to assimilate the new movement. When he finally exhibited the large bronze *Frileuse* in the Salon of 1791, it was greeted by the critics with a complete lack of enthusiasm.[229]

The *Negress* attendant for the fountain in the Duc d'Orléans' garden at Monceau was destroyed during the Revolution and the rococo *Bather* was damaged. This was probably evidence of hostility to the royal house rather than aesthetic judgement; but the treatment of *La Frileuse* and later of the *Diana* at the hands of neo-classical critics was little more sympathetic. When the *Diana* was exhibited in the Salon of 1802, one critic wrote, 'At the time when we were not yet familiar with the beauties of antiquity this statue could have given us pleasure; but today, when we demand purity of design in a statue, it is impossible not to laugh at this unfortunate *Diana* who, to compound her woe, hasn't the slightest garment to conceal her French proportions.' The derogatory use of the term, French, equated to rococo, is of interest. A more tolerant reviewer, whose memory went back a number of years, wrote, 'It is about twenty years since we were shown this figure at the Bibliothèque du Roi in the studio of Houdon. At that time it was not possible to exhibit it at the Salon; bigotry opposed it . . . The statue by Houdon does him much honor despite the criticisms which were then made for his having represented Diana the Huntress nude; this impropriety, it was said, was stipulated by the collector who commissioned the statue. The head is a portrait: as a consequence it does not have the ideal and severe character which the ancients gave to the goddess.' Although this writer, an old-timer, is not actually hostile, his praise is most restrained. He repeats two anecdotes which have entered into and confused subsequent Houdon literature. One is that Girardot de Marigny, who commissioned the first bronze *Diana*, insisted on her being represented completely nude. This is not out of character for an eighteenth-century *amateur des arts* (or for that matter an *amateur* of other centuries); but the bronze of 1782 was preceded by the equally explicit marble of 1780 and the plaster of 1776, and it is highly unlikely that either the Duke of Saxe-Gotha or Catherine of Russia insisted on this degree of nudity.

The other anecdote is even more confusing and totally without evidence. The statement that the head of *Diana* is a portrait has resulted in various searches for the presumed model and even her identification in a bust that is obviously an adaptation from the *Diana*. This anecdote is principally interesting as an illustration of how critics can repeat stories that are refuted by the work before their eyes. The head of the *Diana* is one of the most abstractly classic portrayals ever created by Houdon. This was simply not classicism as a neo-classical critic understood the term. *Diana* probably looked much more rococo in 1802 than she does in the second half of the twentieth century.[230]

During the last twenty years of his career Houdon, like many of his colleagues grown up in the Salon tradition of the old regime, was affected by the major stylistic changes and the accompanying 'new criticism', by vandalism, confiscation, and lack of official commissions. During the periods of the Revolution and the Directory there was little money available for such commissions, and the rising bourgeoisie contained few educated patrons to replace the nobility. In 1790 the National Assembly did decree the erection of a statue to Jean-Jacques Rousseau. Houdon campaigned for the commission as the possessor of Rousseau's death-mask and the only sculptor to have made many portraits of him. Despite his claims the project went to a *concours*; but it was never carried out for lack of funds.[231]

The confusion of the times is illustrated by the following story. In 1794 Houdon completed an over-life-size statue of *Philosophy*, which was placed in the assembly hall of the National Convention. According to various traditions he had transformed a statue of a saint into that of *Philosophy* in order to avoid pro-religious accusations. In one version it was the quick thinking of Madame Houdon that effected the transformation; in another the anecdotist Barrère claimed credit. The definitive version seems to be contained in a document dated 1798 having to do with the new decoration of the Invalides. Here the architect Peyre proposed that various statues of the Virgin and of saints in the Invalides might easily be preserved and changed into non-religious symbols for the Republic. To illustrate the feasibility of his proposal he cited the fact that Houdon had changed a statue of *Saint Eudoxia* into one of *Philosophy*. According to this version the change seems to have been made not for fear of reprisals but merely as a matter of convenience or economy. Of course the temper of the times had abated somewhat by 1798; but there is no reason not to accept this explanation. The large marble *Vestal* by Houdon could equally well be a medieval saint. Another document, dated 1797, reveals that the artist was still having difficulty securing payment for the statue of *Philosophy*; and odder than the anecdotes is the fact that the statue, seven or eight feet high and prominently placed in a public building, should have vanished without trace.[232]

Only four statues from the post-Revolutionary period survive—the plasters of *Cicero* (Louvre and Bibliothèque Nationale), the marbles of *Voltaire Standing* (Panthéon) and *General Joubert* (Versailles), both exhibited in the Salon of 1812; and the stone statue of *Themis* in front of the Palais Bourbon, Paris. The *Themis* has weathered so severely that, despite a restoration of the head in 1954, it must be classed with the lost works. It was designed as a symbol of Justice, while its companion, Roland's *Minerva*, represented Wisdom. Houdon's *Themis* is a heavily draped Pallas-Athena (or Minerva), closely adapted from a Roman statue, the *Pallas of Velletri*, discovered in 1798. It is of interest principally as another instance of Houdon's close study of antiquity when faced with a specifically classic theme. Of his previous works it approximates most specifically to the *Ceres* of the Château Maisons-Laffitte.

A monumental bronze statue of Napoleon was commissioned from the artist in 1804 to be placed on a column in Boulogne, was completed in 1812, and was destroyed with the Restoration.

IF Houdon's career as a sculptor is measured in terms of the Salons, it was half over by 1791. His first Salon was 1769 and his last was 1814. However, by 1791 his major achievements were behind him and, despite a substantial number of notable new works, his Salon entries from 1793 forward add up to a considerably smaller total than those of the earlier years, including many replicas or variants. The Salon of 1800 had no works by Houdon, in several others there was only a token offering of two or three pieces, and there were also increasing numbers of sculptures not identified or for which the subject identification is uncertain. The smaller number of his exhibits was not due solely to the disruption, first of the Revolutionary period, then of the Napoleonic with its continual wars and its attempt to build a new imperial image to replace that of the old regime. Houdon, despite all the changes in fashion, was now a highly respected old master of French sculpture and had no need to make an impressive showing at the Salon. He devoted an increasing proportion of his efforts to seeking major commissions, unfortunately with not a great deal of success. It was in the monumental sculpture of the period that neo-classicism obviously had its greatest impact.

Since my primary concern is with surviving sculptures which can be securely identified and which I believe to be from Houdon's hand, and since, between 1793 and 1814, these are relatively few, it would seem sensible to list them as a group before considering them in detail. I shall concentrate on works which represent some new departure or are of particularly good quality, or involve some historical aspect of interest; and discuss others more summarily.

The key works between 1793 and 1814, aside from those already discussed, include, in chronological order (these are portrait busts unless otherwise indicated):

Abbé Barthélemy (Salons of 1795 and 1802)
Madame Houdon and Sabine? (Medallion, 1798)
Sabine Houdon? (*c.* 1800)
The Princess of Salm-Dyck? (*c.* 1800?)
Adrien Duquesnoy and *Madame Duquesnoy* (*c.* 1800)
Jérôme Le François de Lalande, Astronomer (Salon of 1801)
Edmond Mentelle, Geographer (Salons of 1801 and 1802)
Dorothea von Rodde-Schlözer (Salons of 1802 and 1806)
Pierre-Simon Laplace, Mathematician and Astronomer (1803)
Marshal Ney (Salon of 1804)
Joel Barlow, Diplomat (Salon of 1804)
Robert Fulton, Inventor (Salon of 1804)
Cicero (Statue, Salon of 1804)
The Emperor Napoleon (Salons of 1806 and 1808)
The Empress Josephine (Salons of 1806 and 1808)
Collin d'Harleville, Author (Salon of 1806)
Sabine Houdon? (1807)
General Joubert (Statue, Salon of 1812)
Voltaire, Standing (Statue, Salon of 1812)
Alexander I, Emperor of Russia (Salon of 1814, lost)

THE SALON
OF 1793

BARNAVE

THE Salon of 1793 included a version of the small *Vestal*, a sketch of the Washington statue (disappeared), a small *Frileuse*, and a plaster bust of a child (not identified). The only new work of any apparent significance was a bust of a woman, life-size, in bronze (Madame de Thélusson?).[233] Another problem bust of this period is the portrait of the lawyer-orator, Joseph Barnave (1761–93). As a deputy of the Third Estate, Barnave had a brief but brilliant career as a defender of a constitutional monarchy until his death on the guillotine in 1793.[234] Aside from Mirabeau, who had royalist leanings, and perhaps Barnave, Houdon does not seem to have portrayed any of the active revolutionaries. The sculptor, David d'Angers, records that he made a life-mask of Robespierre, but there is no evidence that he ever completed a portrait bust. Aside from Napoleon and Josephine and Alexander I, the post-revolutionary busts are principally those of scientists, men and women of letters, military men or political functionaries. Foreigners continued to visit the sculptor, and it is perhaps appropriate that his last recorded portrait is that of Alexander I, Czar of Russia (Salon of 1814), grandson of Houdon's first and most notable royal patron, Catherine II.

THE Salon of 1795 included only one entry by Houdon, the *Abbé Barthélemy*. This was probably a plaster since the marble was exhibited in the Salon of 1802. The Abbé Jean-Jacques Barthélemy (1716–95) was the author of the highly popular *Voyage de jeune Anacharsis*, a moral tale of the type beloved at the end of the eighteenth century. He was an antiquarian, curator of coins and medals at the Bibliothèque du Roi, on the ground floor of which Houdon had a studio. The marble bust of Barthélemy, signed through some inadvertence: *hondon f.*, is preserved in the Cabinet des Médailles. He is portrayed without shoulders, undraped, *à l'antique*; belonging thus in Houdon's long line of modern *philosophes* presented as ancient philosophers, the line that extends from Diderot in 1771 to Voltaire, Rousseau, Buffon, for example, and even to Napoleon in 1806. The only real stylistic change in this thirty-year gallery of Great Men is that in the last two, *Barthélemy* and *Napoleon*, the sculptor forms the torso in the rectangular herm shape made popular with neo-classicism. The wrinkled, smiling face of Barthélemy and his few locks of somewhat unkempt hair are as delicately and sensitively modeled as the features of any of Houdon's great men who had preceded him.[235]

THE Salons of 1796 to 1800 included only a reduced marble version of *La Frileuse* by Houdon, other replicas of earlier work, a terra cotta of the *Marquis de Pastoret*, which has disappeared, and unidentified busts.[236]

The identifiable new portraits of these years are a terra cotta medallion in the Petit Palais, Paris, signed and dated: *Houdon f. an 7* [1798], purporting to be a representation of Madame Houdon and her eldest daughter, Sabine, aged thirteen; a plaster bust of Sabine, painted terra cotta, showing her approximately two years older; a supposed portrait of the Princess of Salm-Dyck in plaster and marble; and busts of Monsieur Duquesnoy and his wife. There is no reason to question the authenticity of any of these works although there may be problems about the subject identifications. None of them appeared in the Salons.

The medallion in the Petit Palais is certainly by Houdon, the informality of the presentation strongly suggests a family portrait, and a comparison with the portraits of Madame Houdon and Sabine in the painting of Houdon and his family in his studio, dated 1803, by Boilly (Musée des Arts Décoratifs, Paris), supports the identification. The medallion is an excellent example of Houdon's later style in so far as this can be distinguished from his earlier style: crisp and precise in the hair and hair ribands, but generalized in the features of mother and daughter. The simplified coiffure suggests the radical changes taking place during the Directory in women's fashions as well as in the major arts. The blank eyes as well as the dress *à l'antique* record the moment when neo-classicism penetrates all phases of the life and arts of the time.

The plaster bust of *Sabine*, painted terra cotta, shows the young lady slightly more mature, an attractive girl becoming a woman, her hair drawn back in a large chignon, *à la Grecque*. Although heavily painted, this bust has lost none of the freshness that characterizes Houdon's portraits of children and young women, particularly those of his own family. Sabine has a wide-eyed alertness that reminds one inevitably of her portrait at the age of four, and that is reiterated in Boilly's portrayal of her in 1803 as she looks forthrightly out of the painting at the spectator.[237]

Although it is not signed or dated, another portrait of a lady from Houdon's hand belongs to this period, *c.* 1800. This is Madame Duquesnoy, whose husband, also sculpted by Houdon, was a lawyer and a deputy of the third estate to the States General. Madame Duquesnoy, formerly Mademoiselle Jadelot, seems to have been a simple housewife and has left virtually no other record of her existence or personality. With her portrait Houdon has moved into the full tide of neo-classical sculpture. The hair is elaborately dressed in the Grecian mode, similar to but more formal than that of Sabine at the age of fifteen; it is pulled back with heavy braids around the chignon, while loosely arranged bangs cover her forehead and long curls are arranged about her neck. The shawl around her shoulders over the delicately suggested chemise is particularly happy in its graceful yet ample sweep. Although this detail is reminiscent of the drapery the artist used to lend dignity and amplitude to his portraits of noble ladies and gentlemen of the old regime, as well as to some of his *philosophes*, here the effect is simply that of a shawl arranged comfortably over the lady's dress. The marble conforms to the neo-classical fashion of high finish and precision of details. However, the free and direct carving of the eyes, hair, and eyebrows shows the specific touch of Houdon. The soft, illusionistic rendering of the hair in particular violates the neo-classical tendency to a hard, mechanical stylization. As a classic personification it must be said that *Madame Duquesnoy* is placid rather than withdrawn; but possibly this was the nature of the lady herself.[238]

PRINCESSE
DE SALM-DYCK

Fig. 188

Still another portrait of a woman not recorded in the Salons is that of *Constance-Marie de Theis, Princesse de Salm-Dyck* (1767–1843). She wrote plays and novels, published letters, and was the first woman admitted to the Lycée, later the Athenée des Arts, whose members included artists, scientists, and men of letters, among others Condorcet, Lalande, Marie-Joseph Chénier and the artists Houdon and Carl Vernet. The plaster and the terra cotta show her without shoulders, undraped *à l'antique*, Houdon's preferred formula for men and women of letters since his *Diderot* and *Madame de Charrière* in 1771. Adding to the princess's impact as a classical poet or philosopher is the fact that she wore her hair as short as a man's (underneath his perruque) and arranged in an elegant disarray. Her marble bust, signed on the edge of the right shoulder: *houdon f.* (as is also the plaster), but not dated, shows her in a simple Grecian gown cut in a square *décolleté*.[239]

DUQUESNOY

Fig. 191
Plate 128b

Adrien-Cyprien Duquesnoy (1759–1808), husband of the lady discussed above, is shown in his marble bust in the Louvre (signed *houdon*, undated) in the prosaic civilian garb of the beginning of the nineteenth century. Perhaps because they were friends, perhaps because of his official position, Houdon draped him in the not entirely appropriate toga-like cloak.[240] Duquesnoy was a politician with an eventful career, who apparently played both sides during the Revolution and barely escaped the guillotine. He was elected mayor of the tenth *arrondissement* of Paris, and in this capacity he presided at the marriage of Sabine Houdon to Henri-Jean Pineu-Duval in 1805. Less happy was his officiating at the inappropriate marriage of Lucien Bonaparte with Madame Jouberton in 1804. For this Napoleon dismissed him from office and, in 1808, apparently despondent, Duquesnoy committed suicide. Houdon could not have anticipated Duquesnoy's tragic death and, while he could have been aware of the double-dealing, being himself a moderate he might not have been unsympathetic. Yet, in the light of what we know of his career, this portrait is a marvel of characterization. Duquesnoy is given a furtive smile, a 'lean and hungry look', his long nose, drawn brows, suspicious eyes all framed in lank and thinning hair.

THE SALONS
OF 1801
AND 1802

THE *livrets* for the Salons of 1800 and 1801 contain no entries of works by Houdon. It is possible that the Salon of 1801 contained three busts, those of *d'Alembert*, the astronomer *Lalande*, and the geographer *Mentelle*.[241] *D'Alembert* appears again as a marble in the Salon of 1802, a fact which would suggest that the bust of 1801 was a plaster. The marble shown in 1802 may be that in New Haven, even though it is signed and dated: *houdon f. 1779*. The marble of the *Abbé Barthélemy* listed in 1802 is possibly that in the Bibliothèque Nationale, the plaster of which was shown in 1795. 1802 also included busts in plaster of *Madame la margrave d'Anspach* (disappeared), *Le cit. Mentelle*, and bronze replicas of *La Frileuse* and the *Diana*.

Edmonde Mentelle (1730–1815), geographer, is shown in the newly designed uniform of members of the Institute of France, successor to the Royal Academy. The surviving bust is a terra cotta, signed under the right shoulder: *houdon f.* Heavily brocaded uniforms increasingly became the dress for male functionaries from the Directory to the Empire, with a resulting intricate detail in the portrait busts. While men's everyday dress after 1800 began to assume the drab uniformity that has pertained ever since, under the Empire those who legitimately could sport a uniform did so, seeking in the splendor of these uniforms to recapture the lost elegance of the eighteenth century.[242]

The portrait of *Joseph-Jérôme Le François de Lalande* (1732–1807), the astronomer, presents certain problems typical of a number of Houdon's late busts. There are two known copies of this bust, a plaster painted terra cotta in the Observatory in Paris and a terra cotta in the Lindenau Museum at Altenburg, neither signed nor dated. Both are unquestionably by Houdon; they represent the same man and there is every evidence that the man is Lalande. Houdon's increasing casualness in signing and dating his late works has been noted. The tendency of owners, scholars, or dealers to equate the bust of an unknown subject with a known subject of the right type and period has also been noted. This is a perfectly commendable enterprise, dangerous only when too much wishful thinking is involved. In the case of Lalande there is evidence that a portrait was exhibited in the Salon of 1801. A plaster of the astronomer appeared in the sale of 1828. The bust under discussion is recognizable on the shelf near *Franklin* and behind the *Seated Voltaire* in Boilly's painting of the artist modelling Laplace (Musée des Arts Décoratifs, Paris), as well as in the Cherbourg version where Houdon is working from the model. The terra cotta at Altenburg has a long history of identification with both Houdon and Lalande. Finally, the two busts bear every stamp of Houdon's hand.

Lalande was proud of his purported resemblance to Socrates, and it is as the Socratic philosopher that Houdon has portrayed him. His shirt is open at the throat and over it is flung a cape simulating a toga; his head is bald with attendant hair worn rather long and curling around ears and neck. His face is lifted and breaking out in a wonderful, sardonic smile, which lights up every feature in a manner comparable to that of the *Seated Voltaire*. We know that the astronomer was very much the sort of man he appears to be in this portrait, an authority in his field, witty and amusing, an iconoclast who even challenged the Pope to recognize Copernicus and Galileo.[243]

One other portrait is listed in the *livret* for the Salon of 1802, a plaster of *Dorothea von Rodde-Schlözer* (1770–1825); the marble was shown in the Salon of 1806. Madame von Rodde-Schlözer was a noted intellectual, the first woman to be granted the degree of Doctor of Philosophy at the University of Göttingen, where her father was a distinguished professor. The plaster of her portrait is at Göttingen, the marble in the Museum at Berlin-Dahlem, signed: *houdon f.* on the edge of the right shoulder. Madame von Rodde-Schlözer visited Paris in 1801, where she moved in literary circles. She was a rather heavy lady, not a beauty, although with good features and a calm, reflective gaze. Her hair, in the fashion of the time, is drawn back and gathered in a chignon encompassed with a riband; her shoulders are covered with a simple shawl. Despite its neo-classical austerity this is an extremely fine portrait, a sensitive and beautifully rendered presentation of a woman who was obviously a strong and interesting personality. Details like the delicately rendered lines of the drawnback hair, the rather heavy upper eyelids, which add to the expression of reflection and repose, suggest the personal hand of the sculptor. Above all, and most difficult to define, there is the imperceptible softening of the total surface of the marble, the textural nuances that differentiate a work like this from the mechanical treatment of most neo-classical marbles—even some of this period firmly attributed to Houdon.[244]

A portrait that was not shown in a Salon but that is nevertheless documented as completely as anyone could desire, is the plaster of *Pierre-Simon Laplace* (1749–1827), the great mathe-

LALANDE

Fig. 189
Plate 130

Figs. 205–6

MME VON RODDE-SCHLÖZER

Fig. 192
Plate 129

LAPLACE
Fig. 193, Plate 131

matician-astronomer. It is the last in Houdon's long gallery of French scientists. Both the plaster and Boilly's painting of 1803 showing the sculptor in his studio, accompanied by his wife and three daughters, modelling the clay from which the plaster was made, with Laplace posing, are in the Musée des Arts Décoratifs in Paris.

Laplace was the author, among many other works, of the *Traité de mécanique céleste*, 1799–1825, which corroborated Newton's theory of gravity. Houdon showed him in contemporary dress in the abbreviated version of the bust. The face is not beautiful but has an air not only of intelligence but the quiet authority suggestive of his distinguished administrative, political, as well as scientific career. The plaster has not been painted and, although not immaculate in its surface, is remarkably crisp in its details. The tool marks in the hair and eyebrows as well as the marks of scraping tools over the surfaces are clearly evident, lending to the plaster those qualities of vitality only evident in a work *réparé par le sculpteur lui-même* and not blurred or destroyed by subsequent wear or over-painting.

Another portrait of particular interest from 1803 is that of the Marquise de Créqui (1714–1803). The only known plaster, possibly a recast, is in the Museum at Mans. Madame de Créqui was a friend of Jean-Jacques Rousseau and apparently a remarkable lady in her own right. She seems never to have permitted her portrait to be taken, and Houdon's bust is based on a death-mask. Although the plaster, signed *houdon f.* in cursive under the right shoulder, but not dated, has something of the mechanical quality of a replica, it is a lively interpretation of this eighty-nine-year-old lady, whose face sparkles with humor and intelligence. It is yet another refutation of the cliché that Houdon's genius flagged when he made a posthumous portrait.

THE *livret* for the Salon of 1804 included the *Margrave d'Anspach*, whose portrait has not been securely identified, although she appeared as a plaster in 1802 and in 1804, and as a marble in 1806. It also lists plasters of *Marshal Ney* and of two Americans, *Joel Barlow* and *Robert Fulton*. The most important new commission was the plaster of a statue of *Cicero*, intended to be made in marble for the hall of the Senate. The portrait of *Marshal Ney*, one of the greatest of Napoleon's officers, exists in a plaster cast at Versailles and in a bronze, signed under the right shoulder: *Houdon f. an XII*, in the collection of the Prince of Moscow, a descendant of Marshal Ney.[245]

The busts of *Barlow* and *Fulton* might be considered companion portraits of these two friends, the last of Houdon's series of Americans. Joel Barlow (1754–1812), a poet, a liberal thinker, as well as a diplomat, lived in Europe from 1788 to 1805. From 1790 to 1792 he resided in London, where he was a friend of Thomas Paine. In 1792 he moved to Paris and in 1795 was appointed American Consul to Algiers. In 1805 he returned to America and in 1811 he was appointed American Minister to France, a post he held only briefly until his sudden death in Poland in 1812.

Fig. 194
Plate 132

Barlow's portrait is one of the finest of Houdon's late studies. He appears as a massive, powerful, even belligerent individual, with frowning eyes, compressed mouth and jutting chin. His severely cut coat and simple cravat suggest the new democratic ideal which, since the accession of Napoleon in France, was particularly associated with America. His hair is worn short although he does maintain a queue. A marble version of the bust, formerly in the Barlow family, was recently acquired by the White House, Washington. This is not signed or dated, but on the basis of its quality, its history, and its identity with old plasters, cannot be questioned. Ten plasters were made from this in 1912 and presented to various museums in the United States and Europe, in some of which they are now exhibited as originals.[246]

The portrait of Barlow's close friend, the inventor, engineer, and painter, Robert Fulton

(1765–1815), was also exhibited in the Salon of 1804. Fulton began his career as a portrait painter and established a successful practice in Philadelphia at the precocious age of seventeen. In 1786 he went to Europe, where he remained for twenty years. In England his interest in engineering developed and he was active in many projects, even attempting to build a submarine. In his attempts to sell this project to the French government, he was supported by Joel Barlow, whom he met in Paris. After 1802 Fulton designed a successful steamboat and, returning to the United States in 1807, he built the *Clermont*, which led to a new age in water transport. Others had designed operative steamboats before Fulton, but he was one of the pioneers who applied James Watt's invention of the steam engine in a form that opened up aspects of the industrial revolution and shrank the geographic boundaries of the world. It is only coincidence that one of Houdon's first portraits was that of *Diderot*, whose *Encyclopédie* is filled with early experiments in modern technology, and one of his last should be *Fulton*, who realized some of these early dreams. Yet it is a fact that illustrates the remarkable changes in the world documented by the artist.

The marble bust of *Fulton* in the Detroit Institute of Arts is an even finer example of Houdon's late works than the *Barlow*. Again the dress is of the period, sober and undistinguished, although Fulton, a handsome man, paid somewhat more attention to his cravat than did his friend Barlow. His face is serious and dedicated, sensitive and self-confident, as befits the artist-scientist who is also a man of affairs. His curly hair is worn short and without a queue. Like the original plasters of Barlow, this bust is signed and dated under the right shoulder: *houdon f an XII*.[247]

Fig. 195
Plate 133

Plate 144d

CICERO

The statue of *Cicero inveighing against Catiline in the Roman Senate* was originally commissioned under the Directory in 1798 as one of six sculptures of Greek and Roman legislators and orators for the Council Chamber of the Five Hundred. The statues were to be done in marble, but the commission lagged, and Houdon's *Cicero* was only executed in plaster. Under the Consulate the project was revived on a much enlarged scale, with twenty-eight works proposed, great legislators of antiquity to be placed in the Senate Chamber and their modern counterparts on the grand staircase of the Luxembourg Palace. It was at this time, in 1804, that Houdon exhibited his plaster in the Salon. Again the project was never carried out, and Houdon's *Cicero* survives in two plasters, one in the Louvre and the other in the Bibliothèque Nationale. These casts differ in a slight but interesting detail: the version in the Bibliothèque Nationale points with the right hand, palm turned up; that in the Louvre, palm down. According to the *livret* listing, Cicero is shown at the moment when he denounces Catiline with the words, 'From the Senate and from Rome it is time that you depart'. In view of these words the gesture of the Louvre version would seem to be more logical; the explanation may be that the hand in the Bibliothèque Nationale cast was at some time broken and wrongly repaired. In fact it does seem to have been repaired. A possible confirmation of this suggestion is to be seen in the *General Joubert*, 1812, at Versailles, who points in a manner almost identical with the Louvre *Cicero*.

Fig. 198
Plates 134–5

Almost no figure of antiquity was held in higher esteem by the *philosophes* of the French Enlightenment than Cicero; and his reputation as philosopher-statesman and as defender of the Roman Republic against tyranny made him a symbol in the eyes of the French Revolutionaries. Thus in gaining the commission for Cicero among the legislators of antiquity, Houdon would seem to have had one of his greatest opportunities since his statue of Voltaire. Unfortunately, his *Cicero* was denounced by nearly all critics of his time and has fared little better since.[248] Admittedly the surviving plasters, rough, unretouched piece moulds, give little idea how the finished marble might have looked. The Bibliothèque Nationale cast is in the better condition, despite the fact that it has been heavily painted a dark bronze color, which still further obscures its detail. It must be remembered that it was conceived as a marble, not as a bronze. With all its flaws the *Cicero* deserves more careful examination than it has had in the past. It is one of Houdon's few essays in historical classicism, probably based, like the small *Vestal*, on an ancient prototype. The artist was certainly attempting to be more archaeologically correct than, for instance, in his *Diana* or even his *Apollo*. This was the temper of the times and he felt he must conform in a statue that would take its place in a neo-classical company. Comparison with Roman figures of orators or philosophers of the late Republican and early Imperial periods, such as Augustus and his entourage on the Ara Pacis, would indicate that Houdon's *Cicero* is an authentic approximation of Roman antiquity. When the contemporary critics denounced the heaviness of the robe, the lack of idealism in the head, they were criticizing qualities of Roman rather than of neo-classical sculpture. Even in its unfinished form as a painted plaster rather than a marble, the *Cicero* is remarkable not only as an authentic reproduction, but as an authentic and powerful sculpture in its own right. The emaciated, strongly structured head takes us back to the *Saint Bruno* or more recently and specifically to the second, bronze version of *L'Écorché*. The somewhat awkward gesture of the pointing arm cutting across the figure in counterpoise to the turn of the head authenticates the dramatic moment of denunciation.

THE SALON
OF 1806

NAPOLEON

Fig. 201
Plates 136-7

Plate 144e

COLLIN
D'HARLEVILLE
Fig. 197

'SABINE'
Fig. 180

DESPITE the harsh treatment of the *Cicero* by the critics, Houdon was generally respected during his latter years, although to some extent perhaps as a monument from an earlier era. The number of his portrait commissions did decline during the Empire. Napoleon preferred the idealization and aggrandizement of Canova and of French sculptors such as Chinard, Chaudet, Bosio, and Roland, who adapted to the Imperial ideal. Nevertheless Houdon made three portrait busts of the emperor. The first, showing him as consul, has disappeared, but is recorded in a painting by Boilly, *c.* 1802, showing the artist in his studio modeling Bonaparte.

The definitive portrait is the terra cotta at Dijon, dated 1806, in which the emperor is represented without shoulders, on a rectangular herm base, undraped, *à l'antique*. The artist commemorated the great event of gaining sittings by inscribing the right side of the base in cursive letters: *Sa Majesté L'Empereur et Roy fait d'aprés Nature, St Cloud. Aoust 1806. houdon f.* The inscription is done with a particular flourish. Napoleon is strictly frontalized; the concept is that of a young Augustus Imperator. His short, unruly hair, bound with a riband tied with a bow at the back, falls over his forehead in the manner to be recognized, imitated, and caricatured throughout posterity. This may be the finest portrait of one of the most-portrayed men in history. The artist has carried his classic idealization beyond simple frontalization and generalization to a point of abstract structure, in which he has flattened the planes of the head in the ideal formula of Greek antiquity. The interpretation is one of reflection combined with power. Compared with this, Canova's portrait of *Napoleon* as consul, 1802, is mannered, his 1811 statue of *Napoleon* as the gigantic, nude Mars is a conceit. (It was this statue, incidentally, that the Duke of Wellington happily carried back to England after Waterloo.)[249]

The Salon of 1806 contained portraits of *Sa Majesté l'Empereur et Roi* and *Sa Majesté l'Impératrice*. Since no material was indicated, this could have been the Dijon terra cotta and a companion piece of Josephine that has been lost or not identified. In this Salon Houdon also showed a bust of the poet Jean-François Collin d'Harleville, and marbles of Madame von Rodde-Schlözer and the Margrave d'Anspach.[250] There were also two unidentified ladies designated as *Madame F . . .* and *Mademoiselle H . . . . Mademoiselle H.* is identified by Réau as a lost portrait of Sabine Houdon. There exists in New York a marble bust of a young lady signed and dated on the edge of the right shoulder: *houdon. fecit. 1807,* which Germaine Bapst thought to be Sabine but Réau contends is the Comtesse de Montjay. Whoever she is, this is a lovely example of Houdon's late style; shown without shoulders, undraped *à l'antique,* somewhat reminiscent of the *Unknown Girl* of 1774 and 1775 (the marble version of the *Peasant Girl of Frascati* from the Roman period). She is a classic beauty, the bangs of whose Grecian coiffure are, like the rest of her hair, treated in Houdon's characteristic soft and sensuous manner. Whether or not this actually is Sabine at the age of twenty, the large, veiled eyes, the perfect regularity of nose and mouth, are very like the Sabine who looks directly out at us from the 1803 painting by Boilly. In any event she constitutes an appropriate period point to Houdon's roster of *le siècle de la femme*.[251]

THE SALON OF 1806

Fig. 205

THERE were few contributions by Houdon in the last three Salons for which entries are recorded, but they are of some importance. The Salon of 1808 included the marble busts of *Napoleon* and *Josephine*, presumably those now at Versailles; that of 1812 two marble statues, the *General Joubert* (Versailles) and *Voltaire* (Panthéon), and a plaster bust of the *Comte Boissy d'Anglas* (disappeared); and that of 1814 a bust of *Alexander I, Emperor of Russia* (disappeared). The marble of *Napoleon* at Versailles presents him in an unostentatious uniform as a colonel of cavalry in the guard, a telling contrast to the magnificent, bemedalled uniforms in which his marshals of the army liked to appear. Although based on the 1806 terra cotta, frontalized in the same manner, it is more of a precise portrait than an idealized symbol. The heaviness in the chest and the military collar make the face seem more round than in the earlier version, although it is essentially the same, youthful and reflective. The bust is signed under the right arm: *houdon f.* but not dated.

THE SALONS OF 1808, 1812, AND 1814

NAPOLEON
Fig. 200

Josephine appears in a simple, Grecian tunic, her head turned to her right. This is also an honest portrait and makes no effort to flatter or glorify. The rather small, tight mouth of the empress is, if anything, somewhat accentuated. The hair, bound by an undecorated coronet, is shown at the front in metallic curls, uncharacteristic of Houdon, but at the back the chignon is rendered as a mass of hair in the summary chisel strokes the artist normally uses. The bust is signed and dated under the right arm: *houdon f. 1808*.[252]

JOSEPHINE
Fig. 199

Houdon's portrait bust gallery of notable men of the eighteenth century and the era of Napoleon must end on a somewhat tentative note, although the authenticity of the particular bust is not in doubt. I have not seen the portrait of the *Comte Félix-Julien-Jean Bigot de Préameneu* and so must judge it from photographs.[253] Fortunately these are of good quality. The marble, which does not seem to have appeared in any Salon, is signed and dated under the right arm: *houdon f. 1809*, and thus is the last recorded surviving bust by Houdon. Bigot de Préameneu was a high dignitary under both the Revolution and Napoleon. In 1791 he was a deputy for Paris of the Legislative Assembly; in 1802 he was appointed *président* (chairman) of the section for legislation of the Council of State. In this capacity he collaborated in drawing up the *Code Napoléon*. He was obviously a friend of Houdon since he acted as one of his references in the sculptor's nomination for the Legion of Honor. His portrait shows him in the elaborately brocaded uniform of a high functionary at the court of Napoleon. His face is mobile, good-humored, and intelligent; his hair is worn somewhat long in a rather old-fashioned style. There is no observable decline in the artist's powers as a technician or as an observer of nature.

PRÉAMENEU

Fig. 202

In the Salon of 1812 were exhibited two important marble statues. Both fortunately survive, the *General Joubert* at Versailles and the *Standing Voltaire* in the sepulchral vaults of the Panthéon. The former was commissioned in 1806 by the Comte Daru, *Directeur des Bâtiments* under Napoleon, as one of four life-size statues commanded by the emperor, the others being *General Dugommier* by Chaudet, *Custine* by Moitte, *Caffarelli* by Masson. It was stipulated that they should be completed in time for the Salon of 1808, but Houdon's *Joubert* was delayed as a result of his work on the monumental bronze statue of *Napoleon* to be erected on a column in the city of Boulogne.[254] It was finally exhibited in the Salon of 1812 along with the *Standing Voltaire*.

Joubert's statue, long thought to have disappeared, was rediscovered and identified by Gérard Hubert in 1956.[255] It was actually standing in plain sight in the Palace of Versailles where, at some point it had been misattributed to Jean-Baptiste Stouf. A similar fate is hopefully the case with other documented works by Houdon which now can only be noted as 'disappeared'. The statue is dismissed by Réau, the only serious scholar of Houdon to have commented on it after Hubert's identification, but his opinion does not seem to have been based on a very detailed examination of the work itself. Here we are faced with the enduring tradition that Houdon's powers as a sculptor declined radically after the French Revolution. Like so many of the traditions that have grown up around him this has become a cliché based on inadequate study of the works themselves, on judgements made from bad photographs, on shaky attributions, inferior versions, copies and forgeries, or mere repetitions of earlier opinions. Some of these problems were accentuated in the Revolutionary and post-Revolutionary periods as a consequence of the disruption of the times, periodic lack of patronage, and the emergence of a new generation of portrait sculptors, for some of whose works Houdon is blamed. In his 1794 letter to Bachelier the sculptor was already complaining bitterly about the number of copies and deliberate forgeries then being made of his sculptures.[256]

No one can question the fact that Houdon's achievement as a sculptor reached a climax between approximately 1775 and 1785, when he was a young, mature artist working in a still relatively stable society. But if we concentrate our attention on the surviving and unquestionable sculptures he made after 1790, the achievement shows little if any signs of decline. When he retired in 1814 he was seventy-three years old, but only two years earlier he had completed two remarkable large sculptures, the *Joubert* and the *Standing Voltaire*. The portrait busts after 1790 which may be securely attributed to him constitute an impressive list by any standard.[257]

General Barthélemy-Catherine Joubert (1769–99), one of Napoleon's first officers, accompanied him in the Italian campaign, took Piedmont in 1798, as Chief of the Army in Italy, and was killed in the battle of Novi Ligure in 1799. Thus he was only thirty years old when he died, and Houdon's statue was a posthumous interpretation. Joubert is shown as a very young man with a handsome, intent, idealized face, caught at the moment of giving the command to battle. The pose is an unusual, even awkward one, with the right arm raised and extended horizontally across the chest in a dramatic gesture of pointing. *Joubert* provides an interesting contrast to *Maréchal de Tourville*, also at Versailles, also a posthumous statue, with the figure also in the act of giving the command to battle. Whereas *Tourville*, the seventeenth-century hero, symbolizing the ultimate loyalty to one's king, is conceived in a totally Baroque formula, *Joubert* is a classical image of controlled tension. This is not merely a matter of costume although *Tourville*'s elaborate seventeenth-century dress contributes to the effect of furious energy. *Tourville* is portrayed in a typically Baroque twisting pose, with broken contours and surfaces. *Joubert*, on the other hand, in his comparatively simple uniform contained by the heavy vertical folds of the cloak, is conceived as action held in tension rather than expressed through flamboyant gesture. In the latter figure everything is focused on the outstretched, pointing arm; the sculpture is a column dramatically bisected by the horizontal of the arm. The gesture, which at first seems odd and awkward, becomes convincing as a bold and imaginative device to impart the effect of tension.[258]

The *General Joubert* should also be compared with other works by Houdon that may have contributed to its formulation. The gesture was probably suggested by that of the 1804 *Cicero*, particularly the Louvre version with its similar pointing gesture. This comparison would also support the suggestion that *Joubert* in his modern uniform was conceived as a hero of antiquity. Even the battle plans in his left hand reiterate the scroll in the left hand of *Cicero*. The pointing gesture with its separation of the arm from the torso may suggest those of the first version of *L'Écorché* and the surviving *Saint John the Baptist*; in these works reflecting the commanding gesture of *Augustus Imperator*. That the sculptor was consciously recalling aspects of his youthful classicism may also be inferred from the arrangement of the large and heavy cloak falling in severely columnar folds, comparable to the robe of *Saint Bruno* in Rome.

But the most striking analogy is with the standing portrait of George Washington. It is immediately apparent that the sculptor must have restudied his *Washington* and adapted much of its total effect and many of its details to the *Joubert*. The column-like figure and the pose of the legs are the same, but reversed. The *Joubert* is conceived more compactly, with the exception of the extended arm. His plans and the encompassing cloak act more effectively than Washington's plow and *fasces* as a support and frame for the figure; they are more sculpturally integrated with it. The two heroes differ in concept; Washington, having retired from his campaigns to his peaceful, agrarian role, is dignified, but relaxed and benevolent; Joubert in the midst of battle is tense but controlled. Houdon's initial wish to portray Washington in classical garb as a Roman hero-philosopher will be recalled. With Joubert the classicism resides in the columnar form, the control and economy of masses and contours, the drama focused in the gesture. With all their kinship the *Joubert* is very different from the *Washington* in its impact, yet in many ways not inferior.

The bad reputation of the *Standing Voltaire* in the Panthéon is another instance of the 'standardization of error'. Every responsible Houdon scholar who has mentioned it, including Réau in his monumental posthumous study, dismisses it as a sad monument to the sculptor's final decline. Réau says, 'The comparison which one cannot help making with the *Voltaire Seated* of the Comédie Française only throws into stronger relief the decline of a great artist at the end of his inspiration who has nothing more to say.'[259] These are strong words from one of Houdon's greatest champions, one who has particularly defended the later works of the artist. Rather than argue them in detail I would like here in large part to let the sculptures speak for themselves, as far as this is possible through photographic reproductions. This seems appropriate since the *Standing Voltaire* and its critics constitute an outstanding example of one thesis of this study—that Houdon research has too much neglected the study of the sculptures themselves. Although the *Standing Voltaire* is prominently displayed in the vaults of the Panthéon in Paris among the monuments to the great men of France, and every year is visited by thousands of tourists, it is dimly lighted in an environment of sepulchral gloom, difficult to approach, behind a protecting fence, and almost impossible to see. This has been so ever since it was first installed at the beginning of the nineteenth century; and to the best of my knowledge the only photographs that exist of it give but a dim and shadowy suggestion of its appearance.

The ashes of Voltaire had been interred in the Panthéon, formerly the church of Sainte Geneviève, but dedicated to the great men of France since the beginning of the Revolution. In 1806 Napoleon commissioned a standing statue of *Voltaire* for his tomb and Houdon was selected to execute it. He portrayed the ancient *philosophe* with a knotted scarf around his neck, wrapped in a heavy robe gathered up under the left arm and falling to the ground at the back. The drapery reiterates that of the *Seated Voltaire* in that it is a *robe de chambre* intended to suggest a Roman toga. The manner in which it is gathered over and falls away from the hip also has a curious resemblance to the robe of a High Gothic Madonna—an analogy which, had he known of it, would account for the broad smile on Voltaire's face. In his right hand he holds a quill pen, in his left some writing pads. For the head of the statue Houdon used the bust showing him without perruque and without the simulated, beribboned hair of the seated statue. His smiling, almost laughing face lights up with a wonderfully rendered malicious vitality. Even though this is a reproduction of a portrait done by the artist hundreds of times, the interpretation is incredibly fresh, as are the carving and finishing throughout. There can be no question that even though in the six years he was working on this marble he was seriously interrupted by his work on the monumental bronze statue of *Napoleon*, it was Houdon himself who finished it with loving care. Without contending that it is exactly comparable to the *Seated Voltaire*—which, after all, must rank as one of the first portraits in the history of portrait sculpture—the *Standing Voltaire* is in every way a fitting culmination of Houdon's fifty-year career.

BIOGRAPHICAL details of the latter years of Houdon's life are as sparse and unexciting as those of the earlier years, and may be summarized briefly. The Royal Academies had been suppressed in 1793 and were replaced by the Institute of France, to which Houdon was appointed in 1795. He seems to have made a point of attending the meetings of the Institute and to have taken an active part in the instruction of students. In 1795 he held a sale of works from his studio, an event that provides us with another valuable list of his sculptures. In 1801 he moved his lodgings to the old Collège Mazarin, now the École des Beaux-Arts, while still maintaining his studio in the former Bibliothèque du Roi, now the Bibliothèque Nationale. In 1803 the five orders of the former Academies were formally reconstituted under the Institute. The first six sculptors of the new Academy of Fine Arts were Houdon, Pajou, Roland, Julien, Moitte, and Dejoux. In 1803 Houdon was created a Chevalier of Napoleon's newly formed Legion of Honor and in 1805 he was named professor in the special Schools of Painting, Sculpture, and Architecture of the Institute. This appointment to the position left vacant by the death of the sculptor, Julien, was on the unanimous recommendation of faculty and students. From these details it can be seen that, despite changing fashions in the arts, Houdon continued to occupy an honored place within the Academic hierarchy.

His three daughters were married, all apparently successfully: Sabine to Henri-Jean Pineu-Duval, in 1805; Anne-Ange to Dr Jean-Baptiste-Esprit Louyer-Villermay, in 1808; and Antoinette-Claude to Désiré-Raoul Rochette, in 1810. Pineu-Duval at the time of his marriage was assistant director of the Bureau of Science and Fine Arts of the Ministry of the Interior. Rochette, an archaeologist, was a professor at the Collège Louis-le-Grand and became a member of the Academy of Inscriptions and permanent secretary of the Academy of Fine Arts.

Houdon ceased exhibiting in 1814 and there is no record of any sculptures he produced after that year. He seems to have suffered a stroke that may have impaired his mind. Madame Houdon died in 1823. After the sculptor's death, July 15, 1828, a sale of his sculpture was held from his studio, Bibliothèque Nationale, December 15 to 17, 1828. The prices obtained do not indicate much interest in his work.[260]

As might be expected, Houdon's reputation declined during the era of neo-classicism. But with the rise of romanticism and realism in the second and third quarters of the nineteenth century it was quickly revived.[261] François Rude (1784–1855) not only used Houdon's bust of *Marshal Ney* as a model for his statue of the Marshal (1853) but the figure might be a curious pastiche of the *Tourville* and the *Joubert*. The three leading French portrait sculptors of the nineteenth century, David d'Angers (1788–1856), Jean-Baptiste Carpeaux (1827–75), and Auguste Rodin (1840–1917), were all passionate admirers of Houdon; and his reputation has persisted through all the vicissitudes of twentieth-century art, with artists as diverse as Jacques Lipchitz (1891–1973) and Constantin Brancusi (1876–1957) admitting their debt to him.

Full titles are given in the bibliography, pp. 279 ff.

1. *The Jefferson Papers*, Library of Congress; cited, Chinard, *Houdon in America*, 5–6. See also *Jefferson Papers, Franklin Papers, Washington Papers, Diaries of Washington, Writings of Washington* (Bibliography).

2. The emergence of historical neo-classicism at the end of the eighteenth century saw some adverse criticism of Houdon's figure sculpture; and the auction of the contents of his studio on his death in 1828 brought ridiculously low prices. But all through the nineteenth and twentieth centuries the portraits have consistently been held in high regard. Leading portrait sculptors including David d'Angers, Carpeaux, Rodin, Brancusi, and Jacques Lipchitz have been his devoted admirers.

3. Helen C. Frick, 'Madame Jean-Antoine Houdon', 1947, 207–12. Madame Houdon seems to have been a strong-minded lady who managed the sculptor's business affairs with efficiency and carried on his correspondence as well as personal vendettas against Jacques-Louis David and others. Madame de Vandeul, daughter of Diderot, reported marital friction in 1797; and there is perhaps some evidence of coldness in the terms of Madame Houdon's will in 1815. But there was no separation until her death in 1823. The poverty of biographical information on Houdon and his family tends to give inflated significance to the few documents that exist.

4. Register of baptisms of the parish of Saint-Louis de Versailles, 1741; cited by Augustin Jal, *Dictionnaire . . . 1864*; Giacometti, *Houdon*, 1918, I, 13.

5. Archives Nationales, o¹1094. Letter of the Marquis de Marigny, Director of Art and Architecture (*Directeur des Bâtiments*) for the Crown, August 19, 1764, awarding Houdon his fellowship to Rome. This also documents his first prize in 1761, his studies with Slodtz and at the *École des élèves protégés*. See also Réau, *Houdon*, 1964, I, 25, 26, 137–43.

6. Pevsner, *Academies, passim* for curriculum of the Academies.

7. See p. 17 for documentation of these Roman works. Also, Réau, 'Le premier salon de Houdon', 1923.

8. Bottarius and Foggini, *Musei Capitolini*, III (*Statue*), pl. 23; Jones, *. . . Ancient Sculpture . . . in Rome*, 345–6, pl. 86 and *passim*; Arnason, *Houdon*, 1964, 21–5.

9. Arnason, ibid.

10. Arnason, ibid. See also pp. 82 ff., note 203.

11. Arnason, op. cit., 30–2. Another marble of this bust appeared recently in London at the Heim Gallery, with the differences that the nose is unbroken and the iris is lightly indicated as in the *Peasant Girl of Frascati* and the Gotha *Head of a Vestal*.

12. Von Manlich, *Lebenserinnerungen . . .*, Berlin, 1910, 97, 103, 206; reprinted Réau, *Houdon*, 1964, I, 39.

13. *Correspondance des directeurs de l'Académie de France à Rome*, XII (1902), 119, 140; Réau, *Houdon*, 1964, I, 39–41.

14. Calosso, 'Il San Giovanni Battista di . . . Houdon', 1922; *id.*, 'Houdon a Roma', 1923.

15. See note 13. Also Souchal, *Les Slodtz*, 257–69, pls. 34–5.

16. See Appendix 2; also Vitry, 'Une liste d'œuvres de Houdon . . . en 1784', 1907. An inventory by Houdon *c.* 1784 on the eve of his departure for the United States, listing his recollection of his sculptures to that date. There was appended subsequently a very incomplete summary of later works. The *Priest of the Lupercalia* is No. 10. Une figure sur 2 pieds de hauteur, représentant un prêtre des fêtes lupercal morceau dagréé à l'académie, et a été exécuté en bronze.

17. *Proces-verbaux de l'Académie . . .*, VIII, 1769, 19. It is only noted that Houdon showed some of his works. But, we may assume that these were the Roman plasters, probably some of those now at Gotha.

18. Réau, 'Le premier Salon de Houdon', 1923; Mansfeld, *Jean-Antoine Houdon. Sein Werk in Deutschland*, 1955. Mansfeld's unpublished thesis (Greifswald, 1955, available in microfilm) is the most important study of Houdon's sculptures in Germany, and should be consulted for all references to them.

19. *Collection des livrets . . . 1673 . . . 1800* Paris, 1871–2. See Appendix 1 for Houdon's *Salons*.

20. Letter from Marigny to Pierre, cited Réau, *Houdon*, 1964, I, 155. See also Bogyay, 'Nouveaux documents . . .', 1935; Mansfeld, op. cit.

21. *Diderot Salons*, ed. Adhémar and Seznec. Arthur M. Wilson, *Diderot*, New York, 1972. Many studies of Diderot have recently appeared of which the two noted here are among the most important.

22. F. M. Grimm, *Correspondance littéraire, philosophique et critique*, ed. M. Tourneaux, Paris, 1877–82, 16 volumes.

23. See Appendix 1.

24. Vitry, 'Le "Morphée" de Houdon', 1907; Mansfeld, op. cit.

25. The treatment of the hair, while characteristic, and to be referred to frequently, is in itself no guarantee that a sculpture is actually by Houdon. As will be seen, the problems of unidentified busts are much more complicated than that.

26. *Diderot Salons*, IV, 225–6.

27. Charageat, 'Le Sommeil, étude de Houdon . . .', 1950.

28. See Appendix 1. Salon of 1771.

29. The lost medallion of Alexander the Great is of interest in that, according to the *livret* entry, it was designed as a companion piece to an ancient medallion of Minerva. Alexander appears again as a marble bust in the Salon of 1783 'pour Sa Majesté le Roi de Pologne' (National Museum, Warsaw). Houdon made his own medallion of Minerva (Salon of 1777), identified by Réau in the Gotha Museum, which has since disappeared (Réau, *Houdon*, 1964, II, No. 258, pl. CXXXIX). The inventory, *c.* 1784, lists under the year 1780 medallions of Minerva and Apollo made for the Prince of Holstein-Gottorp. The two high-relief heads of young men, one crowned with myrtle, would also seem to be classical studies, and may anticipate the so-called *Roman Youth* of 1775.

30. Grimm, *Correspondance littéraire*, XII, 104.

31. For Bernini see Rudolf Wittkower, *Bernini*, London, 1966, 2, 7, 9, 57, and *passim*. Houdon might also have learned something from Jean-Baptiste Defernex (1729–83), who undercut the eyes of his portraits in a comparable manner. Defernex was a minor but interesting sculptor, whose contributions to the art of the portrait need further clarification. He also characteristically used the formula of the abbreviated torso without shoulders, undraped, *à l'antique*.

32. Giacometti, *Houdon*, 1928, I, 117–48, on the technique of Houdon. Giacometti, a sculptor, discusses Houdon's technique at length and knowledgeably. His remarks on signatures must be used with caution. See also Réau, *Houdon*, 1964, I, 471–81.

32a. Catherine's marble *Diderot* is not exhibited in the Hermitage. Watson, who has seen it, notes a slight variation in the signatures of the 1773 marbles. See F. Watson, 'Diderot and Houdon', *The Artist and the Writer in France*, Oxford 1974.

33. In his letter of 1794 to Bachelier (Appendix 3) Houdon was already complaining bitterly of the unauthorized casts that were being made of his sculptures; on some of which his name was forged, and on others the forgers put their own names. The process has continued to the present day.

34. Tourneux, 'Hommages rendus à Diderot . . .', 1913, reprints the action of the Municipal Council of Langres. Diderot, *Correspondance*, XV, 185–9, 228–31, 233–6.

35. Madame de Vandeul, 'Mémoires . . .' in Diderot, *Œuvres*, I, lix–lx. A plaster in the Museum at Langres is probably one of these five. The bronze is presumably dated 1780—the date of completion or of delivery.

36. Houdon discusses his work as a bronze caster in the letter to Bachelier (Appendix 3).

37. Vitry, 'Notes sur les différents logements . . .', 1907.

38. Bogyay, 'Nouveaux documents . . .', 1935.

38a. This note is on p. 121 below.

39. As has been noted in his comments on Houdon's *Morpheus*, Diderot enjoyed correcting the iconography of artists; and in many instances advising them on subject, iconography, and composition.

40. This uncharacteristic, shallow indentation of the eyes reappears in the marble of Madame Servat (Fig. 90), signed and dated 1776. Again the technique could have been suggested by the physiognomy of the lady. A marble bust of Catherine, dated 1771, by the Russian sculptor F. I. Shubin (1740–1805) has the same shallow treatment of the eyes. This work, now in the Victoria and Albert Museum, London, is recorded as coming from the Galitzin family. It is tempting to think that Houdon may have seen a version of this bust in the possession of the Russian Ambassador in Paris, but we have no evidence.

41. See Panofsky, *Tomb Sculpture*, a classic survey which, unfortunately does not go beyond Bernini; see also Ingersoll-Smouse, *La Sculpture funéraire en France au XVIIIe siècle*.

42. Ingersoll-Smouse, ibid., 169–77; Réau, *Pigalle*, 86 ff; Souchal, *Les Slodtz*, 323 ff.

43. For recent reappraisals of neo-classicism and its relations to the earlier eighteenth-century traditions of classicism, see: Rosenblum, *Transformations . . .*; Honour, *Neo-Classicism*, 1968; Kalnein and Levey, *Art and Architecture of the Eighteenth Century in France*; *The Age of Neo-classicism*, London, 1972 (Exhibition catalogue). Houdon's classicism is presented throughout this study as a shifting complex of influences from antiquity, the Renaissance, the rococo, and the new wave of historical neo-classicism. With all this it can be argued that in his consciously classical derivations he achieved a synthesis remarkable in its fidelity to the quality of ancient ideal art.

44. Although I have been able to find no absolutely consistent pattern in Houdon's signatures, these tombs provide important evidence for his tendency to date a particular piece as it was about to leave his studio rather than when the original model was made. Thus the *Diderot* marbles based on a model of 1771 are dated 1773 and 1775, presumably the dates when they were commissioned. Original dates are preserved in some recasts by Houdon and recent plasters of certain *Franklins* and other popular heroes of the Enlightenment.

45. Archives Nationales o¹1914; Courajod, *L'École royale . . .*, 1874, 130.

46. Ibid.

47. Desazars de Montgaillard, *Les artistes toulousains . . .*, cited Réau, *Houdon*, 1964, I, 149.

48. Archives Nationales, o¹1914³.

49. Cited by Réau, *Houdon*, 1964, I, 40–1. There is no ascertainable evidence that Catherine actually acquired it.

50. See Appendix 1, *Livrets of Salons*, 1775.

51. Bachaumont, *Mémoires secrets*, Salon of 1775; *Mercure de France*, October 1775. See notes 41, 42.

52. Bogyay, '*Nouveaux documents . . .*'.

53. See note 11.

54. Bachaumont, op. cit.

55. Diderot had a particular passion for Richardson's novels and Greuze's moral tales. Madame Roland on the other hand remarked concerning *The Broken Pitcher* that one doubted that the girl looked sufficiently disturbed not to be tempted to repeat her mistake. (Cited Kalnein-Levey, 145). See also *Diderot Salons*, 'Greuze', *passim*.

56. The Salons of 1775 to 1785 represent Houdon at the height of his powers as a sculptor. Between 1775 and 1777 also he established most of the different types he was to use in subsequent portrait busts. For this reason these initial examples are dealt with at some length. Attention is focused on those I consider to be the best examples. Other superior examples are mentioned in text or notes, with no attempt at all-inclusiveness.

57. Brière, 'Notes sur quelques bustes de Houdon'; Catalogue, *The Frick Collection*, IV, 120–6. Aside from the Frick marble, there is the marble in the Victoria and Albert Museum; a bronzed plaster in the Musée de Peinture et de Sculpture at Orléans; and a marble in the Musée Fabre, Montpellier.

58. Arnason, *Houdon*, 1964, 40–2; Dakin, *Turgot*. Aside from the marble in the Turgot family, Château de Lantheuil, and the plaster in the American Philosophical Society, there is another plaster in the Courty Collection, Châtillon-sous-Bagneux; and a particularly fine plaster in the Art Institute of Chicago.

59. Newman, *Gluck and the Opera*; Einstein, *Gluck*. Joret, 'Houdon et le duc de Weimar'; Bogyay, 'Houdon à Weimar'; *Houdon*, Berlin, 1955; Mansfeld, *Houdon*, Greifswald, 1955.

60. For the marble of *Madame His*, see A. Gilou, in *Connaissance des Arts*, October 1960; for *Sophie Arnould*, E. and J. de Goncourt, *Sophie Arnould*; Beaulieu, 'Le buste de la cantatrice, Sophie Arnould . . .'; for the *Comtesse du Cayla*, Catalogue, *The Frick Collection*, IV, 114–19; for the *Baroness de la Houze*, Wark, *Sculpture in the Huntington Collections*, pls XXXVII–XL and pp. 77–8.

61. While these remarks apply in general to marbles unquestionably from Houdon's hand, particular note should be made of other masterpieces of the latter 1770s, such as: *Sophie Arnould* (Louvre), the *Comtesse du Cayla* (Frick Collection), *Madame Adélaïde* (Louvre), *Molière* (Comédie Française), *Voltaire* (Comédie Française), *Diana* (bust, National Gallery, Washington); a list that can be extended.

62. It is often asserted that a given bust by Houdon that still survives is the one that appeared in the Salon. This lends authenticity to the work; but the claim is usually difficult to prove. In this instance, however, we are safe in assuming that the marble of *Turgot* still in his family is that which was made for him and shown in the Salon of 1777. This being so, the date of 1778 would be another instance of Houdon signing and dating a work at the time he was about to deliver it to his client.

63. *A Catalogue . . . of the American Philosophical Society*, 93–4.

64. See Appendix 3.

65. This is particularly evident in the portraits of the 1770s, when the sculptor might be described as in his most rococo phase. See notably the *Tourville* of 1779; but the Richmond *Lafayette* and the *Bailli de Suffren*, both Salon of 1787, demonstrate that he continued to be capable of a *tour de force* of decorative carving when the particular commission suggested it.

66. Du Pont de Nemours, 'Lettre sur le Salon de 1777 . . .'.

67. Although the marble of *Gluck* was destroyed in the fire of the Paris Opéra, there survive a substantial number of plasters and terra cottas, with and without shoulders. Of the larger type there are three plasters in Germany, in the Schwerin Museum, the State Library in Weimar, and the State Museum in East Berlin. Those at Weimar and Schwerin have impeccable histories and are certainly among the best surviving casts. The Schwerin bust, painted terra cotta, is open at the back and bears the *cachet d'atelier*. The Weimar bust, painted bronze color, of which the letter of transmission from Houdon to Charles-Auguste, Duke of Weimar, exists (cited, Joret, 'Houdon et le duc de Weimar . . .'), has an unusual but important feature for a plaster, in that it is meticulously signed, dated, and inscribed on the base: Houdon Sculpteur du Roy 1775, Bibliotheque Royal. This was probably a special mark of respect from the young sculptor to the duke. The lettering of the inscription, in which Houdon even included his address, is identical with that used on the tombs of the Galitzin in Moscow, notably the signature on that of Prince Mikhail which is dated 1774. There are terra cottas of the *Gluck* without shoulders in the collections of René Huyghe, Paris (signed), and Michael Hall, New York; and a plaster in the Louvre. A signed terra cotta of the version with shoulders is in the Royal Academy of Music, London, but placed so high, above a door, that I could not examine it. The popularity of Gluck led to a large number of reduced bronze replicas, both from Houdon's studio and later copies, all that I have seen of the type without shoulders. Finally, there exist a number of nineteenth-century copies of the larger bust, including a marble in the Hermitage, Leningrad. Comment here has been confined (with the exception of that in the collection of Monsieur Huyghe) to examples I have seen and photographed. Other busts exist, such as the plasters in the Courty Collection, with the *cachet d'atelier*, and in the Châalis Museum;

and still others are recorded. Even more than the *Diderot*, Houdon's first 'Great Man', the *Gluck*, the portrait of an artist whose world reputation has grown continually since the eighteenth century, illustrates the problems of proliferation in such portraits by the sculptor.

68. See Helen C. Frick, 'Madame Jean-Antoine Houdon', for Madame His's relations with the Houdon family. Houdon in 1775 was already engaged on the theme of *Diana*. See p. 43. The diagonal quiver strap appears on the marble *Diana* in Lisbon and the marble bust in Washington. It appears on the bust of *Madame de Jaucourt* (Salon of 1777, Louvre), who is a somewhat more convincing approximation of Diana than is *Madame His*. *Mademoiselle Arnould* (Salon of 1775, Louvre) wears a broad, diagonally arranged riband, decorated with moon and stars to identify her as a priestess of Diana (although at this moment a trifle anachronistically).

69. Mansfeld, *Jean-Antoine Houdon . . . Werk in Deutschland.*

70. R. R. Wark, in his catalogue of the *Sculpture in the Huntington Collection*, has provided a rare example of a museum curator questioning a well-established identification of a subject by Houdon in his own museum. Although this is one of the sculptor's finest portraits of a lady of the old regime, Wark quite correctly points out that there is no positive evidence that the lady is indeed the Baroness de la Houze. See pp. 77–8, and plates XXXVII to XL in his catalogue. The problem deserves recapitulation here. A plaster bust of the 'Baroness' is listed in the *livret* for 1775. A marble bust in the Salon of 1777 is designated, Portrait de Madame de *** (No. 242). The drawing by Saint-Aubin in his copy of the *livret* identifies this unknown lady with the bust in the Huntington Collection. It was frequently Houdon's custom to exhibit the plaster first, followed by the marble in the next Salon. Thus the plaster of the *Comtesse du Cayla* in the Salon of 1775 was followed by the marble in 1777. Since the 'Baroness' does not reappear by name in 1777 but there is an obviously important bust of an unknown lady, it would seem reasonable to the owner or vendor of the bust to assume that it represents the marble of the 'Baroness'. Giacometti and Réau among other critics have assumed this to be the case; but as Dr Wark demonstrates, there is no real evidence. There is one other known bust of the 'Baroness', a plaster in which the torso is reduced in scale, in the possession of the Waresquiel family, where it was known as Madame Rilliet, and accompanied by a plaster of 'Monsieur Rilliet', who is actually Dr Tronchin. (See also Girod de l'Ain, 'Les Thellusson et les artistes'.) In the face of all the mediocre busts that have been attached to the names of lost subjects by Houdon, it is refreshing to find so magnificent and monumental a sculpture as

the 'Baroness' in search of an identity. Dr Wark mentions, perhaps hopefully, Giacometti's original contention that this was Madame du Barry. Again, as he recognizes, there is no evidence, although there is some similarity to existing portraits. In the light of the importance, scale, and quality of the sculpture this is still an intriguing though distant possibility. In 1777 Madame du Barry was thirty-four years old, still beautiful, but living in retirement since the death of Louis XV in 1774. The more prudish Louis XVI or d'Angiviller, *Directeur des Bâtiments*, might well have objected to her splendid presentation in a Salon, particularly a Salon that featured the two elderly aunts of the king and his brother and sister-in-law. The 'Baroness de la Houze' is impressively signed on the base: A. HOUDON FECIT AN. 1777. I have continued to use her traditional name in quotes in the hope that it might some day be confirmed or that she might be presented with an even more impressive identity.

71. Souchal, *Les Slodtz*, 195–200, 658–9, plate 16. *Diderot Salons.*

72. Souchal, ibid.; Wittkower, *Bernini*, plates 20, 19, 75, 7.

73. Marble, Louvre, Paris, signed and dated 1775. 'We the undersigned A. Houdon, on the one part, and Magdelaine Sophie Arnould, on the other part, agree in the following, Know: That I, A. Houdon, will make the bust in marble of Mademoiselle Arnould as Iphigenia, that I promise to deliver it to the said *Mademoiselle Arnould* by next August, and that I shall make 30 more copies of this bust in plaster on bases, finished by myself [réparé par moi], and that I shall deliver these to her by next August. Further that I shall deliver also to Mademoiselle Arnould the bust in clay [en terre] that served as a model, by next August.

'I further engage not to make, nor to give nor sell any other of these busts in marble, plaster or terra cotta, beyond the number above, a total of 32 busts, to any person whatever except to Mademoiselle Arnould or her representative.

'And I Mademoiselle Arnould promise and engage to pay to Monsieur Houdon for the 32 busts specified above the sum of 3,800 livres.†

'900 livres to be paid the end of this April. 900 livres the end of May, and 2,000 livres as soon as the marble bust is finished.

'Further, I, A. Houdon promise Mademoiselle Arnould to furnish her with finished busts in plaster of which she may have need beyond the 30 designated, at a price of 60 livres apiece, under the conditions that I will not be responsible for their delivery, and particularly that I can not be asked, without my specific agreement, for more than 20 extra.

'Agreed between us at Paris the 5 April 1775

Signed: Sophie Arnould
A. Houdon.'

Reprinted, Lami, *Dictionnaire des sculpteurs . . .*, Paris, 1910, I, 416–17.

† The *livre* is generally equated to one American dollar. The prices indicate the relative importance of marbles and plasters; as the entire transaction illustrates the tradition of almost indefinite duplication of plasters. The significant phrase is, 'réparé par moi', the sculptor's guarantee to finish the plaster himself. The contract also documents Houdon's technique of beginning with a clay—then fired to terra cotta model to preserve it.

74. Pope-Hennessy and Hodgkinson, *Sculpture in the Frick Collection*, New York, 1970, IV, 114–119. The sculpture of the *Comtesse du Cayla* is signed and dated on the back of the base: A. HOUDON, F. AN. 1777. The form of the lettering is almost identical with that of the 'Baroness de La Houze', of the same year. To this point the sculptor is still signing a number of his marbles, A. rather than J. A. Houdon. Although the cursive signature occurs on the medallions of the Dukes of Saxe-Gotha (1773), and on the tomb of Prince Alexis Galitzin in Moscow (1774) it does not become common until after 1780.

74a. In his inventory, c. 1784, Houdon lists under the year 1779, No. 68. A group of a kiss of a bacchante. Model to be executed in marble. Under the year 1780: No. 78. Two groups in marble representing the *Kiss Given* and the other *Received*, executed several times in marble. These notes would seem to confirm the date of the marble sculpture, assuming the possibility of a discrepancy of a year or two. On the other hand a letter in the archives of the Louvre, dated 1843, from Monsieur Dubois, Curator of Ancient Art, refers to a date of 1774 on a *Baiser donné* by Houdon then being offered to the Museum. Monsieur Dubois recommended rejection on the ground of its degenerate [rococo] style and its degree of lewdness (Vitry, BSHAF, 1908). Since he emphasizes the date in support of his opinion, this letter would seem to confirm the fact that Houdon had created the *Baiser donné* as early as 1774. This date accords with the style of the piece, its relations to the *Morpheus* and busts exhibited in the Salon of 1775. Since he made many replicas, the date of 1778 on the New York version would be another confirmation of his habit of signing and dating a specific work as he completed it or as it left his studio. See p. 13 for the marble versions dated 1774 and 1775 of the *Peasant Girl of Frascati*, from the Roman period. There exists a marble of *Le Baiser rendu* in New York, but this seems to be a 19th-century variant.

75. *Procès-verbaux de l'Académie Royale*, VIII, 1777, 273. '*M. Houdon, S., received—M. Pigalle*, Assistant Rector, presented to the Company *le sieur Jean-Antoine Houdon*, Sculptor, Agréé, born at Versailles, who had brought the piece commanded from him for

his reception, representing *Morpheus*. By the customary voice vote the Academy received and admits *le sieur Houdon* as Academician, to participate in its meetings and enjoy the privileges, prerogatives and honors belonging to this estate, with the responsibility to observe the Statutes and Rules of the Academy, to which he gave his oath between the hands of *M. Pierre*, Director.' The sponsorship of Pigalle was probably in his capacity as one of Houdon's principal teachers.

76. In 1777 Pigalle was *Adjoint à Recteur* and became *Recteur* in 1779, next to Pierre (a painter) *Directeur*. He was thus, until 1783, not long before his death in 1785, the senior sculptor in the Academy; a fact that gives added significance to his sponsorship of Houdon. See note 75, and *Procès-verbaux de l'Académie Royale*, VIII.

77. *Livrets* of Salons, 1777, 1789 [see Appendix I, pp. 123, 125 below].

78. See note 70.

79. See for instance: *Choiseul-Praslin*, 1780; *Larive*, 1784; *Mirabeau* (with arms), 1791.

80. For *Madame Adélaïde* see Aubert, 'Le buste de Madame Adélaïde . . .'; For *Madame Victoire* see Vitry, 'La sculpture française au Musée Wallace'.

81. Archives Nationales o¹1918; o¹1922ᴬ; o¹1918¹; o¹1922; o¹1918²; Furcy-Raynaud, *Inventaire des sculptures . . .*, 1927, pp. 157, 159, 160, 161, 162; Hart and Biddle, *Houdon*, p. 22, quote the letter from Houdon dated 1789 (Roberts Collection, Haverford College) at which time the sculptor was still seeking payment; Réau, *Houdon*, 1964, quotes the entire correspondence, pp. 75–6.

82. Musée du Louvre, *Les Sculptures . . .*, 1957, pp. XIII–XIV; Arnason, *Houdon*, 1964, pp. 36–9; Vitry, 'Le buste de la comtesse de Jaucourt', 1937.

83. Wildenstein Gallery, New York.

84. Réau, *Houdon*, 1964, I, 400, thought the bust had been destroyed in 1944, in an air raid. Having seen and photographed the marble in the State Museum, East Berlin, in August 1973, I am happy to say that although the surface has been damaged by fire, it is intact.

85. Réau, L'œuvre de Houdon en Russie', 141; Réau, *Houdon*, 1964, I, 399–400, and II, 44, pl. CIII; Vitry, 'Un buste de Houdon au Musée de Berlin'. Réau, who knew the Russian works by Houdon well, refers to two nineteenth-century copies of the Vietinghoff bust at Riga, as evidence that the 1791 marble is the same as the plaster in the Salon of 1777. It may also be pointed out that the dress and perruque of the baron fit better with the 1777 date; the cursive signature is the same as that on the *d'Alembert* (1778) and *Buffon* (1781) at Gotha, among others; and the baron, born in 1722, looks more like a man in his fifties than in his late sixties. Since I have not seen the actual

copies described by Réau, we are dealing here with an hypothesis, but we know that Houdon did—in the case of *Diderot* among others—re-date earlier busts.

86. Arnason, *Houdon*, 1964, 33–5. The two bronzes illustrated I now believe to be later replicas. There are similar replicas in the Hermitage and the Pushkin Museum, Moscow. The two terra cottas in the Louvre are the key versions. Also to be noted are the marbles in the National Gallery, Washington, although *Louise* is of better quality than *Alexandre*. The children's portraits are still being reproduced in Sèvres porcelains and terra cottas.

87. Michel, 'Acquisitions du Département de la sculpture . . .', 1903.

88. Metropolitan Museum, New York, signed and dated: F. P. Houdon, 1779.

89. Aside from the detailed description in the *livret* for the Salon of 1777 (see Appendix I), the *Naiad* is listed in the inventory, *c.* 1784, under the year 1777: No. 46. Une figure représentant une nayade versant avec sa cruche de l'eau dans une coquille posé à ses pieds pour servir de fontaine au jardin de Mʳ Boutin. In the letter to Bachelier, 1794, Houdon lists it: Le modèle d'une *Nayade* grandeur naturelle, à moy. It is also mentioned in the *procès-verbal* of the 1828 sale with a price of 50 francs: *Nayade*. Statue plâtre peint. Bachaumont described the *Naiad* in his description of the Salon of 1777 (*Mémoires secrets*, 1777). The drawing by Saint-Aubin, formerly in the collection of Jean Masson, was acquired, according to Réau, by a Monsieur Goukassov in 1923 (Réau, *Houdon*, 1964, I, 235; II, 15 and pl. CLV).

90. See pp. 62 f. for a recapitulation of Houdon's tomb sculpture.

91. Vitry, 'Houdon animalier'; the *Dead Thrush* is in a private collection; a *Deer Attacked [terrassé] by an Eagle* (Fig. 98) is in another private collection in Paris. See also Giacometti, *Un lévrier, terre-cuite originale par Houdon*, Paris, n.d. This last may be questioned.

92. See *Salon of 1771*, above, p. 19, and note 29.

93. Réau, *Houdon*, 1964, II, pl. CXXXIX (258), refers only to a marble, but the Gotha Museum inventory describes its lost *Minerva* as a plaster. From the illustration it is impossible to distinguish.

94. The *Minerva* of 1777 is of importance, even though it has disappeared, as another example of classical subject to which Houdon returns periodically. Aside from related medallions or busts noted above (Note 29), the Salon of 1781 included a medallion plaster bas-relief representing the head of the *Sun*. This designation would suggest the image in full face surrounded by rays of light rather than the profile view of Apollo, his hair blown by the wind. The medallions of Minerva and Apollo made for the Prince of Holstein-Gottorp (in-

ventory of *c.* 1784 under the year 1780) had Apollo 'repoussé par le vent'. The 1777 *Minerva* was drawn in the margin of the *livret* by Saint-Aubin and, although no *Apollo* by Houdon is noted in that Salon, Saint-Aubin drew, at the top of the same page on which the *Minerva* appeared, a medallion of what must be an *Apollo* in profile with his hair blown back by the wind. There are other references to Apollo and Minerva, but the closest surviving approximation to the lost relief medallion of Apollo is probably the medallion of the aeronauts Montgolfier (1783, Musée de l'Air, Paris). The bronze *Apollo* (1788, Gulbenkian Collection, Lisbon) also has wind-blown hair; as has the *Priest of the Lupercalia* (*c.* 1769, Gotha), who may have been a prototype. Réau cites a marble medallion of *Apollo*, signed and dated, Houdon F. 1792, in the collection of L. Gouvy, Paris. For the *Minerva* formerly at Gotha perhaps the closest parallel is the marble head of a *Vestal* in the Louvre, signed and dated: HOUDON F. 1788. This *Vestal* has a drape over her head rather than a helmet, but her features have something of the same heaviness.

95. Cott, 'A Note on Houdon's Bust of Diana'. Another marble bust of Diana is recorded in the collection of the Comte Mansard de Sagonne. See Darl, *Le buste de Diane*. Despite Darl, this cannot be the bust in the Salon of 1777, since the Diana he describes does not have the quiver strap clearly recorded in Saint-Aubin's drawing.

A third marble, with the strap, formerly in the collection of King Stanislas-Auguste Poniatowski—who ordered the bust of *Alexander the Great* from Houdon—disappeared in World War II. According to Réau this was signed: A. HOUDON F. AN. 1777 on the strap, and also on the end of the right arm stump, in cursive letters: *houdon 1780*. The double signature and date are odd but not impossible (Réau, *Houdon*, 1964, I, 234). The bust of Diana has been reproduced many times after Houdon's death, in bronze, terra cotta, marble, and porcelain. In a number of these the breasts have been chastely draped.

96. Réau, *Houdon*, 1964, discusses the *Diana* at length (I, 223–4; II, 12–13, pls. IV–VIII, and *passim*), and reprints the pertinent documents (I, 43–7, 50); the catalogue of the Frick Collection, IV (1970), 127–39, is the best recent account.

97. Bogyay, 'Nouveaux documents . . .'. Cited Réau, op. cit., I, 43 and 50.

98. The *livret* entry should be noted: 'No. 248. Marble bust of a *Diana*, of which the model, life-size, was made at the Bibliothèque du Roy. This *Diana* to be executed in marble and placed in the gardens of his Highness the Duke of Saxe-Gotha.' The statue exhibited in Houdon's studio, Bibliothèque du Roi, was a plaster, as noted by the commentator in the *Mercure de France*, October 1777, and by

Bachaumont, *Mémoires secrets*, April 21, 1778. Since a life-size plaster figure, in contrast to a marble, is relatively easily transported, it may have been its explicit nudity that prevented its exhibition at the Salon. Roger-Milès, *Les Dianes de Houdon*, discusses 'les caprices de la pudeur esthétique à la fin du XVIIIᵉ siècle'.

99. See above, pp. 1, 3, for sculptures of *Diana* before Houdon.

100. *Mémoires secrets*, Salon of 1777.

101. Although male and female nudes have been primary subjects for the sculptor since the beginning of art and religion, and it has been customary to represent the male genitals, except in periods when puritanism demanded a fig leaf (see note 225a) or some comparable covering, in the Western tradition, stemming from Greece and Rome, the delusion has been perpetuated that the female nude is devoid of external genitalia. Perhaps the major exception is representational sculpture of the latter twentieth century. In the eighteenth century certain sculptors of the erotic, such as Clodion, on occasion did add this detail, but only in small *sculptures d'appartement* intended for a special clientele of *amateurs des arts et des curiosités*. Most versions of Houdon's *Diana* have been subsequently 'corrected', with the exception of the marble and the posthumous bronze at Tours. The latter, as noted below, was cast from a plaster dated 1776. When the Louvre acquired its bronze cast in 1829, orders were given to hammer out what is somewhat indelicately described as 'le bas du ventre que l'artiste avait représenté d'une façon indécente' (MS. Desloynes Collection, Bibliothèque Nationale). Giacometti, *Houdon*, 1928, II, 230 ff, classifies the *Dianas* as 'les *Dianes* sexuées' and 'les *Dianes* corrigées'. See also L. Roger-Milès, *Les Dianes de Houdon et les caprices de la pudeur esthétique à la fin du XVIIIᵉ siècle*.

102. Bogyay, 'Nouveaux documents . . .', 1935; Archives Nationales, *Minutier central* LXXI, file 35. The contract between Houdon and Grimm, representing the Duke of Saxe-Gotha, is quite explicit in stating that the statue has been paid for and belongs to the duke.

103. Réau, *Correspondance artistique de Grimm avec Catherine II*, 1932, 151–2; *Catalogue de la Collection . . . Gulbenkian*, 1960; Réau, 'La Diane et l'Apollon de Houdon à la Fondation Gulbenkian', 1960.

104. The marble *Diana*, after all, was Grimm's idea, not that of the duke. The latter's feelings about the entire transaction are not recorded, but Grimm certainly remained in good standing. I have a suspicion, undocumented, that Saxe-Gotha had agreed to the change before Grimm approached Catherine. It may be that the duke, whose extensive collection of works by Houdon consisted almost exclusively of plasters, was relieved to be relieved of this very expensive marble. He continued to acquire plaster

portraits by Houdon, including *Franklin*, *Molière*, *Rousseau*, *Lalande*, and *Bailly*; and as late as 1806 members of the house of Saxe-Gotha remained on close and cordial terms with the artist and his family.

105. *Livret*, Salon of 1783 (See Appendix 1): 'A statue of *Diana* in bronze, at Monsieur Girardot de Marigny, Rue Vivienne'; Wark, *Sculpture in the Huntington Collection*, 78–9 and pls. XLI, XLII; Courajod, 'La Diane . . . au Musée du Louvre', 1879; *Les Sculptures . . . au Louvre* (Insert, XVIIIᵉ–XIXᵉ *Siècles*), VI–VIII; Catalogue, *The Frick Collection*, IV, 1970, 127–39. The posthumous cast at Tours has the signature, Houdon 1776, and the founder's signature, Carbonneaux 1839. It was cast after a plaster, not impossibly the painted plaster listed in the 1828 sale of the contents of the artist's studio. (See Appendix 5.) This plaster has disappeared as has a lead version listed in the inventory, c. 1784, under the year 1781. The Louvre bronze was also in the 1828 sale, but apparently was withdrawn, and in 1829 was presented to the Louvre by the artist's son-in-law, Raoul Rochette. Houdon made a number of reduced statues in bronze, marble, and terra cotta, and, needless to say, these continued to be made throughout the nineteenth century. Houdon's *Diana* has been adapted by several nineteenth-century sculptors, notably Augustus Saint-Gaudens, whose bronze *Diana* is in the Philadelphia Museum of Art.

The bronze *Diana* made for Girardot de Marigny in 1782 was Houdon's first life-size figure cast in bronze. The *mémoire* addressed to Bachelier, dated 1794, is a most important document, describing among other things the sculptor's experiments in bronze casting. (See Appendix 3.)

106. When Houdon exhibited a bronze of his *Diana* in the Salon of 1802, critics, now conditioned to the archaeological neo-classicism of Canova and his French followers, were predictably not kind. See text p. 94.

107. The most comprehensive recent study of the Enlightenment is Peter Gay, *The Enlightenment: An Interpretation*, Vol. I, 1966, Vol. II, 1969, New York. This contains a monumental critical bibliography.

108. Collection the Comte and Comtesse de Contades. There is a plaster in the Louvre. Mention has been made of the difficulties in identifying many of Houdon's subjects when we move outside the circle of figures like Voltaire, Rousseau, or Washington, known to posterity. The marble of *de Nicolay* has the sort of documentation that one wishes were more common. There is first the inscription. The Comtesse de Contades is a de Nicolay and the bust came down directly in her family. De Nicolay is clearly recognizable in two of the paintings by Boilly of Houdon's studio. A portrait of de Nicolay's son, by the Swedish

painter, Roslin, displays the bust in the background.

109. Brière, 'Le buste de Caumartin par Houdon'. There is a bronzed plaster at the Hospital at Lille, where Caumartin was a financial administrator before proceeding to Paris.

110. *Registre des délibérations de la Comédie-Française*, September 30, 1776. Arnason, *Houdon*, 1964, 43–7; Dacier, *Le Musée de la Comédie-Française*, 8–9, 139, 146, 181–3, and *passim*.

111. *Journal de Paris*, March 10, April 14, 1778; *Correspondance littéraire*, May 1778, November 1778. In the latter d'Alembert, the permanent secretary, announced the donation to the Académie Française of the bust of *Molière* with that of Voltaire. An inscription was voted in honor of Molière—he had never been a member of the Academy—*Rien ne manque à sa gloire, il manquait à la nôtre*.

112. Reprinted in Guiffrey, *Les Caffieri*, 287.

113. In 1784 and 1785 several letters were exchanged between Caffieri, Franklin, and Franklin's grandson, who acted as his secretary, in which Caffieri protested and the Franklins turned him off rather brusquely. Ingersoll-Smouse, 'Lettres inédites de J.-J. Caffieri', *Franklin Papers*, February 19, April 3, June 20, 1785; Guiffrey, *Les Caffieri*, reprints a substantial portion of Caffieri's correspondence, particularly with d'Angiviller, *Directeur des Bâtiments*. These are fascinating illustrations of Caffieri's almost paranoid personality and of d'Angiviller's remarkable patience with hysterical demands. In comparison, Houdon's few requests of the *Directeur* are modest and restrained. Nevertheless it must be recalled that Caffieri was an excellent and established portrait sculptor when Houdon appeared on the scene; and the acclaim of the younger man must have been at times frustrating and infuriating.

114. Stein, *Pajou*, 384.

115. Montaiglon and Duplessis, *Houdon*, 1855, 347–50, reprint the exchange between Madame Houdon and David.

116. Buffenoir, 'Jean-Jacques Rousseau et Houdon', publishes the letter of the Marquis de Girardin to his daughter, Sophie, describing the event. See also, Arnason, *Houdon*, 1964, 66–9, with bibliography.

117. Seymour, 'Houdon's Marble Bust of d'Alembert'; Arnason, *Houdon*, 1964, 63–5. Despite the date of 1779 on the marble, Seymour believes that it was made between 1790 and 1800. Although in 1964 I tended to accept his dating, further study of Houdon's pattern of dating raises some questions. I know of no other instance where the artist has pre-dated a later bust in this manner. The statue of Washington is dated 1788 although not delivered until 1796. Presumably it was finished in 1788, and delivery was delayed by the French Revolution among other events the sculptor

could not anticipate. On the other hand, the marble in Berlin of the *Baron de Vietinghoff*, dated 1791, seems to be a replica of the plaster in the Salon of 1777. The artist's tendency to sign and date a work as it left his studio has been noted. We do not know certainly that the Yale *d'Alembert* is actually the marble exhibited in 1802. Even if it is, after 1790 Houdon was submitting to the Salons busts of earlier works. Stylistically, I think the *d'Alembert* is quite comparable to other portraits of the late 1770s. The problem of Houdon's late style is a difficult one, compounded by doubtful attributions. Portraits of his children in marble, such as the *Sabine* in the Huntington Collection, or the *Claudine*, at Worcester, both *c.* 1791, are in every way comparable to the *Brongniart* children, *c.* 1777. Distinctions can be drawn after 1800, but the *Fulton* at Detroit, the *Dorothea von Rodde-Schlözer* in Berlin, and even the *Standing Voltaire*, 1812, in the Panthéon, retain to a remarkable degree the earlier virtuosity in the carving of the marble.

118. The scene was engraved by Gaucher after a drawing by Moreau. The engraving is inscribed: *Hommages rendus à Voltaire sur le Théâtre françois le 30 mars 1778 après la 6e représentation d'Irène.* (Reproduced Hart and Biddle, pl. XXXI).

119. Discourse of the Marquis de Villevieille at Montpellier. See note 121.

120. Archives Nationales 0¹845. Letter of Houdon to d'Angiviller, February 10, 1780.

121. *Rapport fait à la Société des sciences et belles-lettres de Montpellier sur l'inauguration de la statue de Voltaire au musée de la même ville*, January 5, 1803. This is the terra cotta version of the *Seated Voltaire* at Montpellier. Guiffrey, *Les Caffieri*, 276–89, reprints and discusses the account. He argues that the bust of Voltaire shown at the performance of *Irène* could not have been that of Houdon, but was a lost bust by Caffieri. His argument is not convincing, as a glance at the Gaucher engraving would make evident. (See note 118).

122. Réau, *Pigalle*, 60–7.

123. Sauerländer, *Jean-Antoine Houdon, Voltaire*, 1963, is the best account. See also Arnason, *Houdon*, 1964, 48–53, bibliography; Benisovitch, 'Houdon's Statue of Voltaire Seated'. The marble of the *Seated Voltaire* in the Hermitage has been somewhat neglected by students of Houdon, perhaps because the Comédie-Française version is more accessible and has been reproduced much more frequently. Réau refers to it as a 'replica', a description that is perhaps correct in that it was the second of the two marbles. On the other hand, it is a work of magnificent quality, comparable in every detail with the first marble. Houdon, ever conscious of the importance of pleasing Catherine, seems to have exercised particular care in finishing the sculpture himself. The illustrations, as far as I know the first details to be published of this marble, may suggest something of its quality. Also to be noted are the terra cottas at Montpellier and the Voltaire Institute, Geneva. See also Réau, 'L'œuvre de Houdon en Russie'; *Correspondance artistique de Grimm avec Catherine II*; Besterman, *The Terra Cotta Statue of Voltaire . . .*, 1960.

124. Réau, *Houdon*, 1964, I, 54–6, reprints the documents on the Madame Denis-Duvivier affair: See also Benisovitch, op. cit.

125. I have in my files photographs of over seventy surviving examples of Houdon portraits of Voltaire—of all different types and quality ranging from the impeccable to the impossible.

126. Periodically it must be re-emphasized that, in the case of multiple examples of a portrait subject by Houdon, I have made no attempt to be inclusive. With *Voltaire, Rousseau, Franklin*, and others of which a great number of replicas exist, I am merely mentioning a few that I have studied and photographed in detail, and which I feel to be authentic. In the case of *Voltaire* there are many others of good quality, which will be described in a *catalogue raisonné*. Of this first type, for instance, truncated, undraped, *sans perruque, à l'antique*, there are, aside from those I have mentioned, marbles at the Musée Saint-Jean, Angers and the National Gallery, Washington; bronzes in the Louvre, the Courty Collection, and the Davies Collection, Washington, among others. There are also many later copies, particularly of this bronze type.

127. There is also an old plaster of this type in the Musée des Arts Décoratifs, Paris, and a terra cotta, signed: HOUDON F. 1778, in the Courty Collection.

128. The marble bust ordered by Frederick is still in the Berlin Academy (Deutsche Akademie der Wissenschaften). See illustration, *Jean-Antoine Houdon*, exhibition catalogue, Berlin, 1955, pl. 43. This is a work of unusually high quality, inscribed and signed on the back: VOLTAIRE. HOUDON. F. ANNEE 1778. The plaster in the Staatliches Museum, Schwerin, although heavily painted, is also important for its unbroken history.

129. A plaster in the Schlossmuseum, Gotha, unsigned, painted bronze color, differs from the marble in Leningrad, in that the toga is undecorated. This fact indicates that it is an original plaster, since it would be normal to add the decorative carving in the marble. Illustrated, *Houdon*, Berlin exhibition catalogue, 1955, pls. 44, 45. The correspondence of Catherine with Grimm records that the empress received a bronze and a plaster of Voltaire in 1778. (She much preferred that without the perruque, since she felt perruques were laughable.) These would probably be a bronze of the undraped *à l'antique*, without shoulders or perruque (there is such a bronze in the Pushkin Museum, Moscow); and a plaster of that in modern dress with perruque. The letter from Grimm, November 8 1778, also refers to a marble on which Houdon was still working and which should be ready by the end of the year. This was undoubtedly the beautiful marble now in the Hermitage draped *à l'antique*, and so carefully inscribed to Catherine, which was in the Salon of 1779. See Réau, *Correspondance artistique . . .*, 30–4.

130. The Comédie-Française category includes the largest proportion of later copies. At some point casts were made from the head of the marble statue, and some of these have subsequently become originals. There are a number of variants of this type in which more or less of the torso is indicated. On the other hand an old plaster in the Petit Palais, Paris, bears a characteristic cursive signature on its right edge: *f. p. houdon. 1780.*, that seems to have been cast. There is no reason to doubt that this comes from Houdon's studio, or that he made a separate bust in process of making the marble statue. The marbles, with the masks of Comedy and Tragedy, in which Voltaire has a particularly fixed smirk, need further study.

131. Verse addressed to Houdon by the Chevalier de Cubières on behalf of the members of the Lodge of the Nine Sisters, on the day of his reception. *Journal de Paris*, February 20 1779. Reprinted, Réau, *Houdon*, 1964, I, 28.

132. Arnason, *Houdon*, 1964, 54–62; bibliography; Massengale, *The Angers-Athenaeum Bust of Benjamin Franklin by Houdon*, 1964 (unpublished thesis New York University bibliography). Massengale, 'A Franklin by Houdon Rediscovered', *Marsyas*, vol. XII, 1964–5, 1–15 (summary of thesis).

133. Massengale, ibid.; Swan, *The Athenaeum Gallery*. Mrs. Massengale gives the most thorough account of the Athenaeum bust of Franklin. Although I reserve judgment on some of her opinions concerning the relationship of the 1778 bust to the Athenaeum bust, and the exact date of the latter, her thesis is most valuable.

134. Arnason; Massengale; Swan, op. cit.

135. Hubert, 'Une œuvre de Houdon identifiée . . . Joubert'.

136. Ingersoll-Smouse, 'Lettres inédites de J.-J. Caffieri', 1913; Franklin Papers; Reprinted Réau, *Houdon*, 1964, I, 57.

137. See Appendix I: 'No. 252. Statue in marble of Monsieur de Voltaire, which was to have been placed in the Académie Française, but is destined to decorate the New Hall of the Comédie, rue de Condé'.

138. Since Houdon's Christian religious sculpture, with the exception of *Saint Bruno* and *Saint John the Baptist*, has disappeared and presumably been destroyed, it is noted here only in passing. For the decoration of Sainte Geneviève and the *Saint Paula* for the In-

valides, see: Archives Nationales, o¹1698, and Archives of the Invalides, Paris. Réau, *Houdon*, 1964, I, 49, 250–4, discusses the religious sculpture at length.

9. Réau, 'La sculpture funéraire dans l'œuvre de Houdon', 1943. The tomb of the Comte de Valbelle consisted of a portrait bust and four figures representing Power or Authority [La Force], Hope, Saint Monica, and Provence. The marble bust is now in the Museum of Draguignan; there is a terra cotta (Fig. 121) in the Wildenstein Gallery, New York; a plaster at Versailles is presumably that formerly in the Institute of France, mentioned by Houdon in his inventory, *c.* 1784: No. 57 *bis*. Buste de Mr. le comte de Valbel pour l'académie françoise. This is under the date 1779; the count died in 1778 so this could have been made from life or, like the Rousseau, from a death-mask. Compared with his other tomb sculptures this seems to have been something of a patchwork. According to Réau the allegorical figures were not by Houdon but probably by a Provençal sculptor, J.-P. Chastel, and a Marseillais, Christophe Fossaty; and are now at the Museum of Fréjus, the Palace of Justice at Draguignan, the church of Sainte-Beaume and the Museum of Toulon.

0. Réau, 'Documents sur Houdon: le projet d'un monument au Parc de Bruxelles', 1922, 1923; 'Houdon et la Belgique', 1943. Houdon in 1783 also participated in and submitted maquettes, now lost, for a monument to the aeronauts, the brothers Montgolfier. In 1785 he presented a model and a program for a statue of Louis XVI at Brest. There was a project for the painter-poet Gessner at Zurich, projects for a monument to Rousseau for the Panthéon, the equestrian statue of Washington, and others, none realized. The monumental bronze statue of Napoleon for Boulogne, actually completed about 1812, was destroyed with the Restoration. See Réau, *Houdon*, 1964, I, 64–6 and *passim*.

1. The inventory, *c.* 1784, lists under 1783, No. 110, a model of the statue of Henri IV life-size; see Appendix 2. Grimm, *Correspondance littéraire*, XII, 149, mentions in the garden of the Palais-Royal a statue of Henri IV on a pedestal, from the chisel of Houdon.

2. Of particular importance in salvaging works of art which might have been destroyed was the establishment of the *Musée des monuments français*, and the diligence of its curator, Alexandre Lenoir, during the Revolutionary period. His valiant if unsuccessful attempt to have Houdon's noble tomb of the Comte d'Ennery acquired by the museum is recorded in letters to the Minister of Fine Arts in 1801. *Archives du Musée des monuments français*, I, 218. Despite his lack of success in this instance, the tomb was fortunately preserved intact and is now the chief ornament of the Houdon room in the Louvre.

143. Ancestors of Choiseul-Praslin are recorded by Saint-Simon at Versailles, and descendants by Proust. The marble, signed and dated: HOUDON FECIT. 1780, is on loan from the Louvre to the Castle at Angers. Since accounts of portrait busts in this essay become increasingly summary, with the exception of those that involve some unusual historic, iconographic, or stylistic element, it should be added that this, in my estimation, is one of the very fine lesser known portraits by the sculptor. The Louvre could well put the plaster on exhibition together with the marble.

144. See above, note 139; Bachaumont, *Mémoires secrets*, August 25 and 30, 1779. Teissier, *Un grand seigneur au XVIIIᵉ siècle, le comte de Valbelle*, Paris, 1890.

145. Réau, 'Les bustes de l'avocat Gerbier par Lemoyne et Houdon', 1922. Rodin, speaking of Houdon's *Mirabeau*, describes the attributes, in portrait sculpture, of the orator; 'Profession: the tribune. The mouth protrudes like a speaking-trumpet ready to fling his voice abroad. He lifts his head because, like most orators, he was short. . . . The eyes are not fixed on any one; they rove over a great assembly. It is a glance at once vague and superb. Tell me, is it not a marvellous achievement to evoke in this one head a whole crowd—more, a whole listening country?' *On Art and Artists*, 139.

Although Rodin is really speaking of himself, he is right in insisting on Houdon's sense of the dramatic moment, when it was appropriate, in sculptures like *Gerbier*, *Mirabeau*, *Larive*, *Molière*, or *Mademoiselle Arnould*.

146. Bovy, 'Quelques bustes français . . .'; Gielly, 'Le buste de Théodore Tronchin . . .'; Girod de l'Ain, 'Les Thellusson et les artistes'.

147. Grimm, *Correspondance littéraire*, May 1780.

148. Aside from the Boston plaster, there are good plasters in the Columbus (Ohio) Gallery of Fine Arts, the Pennsylvania Academy, Philadelphia (heavily painted bronze color), the National Academy of Design, New York, and the Musée de Blérancourt.

149. Arnason, *Houdon*, 1964, 70–3, bibliography. Pudelko, 'A Marble Bust of John Paul Jones', draws an interesting comparison between the face of Jones in this bust and that of Donatello's condottiere *Gattamelata*. Seen in profile the resemblance is striking.

150. Giacometti, *Houdon*, 1928, II, 99–101.

151. Two other marble busts of *Madame de Sérilly* have recently appeared on the art market in New York. These are both signed and dated: Houdon. F. 1780., in an almost identical style, although one of the signatures, curiously, is upside down. Both differ from the Wallace Collection version in some details of drapery as well as in the date; and both need further research.

152. Steinmann, 'Houdon in . . . Schwerin', 1911; Callataÿ, 'Les bustes genevois . . . , 1954; Girod de l'Ain, *Les Thellusson*, 1956; *Jean-Antoine Houdon*, exhibition catalogue, Berlin, 1955, pls. 38–9. The Metropolitan Museum, New York, plaster is similar to that at Schwerin. The plaster with the shawl over the shoulders is in the collection of Henry P. McIlhenny, Philadelphia.

153. Vitry, 'Un buste de négresse par Houdon au Musée de Soissons', 1897; 'La tête de négresse . . . .', 1931; 'Un buste de la collection de M. de Camondo . . .', 1931; *Musée Nissim de Camondo*, Handbook, 1954, 56–7. The bust in the Musée Camondo, listed in the handbook as *after* Houdon, is a splendid bronze that apparently was too good to be true. It combines qualities of the Soissons fragment and the miniature bronze in the Musée des Arts Décoratifs, including the fact that the torso is closed at the back. This is appropriate to a miniature bronze but not to a life-size bronze bust of the eighteenth century.

154. See above, note 94.

155. Obviously d'Angiviller's Great Men represented an official selection approved by the king. The *philosophes* would not necessarily have subscribed to many of his nominations; and the basis of selection changes radically after the Revolution. See Appendix 1, *Livrets* of Salons, 1777 *et seq.* Dowley, 'D'Angiviller's Grand Hommes and the Significant Moment', Art Bulletin, vol. 39, 1957, 260–63.

156. Archives Nationales, o¹1915. Réau, 'Documents sur Houdon', 1922, 368. Jean-Baptiste Pierre (1713–89), a minor painter, was *Premier Peintre* to the king, and *Directeur* of the *Académie Royale de Peinture et de Sculpture*. His principal distinction was acting as a loyal assistant to d'Angiviller.

157. Bachaumont, *Lettres sur les peintures . . .*, Salon of 1779.

158. Although most of the previous statues of the Great Men in the series (and the other three for 1781) were presented first in plaster and only two years later at the subsequent Salon in marble, Houdon, anxious to present his *Tourville* immediately in marble, provided his own block with the understanding that it would be replaced from the royal depots when a suitable piece was available. There was considerable difficulty in achieving the replacement, and it was not until 1785 that he received the last payment for the statue itself. What with all the other strains on it at the time, the royal purse was notoriously reluctant to yield up even small amounts. One letter from d'Angiviller to Houdon, dated June 24, 1783, is of some interest. This is a request urging the sculptor to finish as soon as possible the model of the *Tourville* for the Sèvres porcelain factory. The Great Men, like other royal commissions, were regularly presented to a wide public through these popular Sèvres

reproductions. Archives Nationales, o¹1916; Réau, 'Documents sur Houdon', 1922, 372; Archives Nationales, o¹2086. This is a letter from Mazetti, *sculpteur*, December 11, 1780, to d'Angiviller, giving Pajou and Houdon as references. He says, 'M. Pajou pour qui j'ai exécuté la statue de *Bossuet* . . . M. Houdon sous lequel je travaille à la figure de Tourville . . . .'. The distinction he draws between his work for Pajou and for Houdon may or may not be of significance.

Houdon's terra cotta maquette is still at the museum of the Sèvres porcelain factory. Another terra cotta maquette in the Courty Collection shows some significant differences that may suggest it to be a preliminary study.

159. See above, p. 28 f.

160. Lotte, 'Un mausolée de Victor Charpentier par Houdon', 1920; Aubert, 'Le mausolée du Comte d'Ennery par Houdon', 1943; Aubert and Picard, 'Le mausolée du Comte d'Ennery par Houdon', 1944; Réau, 'Un nouveau chef-d'œuvre . . .', 1946; Gagneur, 'Le mausolée de Victor Charpentier . . .', 1947; Picard, 'Houdon et l'antique', 1943. The monument is signed (Plate 143i): J. A. Houdon, F. 1781.

160a. See Deshairs, *Le château de Maisons*, 1907; Vitry, *Le château de Maisons-Laffitte . . .* 1912; Réau, *Houdon*, 1964, I, 245.

161. Réau, 'L'œuvre de Houdon en Russie', 1914. Soltykov's dress, including the elaborate brocade of his coat, meticulously reproduced in marble, shows nothing of that approaching sobriety in men's clothes discussed above.

162. Legrand, *Les collections artistiques de la Faculté de médecine*, 1911.

163. Réau, *Correspondance de Grimm avec Catherine II*, 1932. We know further from the correspondence that Buffon sent his son with the bust; and on June 29, 1782, Catherine reported having received the son and the bust.

164. Jean-Baptiste Defernex (1729–83), whose modest portrait busts Houdon may have studied with interest, did a portrait of Buffon c. 1772 (Courty Collection). Réau, 'J.-B. Defernex, sculpteur du duc d'Orléans', 1931; Bourdier, *L'iconographie de Buffon*, 1952; Arnason, *Houdon*, 1964, 74–7, bibliography. The marble in the Hermitage is signed and dated: HOUDON. F. 1782. The marble in the Louvre is signed: *houdon f.* Aside from the plaster at Schwerin, signed and dated *houdon f. 1781.*, there is a plaster of the Hermitage-Louvre type in the Dijon Museum of Fine Arts and another in the Hirshhorn Museum, Washington, signed and dated: *houdon f. 1782.*, and with the *cachet d'atelier*; and a terra cotta, signed on the lower front edge: *houdon f. 1782*, in the California Palace of the Legion of Honor, San Francisco. An important bronze in the Neuchâtel Museum, Switzerland, is signed and dated: Houdon f. 1781. A number of other versions and copies exist.

Réau, who published the works of Houdon

in Russia, claims the Louvre marble to be a workshop replica of the marble in the Hermitage (*Houdon*, 1964, II, 27). Having studied and photographed both marbles in detail in August 1973, I would agree that the Hermitage version is superior, but see no reason to question the Louvre example as a work by Houdon. Equally, but the other way round, Réau regarded the *Seated Voltaire* in the Hermitage merely as a replica, because it was made later than the Comédie-Française marble. It is, in fact, in every way comparable. He also refers to the Dijon plaster, which bears the *cachet d'atelier* on the back, as the 'original' plaster from which the Hermitage marble was made. Admittedly this is a fine plaster, but what the evidence is for its being the 'original' he does not state (Réau, 'Le buste de Buffon du Musée de Dijon', 1923; see also, Querré, 'Sur un buste de Houdon au Musée de Dijon', 1958). Claims for plasters or terra cottas as being the 'originals' are clichés of the Houdon art market.

165. The marble of Larive in the Comédie Française is signed and dated on the end of the stump of the right arm: HOUDON. F. 1784, a formula that Houdon uses increasingly in late busts. Dacier, *Le musée de la Comédie Française*, 1905.

166. Guiffrey, *Les Caffieri*, 333 ff and *passim*. Houdon may well have been unhappy, after the success of his bust of *Molière*, that Caffieri should have been given the commission for the statue in the Great Men series. The plaster of Caffieri's work was also exhibited in the Salon of 1783, and Houdon could have been consoled by the bad press it received.

167. National Museum, Warsaw. The *Alexander* is an unusual and important work by Houdon which I regret I have not yet seen. The Girardon *Alexander*, which Houdon could well have used as a model, is in the Louvre.

168. Arnason, 'Jean-Antoine Houdon's Jean de La Fontaine', 1968. The marble in the Philadelphia Museum is signed: HOUDON. F. Aside from the terra cotta in the Orléans Museum, there is another terra cotta in the collection of Monsieur Sommier at Vaux-le-Vicomte, signed and dated, Houdon. F. 1782. and a plaster, painted terra cotta, with the *cachet d'atelier*, at Schwerin.

169. Steinmann, 'Houdon in . . . Schwerin', 1911; *Jean-Antoine Houdon*, exhibition catalogue, Berlin, 1955, pls. 54–5; Mansfeld, *Der Bildhauer Jean Antoine Houdon . . . in Deutschland*, 1955.

170. The *Diana* has been discussed above. For *La Frileuse*, see Phillips, 'Monsieur Houdon's *Frileuse*', 1963, and Arnason, *Houdon*, 1964, 96–101, bibliography.

171. Appendix 2, 1781, No. 93.

172. The *Summer*, as far as I know, exists only in the marble at Montpellier, although there are modern bronze casts. Two busts by

Houdon, one in marble and one in plaster painted terra cotta with the *cachet d'atelier*, a in the Musée Camondo, Paris. Of *La Frileu* much the more popular of the two figure the marble at Montpellier and the bronze the Metropolitan Museum, New York, sign and dated on the base: HOUDON. F. 1787, a the key surviving examples. The bronze do not have the supporting urn and drapery of th marble. A life-size plaster in the Galer Souffrice, Paris, has the interesting varia that the supporting element is a tree tru rather than the urn. There is a terra cott reduced scale (48 cms) in the Nation Museum, Warsaw, signed: HOUDON, in whic the shawl she wears is heavily textured. Th legs of the figure have been damaged. I ha only seen photographs of the last two. There in the Musée Royal des Beaux-Arts, Brusse an almost literal marble copy of *La Frileuse*, the Belgian sculptor Godechar, signed a dated, 1803—somewhat more elegantly elo gated than Houdon's version. Reduced bron replicas of Godechar's adaptation of Houdor Frileuse have appeared, attributed to Houdo

173. Archives Nationales, o¹1918; Réau, 'Doc ments sur Houdon', 1922.

174. Papier-mâché was used frequently in th eighteenth century for sculptures to be use in fêtes or other theatrical performances. papier-mâché statue of Houdon's *Seat Voltaire*, in the Library at Rouen, was ma in 1791 for the ceremony in which Voltaire ashes were transferred to the Panthéon. (*La Frileuse* there is a papier-mâché version the Staatliches Museum, Weimar, another the Courty Collection, painted bronze col and a third, painted white, in the entrance ha of the country home of Anna-Amalia, Duche of Saxe-Weimar, patroness of Goethe, Schille and Herder, among others. This last, accordi to local legend, commemorated the sufferin of a noble lady who boasted that all doors Weimar were open to her; whereat Goeth and the reigning duke locked her in th unheated entrance on a cold and frosty night

175. Pradel, 'Une "Petite Frileuse" par Houdor 1946.

176. See below, pp. 92 f. and Appendix Letter to Bachelier, 1794. For Thomire, th greatest foundryman trained by Houdon, s Niclausse, *Thomire, fondeur-ciseleur*, Paris, 194 Thomire, of course, was even more of a artist than a technician.

177. The *Bather* for the Monceau fountai Metropolitan Museum, New York, is signe and dated: HOUDON F. 1782. Although acquire by the Duc d'Orléans and installed in h garden, Houdon apparently designed th fountain group independently and first offere it to the *Direction des Bâtiments* for the kin The price seems to have been too high, so th Duc d'Orléans, who was married to one the richest ladies in Europe and thus did n

need to quibble acquired it (Furcy-Raynaud, 'Correspondance de M. d'Angiviller avec Pierre', 237–8). L. V. Thiery, *Guide des amateurs et des étrangers voyageurs à Paris*, 1787, I, 70, describes the installation at Monceau: 'Proceeding a few steps one will enter a small area occupied by a basin of white marble in which is a charming group by Monsieur Houdon, sculptor to the king, representing a superb figure in white marble, bathing; behind her, another woman, executed in lead and painted black, represents a negress holding in one hand a drapery of white marble and in the other a ewer *doré* from which she pours the water over the form of her mistress, from whom it falls to the pool in the basin.

'A ruined gate opposite this group leads one to the colonnade which surrounds part of the *Naumachie*.' The ruined gate or portal is of interest as a touch of eighteenth-century romantic garden design. The *Procès-verbaux de la Commission temporaire des arts*, October 17, 1795, II, 354 (ed. A. Tuetey), describes the vandalism of the fountain, specifically of the figure of the black attendant. See also Metropolitan Museum Bulletin.

The Monceau fountain was Houdon's most elaborately rococo garden sculpture, involving as it did the use of different materials and strongly contrasting colors. The marble *Diana* was intended originally as a garden sculpture for the Duke of Saxe-Gotha, but as a single figure. The *Naiad* fountain of the Salon of 1777 was the only comparable work by the sculptor, but as far as is known this was never carried beyond the stage of the model. Although from the drawing by Saint-Aubin, the only surviving indication, this was a highly decorative concept, it does not seem to have involved the colorism of the later work.

78. As noted above under *Caumartin*, Houdon rather collected *Prévôts des marchands*, men of substance. Unfortunately he has lost two out of his three. The bust of Gustave III in the Palace of Justice, Stockholm, may be a work of the Swedish sculptor Sergel; it is certainly not by Houdon.

79. The plaster is in the State Library, Weimar (Nationale Forschungs- und Gedenkstätten der klassischen deutschen Literatur in Weimar), the bronze at Potsdam-Sanssouci. See Bogyay, 'Houdon à Weimar', 1935; *Jean-Antoine Houdon*, exhibition catalogue, Berlin, 1955, pl. 56; Mansfeld, *... Houdon ... in Deutschland*, 1955; Niclausse, *Thomire ...* , 1947.

79a. Although I have not seen this bust, from the photographs it looks like a work of unusual interest and quality, aside from being impeccably documented. See Réau, 'Le buste de la comtesse de Moustier', 1924; id., *Houdon*, 1964, I, 320–1, and II, 38 and pl. LXXX.

80. Boston Museum of Fine Arts, The Forsyth Wickes Collection. Arnason, *Houdon*, 1964, 92–5.

181. Réau, *Houdon*, 1964, I, 77.

182. Wilson, *Diderot*, *passim* on Malesherbes; Michel, 'Le buste de Malesherbes . . .', 1912. A plaster of the *Malesherbes* is in the Courty Collection. The Louvre does not have definite proof that its bust is Malesherbes; a posthumous bust of *Malesherbes* in the Louvre, done in 1801 by Denis-Antoine Chaudet, has no resemblance to the Houdon bust. So this seems to be a triple problem of identification. *Lenoir* could be *Malesherbes* or *Malesherbes* could be *Lenoir*, or both could be an unknown. But both are certainly outstanding portraits by Houdon.

183. Ingersoll-Smouse, 'Houdon en Amérique'; *Catalogue . . . American Philosophical Society*, 1961; Arnason, *Houdon*, 1964, 78–80.

184. The *Esquisse*, written under the greatest difficulties, is one of the most remarkable statements of eighteenth-century optimism for the perfectibility of man. Condorcet's suicide has been questioned. All that is certain is that he died in prison.

185. Op. cit., 15–16, fig. 11. Cited from the *Massachusetts Historical Society Collections*, I, 1900, 288–9.

186. Vigée-Lebrun, *Souvenirs*, 1835; Delpech, *L'Amour le plus tendre*, 1964; *Jean-Antoine Houdon*, Berlin, 1955, pl. 57; Mansfeld, *Houdon . . . in Deutschland*, 1955.

A plaster, painted terra cotta with the *cachet d'atelier*, formerly in the collection of Prince Henry, is now in the National Gallery, [West] Berlin. Other plasters are in the Thüringer Museum, Eisenach, and the Schlossmuseum, Gotha. There exist many replicas in marble, plaster, and terra cotta.

187. Chinard, ed. *Houdon in America*, 1930, *passim*. Chinard reprints almost all the pertinent documents relative to Houdon's trip to the United States. Unless otherwise indicated, quotations are taken from Chinard. Arnason, *Houdon*, 1964, 86–91, bibliography; Eisen, *Portraits of Washington*, 1952; Flexner, *George Washington*, 5 vols. See also Bibliography on American subjects.

188. Ingersoll-Smouse, 'Lettres inédites de J.-J. Caffieri', 1913; *Franklin Papers*, New Haven; cited, Réau, *Houdon*, 1964, I, 57.

189. An equestrian statue of Washington had been proposed in the Continental Congress in 1783 and passed on August 7 of that year. This was to be a bronze statue showing Washington in Roman dress, his head encircled with a laurel wreath; to be executed by the best artist in Europe. The American painter-sculptor Joseph Wright was recommended to make a bust from life to serve as a model for the statue. Wright presumably made life-mask, busts, paintings and a relief that survives—assumed to be the earliest sculptured portrait of Washington. See Richard B. Morris, '*The Wright Plaque of Washington*', 1961 (manuscript).

This project was not realized at the time, but it would seem probable that Houdon had heard of it—which would account, even more than the example of Falconet, for his obsession with the project for an equestrian statue. Jefferson very likely told him about it as an added inducement. In fact, on July 12, 1785, he wrote to the Virginia delegation in Congress, urging Houdon's claims. The stipulation by the Congress that Washington should appear in 'Roman dress' complete with laurel wreath, may also help explain Houdon's passion to show the Commander-in-Chief *à l'antique*.

190. Seymour, 'Houdon's Washington . . .', 1948, 137–58. An important account, particularly valuable for the light it sheds on Houdon's technique.

191. George Washington, John Adams, whom Jefferson consulted on Houdon's insurance, Thomas Jefferson, James Madison, and James Monroe.

192. A final problem of the Washington commission is the 'life-mask' now in the Pierpont Morgan Library, New York. Whether this is the actual life-mask taken from Washington cannot be determined. The fact that the eyes are open rather than closed as they normally would be in a mask taken from life, would suggest that this may be a cast taken from the original mould. The eyes could have been recut on the mask. Whatever it is, it is a remarkable work and has some place in the intricate story of the statue of George Washington by Houdon. See also Seymour, 'Houdon's Washington . . .', *op. cit.*

In terms of their general quality, the Versailles *Washington* and also the Versailles *Mirabeau* are probably studio works.

193. For the correspondence concerning Houdon's mother's pension, see Archives Nationales o¹1919. For the artist's marriage and the birth of his three daughters, the Register of the Church of Saint-Philippe-du-Roule. Reprinted Réau, *Houdon*, 1964, I, 27. See also Réau, 'La vie intime de Houdon', 1950; Helen C. Frick, 'Madame Jean-Antoine Houdon', 1947. The *Journal de Versailles*, 1891, contains an account by Monsieur Perrin, one of Houdon's descendants, of the family lineage to that date, Réau, op. cit.

194. Archives Nationales o¹2086 and o²1917¹.

195. According to Réau, *Houdon*, 1964, I, 305, the bust of Louis XVI in the Salon of 1787 was a plaster, and 'the marble destined for the Compagnie des agents de change could not be inaugurated in the hall of the Bourse until 1789. Saved from destruction by the Abbé Leblond, who ceded it in 1792 to Lenoir for the depot of the Petits-Augustins, later the Musée des Monuments Français, in exchange for a group of maps and manuscripts, this bust, dated 1790, thus escaped by a miracle the Jacobin vandalism; it is this which is conserved

at the Musée de Versailles.' The *livret* of the 1787 Salon lists the *Louis XVI* under marbles. If Réau is correct on the date of its installation, Houdon could have deferred signing and dating it until it had left his studio. There is still a discrepancy of a year, and Réau recognizes in a footnote that the Versailles marble could be a second version. Houdon did make a second marble in 1790, for the Hôtel de Ville in Paris, presumably destroyed in 1792, and a third for Strasbourg, destroyed in 1870. Aside from the marble there survives an old plaster in a private collection, probably taken from the marble at Versailles. See Levallet-Haug, 'Le buste de Louis XVI . . .', 1937.

196. Cited, Réau, *Houdon*, 1964, I, 305.

197. Staring, 'Houdon en Nederland', 1940; Réau, 'La sculpture française en Hollande au XVIIIe siècle, 1952. A plaster of Suffren, painted terra cotta, is in the Musée d'Aix-en-Provence, signed and dated: Houdon f. 1786 and with the seal of the atelier. This is of a quality and uniqueness that merits the description, 'original plaster'. The simplification, as in the case of the Schwerin plaster of Catherine, would confirm this.

198. Chinard, *Houdon in America*, 1930, 1–2, 21–2, 28, 30–4, 37, 41; Lafayette, *Mémoires . . .*, 1837; Ingersoll-Smouse, 'Houdon en Amérique' 1914; Swan, *The Athenaeum Gallery*, 1940, 160–8; Kimball, *Jefferson . . .*, 1950; *Exposition Lafayette*, 1957 (catalogue); Arnason, *Houdon*, 1964, 81–5.

A plaster of the Richmond, Virginia, type is in Berlin (ill. Réau, *Houdon*, 1964, II, pl. LXX, 142B); and a 'life-mask' at Cornell University in Ithaca, New York (ibid., pl. LXXI, 142A). Both of these look interesting but I have only seen the illustrations. There is an old plaster of the Athenaeum type at Girard College, Philadelphia, recently painted bronze color. There are also a large number of modern bronze replicas of the *Athenaeum* type.

199. Aside from the 1790 Versailles marble of Lafayette, there is another marble in a private collection in Flushing, New York. This has a different, but equally questionable signature. Otherwise it is identical with the Versailles version and comparable in quality. The Versailles marble has been the source for a large number of modern bronze replicas, as well as at least one plaster, that at the Musée at Mans.

Full-size Sèvres replicas exist in the Fogg Museum, Harvard University and the collection of Samuel Barlow, New York, differing in details of the base.

200. *Jean-Antoine Houdon*, exhibition catalogue, 1955, 58. Mansfeld, *. . . Houdon . . .*, 1955; Pérey, *. . . le duc de Nivernais*, Paris, 1891. Although the bust of the Duc de Nivernais, in its Baroque elaboration, seems to have been designed to be executed in marble, no marble is known to exist. I know of five plasters, four

of which I have examined, those in the Musée des Arts Décoratifs, Paris, at Nevers, Besançon, and Schwerin; the other is at Potsdam, from the collection of Prince Henry of Prussia, a friend of de Nivernais. That at Schwerin, which bears the *cachet d'atelier*, is the best in quality or condition of those I have seen.

201. Aude, 'Le marquis de Méjanes', 1933; Villard, 'Sur le buste du marquis de Méjanes', 1952. Two more portraits in marble, of which the subjects are unidentified, should also be noted at this point. These are: a '*Magistrate*', signed and dated under the right shoulder: *houdon f. 1787*, noted by Ingersoll-Smouse 'Houdon en Amérique', 1914, in the collection of S. R. Bertrou, New York, later in the Wimpfheimer Collection, New York. Present owner unknown (ill. Réau, *Houdon*, 1964, II, pl. CXLV), and a '*Magistrate*', Musée Fabre, Montpellier, signed and dated: *houdon f. 1788*. From their robes, both seem definitely to belong to the legal or academic professions (cf. *Miromesnil* and *Louis*). The Montpellier '*Magistrate*' is a work of fine quality, and the New York example seems to be, from the photographs. I have not as yet been able to trace it. The two '*Magistrates*' are of interest as indicating that in this flurry of 'noblemen of the sword' Houdon was not neglecting the gentlemen of the robe. In fact, de Nivernais and de Méjanes might have preferred to be classified with the latter.

202. Brière, 'Notes sur quelques bustes de Houdon: . . . Cagliostro . . . , 1913; Vaudoyer, 'Les Houdon d'Aix', 1925; Coppoler-Orlando, 'Il ritratto di Cagliostro', 1953. The two marbles of Cagliostro, at the Musée d'Aix-en-Provence, and the National Gallery, Washington, both signed and dated: *houdon f. 1786*, seem to be identical, with variations in the marble. See also, *Paintings and Sculpture from the Kress Collection*, 1956, 236–7.

203. A list of mentions, exhibitions, and sales of various versions of the *Vestal*, between 1774 and 1828.

1774. 17 January [Sale]. Vassal de Saint-Hubert, No. 152: Terre cuite. *Une prêtresse antique* portant un vase de libation, par Houdon. H. 22 pouces.

1777. *Livret* of Salon: 255. Une *Vestale* en bronze. L'idée est prise d'après le marbre que l'on voit à Rome, appelé vulgairement *Pandore*. Cette Figure, de 23 pouces, doit servir de lampe de nuit.

c. 1784. Houdon's inventory of his sculpture. Under 1779, No. 61. Buste d'une Vestail. No. 62. Une grande Vestal exécuté pour l'escalier de M. le duc d'Aumont. No. 67. Une Vestale de 2 pieds en terre cuite et exécuté en bronze. Under 1782, No. 103. Une petite statue de 18 pouces de haut, en marbre, représentant une vestale qui tient son feu sacré.

1787. *Livret* of Salon: 257. Une *Vestale*.

1793. *Livret* of Salon: 121. Une *Vesta* Statue de 20 pouces de hauteur.

1794. Houdon Letter to Bachelier. U *Vestale* grandeur naturelle en marbre, à moy

1795. Houdon Sale from his Studio: No. 6 Une *Vestale*, drapée dans le goût antiqu Elle tient le vase du feu sacré; près d'elle un autel. Ce précieux morceau porte pouces de haut. [Under bronzes.]—72. U *Vestale* debout, portant le feu sacré; elle drapée dans le goût antique, la tête en part couverte d'un voile et posée sur un piédest H. de la figure: 6 pieds; celle du piédesta 3 pieds 4 pouces. [Marble.]—93. Une *Vesta* elle est drapée et tient l'urne du feu sacré; pr d'elle est un autel de style antique. H. 21 pouc [Terra cotta.]

1797. August 30 [13 fructidor an v]. [Sal Porché-Vaubal: *Bronzes*, Nos. 108: U *Vestale* tenant le feu sacré dans un vase: figu drapée et étudiée à Rome d'après un fragmen antique très bien exécutée. H.: 22 pouces.

1798. December 26 [6 nivôse an v] [Sa Verdun-Bouquet: *Bronzes*, 178: Une *Vest* tenant le feu sacré dans un vase, figure, drap et étudiée à Rome, d'après un fragmen antique, très bien exécutée par l'artiste mêm 1821. May 8. [Sale.] Mme Philippe de Sai Maurice: no. 46: Une figure de *Vestale* drap et tenant une urne. Bronze de 22 pouces de ha 1828. Sale of the contents of Houdon's stu after his death. Procès-verbal with pri obtained. Under *Statues and Statuett Vestale*. Plâtre. 70 francs.

204. A marble bust of the small *Vestal* is in t Musée Cognacq-Jay, Paris.

205. See pp. 11–13.

206. The *livret* listing for the Salon of 1787 somewhat ambiguous. There is first a gene heading, *Bustes en marbre*, followed by the fi busts already discussed. The sixth item, 2 is Une Vestale. This would suggest that t was a bust of a *Vestal*, but the reviewers the Salon are clearly talking about a stat As pointed out, these *livrets* were put togeth hurriedly.

207. Reviews of the 1787 Salon, reprinted Réau, *Houdon*, 1964, I, 39.

208. For the various *Vestals*, see Arnaso Houdon, 1964, 21–25, bibliography. Desha Dijon, *Architecture et décoration aux XVII XVIIIe siècles*, Paris, 1910, pl. 63, reprodu a plaster replica of the large *Vestal* in the Hô de Bretenières (École Saint-François de Sal in Dijon.

209. *Tarare au Salon de Peinture*, 1787. Cited Réau, 1964, I, 417–18. Vitry, 'Houdon p traitiste de sa femme et de ses enfants', 19 feels that the young lady of the Louvre b looks older than twenty years. This is matter of judgement, and it cannot be tak as proved beyond all question that this Madame Houdon. The Louvre bust com from the Perrin-Houdon family. There

another plaster in the Courty Collection, and a terra cotta in the collection of Helen C. Frick, New York. See also Arnason, *Houdon*, 1964, 109–15, with bibliography, on the portraits of Madame Houdon and the three daughters.

210. While unquestionably a work by Houdon, this portrait of a baby presents some still unresolved questions as to the identification of the subject. Aside from the plaster at Schwerin with the *cachet d'atelier*, there were formerly a plaster (with pointing marks) and a marble, on an elaborately veined base, in the Larcade Gallery, Paris. These were published by Giacometti, *Houdon*, 1928, II, 197–9, and the marble is illustrated, as the portrait of a very young, unidentified child. In 1955 the marble had been sold by Larcade, but the present owner was unknown. The same year a bust, signed on the back: *houdon f.* was on the market, identified by the owner as an ancestor, portrayed in 1786 at the age of a few months. Although this bust is identical with that at Schwerin, with the exception that it is signed whereas that at Schwerin has the *cachet d'atelier* and is painted terra cotta, a comparison of the two illustrations will reveal how different they can look under different photographic conditions.

See *Jean-Antoine Houdon*, 1955, exhibition catalogue, pl. 60; Mansfeld, . . . *Houdon . . . in Deutschland*, 1955.

211. A plaster of this bust with the *cachet d'atelier* is in the Louvre. Another bust of Sabine, aged two years, dated 1789[?] is recorded formerly in the palace of Gatchina, near Leningrad.

212. Aside from the marble in the Huntington Collection and the plaster in the Louvre, there is a bronze in the Courty Collection, that should be noted. There are other marbles I have seen that I do not question, and, as indicated, copies in all materials. The best version of the *Sabine* with drapery is that in the Heim Gallery, London, signed and dated 1791 (see Plate 144b).

213. Another plaster of Anne-Ange, with the *cachet d'atelier*, is in the Courty Collection.

214. There are plasters of Claudine in the Courty Collection, the Musée Carnavalet, Paris, with marks of the *cachet d'atelier*, painted bronze, a terra cotta in the collection of Miss Alice Tully, New York, and several others recorded.

215. From the expanded activity in bronze casting emerged a number of bronze versions of busts, including the *Prince Henry of Prussia* (Salon of 1789) and a *Voltaire drapé à l'antique*; as well as a second bronze version of the *Diana* (1790, Louvre), a bronze *Frileuse*, probably that dated 1787 (Metropolitan Museum, New York), the bronze statue of the *Apollo* (1790, Gulbenkian Collection, Lisbon) ordered by Girardot de Marigny as a companion piece for his *Diana* of 1782; and a

second version of *L'Écorché*, modified, with the right arm raised over the head (1792, École des Beaux-Arts, Paris).

216. A marble of Jean-Baptiste Mercier du Paty is in the collection of the Marquis du Paty de Clam. Ill. Réau, 1964, II, pl. LVI. I have not seen the original.

217. Arnason, *Houdon*, 1964, 102–5, bibliography. There are plasters in the American Philosophical Society, Philadelphia, and the New York Historical Society, with long histories, as well as modern bronze replicas.

218. For the general remarks on the Salon of 1791 see Pevsner, *Academies; Livrets*, ed. Guiffrey, Salon of 1791, 8, and index.

219. For the 1791 *Franklin*, see Massengale, *The Angers-Athenaeum Bust of Benjamin Franklin by Houdon*, 1965 (unpublished thesis New York University). See also, Arnason, *Houdon*, 1964, 54–61, bibliography. As suggested in the discussion of the 1778 bust of Franklin, p. 54, it is my conviction that Houdon adapted the head from the first version for this monumental version. This conviction results from having seen and photographed in detail most surviving busts of Franklin by Houdon. Close comparison of identical views show no significant difference, such as would have arisen from an entirely new sitting. The head in the later bust seems to be lifted more than that of the earlier one, giving Franklin a more magisterial appearance. Lighting and angle can give a photograph of a portrait sculpture a wide variety of expressions not necessarily accurate or intended by the sculptor.

220. In his listing of the *livrets*, Réau appends to that of 1791 an enlarged and 'corrected' version of Houdon's listing. Since he gives no source and I have been unable as yet to trace any, I have used the list of the original *livret*. The amended list does not really add any new, surviving subjects to those we already know.

In the original *livret* entry, the statue of *La Frileuse*, mentioned as 'bronze, achetée par le Roi de Prusse', poses a somewhat intricate problem which may be summarized here. There seems to be no evidence that the King of Prussia ever received this statue. About 1957 the Staatliches Museum in Berlin acquired a bronze figure of a girl that was published as the 1791 version of Houdon's *La Frileuse* (ill., Réau, 1964, II, pl. XV). This statue is quite different from the earlier marble and bronze, showing the maiden in a wind-swept fragment of drapery, her arms crossed in an attempt to conceal her breasts, her head drooping on her right shoulder while she peeks coyly at the spectator. She is 4 feet 2¾ inches high or approximately life-size and bears a signature: HOUDON—improbably lettered on the base. She is also obviously a sculpture of the mid or latter nineteenth century by someone influenced by Carpeaux. One of the laughing

bacchantes in the group of the *Dance* in front of the Paris Opera would be a possible source, although Carpeaux also did a sculpture of his own *La Frileuse* in 1871. The Berlin Museum has since withdrawn the attribution to Houdon, but while it was still a question, this young lady, who apparently was popular during the nineteenth century, began to reappear in various contexts. Another cast of better bronze quality has long been in the Huntington Library in California. Although this also bears Houdon's signature on the base crudely lettered, it is catalogued simply as *French, XIX Century* at the Huntington. In 1967 another cast was brought to my attention, in Virginia with a somewhat different but equally improbable signature; and still another with a similar signature in a South American collection. Then busts drawn from the statue began to proliferate in New York in 1967; a bronze, a marble, and a terra cotta with similar, crude, added signatures. The flood has since dried up, but for a time it was bewildering. In all instances we have to do with a perfectly genuine nineteenth-century sculpture by an inferior but technically accomplished sculptor, to which someone at some point has added an Houdon signature. Even if the signature had been cleverly forged, the figure should never have been mistaken for a work by Houdon— although for a period it seems to have been.

I should perhaps add that I have recently isolated what I believe to be a group of genuine forgeries, of diverse subjects but all, hopefully, from the same *atelier*, in which the signature is so perfect that it transcends any original.

221. A perhaps to be expected manifestation of the periods of Revolution, the Directory, and the Empire of Napoleon is the increase in documentation in general and specifically for artists. Letters were exchanged frequently between Houdon and various government agencies, at first as though he were anxious to record the fact that he was on the right side and later as evidence of a growing pattern of bureaucracy. Under the old regime it is sometimes surprising how casually and informally commissions and arrangements between artists and the *Direction des Bâtiments* were carried on. Now there frequently seemed to be uncertainty on the part of artists exactly with whom they were dealing. For Houdon also it must be recalled that after his marriage Madame Houdon, more literate than he and an inveterate letter writer, conducted much of his correspondence.

Thus, for the bust of Necker we have extensive communications between Houdon and the Commune of the City of Paris in which, after the bust is voted, he offers—in the interest of good relations—to make it free of charge. There is a long series of expressions of admiration and good will recorded in the

Actes de la Commune de Paris (1789), I, 497, 504; III, 319, 383, 501. Then on August 10, 1792, with a radical change in the temper of the times, busts of Louis XVI, Necker, Lafayette, and Bailly (all, it happened, by Houdon) were ordered to be immediately destroyed. Reprinted Réau, 1964, I, 86–8.

222. Böhme, 'Unbekannte Büsten Houdons. Die Büsten von Lalande und Bailly in Altenburg', 1926. Le Châtelier, *L.-P. Deseine*, Paris, n.d. Although born in 1749, only seven years after Houdon, Louis-Pierre Deseine did not begin exhibiting in the Salons until 1785, and most of his sculpture belongs within the orbit of neo-classicism at the beginning of the nineteenth century. His bust of *Bailly* is so much superior to his other portraits that one wonders whether it could have been one of those copies about which Houdon complained so bitterly in his letter to Bachelier (Appendix 3 below).

223. Translated from the account of the meeting, June 5, 1791, of *la Société des amis de la Constitution*. Reprinted, A. Aulard, *La Société des Jacobins*, II, 481; and Réau, 1964, I, 88. For *Mirabeau* and the problems of the *concours*, see Arnason, *Houdon*, 1964, 106–8, bibliography.

223a. Comte LeLorrain Roederer, *Mémoires sur la Révolution, le Consulat et l'Empire*, Paris, 1942, p. 86.

224. Vitry, 'Notes sur les différents logements et ateliers occupés par J.-A. Houdon', 1907.

225. *Letter to Bachelier*, 1794. Published by Delerot & Legrelle, 1856. See Appendix 3 for full text.

225a. This note is on p. 121 below.

226. See note 94. Vitry, 'La *Diane* et l'*Apollon* de Houdon', 1907; Réau, 'La *Diane* et l'*Apollon* de Houdon . . . à Lisbon', 1960.

227. Arnason, *Houdon*, 1964, 18–20, bibliography. Also p. 14 above and notes 13, 14. In the *Letter to Bachelier* Houdon refers to the changes in the second, large version; 'L'ayant exécuté [L'Écorché] en bronze, il y a trois ans, j'y fis des changements. . . .'

228. Pevsner, *Academies of Art*, 140–42; Novotny, *Painting and Sculpture in Europe, 1780–1880*, 17–23, 209–17; Rosenblum, *Transformations in Late Eighteenth-Century Art*, 1967; Honour, *Neo-classicism*, 1967; *The Age of Neo-classicism* [exhibition], 1972.

229. For instance, *M. D. citoyen patriote et véridique* describes her as 'Une *Frileuse* qui se couvre la tête et qui met son cul à l'air'. Réau, 1964, I, 48, gives other examples. This bronze, incidentally, belonging to the Duc d'Orléans, was confiscated as the property of an émigré; as were a number of other works by Houdon belonging to noblemen or otherwise suspect collectors. Houdon himself brought *La Frileuse* to the depot as a token of his loyalty to the new regime.

230. *Revue du Salon de l'an X*; *Journal des arts: Exposition faite en 1802 par les artistes vivants*; reprinted Réau, 1964, I, 46.

231. Arnason, *Houdon*, 1964, 66–9, bibliography. A number of small maquettes exist, purporting to represent Houdon's ideas for the *Rousseau* monument. Réau illustrates two (Houdon, 1964, II, pl. XXXV). In judging these maquettes or reductions of Houdon's statues, such as the many small versions of the *Seated Voltaire*, these *Rousseau* sketches, or a sketch showing the *Monceau Fountain* in its original state, the criterion of quality is probably the maquette of the tomb of Prince Pjotr Mikhailovitch Galitzin, in the Louvre.

232. Vitry, 'La statue de la Philosophie de Houdon', 1907; Documents reprinted by Réau, 1964, I, 69–70.

233. The *livret* entry reads: '120. Un buste de femme grand comme nature et en bronze.' Réau, 1964, I, 339–40; II, 53–4, pls. CXXXVII and CXXXVIII, associates this entry with a Madame de Thélusson de Sorcy, of whom there exist three busts attributed to Houdon. A plaster, now in a private collection, Paris, is signed on the back in cursive script; *houdon*, and also has a *cachet d'atelier*. The face has pointing marks as though another bust had been made from it. On the other hand, the back of the plaster is closed in a manner unusual for Houdon, unless it had been made from a marble. There is a marble of the bust in the Courty collection also signed: *houdon*, essentially identical with the plaster. The third version is a bronze in the Detroit Institute of Arts in which an elaborate shawl covers the head and envelops the figure. The back is closed in a manner I have not been able to find in demonstrably eighteenth-century bronze busts; and in fact, the back of the bronze is textured in a manner suggestive of a marble (though a different marble than the Courty version). The bronze is signed and dated: *houdon. f. 1791*, with a precision and flourish beyond the signature on any of the major Houdon bronzes. The plaster and marble have an indefinable nineteenth-century look —which might be perfectly possible in a full-faced lady around 1791—but the elaboration of the bronze strongly accentuates this look. So this, in my estimation is a problem piece. [The detail of the marble illustrated by Réau, pl. CXXXVIII is my photograph, as are several other photographs in his book. I photographed all three busts of *Madame de Thélusson* in considerable detail.]

234. A terra cotta of Barnave, unsigned, in the Musée de Grenoble, was presumably given to the museum by Barnave's sister. Here the dangers of apparently conclusive documentation may be illustrated. If the sister were in Grenoble when Barnave had his bust made in Paris, she could have thought it was by Houdon. A plaster in the Musée Carnavalet, Paris, is similarly unsigned. Another plaster, bronzed, in the Courty Collection has a signature of Houdon. Although I have photographed

all three busts, I do not have a photograph of the signature, so cannot speak of it. Reserving judgement at this point, the portrait is a fine one, unquestionably of the time, but has a hardness in the modeling of details characteristic of Houdon's younger contemporaries. The treatment of hair, eyebrows, eyelids, mouth, has a sharp precision more characteristic of an L.-P. Deseine, than an Houdon. If Deseine had made the *Barnave* he would probably have signed it in detail, as was his habit. But, aside from his *Bailly* there are in the Musée Carnavalet, busts by L.-P. Deseine of *Jacques-Guillaume* and of *Michel-Augustin Thouret*, both signed and dated 1791. That of *Jacques-Guillaume* particularly, even though he is in modern dress rather than the toga worn by Barnave, is remarkably similar in technique, pose, and concept. These portrayals of young revolutionaries have a fiery, romantic melodramatic quality that is foreign to Houdon or that he reserved for the stage. In short it is my conclusion that the *Barnave* is a work comparable to those by Houdon in its power and distinction, but not in its style or concept.

235. Réau, 'Houdon sous la Révolution et l'Empire', 1924. A plaster, signed and dated HOUDON F. 2e année R., is in the Institute of France, and a second plaster is in the Courty Collection.

236. Réau, 1964, I, 102, adds to the list of the Salons an *Exposition de l'Élysée*, in 1798, that included plasters of *Molière*, *Voltaire*, and *Rousseau*; and marbles of *Voltaire* and *Rousseau* after the model of Houdon. The only new item was: 91. A little bronze portrait of *Voltaire* standing. A type of small standing *Voltaire* usually with Rousseau as a companion piece, both in modern dress, is common. Although many of these date from the late eighteenth and early nineteenth centuries, I have found none attributable to Houdon.

237. Réau remarks without documentation that this relief probably represents Houdon's sister-in-law and his niece. The plaster bust of *Sabine* I have not seen although there exist unusually good photographs. From the profile view I would say that this looks very much like the young lady portrayed in the medallion, and that if one is the other is. Both could certainly be the Sabine who looks out at us from Boilly's painting of Houdon's studio (1803, Musée des Arts Décoratifs) although this last is idealized in a neo-classical sense, and begins to look like the purported *Sabine* of 1807 who, Réau says, is the Comtesse de Montjay, again not giving his source. In any event I would not question that they are all admirable works by Houdon from the late neo-classical phase, and representations of a charming young lady (ladies?).

238. The marble bust of *Madame Duquesnoy* in the De Young Museum, San Francisco, is recorded as coming from the Jadelot family

It is shown very clearly in the 1803 painting by Boilly in the Musée des Arts Décoratifs on the stand immediately behind the legs of the *Seated Voltaire*. Here again, I regret to say I must differ with Réau. He identifies this bust in the Boilly painting with a marble bust of the Princess Lucien Bonaparte (1964, II, pl. CXVII). He also reproduces *Madame Duquesnoy* (pl. CXXII). The photograph of the entire bust he reproduces is from the same angle as Boilly's representation, and from detail photographs of the painting there is no question that this is Madame Duquesnoy. Coiffure, profile, and dress are the same, whereas these details in the princess differ markedly. I do not know whether Réau ever saw the actual bust of the *Princess Lucien Bonaparte*, the location of which, according to his account, is kept a secret; and the photographs of *Madame Duquesnoy* were taken after his death, at my request, when I was asked to examine the bust by the De Young Museum. I think if he had seen them, he would probably have agreed with me.

I should add that I have only seen a photograph of the bust of the *Princess Lucien Bonaparte*, which is unsigned and, apparently, not available. From the photograph I would only say that it seems untypical of Houdon, even *c.* 1800.

239. Réau, 'Houdon sous la Révolution et l'Empire', 1924. Aside from the marble and plaster in the Courty Collection, an unsigned terra cotta is recorded. The identification as the Princess de Salm-Dyck seems reasonable but could be argued.

240. It is possible that the busts of Monsieur and Madame Duquesnoy were conceived together; in which case his cape parallels her shawl. The *Journal d'Adrien Duquesnoy*, edited by Robert de Crèvecœur, was published in Paris, 1894.

241. A letter from Madame de Vandeul, Diderot's daughter, refers to busts of d'Alembert, Mentelle, and Lalande in this Salon. Reprinted Tourneaux, BSHA, 1912, cited by Réau, 1964, I, 102. For d'Alembert, see p. 49 and note 117.

242. A terra cotta is reported by Réau in the collection René Charlier, Paris. Although I know this only from the photograph, it seems completely characteristic of Houdon *c.* 1800. Réau, 'Houdon sous la Révolution et l'Empire', 1924.

243. Böhme, 'Unbekannte Büsten Houdons. Die Büsten von Lalande und Bailly in Altenburg', 1926. We know from the *Mémoires secrets* of Bachaumont that Houdon exhibited a bust of *Lalande* in the Salon of 1773, thus placing him among the first *philosophes* shortly after *Diderot*. And finally, despite certainty that the bust discussed here is *Lalande* by Houdon, there is in the Museum of Natural History in Paris a plaster bust presumed to be the naturalist, Joseph Dombey, which bears an astonishing resemblance to Lalande, although a rather sour, dyspeptic Lalande.

244. Metz, 'Das Marmorbild der Dorothea von Rodde-Schlözer von Jean-Antoine Houdon', 1958; L. von Schlözer, *Dorothea von Schlözer*, 1925. We must always recall that Houdon worked with assistants, and increasingly in the later stage of his career. These assistants, sculptors in their own right, prepared the moulds for the plaster casts and did much of the preliminary work on the marbles. Questions may be raised about certain marbles which seem to be perfectly authentic, but whose surfaces and even characterizations lack the subtlety that we associate with his own hand. His guarantee on certain works, principally plasters, 'réparé par l'auteur lui-même', certainly has significance. There are works that emerged from his studio, particularly after 1800, which must have felt little of the sculptor's finishing touch. The marble bust of *Dorothea von Rodde-Schlözer*, with all its subtlety of surface and characterization, is a late work that we can be quite sure came from the sculptor's own hand.

245. Unfortunately discussion of the *Marshal Ney* must be deferred, since I have not seen the bronze, and the plaster at Versailles is an inferior example. One comment may be made, the simplicity and honesty in the presentation of the marshal's youthful (he was then thirty-five years old) but impressively unostentatious head, contrasted with the imperial magnificence of his bemedalled uniform.

246. Original plasters exist in the Pennsylvania Academy of Fine Arts, where it has been since 1812, the National Academy of Design, New York, and the New York Historical Society. These are signed and dated under the right shoulder (on the end of the arm stump): *houdon f. an. XII* [1804], and inscribed under the left shoulder: *J. Barlow 50 ans.*, probably at the request of Barlow. These plasters are finished and closed at the back in a manner suggesting that they may have been made from a marble. There are also instances where eighteenth-century plasters open at the back have been filled in at a later date. Since it is known from the letter of Fulton to Ruth Baldwin Barlow, dated June 12, 1813, that Fulton ordered a marble of *Barlow* and that Barlow himself owned one, it is conceivable that one of these, probably the original, was signed, dated, and inscribed, and the later one, made nine years later, was unsigned. See Arnason, *Houdon*, 1964, 120–3, and 124–7, bibliography, reprint of Fulton letter to Mrs Barlow.

247. A number of original plasters exist, open at the back, of which one of the finest is that in the collection of Mrs Sarah Hunter Kelly, New York. Fulton's bust has also been copied frequently in modern times, in plaster and bronze. Arnason, op. cit.

248. Picard, 'Houdon et l'antique', 1943, gives the source of the *Cicero* as an *Augustus Imperator*. Documents and contemporary reviews cited by Réau, 1964, I, 71, 431–2.

249. The head of the Canova statue of Napoleon is a classical mask, as are most of its French offshoots. The bust by Chaudet is a somewhat more realistic version of that of Canova. Roland's statue of *Napoleon Imperator*, in all his imperial robes, is a celebration of the office rather than the man. David's similar exaltation of Napoleon, Emperor, in the vast painting of the *Coronation* appeared in the Salon of 1808 at the same time as Houdon's marble portrait bust. The iconography of Napoleon is immense and complex, but of the portrait busts perhaps the only one to compare with Houdon's 1806 terra cotta is Charles-Louis Corbet's portrait of 1798 (Lille). Made under the Directory before Napoleon had seized power to become First Consul and then Emperor, the bronze at Lille shows him in uniform, wearing his hair somewhat longer than in Houdon's bust or in later representations, as a young eighteenth-century soldier, his handsome face in no sense generalized, but already reflecting a quality of poetic intensity (Fig. 51).

The importance to Houdon of his session with Napoleon is documented in a letter to Daru, *Intendant Général* of the Emperor's household. Archives Nationales o²202.

Paris, August 17, 1806

Monsieur,
I do not know if you have been informed that His Majesty the Emperor granted me sittings to make his bust. I am happy to say that he is satisfied with the resemblance. I subsequently obtained the same favor and the same success with her Majesty the Empress.

Yesterday I submitted my work to the Emperor. He did me the great kindness to talk with me about the difficulties presented by sculpture devoid of the charm of color in creating a resemblance; I said that marble by its transparence and its grace removed some of these difficulties and I indicated my desire to execute the busts of their Majesties in this material.

The Emperor approved this wish on my part with the benevolence with which he has continued to honor me since I have had the good fortune of working from his august person. . . .

Houdon's elegant letter—undoubtedly composed by Madame Houdon—continues with queries concerning authorization for payment. The details were worked out in correspondence between Houdon and Daru. Archives Nationales, o²1840; o²840; o²838. Reprinted Réau, 1964, I, 90–1. See also G. Brière, 'Une lettre de J.-A. Houdon relative aux bustes de Napoléon et de Joséphine,' 1907. Unfortunately there is no evidence that the magnificent terra cotta at Dijon was ever translated into marble.

250. Since the terra cotta was finished and presented to the emperor for approval, according to Houdon's letter, on August 16, and since the Salon was held during the latter part of August, even Houdon would have had difficulty in completing the two marbles before the Salon opened.

The bust of *Madame von Rodde-Schlözer* has been discussed; that of the *Margrave d'Anspach* has not been securely identified. See Helen Clay Frick, 'Un buste présumé de Lady Craven par Houdon', 1948; and Réau, 1964, I, 463–4. A signed plaster bust of the comic poet, *Collin d'Harleville* (1755–1806) is in the Musée at Chartres. This has the neo-classical, herm treatment of the torso as a base, comparable to Houdon's 1806 terra cotta of Napoleon, and his marble of the Abbé Barthélemy. It is a posthumous portrait, made after a death-mask, and the extreme emaciation of the poet's face reflects his suffering during his long mortal illness. The plaster has been so heavily painted that most of the detail has been lost. I reproduce the bust (a recast) in the Musée Lambinet at Versailles (Fig. 197).

251. Bapst, 'Le buste en marbre de Madame Pineu-Duval, née Sabine Houdon', 1917; Réau, 'Houdon sous la Révolution et l'Empire', 1924. Bapst's original case is speculative. Réau's is based on the fact that a signed plaster of the young lady, in the Courty Collection, which is identical to the marble in the Wildenstein Gallery, New York, was formerly in the collection of Comte Jean de Segonzac, a descendant of the Comtesse de Montjay. Here I must admit to a prejudice. Questions can be raised about the identification of the subjects for the medallion in the Petit Palais, and, probably, for the bust in the Perrin-Houdon family (if it is still there). The only unquestioned evidence we have of Sabine's appearance as an adolescent girl already a young lady, is the 1803 painting by Boilly of Houdon and his family in his studio, in the Musée des Arts Décoratifs, Paris. Until I have positive, documentary evidence that the 1807 bust is actually the Comtesse de Montjay, I shall continue to think of her as Sabine; as I shall continue to think of the medallion and the plaster bust as representing Sabine in the process of growing up. The fundamental points are probably the authenticity and the quality of these late sculptures by Houdon. See also, Arnason, *Houdon*, 1964, 109–15, bibliography.

252. The marble busts of Napoleon and Josephine at Versailles, exhibited in the Salon of 1808, are most likely based on the models executed by the artist in 1806. There is no evidence of another sitting by either of them after this date. Although the head of Napoleon in the 1808 version looks somewhat heavier, it is essentially the same as the 1806 terra cotta. Even the famous lock of hair falling over the forehead is arranged in an identical manner. This illustrates the difference in effect arising from a difference of dress. The stand-up military collar of the period—continued in uniforms through World War I—creates a somewhat choking effect. Marshal Ney is dominated by his collar.

The date of 1808 on the marble of Josephine would indicate the date of exhibition or of delivery of this particular marble bust. Both busts have an effect more uniform and even colder than earlier works by the artist, indicative of his acceptance of neo-classical criteria, particularly in official works such as these. He was probably well aware of the preferences of the emperor and his court.

Houdon's modeling of the hair has frequently been commented on as a signature that differentiates his sculptures from that of most of his contemporaries, both of the old regime and—particularly—of the post-revolutionary period of neo-classicism. Neo-classical sculptors carried the tendency of antiquity, to treat hair as carved stone rather than simulated hair, to an extreme of non-naturalism. In surviving portraits of men and women of the post-revolutionary period, such as the *Dorothea von Rodde-Schlözer* and the 'Sabine' at the age of twenty, Houdon continued to resist this tendency. Thus, Josephine's enamelled ringlets are something of an oddity, but they do occur in other busts of women from the same period attributed to the sculptor. The fact that these curls over the forehead are combined with the main mass of the hair shown as hair, in his customary technique, suggests that they represent a fashion of the time, in which they were actually shaped and fixed as they appear. Deriving in all probability from ancient sculpture, they represent another aspect of the classic mode that permeated not only painting, sculpture, and architecture, but all aspects of decoration including women's fashions. Houdon as always was imitating nature, but in this instance nature was imitating art.

In a fine plaster in the Courty Collection, Josephine's hair throughout is treated in Houdon's characteristic manner. This bust differs in several details from the marble and may well be an earlier version. Josephine is shown without shoulders, undraped, *à l'antique*, in the sculptor's basic classical formula. She also wears a different tiara. G. Brière, 'Une lettre de Houdon relative aux bustes de Napoléon et de Joséphine', 1907; Réau, 1964, I, 89–91, reprints of documents. A plaster of the actress, Mme de Grandménil (Heim Gallery, London), signed Houdon and dating circa 1800, features the same shaped curls as Josephine.

253. The marble bust of Bigot de Préameneu i[s] in the collection of his descendant, Comt[e] Boulay de la Meurthe, in Paris.

254. Archives Nationales o³1387. 'It is the leas[t] advanced of those of the dead generals. H[e] [Houdon] excuses himself, having been occu[pied with the colossal statue of the empero[r] for the column at Boulogne. The model is a[t] the point of being finished.' Report of Denon August 15, 1808. Archives Nationales, o²841[.] '. . . M. Houdon, charged with that of Genera[l] Joubert, having been occupied to the presen[t] time with the statue of His Majesty th[e] Emperor, which is to surmount the colum[n] at Boulogne-sur-Mer.' Denon to the Comt[e] Daru, September 3, 1810.

255. Hubert, 'Une œuvre de Houdon identifiée[:] la statue du général Joubert à Versailles'[,] 1956; The commission of 1806 is given in letter in the archives of the Louvre, reprinte[d] by P. Marmottan, 'Commandes de Napoléo[n] aux artistes entre 1805 et 1810', 1921.

256. See Appendix 3: '. . . under the Old Regim[e] my works were constantly being recast wit[h] my name forged, and others even less hones[t] simply copied them putting their name o[n] them; and now, despite formal decree of th[e] Convention for the protection of the art[s] and artists' rights, they continue to sell, t[o] exhibit, to parade publicly [my works] an[d] thus to rob me of my labors.' How lucky it i[s] that Houdon could not know what was t[o] happen after his death.

257. We need only mention the *Mirabeau[,] Bailly*, *Necker*, *Barthélemy*, *Lalande*, *Madam[e] von Rodde-Schlözer*, *Barlow*, *Fulton*, *Napoleon[,] Josephine*, *Dumouriez*, *Bigot de Préameneu*, an[d] portraits of his children.

258. Michelangelo's use of the pointing hori[-]zontal arm cutting across the vertical mass o[f] the figure (as in his *Moses*, which Houdo[n] could have known at Rome) would be a[n] obvious prototype for this use of opposites i[n] tension.

259. Aside from the *livret* for the Salon of 1812[,] the *Standing Voltaire* is documented by th[e] *Mercure de France*, July 1806: 'The presen[t] tomb of Voltaire in the church of Sainte[-] Geneviève will be replaced at once by [a] monument in marble which will be place[d] against one of the walls of the sepulchra[l] chapel. The celebrated sculptor, Monsieu[r] Houdon, is charged with the commission.'

The quotation from Réau is *Houdon*, 1964[,] I, 450. See also, Réau, 'Houdon sous la Révo[-]lution et l'Empire', 1924.

260. Documents on Houdon's life during th[e] Revolutionary and post-Revolutionary era[s] are reprinted in Réau, 1964, I, 31–6; See als[o] Helen Clay Frick, 'Madame Jean-Antoin[e] Houdon', 1947. For the sale of the content[s] of his studio, see Appendix 5.

261. A mundane but accurate index of Houdon's steadily increasing reputation during the second half of the nineteenth century and the twentieth century is to be found in sales catalogues. Despite the enormous number of replicas created by Houdon, many of which have been on the market during the last hundred and fifty years, there has been a steady and at times dramatic increase in prices paid for them. In the last fifty years prices for important examples have reached astronomical heights. Réau, who has a passion for such statistics, gives a comprehensive list: *Houdon*, 1964, I, 118–27. The most telling evidence is still the number of later replicas and forgeries.

ADDITIONAL NOTES

38a. The plaster bust of a woman in the Gotha Museum is catalogued as Marie-Charlotte, wife of Duke Ernest-Louis. The *livret* for the Salon of 1773 lists the late duke, Frederick III (No. 232); the reigning duke, Ernest-Louis (No. 233); Marie-Charlotte, wife of the reigning duke (No. 234); and Fredericka-Louisa, sister of the reigning duke (No. 235). Neither the material nor the form of these sculptures is indicated. However, in the list of Houdon's works, c. 1784 (Appendix 2 below), the following are mentioned: No. 17, Bust of the Duchess of Saxe-Gotha; and No. 18, Medallions of the Duke and the Duchess of Saxe-Gotha and of the late Duke (*duc Père*). In the Gotha Museum there exist, as described in my text, two plaster medallions, painted bronze color and carefully finished, of the reigning duke, Ernest Louis, and his father, the late Duke Frederick III. The medallion of the duchess has disappeared. There is also an original plaster bust of a lady, sketchily modeled, which is traditionally identified as the reigning duchess, presumably on the evidence (No. 17 in the list of c. 1784) that Houdon had made a bust of a duchess of Saxe-Gotha. It seems to me odd that Houdon should have made both a medallion and a bust of the duchess while making only medallions of the dukes. Therefore I incline to think that the bust is actually that of the sister, Fredericka-Louisa, referred to in the *livret* of 1773. Although I know nothing about the lady, she looks more like a bluestocking spinster than like the bride whom the handsome young duke might have chosen. This is, of course, pure speculation, but Houdon could easily have referred to the sister also as a duchess.

225a. When I saw Houdon's bronze *Apollo* in the Paris home of Mr. Gulbenkian before it was sent to Lisbon to become part of the Gulbenkian Foundation, I was somewhat disturbed by the fact that the god wore a fig leaf. This did not seem characteristic of the sculptor's almost fanatical devotion to nature and antiquity. Hence I was delighted when I received a new photograph from the Gulbenkian Foundation and found that the fig leaf had been removed and that Apollo was shown in the appropriate Greek state of godlike nudity. The fig leaf had obviously been an accretion of the nineteenth century. See also Note 101 above.

APPENDIX 1

The Roman Sculptures

The Small *Vestal*.
Head of a *Vestal*. Plaster, Gotha; marble replica, 1788, Louvre.
Peasant Girl of Frascati.
Unknown Girl, 1774, Paris, 1775, Leningrad. Marble replicas of
    Peasant Girl of Frascati.
Roman Youth, 1775, New York and London. Possibly after an original
    made in Rome.
L'Écorché.
Saint John the Baptist.
Saint Bruno.
Priest of the Lupercalia.

NOTE. The surviving sculptures from the Roman period, 1764–8, and
later replicas derived from them, are all classic in their common
qualities of simplicity, control and emotional restraint. This is in
general a classicism stemming from Raphael and the High Rennais-
sance as well as from Roman antiquity. The later replicas indicate
Houdon's re-use of earlier themes when they were appropriate to the
time.
The *Priest of the Lupercalia*, while related to ancient statues such as the
Borghese Warrior, derives more immediately from Bernini's *Apollo*
of his *Apollo and Daphne* and from Nicolas Coustou's *Apollo*, also
stemming from Bernini.

Livrets of the Salons of Paris—1769–1814—Entries by Houdon.
Surviving, identified works marked with an
asterisk. These are not always necessarily the specific
example exhibited in the Salon. The spelling follows the
original text.

1769

Sculptures by Houdon not listed but reconstituted from the drawings
by Saint-Aubin and from contemporary reviews:
Un prêtre lupercal.*
Saint Jean-Baptiste prêchant.*
Saint Bruno en méditation.*
Buste d'une paysanne de Frascati.*
Tête d'enfant en marbre blanc.

NOTE. Aside from the unidentified marble head of a child, the four
other works were undoubtedly the plasters from Houdon's work in
Rome which are now in Gotha. They represent different explorations
of classical themes and forms.

1771

279. *Morphée.* L'un des enfants et ministres du dieu du Sommeil.
    C'est le plus habile de tous les songes pour prendre la démarche,
    l'air, le visage et le son de la voix de ceux qu'il veux représenter.
    C'est lui qui fut envoyé par le dieu à Alcione sous la figure de son
    époux. Modèle de grandeur naturelle.
280. Les portraits de *M. Bignon*, prévôt des marchands, et de Mme.
    son épouse.
281. Le portrait de *M. Diderot*.*

282. Le portrait de *Mme de Mailly*, épouse de M. de Mailly, peintre
    en émail.
283. La tête d'*Alexandre*. Médaillon plus grand que le naturel pour
    faire pendant à une tête antique de *Minerve*, de même grandeur et
    de même relief.
284. *Deux têtes de jeunes hommes*, l'une couronnée de myrte, l'autre
    ceinte d'un ruban. De ronde-bosse et de grandeur naturelle.

NOTE. The classical theme continues, notably in the life-size *Morpheus*,
repeated in 1777 in a reduced scale marble as Houdon's *morceau de
réception* for the Academy. The portrait of *Diderot*, first of the great
series of *philosophes*, is without shoulders, undraped *à l'antique*, in
the formula to be used for scientists, philosophers, and men of
letters, throughout the artist's career. Also to be noted, although not in
the Salon, is *Mme de Charrière*, a woman of the Enlightenment.

1773

229. Un monument érigé en l'honneur de M. *le prince Miche*
    Michaïlowitsch Gallitzin.*
    Un génie militaire, appuyé sur une urne cinéraire, éteint un flam-
    beau; à ses pieds est un trophée du casque, de l'épée et du bouclier
    de ce prince; des palmes, des lauriers et différentes couronne
    désignent les genres de victoires qu'il a remportées.
    Cette figure, de grandeur naturelle, est appuyée sur un fond forman
    une pyramide, qui doit être accompagnée de deux cyprès.
    Ce morceau, dont la pyramide a 10 pieds de haut sur 4 de large
    s'exécute en marbre au Roule, dans les ateliers de la Ville.
230. Autre monument à l'honneur du *prince Alexis de Mitricewitsc*
    [Dmitrievitch] *Gallitzin*.*
    La Justice est appuyée sur une table destinée à recevoir l'inscrip-
    tion. Sur le socle qui porte cette figure est une urne cinérair
    groupée avec une branche de cyprès. Au-dessous sont deux fais
    ceaux qui désignent la qualité de sénateur dont le prince étai
    revêtu. Ce morceau, de même grandeur que le précédant, s'exécut
    dans le même atelier.
231. *L'Impératrice de Russie*. Buste en marbre.*
232. Le portrait de feu Frédéric III, duc de Saxe-Gotha et Alten
    bourg.*
233. Ernest-Louis, duc régnant.*
234. *Marie-Charlotte de Saxe-Meiningen*, épouse du duc régnant.
235. Frédérique-Louise, sœur du duc régnant.*
236. Une tête de vieillard aveugle représentant *Bélisaire*.*

NOTE. The two tombs of the Galitzin are unusual for eighteenth
century tomb sculpture in their classical austerity. The medallion
of the dukes of Saxe-Gotha also continue the classical formula, a
does the bust of Fredericka-Louisa. The *tête d'expression* of *Belisariu*
employs a more dramatic, expressionist approach; and the portrai
of *Catherine the Great* is Houdon's first essay in the Baroque, officia
portrait.

1775

252. *Une femme sortant du bain*. Modèle en plâtre; il doit être exécut
    en marbre.
253. Le buste de *M. le marquis de Miromesnil*, garde des sceaux.*
254. Le modèle du buste de *M. Turgot*, contrôleur général. Plâtre.*
255. Le Buste de *Mme. la Comtesse du Caila*.
256. Le Buste de *Mme. la Baronne de la Houze*.

257. Le Buste en marbre de *Mlle. Arnould*, dans le rôle d'Iphigénie.*
258. Le Buste de M. le *Chevalier Gluck.**
259. Le Modèle d'une Chapelle Sépulcrale, en mémoire de *Louise-Dorothée, Duchess de Saxe-Gotha.*

Au fond de cette Chapelle est la porte du Temple de la Mort, qui, sous la Figure d'une squelette, lève, pour en sortir, les rideaux dont elle est en partie voilée, & se saisit, avec précipitation, de la Duchesse. La Duchesse, les cheveux épars, est couverte d'une linceul; elle doit exprimer son attachement pour tous ceux qui lui étoient alliés, & son affection pour le Peuple.

260. Un Buste en marbre de *Mme. His.**
261. Plusieurs Têtes ou Portraits en marbre sous le même Numéro.
262. Une Tête de Méduse, imitée de l'Antique.
263. Une Tête de Femme. Plâtre bronze.

NOTE. With the Salons of 1775 and 1777 the classical theme is subordinated to the rococo, particularly in the portraits of ladies of the court, where the emphasis is on elaborate elegance expressed in virtuoso techniques. There can be no doubt that the preferences of the patrons played a large role, but the style was by no means uncongenial to the artist. Even the portrait of *Turgot* is an elegant court image. That of *Miromesnil*, on the other hand, inaugurates the impressive sobriety of the professional portrait. The model of the sepulchral chapel for the Duchess of Saxe-Gotha, probably the first of Houdon's designs for tomb sculpture, is very much in the manner of eighteenth-century adaptations of Roman Baroque tombs. Although all that is left is the description, the drawing for the tomb of Monsieur Guillard,* dated 1774, may indicate something of its elaborate emotionalism. The bust of *Gluck* is unusual in its direct, expressive statement of materials; in this it is related to the *Belisarius* of 1773.

1777

233. Portrait de Monsieur.*
234. Portrait de Madame.
235. Portrait de Madame Adélaïde.*
236. Portrait de Madame Victoire.*
Ces quatre bustes sont en marbre.
237. Deux Têtes d'Étude. En terre cuite.
238. Portrait de M. le Baron de Vietinghoff [marbre*]. Buste en plâtre.

Bustes en marbre

239. Portrait de Madame la Comtesse de Cayla.*
240. Portrait de Madame la Comtesse de Jaucourt, sa mère.*
241. Portrait de M. Turgot, ancien Contrôleur-Général, Honoraire-Associé-libre de l'Académie.*
242. Portrait de Madame de ***.[*?]
243. Portrait de Madame Servat.*
244. Portrait de Mademoiselle Servat.
245. Portrait de M. le Chevalier Gluck. Il doit être placé dans le foyer de l'Opéra.
246. Deux autres Portraits des Enfans de M. Brognard.*
247. Portrait de Mademoiselle Bocquet. En terre cuite.
248. Buste en marbre d'une Diane, dont le modèle, de grandeur naturelle, a été fait à la Bibliothèque du Roi.* Cette Diane doit être exécutée en marbre & placée dans les Jardins de S.A. le Duc de Saxe-Gotha.
249. Buste de Charles IX, en plâtre. Il doit être exécuté en marbre pour le Collège Royal.
250. Plusieurs Portraits en médaillons, de grandeur naturelle.
251. Médaillon de Minerve, en marbre.

Une Nayade, de grandeur naturelle, devant servir à former une Fontaine.
Cette Figure doit être exécutée en marbre. Le modèle se voit à la Bibliothèque du Roi, sur le premier pallier du grand escalier.
252. Plusieurs Animaux, en marbre.* [One identified.]
253. Plusieurs Portraits, en cire.
254. Deux Esquisses de Tombeaux pour deux Princes Gallitzin.* [One survives.] Ces Monuments doivent être exécutés en marbre, de grandeur naturelle.
255. Une Vestale, en bronze.* L'idée est prise d'après le marbre que l'on voit à Rome, appellé vulgairement *Pandore*. Cette Figure, de 23 pouces, doit servir de lampe de nuit.
256. Morphée.* Cette Figure, en marbre, est le morceau de Réception de l'Auteur.

NOTE. The rococo approach continues with marbles of plasters shown in 1775, new portraits of members of the royal house, and an elaborate fountain figure of a Naiad, lost, but preserved in a drawing by Saint-Aubin. The Brongniart children inaugurate the subject of children. There is a return to classical themes with the *Diana* and the medallion of Minerva, as well as the bronze cast of the small *Vestal*—first evidence of the new interest in bronze. The surviving maquette for the monument to Prince Pjotr Mikhailovitch Galitzin also suggests an attempt on the part of Houdon to reconcile the tradition of Roman Baroque tomb sculpture with a more formally classical organization. The marble reduction of the *Morpheus* (Houdon's *morceau de réception* for the Academy) is more rococo in feeling than the life-size plaster exhibited in 1771, in part as a consequence of the virtuoso carving and polishing of the marble. The Salon of 1777 is a high point in the quantity and quality and variety of the entries.

1779. Par M. *Houdon*, Académicien.

Bustes en marbre

216. M. de Nicolai, Premier Président de la Chambre des Comptes.*
217. M. de Caumartin, Prévôt des Marchands.*

Bustes en terre cuite

218. Molière.* Il est tiré du Cabinet de M. de Miromesnil, Garde-des-Sceaux. [plasters and marble]
219. Voltaire.*.
Ces deux bustes sont exécutés en marbre, & placés dans le Foyer de la Comédie Françoise.
220. J.-J. Rousseau.* Appartenant à M. le Marquis de Gerardin [Girardin].
221. Buste de M. Franklin.*
222. Statue de Voltaire, représenté assis.* Cette Figure est exécutée en bronze dors. [Others exist]
223. Autre Buste de Voltaire, drapé à la manière des Anciens.* Il est exécuté en marbre.
Ces deux objets sont placés dans le Cabinet de l'Impératrice de Russie.

NOTE. *Nicolai* and *Caumartin* continue the formula of the official, professional, portrait of *Miromesnil*; *Molière* the informal presentation of the poet or musician, inaugurated with *Gluck*. Portraits of the *philosophes*, Voltaire, Rousseau, and Franklin, are presented first in contemporary dress, with perruque, and then variations begin to be played, showing them draped and undraped, *à l'antique*. The gilt-bronze 'statue' of Voltaire for Catherine is a small sketch of the great marble statue on which the sculptor is working. The Salon of

1779 is the first major presentation of a group of the great men of the Enlightenment.

1781. Par M. *Houdon*, Académicien

251. Le Maréchal de Tourville. Statue en marbre de 6 pieds de proportion, pour le Roi.*

Le Maréchal est représenté à l'instant où il fait voir au Conseil de Guerre la lettre du Roi, qui lui commande de donner le signal d'ordre de battaille. Cette action se passa au mois de Mai, 1692, suivant les mémoires du Duc de Barvick. En voici l'extrait: Le rendez-vous de la Flotte, étoit, au mois de Mai à l'hauteur d'Ouessant, mais les vents contraires empêchèrent le Comte d'Etrées, pendant six semaines, de sortir de la Méditerranée avec les Vaisseaux de Toulon; de manière que le Roi, impatient d'exécuter son projet, envoya ordre au Chevalier de Tourville, Amiral de la Flotte, d'entrer dans la Manche avec les Vaisseaux de Brest, sans attendre l'Escadre du Comte d'Etrées, & de combattre les ennemis forts ou foibles, s'il les trouvoient. Cet Amiral, le plus habile homme de Mer qu'il y eût en France, & peut-être même dans le monde entier, ne balança d'exécuter l'ordre qu'il avoit reçu.

252. Statue en marbre, de M. de Voltaire,* qui devoit être placée à l'Académie Françoise, mais destinée depuis à décorer la nouvelle Salle de Comédie, rue de Condé.

Bustes en marbre

253. M. le Duc de Praslin.*
254. M. Tronchin, Médecin.*
255. Mademoiselle Odeoud [Audéoud] [plaster*]. Ce Buste appartient à M. Girardot de Marigny.

Bustes en plâtre, *couleur de terre cuite*

256. Mme. la Princesse d'Aschkoff [Dachkov].
257. Mme. de Sérilly.
258. M. le Comte de Valbelle.*
259. M. Qesnay, Médecin.
260. M. Gerbier, Avocat.*
261. Paul Jones.*
262. M. Palissot.*
263. Médaillon, bas-relief en plâtre, représentant la tête du Soleil.
264. Le Buste d'une Négresse en plâtre, imitant le bronze antique.*

NOTE. The most notable event of this Salon was the appearance of the marble statue of the seated *Voltaire* for the Comédie Française, although the place of honor is given to the *Maréchal de Tourville*, Houdon's contribution to d'Angiviller's series of the Great Men of France. This *tour de force* of Baroque emotion was the artist's only royal commission for a statue under the old regime. The portrait busts include a range of professional men, nobles, ladies of the court, and the second of the American portraits, *John Paul Jones*. *Mademoiselle Audéoud* is another in the delightful children's series.

1783. Par M. *Houdon*, Académicien

Bustes en marbre

241. Du Général Soltikoff.*
242. Du Comte Soltikoff son fils, aussi Général.
243. De Madame de Sérilly.*
244. De Mademoiselle Robert, fille de M. Robert, Peintre du Roi.
245. De M. Louis, Chirurgien.*
246. Le Buste d'Alexandre, pour S.M. le Roi de Pologne.*

247. Le Buste de La Fontaine.* Le modèle a été fait en 1781 pour M. le Président Aubry.
248. Buste de M. le Comte de Buffon;* il a été exécuté en marbre aux frais de S.M. l'Impératrice de toutes les Russies.
249. Madame la Princesse Achkow [Dachkov], Directrice de l'Académie des Sciences de Saint-Pétersbourg. *Buste en bronze.*
250. Leurs Altesses le Prince & la Princesse de Mecklimbourg-Schwerin.*
251. M. de la Rive, de la Comédie Françoise, dans le rôle de Brutus. Une jeune Fille en marbre de grandeur naturelle exprimant le froid, surnommé la Frileuse.* Elle est chez l'Auteur à la Bibliothèque du Roi. Une Statue de Diane en bronze chez M. Girardot de Marigny, rue Vivienne.* Une Fontaine composée de deux figures de grandeur naturelle, l'une en marbre blanc, & l'autre imitant une Négresse, exécutées & placées dans le Jardin de Monseigneur le Duc de Chartres, à Monceaux, près de Paris.* [The marble statue of the *Bather* survives.]

NOTE. The portrait busts continue the pattern of variety and quality evident in the Salon of 1783; a great scientist, Buffon, a great poet, La Fontaine, a noted medical man, and a famous actor, nobles from France, Germany, and Russia, and a commission from the King of Poland. The sculptor continues to adapt his approach to the individual, his profession or interests, or his station; ranging from *Buffon* undraped, *à l'antique* to the rococo elegance of *Madame de Sérilly*. The same range is evident in the three statues, the bronze *Diana*, the marble *Frileuse* and the Monceau Fountain.

1785

Par M. *Houdon*, de l'Académie de Toulouse, Académicien.

Bustes en marbre

225. M. le Noir, Conseiller d'Etat, Bibliothécaire du Roi, &c.* (?) [bronze]
226. M. de Biré.* (?)
227. M. de la Rive, dans le rôle de Brutus.*

Bustes en plâtre

228. Sa Majesté le Roi de Suède.
229. Le Prince Henri.*
230. M. le Pelletier de Morfontaine, Prévôt des Marchands.
231. Plusieurs Portraits sous le même numéro.

NOTE. Of the few entries for the Salon of 1785 only two securely identified busts remain: the superb marble of the actor, *Larive*, in the Comédie Française, and the plaster of *Prince Henry of Prussia*, in the State Library at Weimar. *Lenoir* and *de Biré* are problems of subject identification, discussed in the text. The paucity of entries was the consequence of Houdon's departure for the United States to take the likeness of George Washington.

1787

Par M. *Houdon*, Académicien, Membre de l'Académie de Toulouse.

Bustes en marbre

252. Le Roi.*
253. Le Prince Henri de Prusse, pour le Roi.
254. M. le Bailli de Suffren.* Pour MM. les Directeurs de la noble Compagnie des Indes Hollandoises du département de Zélande.

255. M. le Marquis de Bouillé.*
256. M. le Marquis de la Fayette, pour les Etats de la Virginie.*
257. Une Vestale.*
258. Tête de jeune fille. (*?) En plâtre.
259. Le Général Washington, fait par l'Auteur dans la Terre de ce Général en Virginie.*

NOTE. Because several of the busts were commemorative sculptures ordered for public presentation, and were of royalty and nobility, Houdon used a Baroque formula, with full torso, encompassed in drapery acting as transition to the base. *Henry of Prussia*, in the surviving bronze version at Potsdam, is in armor surmounted by a toga. The plaster head of a young girl is possibly Madame Houdon. Among works of that time not presented in the Salon, the busts of the *Duc de Nivernais*, the *Marquis de Méjanes*, and *Cagliostro*, should also be noted.

1789

Par M. *Houdon*, Académicien, Membre de l'Académie de Toulouse.
240. Le Prince Henri de Prusse.* Buste en bronze de grandeur naturelle.
241. M. Sesserson, Envoyé des Etats de Virginie.*
242. M. le Chevalier de Boufflers.
243. M. le Président du Paty.*
244. Mlle. Olivier. Pensionnaire du Roi.
245. Pilastre de Rosier.
Ces Bustes sont en plâtre.
246. Tête d'Enfant à l'âge de 10 mois (*?)
247. J.-J. Rousseau.
248. Buffon.
249. Diderot.
Têtes en marbre de petite proportion.

NOTE. This last Salon before the French Revolution features a rather mixed bag, of which only the bronze of *Prince Henry*, and a marble and plasters of *Thomas Jefferson* (No. 241, 'M. Sesserson'), and *Monsieur du Paty*, survive and can be identified. These suggest the increasing sobriety in the presentation of men's dress. The head of a child (No. 246) may be a portrait of Sabine, one of Houdon's delightful portraits of his own children.

1791

484. Onze morceaux de Sculpture. Bustes tant en Marbre qu'en Terre cuite, Plâtre, & Bronze. M. la Fayette* (?), deux Têtes grouppées, Voltaire, deux Têtes d'Enfants, Franklin* (?), Têtes de jeune Fille, M. Bailly,* Tête d'Enfant, M. Necker* & Mirabeau.* Par M. *Houdon*, Ac.
492. Bustes de Femme en plâtre. Par M. *Houdon*, Ac.
788. Figure de Bronze, représentant une Frileuse.* Par M. Houdon, Ac.

NOTE. The Salon of 1791, the first after the Revolution, saw the opening up of the exhibition to all artists, French or foreign, whether or not members of the Academy. Works were listed in the *livret* in accordance with their placement in the galleries, resulting in the separation of numbers. Surviving by Houdon are the *Lafayette* (the later type of the Versailles marble, if not the original); very probably the *Franklin à l'antique* (Boston and Angers); *Bailly*, *Necker*, and *Mirabeau*; and the bronze *Frileuse*. The children *may* be his own.

Réau (1964, I, 102) gives a supplementary list, overlapping the one of the *livret* and more specific in identification. I have not yet traced its source. From this point forward, Houdon's entries are few, and an increasing number are not identified. Among them, however, despite increasing concessions to neo-classicism, there are a number of excellent portraits, indicating little decline in his powers.

1793

120. Un Buste de Femme, grand comme nature & en bronze. Par *Houdon*.
121. Une Vestale. Statue de 20 pouces de hauteur. Par le même.*
122. Le Général Washington. Statue esquisse en plâtre d'environ 1 pied. Par le même.
123. Un Buste d'Enfant en plâtre. Par le même.
124. Une petite Frileuse.* Par le même.

NOTE. From this point forward Houdon exhibits little, except replicas of earlier busts or reduced versions of *La Frileuse*, etc. As a senior Academician, Salon showings were of less importance to him except when he had in hand a portrait of Napoleon or a major commission such as the *Standing Voltaire*, the *Cicero*, or the *General Joubert*. He seems to have continued working energetically, producing replicas of his more popular earlier busts and seeking large commissions, in most cases with little success.

1795

Par le C. *Houdon*, au Louvre
1040. Le buste de Barthélemy, auteur d'Anacharsis, grandeur naturelle.*

NOTE. With this Salon the *livret* reverted to the traditional form of listing the artists alphabetically under each medium—Painting, Sculpture, Printmaking, Drawings, etc.

1796 [Year V]

Houdon (Jean-A.), élève de Michel-Ange Slodtz, cour du Louvre.
617. La frileuse. Statue en marbre: hauteur 20 pouces. Cette figure appartient à l'Auteur.
618. Buste de Pastoret. Terre cuite. Fait l'an 1er de la République.

1798 [Year VII]

No entries.

NOTE. Réau (1964, I, 102) notes in an *Exposition de l'Élysée*, three plaster busts of *Molière*, *Voltaire*, and *Rousseau*, réparés par Houdon; a small bronze portrait of a standing *Voltaire*; and marble busts of *Voltaire* and *Rousseau* d'après le modèle de Houdon. The small, standing *Voltaire* has not been identified, although there are many of this type by other sculptors, frequently with a *Rousseau* as companion. The notes on the busts, *réparés par Houdon* and *d'après le modèle de Houdon*, are of interest as indications that questions of authenticity were already being raised.

1799 [Year VIII]

No entries recorded.

1800 [*Year IX*]

Houdon, membre de l'institut national
438. Plusieurs bustes en marbre et en plâtre, sous le même numéro.

1801 [*Year X*]

NOTE. From this point forward I am following the listing of Salons in Réau, 1964, I, 102–3. For 1801 he states that the listing was the same as in 1800, but notes that according to a letter from Madame de Vandeul, Diderot's daughter, busts exhibited included *Lalande*, *Mentelle*, and *d'Alembert*.

1802 [*Year X*]

Bustes en marbre
429. *D'Alembert.**
430. *L'abbé Barthélemy.**
431. Étude de femme.

Bustes en plâtre
432. *Mme. Rodde.**
433. *Mme la margrave d'Anspach.*
434. *Le cit. Mentelle*, membre de l'Institut.
Ils appartiennent à l'auteur.

NOTE. The *d'Alembert* may well be the marble in New Haven, even though this is dated 1779, and in my opinion was probably made about that time. The *Barthélemy* is probably the marble now in the Bibliothèque Nationale, Paris, of which the version in the Salon of 1795, in accordance with Houdon's practice, was likely a plaster. We have no idea why the *d'Alembert* was not exhibited earlier, but the artist was now sending in versions of earlier portraits—*Diderot*, *Voltaire*, *Rousseau*. If the marbles of *d'Alembert* and *Barthélemy* do date sixteen years apart, they indicate how consistent were Houdon's style and technical quality. Both are beautiful; the principal difference is the use of the squared-off herm base for the *Barthélemy*.
According to the *Salon of the year X* Houdon also exhibited statues (probably reduced scale) of *La Frileuse* and the *bronze Diana*.

1804

636. *Mme. la margrave d'Anspach.*
637. *Le maréchal Ney.**
638. *M. Barlow.**
639. *M. Fulton.**
641. *Cicéron.* Statue en plâtre.*
L'artiste a choisi le moment où Cicéron adresse, en plein Sénat,

ces paroles à Catalina: *Du Sénat et de Rome, il est temps que tu sortes.*
Cette statue doit être exécutée en marbre pour le Sénat conservateur.

NOTE. Of particular interest here is the *Cicero*—although never realized in marble—as an instance of Houdon's adherence to historical classicism, contrasted to the mannerism of neo-classicism. The portraits of *Barlow* and *Fulton*, the last American portraits, are fine examples of his late portraits.

1806

601. Buste de *Sa Majesté l'Empereur et Roi.**
602. Buste de *Sa Majesté l'Impératrice.*
603. *Madame F . . .*
604. *Mademoiselle H . . .** (?)
605. *Collin d'Harleville.**
606. Buste en marbre de *S.A.S. Madame la margrave d'Anspach.*
607. *Madame Rodde.* Buste en marbre.*

NOTE. The bust of *Napoleon* is almost without question the magnificent terra cotta at Dijon, the finest example of Houdon's late classical portrait bust. The marble of *Dorothea von Rodde*, in Berlin, illustrates how well the artist was able to maintain his characteristic quality of generalization in the face of the cold and mechanical surfaces becoming customary in neo-classical sculpture. The degree to which this is evident in Houdon's late marbles is probably an index of the degree to which he himself finished the marble.

1808

703. *Sa Majesté l'Empereur.**
704. *Sa Majesté l'Impératrice.**

NOTE. These are probably the marbles at Versailles.

1812

1089. *Général Joubert.* Statue en marbre.*
1090. *Voltaire.* Statue en marbre.*
1091. *M. le comte de Boissy d'Anglas*, sénateur. Buste en plâtre.

NOTE. The *Joubert* at Versailles and the standing *Voltaire* in the Panthéon, Paris, are the last surviving full-scale sculptures by Houdon.

1814

Buste de l'empereur de Russie *Alexandre Ier.*

APPENDIX 2

A List of Sculptures Drawn up by the Artist about 1784, with a Partial Supplement after that Date.

Note: This list has been reprinted by Délerot and Legrelle, Montaiglon and Duplessis, Dierks and Réau. The definitive version is Paul Vitry, 'Une liste d'œuvres de J.-A. Houdon rédigée par l'artiste lui-même vers 1784', *Archives de l'art français*, series 1, 1907, pp. 193–220. The list is valuable, despite its incompleteness, certain inaccuracies in listing, and the peculiarities of Houdon's spelling. It indicates the quantity of works that have disappeared or been destroyed.

Nº 1. Un grand Ecorché de grandeur naturel. Plus fait un petit Ecorché de 18 pouces d'auteur pour servir d'étude aux Elèves.

Nº 2. Un *St Brunot* sur dix pieds de proportion exécuté en marbre pour l'Eglise des Chartreux de Rome.
Plus le même sur 2 pieds et demit d'auteur.

Nº 3. Un *St Jean Baptiste* de grandeur naturel.

Nº 4. 3 têtes de caractère en terre cuite, représentant le ris, la douleur et le dédain.

Nº 5. Buste en terre de Mad. Charlier [de Charrière] en Suisse.

Nº 6. Buste en terre de Mad. Préville, de la comédie françoise.

Nº 7. Buste en terre de Mad. Mailly [de Mailly].

Nº 8. Buste en terre de Mad. Petit.

Nº 9. Buste en terre de M . . ., Banquier, rue de la Verrerie.

Nº 10. Une figure sur 2 pieds de hauteur représentant un prêtre des fêtes lupercal, morceau dagréé à l'académie, et a été exécuté en bronze.

Nº 11. Buste de Mr Diderot, et a été exécuté en marbre.

Nº 12. Buste de Mr Capperonnier, garde de la Bibliothèque du Roy et de lacadémie des science.

Nº 13. Buste de Charles IX, roy de France.

Nº 14. Buste de Mr Dauvergne, directeur de lopéra.

Nº 15. Buste en terre de Mr Mellon.

Nº 16. Buste en terre de M. le Barron de Fitinioff [Vietinghof].

Nº 17. Buste de la duchesse de Saxe-Gotha.

Nº 18. Médaillons du duc et de la duchesse de Saxe-Gotha et du duc Père.

Nº 19. Buste en terre de Mlle Boquet.

Nº 20. Buste de Mr Bignon, Prévôt des marchands.

Nº 21. Buste de Mad. Bignon, Prévote des marchands.

Nº 22. Buste de Mad. Bignon, conseiller d'état.

Nº 23. Medaillon de Mad. de Miroménil.

Nº 24. Buste de Mad. la Baronne de la Houze, Embassadrice de France en Dannemark.

Nº 25. Medaillon de Mr Courlevau, procur[eur].

Nº 26. Médaillon de M. Mayer, Peintre.

Nº 27. Buste en terre d'un enfant de Mr le vicomte de Noyalles [Noailles].

Nº 28. Un petit chien en marbre.

Nº 29. Un tête d'étude représentant un viellard.
Un autre à tête chauve.
Une autre représentant un ivrogne.
Une autre représentant un rabin juif.

Nº 30. Un serin couché sur son tombeau, en marbre.
Une perderix, en marbre.

Nº 31. Un grand Bats-reliefs représentant la reine de Sabat aportant des présent à Salomon.

Nº 32. Deux autre bats-reliefs exécuté en pierre pour une chapelle à St Cloux representant la Religion et l'Espérance.

Nº 33. Un bat-relieffe exécuté en pierre pour le portail de l'Église de Ste Geneviève de Paris representant Notre Seigneur donnant les clefs à St Pierre.

Nº 34. Saints exécuté sur 18 pieds de proportion en pierre pour l'Église de Ste Croix d'Orléans representant Ste Caterine, St Etienne, St Pierre et St Barthelemy.

Nº 35. Un monument en marbre pour le feld maréchal Prince de Galizin, déposé dans l'église basse de Moscou.

Nº 36. Un autre monument pour un Sénateur prince de Galizin, déposé dans la même église.

Nº 37. Un buste en marbre de l'imperatrice de Russie pour Mr le Comte de Stragonof.

En 1777

Nº 38. Le buste en marbre de Mad. la comtesse de Jaucourt.

Nº 39. Le buste en marbre de Mad. la comtesse de Caylas [sa fille].

Nº 40. Le Buste en marbre de Madame His.

Nº 41. Le Buste en marbre de Madame Servat.

Nº 43. Les Bustes d'enfans de Mr Brognard [Brongniart].

Nº 44. Un figure de grandeur naturel en terre cuite et en plâtre représentant une baigneuse sortant du bain.

Nº 45. Le modelle d'une figure représentant Dianne s'élance pour la chasse armé de son arc et de sa flèche.

Nº 46. Une figure représentant une nayade versant avec sa cruche de l'eau dans une coquille posé à ses pieds pour servir de fontaine au jardin de Mr Boutin.

Nº 47. Un modelle de monument pour la duchesse de Saxe-Gotha.

Nº 48. Un modelle de monument pour le prince de Galizin, vice chancelier de Russie.

Nº 49. Un modelle de monument pour le prince de Galizin, mort d'un duelle.

Nº 50. Le buste de marbre de Mr de Miroménil, garde des sceaux de France.

En 1778

Nº 51. Le Buste de marbre de Monsieur frère du Roy.

Nº 52. Le Buste de marbre de Madame.

Nº 53. Le Buste de marbre de Mad. Adélaïde de France.

Nº 54. Le Buste de marbre de Mad. Victoire de France.

Nº 54 *bis*. Le buste de Mr chevalier Glouk [Gluck], pour le foyer de l'Opéra, en marbre.

Nº 55. Le Buste de Molière, en marbre, pour le foyer de la cadémie française.

Nº 56. 4 buste de différents costumes de Mr de Voltaire, tous exécutés en marbre et en bronze.

Nº 57. Le Buste en marbre de Mad. la baronne de Vermenon [Girardot de Vermenoux].

Nº 58. Le buste en marbre de Mlle Arnoud [Arnould] dans le rolle d'iphigénie en Thauride.

No 59. Le buste en marbre de Mr Turgot, ancien contrôleur général.
No 50 bis. Buste de J. J. Rousseau.
Une tête à l'antique.

En 1779

No 51 bis. Un groupe en marbre représentant un baisé pour Mr le duc de Chartre.
No 53 bis. Deux têtes en marbre représentant la petit lisse [Lise] et lautre une tête entique en marbre.
No 53 bis. Deux petite figure de *Voltaire* assit dans un fauteuil drapé à lentique, en terre cuite et en marbre et en bronze.
No 54 ter. Le buste en marbre de M. de Caumartin, prévôt des marchands.
No 55 bis. Le buste de M. le Premier Président de Nicolay, en marbre.
No 56 bis. Buste de M. Le Noire, lieutenant général de police, en terre cuite.
No 57 bis. Buste de Mr le comte de Valbel[le] pour lacadémie françoise.
No 58 bis. Buste de M. Voltaire dans le costume francois et draperie pour le foyer de la comedie françoise.
No 59 bis. Buste de M. le docteur franklin.
No 60. Buste en marbre de Dianne.
No 61. Buste d'une Vestail.
No 62. Une grande Vestal exécuté pour lescalier de M. le duc d'Aumont.
No 63. Buste de Mr D'alembert, secrétaire de l'Académie françoise.
No 64. Un médaillon en marbre représentant une tête de Minerve pour le Prince de Holtin Gotorpe (Holstein-Gottorp).
No 65. Buste de M. Palissot.
No 66. Buste de Mr de La Lande.
No 67. Une Vestal de 2 pieds de haute en terre cuite et exécuté en bronze.
No 68. Un groupe de baisé d'une bacante. Modelle pour être exécuté en marbre.
No 69. Un modelle de monument pour être exécuté en marbre pour l'eglise de... [Ennery près Pontoise].
No 70. Un modelle de figure de grandeur naturelle de Voltaire assit dans un fauteuil et drapé à l'entique pour être exécuté en marbre pour lac...
No 71. Un figure de hauteur naturel de St Louis.
Et une autre de Charlemagne pour le reposoire de la fête Dieu à Versailles.
No 73. Une figure de Minerve exécuté en carton pour la salle de la Comédie de Versailles.
No 74. L'Ecusson de la France soutenut par deux anges placé au dessus de la toile de la Salle de la Comédie de Versailles, exécuté en carton doré.
[75]. Buste en marbre de M. le duc de Pralin [Choiseul-Praslin].

En 1780

[76]. Buste de M. Le Noire, Lieut. de Police, terre cuite.
[77]. Buste du docteur Queney [Quesnay], en terre cuite.
[78]. Deux groupe de marbre représentant le baisé donné et l'autre rendu, exécuté plusieurs fois en marbre.
[79]. Deux medaillons en marbre representant Minerve et l'autre Appollon repoussé par le vent pour le prince de Holstin Gotorpe [Holstein-Gottorp].

En 1781

[80]. Une statue de Dianne de cinq pieds 8 pouces armé de son arc et de sa flèche pour le prince de Saxe-Gotha.

[81]. Une nayade de grandeur naturelle, en marbre, assisse dans une couvette se lavant, et une négress de grandeur naturell, ne plomb, lui versant de leau sur les épaules, groupe pour servir de fontaine au jardin de Monceaux de M. le Duc de Chartres.
[82]. Deux statues en marbre de Voltaire, assis dans un fauteuil antique, drapé du manteau de filosope et la tête sein du ruban de l'immortalité, lune sera placé au foyé de la comédie françoise et lautre dans le museum de l'imperatrice de Russie.
[83]. Une statue en plomb de Dianne.
[84]. Une autre statue de Dianne exécuté en bronze pour Mr de Marigny de Girardot.
[85]. Une statue en marbre pour le Roy représentant le maréchal de Tourville de la hauteur de six pieds quelques pouces.
[86]. Buste de la princesse d'Aschkopf [Dachkov], de Russie, en marbre.
[87]. Buste en marbre de Mad. de Sérilly.
[88]. Buste en marbre de Mr Tronchain [Tronchin], médecin.
[89]. Buste en marbre de la fille de Mr Odeo [Audéoud] de Genève.
[90]. Buste en terre cuitte du commodore Paul-Jones.
[91]. Buste en bronze de M. Gerbier, avocat.
[92]. Monument en marbre à la mémoire de Mr le comte d'Ennery representant en bas-relief trois figures éplorée, Mad. la Comtesse de Blot, Mad. la comtesse d'Ennery et Mlle sa fille, et le médaillon de Mr le comte d'Ennery et d'autre attributs cinéraire; ce monument et déposé en l'eglise d'Ennery, près Pontoise.
[93]. Modelle d'une frileuse representant l'hiver pour être exécuté en marbre sur quatre pieds de haut.
[94]. Modelle d'une autre figure pour faire pendant représentant l'été.
[95]. Figure assise représentant le délassement de la moisson sera exécuté en marbre.
[96]. Modelle d'une statue de Cérès de 6 pieds pour être exécuté en pierre pour la salle à mangé de Maison a M. le comte Dartois.
[97]. Un buste en bronze de Mr Diderot, déposé dans l'hôtel de ville de Langre, sa patrie.

En 1782

[98]. Une statue de Diane de grandeur naturel, en bronze, placé che Mr Girardot de Marigny.
[99]. Un buste en bronze de Mad. la princesse Daschow.
[100]. Un buste en marbre de Mr Louis, secrétaire de l'accadémie de chirurgie pour y être placé.
[101]. Une tête à l'antique de Mr le comte de Buffon, en marbre, envoyé à l'imperatrice de Russie.
[102]. Buste en terre cuite de La fontaine.
[103]. Une petite statue de 18 pouces de haut, en marbre, représentant une vestale qui tien son feu sacré.

En 1783

[104]. Bustes en terre cuite du Prince et de la Princesse de Mecklenbourg Schwerin.
[105]. Buste en marbre du général comte Soltikof.
[106]. Buste du roy de Suède pour le comte de Cr[eutz].
[107]. Buste en marbre de la petite Robert.
[108]. Petit modelle de statue de Tourville, de 18 pouces, pour être exécuté à la manufacture de Sève [Sèvres].
[109]. Modelle d'une statue d'Apollon de grandeur naturel.
[110]. Modelle de la statue de Henry quatre, même grandeur.

[111]. Statue en pied de Voltaire pour son tombeau au Panthéon.
[112]. Buste de Napoléon Ier, en marbre et en terre.
[113]. Buste d'Alexandre, empereur de Russie.
[114]. Buste de Mirabeau.
[115]. — Diderot.
[116]. — Franklin.
[117]. Buste et statue de Washington.
[118]. Un Cicéron colossal au Palais-Royal.

[119]. Un buste de Condorcet.
[120]. — Buffon.
[121]. — Lafontaine.
[122]. — Jefferson.
[123]. — Le bailly de Suffren.
[124]. — Dalembert.
[125]. — Barthélemy.
[126]. — Henry de Prusse.
[127]. — La Fayette.

APPENDIX 3

Memorandum from Houdon to Bachelier, 1794

Note: This important memorandum was published in part by Délerot and Legrelle, in 1856; in the *Intermédiaire des chercheurs et des curieux*, 1886; by Giacometti, *Quelques notes sur Houdon*, 1900 (under the signature, Gandouin); by Giacometti in the two editions of his book on Houdon; and by Réau, *Houdon*, 1964. A translation in part appears here, p. 92.

Paris, 20 vendémiaire troisième année républicaine [11 octobre 1794]

Vous m'avez demandé, citoyen, des renseignements sur la nature de mes travaux et pour qui je les avais faits: j'ai mis par écrit ceux que ma mémoire a pu me fournir et je vous le envoye.

Né pour ainsi dire au pied de l'Académie, dès l'âge de neuf ans, j'ai fait de la sculpture; j'ai gagné le grand prix à seize ans; je suis parti pour Rome à dix-neuf ans où je suis resté quatre ans, ce qui fait en tout sept ans de pension.

J'ai employé ce temps à des études profondes sur l'anatomie considérée comme base du dessin et je fis un *Écorché* de grandeur naturelle placé maintenant dans les diverses écoles de l'Europe et dont je donnai un plâtre à celle de Paris à mon retour de Rome. L'ayant exécuté en bronze, il y a trois ans, j'y fis des changements et j'en redonnai un deuxième plâtre à l'École; le bronze est à moi dans mon atelier.

J'ai de plus fait à Rome un *Saint Brunehaut* [sic] en marbre de 9 pieds 1/2, un *Saint Jean-Baptiste*.

A mon retour, pour mon morceau de réception, un *Morphée* en marbre demi-nature; depuis un *Prêtre des Lupercales* en bronze, à moy.

Plusieurs grands bas-reliefs, un entre autres représentant *Jésus-Christ donnant les clefs à Saint Pierre*, placé au fronton de Sainte-Geneviève et détruit lorsqu'on a changé la destination de cette église en Panthéon.

Deux tombeaux en marbre pour la Russie.

Un groupe: une *Baigneuse* en marbre sur laquelle une négresse en plomb verse de l'eau, pour le jardin de Monceau. La négresse est en mauvais état et a besoin d'être restaurée.

Le modèle d'une *Nayade* grandeur naturelle, à moy.

Une *Diane* grandeur naturelle en bronze au citoyen Girardot, un *Apollon* au citoyen Girardot. Le marbre de ma *Diane* est à la Russie; le marbre de petite proportion était à feu d'Ormesson; le bronze à moy.

Une *Vestale* grandeur naturelle en marbre, à moy.

La statue de *Voltaire*, deux marbres: l'un à la Russie, l'autre donné par sa nièce à la Comédie Française.

Le *maréchal de Tourville*, à la nation, 6 pieds, en marbre.

Un tombeau en marbre composé d'un groupe de trois personnes, grandeur naturelle, à Ennery près Pontoise.

Une *Frileuse* et *L'Été*, grandeur naturelle, en marbre, à un particulier. Le bronze de la *Frileuse* était à feu d'Orléans.

Cérès en pierre, à Maisons, château qui appartenait à d'Artois.

Washington en marbre pour les États de Virginie.

La *Philosophie* en marbre, 7 pieds 1/2, pour être placée dans la première salle de la Convention.

Plusieurs statues petite proportion, des groupes en marbre et bronze, des têtes de fantaisie et d'étude, presque toutes à moy.

Beaucoup de bustes, presque tous d'hommes célèbres: *Molière, La Fontaine, Diderot, d'Alembert, Palissot, Buffon, Voltaire, Rousseau, Franklin, Washington, Barthélemy*, etc..., en bronze, en marbre, plusieurs à moy.

Je ne puis m'empêcher d'observer, en finissant cette espèce de nomenclature que votre amitié exige de moy, que c'est toujours pour moy que j'ai fait les bronzes et qu'on ne me les a achetés qu'après, que ce n'est que mon amour pour la gloire et non l'intérêt qui m'ont fait faire la plupart de ces bustes, entre autres celui de *Rousseau*; que, malgré les lois, sous l'Ancien Régime, on a surmoulé constamment mes ouvrages, on les a défigurés en y mettant mon nom, que d'autres, encore moins honnêtes, les copiaient tout simplement en y mettant le leur; que maintenant, au mépris des décrets formels de la Convention en faveur des arts et des propriétés, on continue à les vendre, à les exposer, à les promener publiquement et à me fruster ainsi de mon labeur. Tel de mes ouvrages qui aurait dû beaucoup me rapporter, au moyen de ce brigandage, n'a enrichi que les voleurs, tandis que moy je ne recouvrais même pas mes frais, tels que mon *Écorché, J.-J. Rousseau*, etc...

En résumant le récit de mes travaux, je puis dire que je ne me suis livré véritablement qu'à deux études qui ont rempli ma vie entière, auxquelles j'ci consacré tout ce que j'ai gagné, et que j'aurais rendues plus utiles à ma patrie si j'eusse été secondé et si j'eusse eu de la fortune: l'*anatomie* et la *fonte des statues*.

Longtemps logé aux ateliers de la Ville, je profitai de cette position pour être à la fois *statuaire* et *fondeur* (dans les temps modernes les deux professions étaient toujours exercées par des personnes différentes), et pour faire revivre dans ma patrie cet art utile qui pouvait se perdre, attendu que tous les fondeurs y étaient morts lorsque je m'en occupai. Je construisis des fourneaux, je formai des ouvriers et, après beaucoup d'essais infructueux et dispendieux, je parvins à fondre moi-même deux statues: la *Diane* dont une m'appartient encore et ma *Frileuse*. Chassé en 1787 de ces ateliers par Breteuil en trois semaines j'achetai une maison en face, je construisis de nouveaux fourneaux et j'y fondis mon *Apollon*.

Depuis la Révolution, n'ayant plus d'ouvrage, (n'ayant jamais travaillé que pour les particuliers ou l'étranger, excepté *Tourville*), je voulus soutenir mon atelier et conserver à mon pays des ouvriers précieux qui auraient porté leurs talents à nos voisins. Je pris sur les fonds d'une fortune modique de quoi continuer mes travaux en ce genre: je fondis des bustes des grands hommes: *Molière, Buffon, Voltaire, Rousseau,* etc..., toujours entraîné par l'amour de mon art,

par le désir de laisser à la postérité un monument durable et un sujet d'études aux jeunes artistes.

Quoique père de famille, je fondis mon grand *Écorché* en 1792. Lorsqu'on voulut fondre la statue qui est placée sur le dôme du Panthéon, ce fut dans mon atelier qu'on fut obligé de chercher un fondeur: on y prit un homme de beaucoup de mérite, mais qui n'avait jamais travaillé que sous moy et qui devait à moy seul, à ma persévérance, à mon argent et à mes conseils mes connaissances sur cet art. Il était mouleur en entrant chez moy.

Voilà, citoyen, le rapport que vous avez exigé de moy.

Il en résulte que l'on peut me considérer sous le double rapport du *statuaire* et du *fondeur*. Sous le premier aspect, je puis créer; sous le second, je puis exécuter d'une manière durable les créations des autres, à beaucoup moins de frais que tout autre. N'ayant jamais eu pour m'occuper de cet art d'autre argent que celuy de mes économies, il en résulte que j'ai appris aussi à diminuer les dépenses et à retrancher celles superflues.

APPENDIX 4

Sale by Houdon from his Studio in the Bibliothèque Nationale, October 8, 1795.

I. *FIGURES ET BUSTES EN BRONZE*

63. *Diane*, debout, armée d'une flèche et de son arc et dans l'action de chasser. Cette figure, de grandeur naturelle (hauteur totale 6 pieds) est posée sur une terrasse en bronze.

64. *Un prêtre des fêtes lupercales.* Il tient d'une main des courroies et de l'autre un couteau. Cette figure sur terrasse porte 31 pouces de haut.

65. Une figure d'*Écorché*, le bras droit élevé. Il est posé sur terrasse. H.: 18 pouces.

66. Une *Vestale*, drapée dans le goût antique. Elle tient le vase du feu sacré; près d'elle est un autel. Ce précieux morceau porte 21 pouces de haut.

67. Le buste de *Saint Bruno*, extrait de la statue en marbre faite pour l'église des Chartreux à Rome. Il est posé sur piédouche en bronze doré. H. totale: 8 pouces 9 lignes.

68. Le buste de *Diane*, coiffée en cheveux tressés, ornés d'un croissant. Il est posé sur un piédouche en marbre. H. totale: 29 pouces 6 lignes.

69. Le buste de *Buffon*, posé sur piédouche en marbre. H. totale: 22 pouces.

70. Le buste d'*Arouet de Voltaire*, tête nue et posé sur piédouche et socle de même matière. H. totale: 16 pouces 6 lignes.

71. Le buste d'un homme en cimare† [simarre]. Médaillon demi-relief. Diamètre: 29 pouces.

82. *Henri IV et Sully.* Groupe en bronze posé sur piédestal en marbre blanc. H. totale: 15 pouces.

I. *FIGURES ET BUSTES EN MARBRE*

72. Une *Vestale* debout, portant le feu sacré; elle est drapée dans le goût antique, la tête en partie couverte d'un voile et posée sur un piédestal. H. de la figure: 6 pieds; celle du piédestal: 3 pieds 4 pouces.

73. Une tête d'*Amour*. Il est coiffé en cheveux naturellement bouclés et couronné de branches de myrte,‡ posé sur piédouche et socle de même matière. H. totale: 19 pouces.

74. Une tête d'*Enfant* coiffé en cheveux et posé pié-douche en marbre bleu turquin. H. totale: 13 pouces.

75. Le buste d'*Apollon*, demi-relief en médaillon de 15 pouces 6 lignes de diamètre.

76. *Méduse*, coiffée en cheveux mêlés de serpents. Médaillon demi-relief, de 6 pouces 9 lignes de haut sur 6 pouces de large.

77. Le buste de *Buffon*, sur piédouche de même matière. H. totale: 22 pouces.

78. Le buste de *Voltaire*, coiffé en perruque et posé sur piédouche. H.: 24 pouces.

79. Le buste du même: il est tête nue et posé sur piédouche en marbre blanc. H.: 34 pouces.

80. Le buste de *Mirabeau*, posé sur piédouche en marbre blanc. H.: 34 pouces.

81. Une *Grive morte*: elle est posée sur un socle en marbre blanc.

83. Une jeune fille à genoux, tenant une colombe en captivité: elle est posée sur socle et marbre portor.§ H.: 16 pouces.

‡ In antiquity the myrtle was sacred to Venus.
§ Black marble with yellow veins.

† In Italian *zimarra* or *cimarra*: a magistrate's long robe. Cf. French *chamarre*

84. Deux vases de forme Médicis en marbre vert antique, posés sur piédouche et socle de même matière; ils sont garnis de roseaux en bronze formant anses. H. totale: 13 pouces.

85. Une cassolette couverte, l'intérieur évidé.

III. *TERRES CUITES*

86. *Diane.* Figure de 6 pieds de haut, compris l'épaisseur du socle.

87. La même figure en petit, sur socle bleu turquin. H.: 24 pouces.

88. *Voltaire*, figure de proportion naturelle: il est assis dans une chaise curule. Cette terre est celle de la figure de marbre qui orne le péristyle du Théâtre français. H.: 4 pieds.

89. La même figure, en carton doré, posée sur socle peint en porphyre.

90. *L'Écorché*, figure de petite proportion. H.: 18 pouces.

91. Une jeune fille, la tête et les épaules couvertes d'une draperie, le reste du corps nu. Ce joli morceau, connu sous le nom de *La Frileuse*, porte 53 pouces de haut.

92. La même figure, de petite proportion. H.: 19 pouces.

93. Une *Vestale:* elle est drapée et tient l'urne du feu sacré; près d'elle est un autel de style antique. H.: 21 pouces.

94. *L'Été*, figuré par une jeune fille coiffée en cheveux couverts d'un mouchoir, la gorge en partie couverte d'une draperie. Ce buste est posé sur piédouche en marbre bleu turquin. H. totale: 20 pouces.

95. *Le baiser*, groupe de deux figures vues à mi-corps, posées sur piédouche en marbre blanc. H. totale: 17 pouces.

96. Le buste de *La Fontaine:* il est posé sur piédouche en marbre blanc. H. totale: 29 pouces.

97. Le buste de *Paul Jones:* il est vêtu en uniforme et posé sur piédouche en marbre bleu turquin. H. totale: 24 pouces.

98. Le buste de *Franklin*, sur piédouche en marbre. H. totale: 20 pouces.

99. Le buste de *D'Alembert*, sur piédouche en stuc. H. totale: 18 pouces.

100. Le buste de *Mirabeau*, en costume de député, posé sur piédouche en marbre de Flandre. H. totale: 24 pouces.

101. Deux bustes de jeunes femmes, têtes d'expression, l'une coiffée en cheveux, l'autre la tête couverte d'une draperie; elles sont posées sur piédouches en marbre. H. totale: 23 pouces.

102. Deux têtes d'enfants; elles sont coiffées cheveux, posées sur piédouche en marbre bleu turquin. H.: 13 pouces.

103. Deux oiseaux morts, posés sur socle.

IV. *MODELES EN PLATRE*

104. *Morphée.* Le dieu est couché sur un rocher, entouré d'une guirlande de pavots. H.: 23 pouces.

105. *Tourville*, debout et montrant avec son épée l'ordre de combattre à La Hogue: modèle de la grande figure en marbre qui appartient à la nation. H.: 25 pouces.

APPENDIX 5

Auction of the Contents of Houdon's Studio, after his death
December 15–17, 1828

15–17 décembre. FONDS DE L'ATELIER HOUDON, après décès, à la requête des trois filles de l'artiste.

1. Marbre blanc. Tête de *Minerve* vue de profil: ouvrage en bas-relief et destiné à être appliqué sur un fond.

2. Bronze. *Diane* nue et la tête un peu détournée, se livrant à une course légère [*sic*]: la déesse tient une flèche de la main droite et sa main gauche soutient un arc de petite proportion. Cette statue, dont la pondération est parfaite et qui, par sa nudité et le caractère gracieux de ses formes, représenterait peut-être mieux une *Vénus chasseresse*, offre certainement l'une des productions les plus remarquables de la statuaire moderne et mérite encore plus l'estime si l'on considère qu'elle est l'un des ouvrages qui ont le mieux concouru à rappeler à l'imitation de la nature et de l'antique, à l'époque où il fut exécuté. Cette statue de grandeur naturelle et d'une belle fonte est parfaitement ciselée et réparée.

3. Plâtre peint. Empreinte prise sur la figure précédente.

4. Bronze. Jolie copie réduite de la statue précédente.

5. Plâtre peint. Empreinte prise sur la réduction qui vient d'être décrite.

6. Cire. *Vénus et Mars*, groupe d'une petitesse extrême, supporté par une console formée par un masque humain.

7. Milon of Crotona by Falconet.

8. Terre cuite. Un bas-relief représentant *la reine de Saba apportant des présents à Salomon.* Cette composition est celle du grand. prix de sculpture remporté par M. Houdon vers 1760 [en 1761] A l'École des beaux-arts.

9. Plâtre peint. Petit modèle de la belle statue de *Saint Bruno*, exécutée en marbre par M. Houdon et placée à Rome dans l'église des Chartreux.

10. Marbre blanc. Portrait de *Louis XIV*, vu de profil. Bas-relief de forme ovale.

11. Marbre blanc. Buste habillé de *Voltaire*.

12. Marbre blanc. Buste de *Voltaire*, sur socle en marbre veiné.

13. Carton bronzé. Statue assise de *Voltaire*, maquette qui a servi

dans la translation des cendres de ce grand homme au Panthéon français.— A la Bibliothèque de Rouen.

14. Plâtre. Modèle réduit de la statue de *Voltaire*, par M. Houdon, qui était placée au Panthéon français.

15. Plâtre. Masque moulé sur le visage de *J.-J. Rousseau*, peu d'heures après sa mort. Cette précieuse empreinte, qui est unique, a été faite par M. Houdon, sur l'invitation de feu M. le comte de Girardin, chez lequel ce philosophe mourut, le 3 juillet 1778.

16. Plâtre peint. Buste de *D'Alembert*, mort le 29 octobre 1783.

17. Terre cuite. Buste de *Diderot*, mort le 30 juillet 1784.

18. Buste du prince *Henri de Prusse*.

19. Plâtre. Buste de *John Paul Jones*, général [*sic*] américain.

20. Plâtre coloré. Buste de *J.-F. Pilâtre de Rosier*, physicien, tué près de Boulogne le 15 juin 1785.

22. Plâtre. Buste de *C. Gluck*, mort le 15 novembre 1787.

23. Plâtre coloré. Buste de *Gerbier*, avocat général, mort le 26 mars 1788.

24. Plâtre. Buste du comte de *Buffon*, mort le 16 avril 1788.

25. Plâtre coloré. Buste du président *Dupaty*, mort le 17 septembre 1788.

26. Plâtre bronzé. Buste du docteur *Tronchin*.

27. Terre cuite. Buste de *B. Franklin*, mort le 17 avril 1790.

28. Plâtre. Buste du *comte de Guibert*, membre de l'Académie des sciences, mort vers 1790.

29. Terre cuite. Buste de Riquetti, comte de *Mirabeau*, mort le 2 avril 1791.

30. Plâtre. Buste de l'*abbé Barthélemy*, mort le 30 avril 1795.

31. Plâtre peint. Buste de Joseph Balsamo, dit *Cagliostro*, mort au château de Saint-Léon en 1795.

32. Marbre blanc. Buste de *Hue de Miromesnil*, garde des sceaux, mort le 6 juillet 1793.

33. Plâtre. Buste de *M. de Nicolai*, premier président de la Cour des aides.

34. Plâtre. Masque de la statue de *Joubert*, général en chef de l'armée française en Italie, tué à la bataille de Novi en 1799.

35. Plâtre. Buste de *Washington*, général en chef des armées américaines pendant la guerre de l'Indépendance.

36. Plâtre. Buste de *J. Lalande*, astronome, mort le 4 avril 1807.

37. Marbre blanc. Buste de *M. Lenoir*, ancien lieutenant de police, mort en 1807.

38. Plâtre peint. Portrait en bas-relief de *J.-M. Montgolfier*, mécanicien [*sic*], l'un des inventeurs des aérostats, mort le 26 juin 1810.

39. Terre cuite. Buste de *M.-J. Chénier*, membre de l'Institut, mort le 10 janvier 1811.

40. Terre cuite. Buste de l'*Impératrice Joséphine*, sur piédouche en marbre veiné.

41. Plâtre. Buste de *M. Barlow*, ministre des États-Unis près la Cour de France, auteur du poème de la *Colombiade*.

42. Plâtre. Buste de feu *M. le maréchal Ney*, prince de la Moskowa.

43. Terre cuite. Buste taillé en hermès et diadémé de *Napoléon Bonaparte*, modelé à Saint-Cloud en 1806. Ce buste, pour lequel l'artiste obtint beaucoup de séances, passe avec raison pour celui de tous les portraits de Napoléon où sa physionomie est rendue avec le plus de vérité.

44. Terre cuite. Buste de *Napoléon* en uniforme militaire.

45. Plâtre. Buste de Mme la comtesse *Regnault de Saint-Jean-d'Angély*.

46. Plâtre. Masque de feu M. le comte *Boissy d'Anglas*, pair de France et membre de l'Institut. Ce masque a été moulé pendant la vie de ce personnage.

47. Plâtre. Buste de *Jefferson*, ancien président de la République des États-Unis.

48. Plâtre. Buste de feu *Larive*, tragédien célèbre.

49. Marbre blanc. Buste de *M. Camus-Gréneville* [de Néville], ancien magistrat.

50. Plâtre. Buste de *R. Fulton*, inventeur des bateaux à vapeur.

51. Marbre blanc. Buste de M. le général *Lafayette* en uniforme de commandant de la garde nationale de Paris. Ce buste, voté en 1791 par la Commune de Paris, a éprouvé en 1793 une mutilation qui a été réparée.

52. Terre cuite. Buste de Mme ***, les cheveux relevés derrière la tête et le sein et les épaules enveloppés d'une draperie.

53. Plâtre. Buste de *M. le maréchal Soult*, duc de Dalmatie.

54. Plâtre. Buste de feu *M. Moitte*, statuaire.

55. Plâtre. Buste de Mme *la princesse de Salm*.

56. Plâtre. Portrait à mi-corps de Mme *de Sérilly*.

57. Terre cuite. Buste de Mme *de Vermenon* [Vermenoux].

58. Plâtre. Buste de Mme *de Bervick*.

59. Marbre blanc. Buste de jeune homme couronné de myrte.

60. Plâtre coloré. Buste de feu Mlle *de Tarente*, exécuté après sa mort.

61. Terre cuite. Buste d'une jeune femme, les cheveux noués derrière la tête.

62. Marbre blanc. Copie réduite de *La Frileuse*.

63. Marbre blanc. Buste de jeune femme, les cheveux attachés derrière la tête: cette jolie tête d'étude présente le caractère de la douceur.

64. Plâtre. Le grand *Écorché*, épreuve peinte à l'huile et offrant les couleurs des muscles, veines et tendons.

65. Plâtre. Le moule de la figure précédente. L'acquisition de ce moule conférera la propriété de la figure, l'une des plus estimées de notre école.

66. Plâtre. Tête de l'*Écorché*, peinte à l'huile.

67. Marbre blanc. Deux petites têtes d'enfants, dont l'une pleure et l'autre rit.

68. Marbre blanc. Un oiseau mort et les pattes attachées à un clou.

73. Un grand nombre de masques de personnages célèbres la plupart moulés de leur vivant, tels que ceux de *M. Moitte*, statuaire, *M. Arnaud*, de l'Académie française, etc.

PROCES-VERBAL
DE LA VENTE APRES DÉCES DE 1828
AVEC INDICATION DES PRIX OBTENUS

I. *STATUES OU STATUETTES*

	Francs
La Frileuse. Petit modèle bronze.	230
La Frileuse. Statuette en plâtre.	10
Vestale. Plâtre.	70
Saint Bruno. Petite statuette plâtre.	49
Nayade. Statue plâtre peint.	50
Baigneuse. Groupe en terre cuite.	7
Écorché. Plâtre peint.	35
Cicéron. Plâtre.	10

II. *BUSTES ISOLÉS*

Miromesnil. Marbre.	81
Nicolaï. Marbre.	129
Lenoir. Marbre.	100
La Fayette. Marbre.	50
Voltaire. Marbre.	7,50
Deux bustes d'enfants. Marbre.	30
Tronchin. Plâtre bronzé.	11
Barthélemy. Plâtre.	11
Cagliostro. Plâtre.	16
La Fontaine. Plâtre.	7

Duquesnoy. Terre cuite.	6
Napoléon Ier. Terre cuite.	41
Joséphine. Terre cuite sur piédouche en marbre veiné.	41
Soult. Plâtre.	10,50
Mme Renaud [Regnault de Saint-Jean-d'Angély].	10

III. *BUSTES GROUPÉS*

Gerbier et Henri de Prusse. Terre cuite.	23
Le prince Henri et la tête de l'Écorché.	3
Gluck et Moitte. Plâtre.	11
Lalande, Barlow. Plâtre.	4,50
L'empereur Alexandre et l'impératrice Joséphine.	2,50
Bailly, Dupaty et deux autres. Plâtre.	12
Barthélemy, Voltaire. Plâtre.	29
D'Alembert, Fulton, Buffon. Plâtre.	9
Mme de Vermenon, Guibert, Chénier. Plâtre.	2

IV. *MASQUES*

Masque de *J.-J. Rousseau* [A M. Hazard].	655
Masque *d'Arnaud.*	50

V. *ANIMAUX*

Cerf. Groupe plâtre.	7
Trois pièces en marbre dont *un chien.*	7
Oiseau mort. Marbre.	18

NOTE ON THE PLATES

SINCE Houdon's portrait busts and portrait statues are all life size, it has seemed to me superfluous to give exact measurements. Where figure sculptures are over-lifesize (e.g. *Saint Bruno*, the original *Saint John the Baptist*) this is usually indicated in the text. The *Cicero* and the *Themis* are over-lifesize, and the destroyed *Napoleon*, formerly at Boulogne, was described as 'colossal'. The *Diana* is tall (about six feet), but not extravagantly so for a goddess. Réau refers to certain busts, such as Catherine II, as 'colossal', but actually these are life-size with the torso lengthened or expanded with swags of drapery. In the case of works which are below life-size, such as the small *Vestal*, the *Priest of the Lupercalia*, or the second version of the *Morpheus*, this fact is noted in the text.

Nearly all the Plates show details from Houdon's sculptures; for complete views see Figs. 55–204.

Corrigenda to the captions:
Plate 30 (and Fig. 85). *Monsieur, le Comte de Provence*: For *1776* read *1775*.
Plate 41. *Diana*, Frick Collection. Read: *about 1778*.
Fig. 13. Coysevox, *Robert de Cotte*. For *1707* read *1704*.
Fig. 42. Lecomte, *d'Alembert*. Read: *Le Rond*.
Fig. 98. Houdon, *Eagle*. For *Plaster* read *Marble*.
Fig. 113. Houdon, *Voltaire*, Baltimore. For *about 1779* read *1778*.

A Vestal. Detail of Fig. 56. Plaster, about 1768. Gotha, Schlossmuseum

2. *An Unknown Girl*
   (Peasant Girl of Frascati
   (Cf. Fig. 62.)
   Marble, 1775.
   Leningrad, Hermitage

A Roman Youth. Detail of Fig. 64. Marble, 1775. New York, Dr. Peter Guggenheim

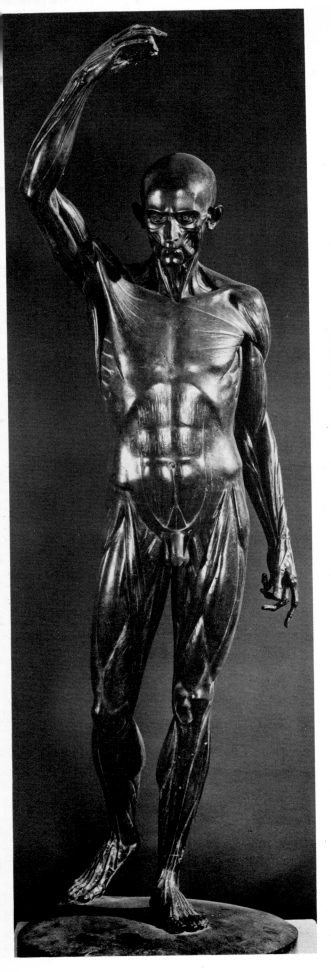

5. *L'Ecorché*. Detail of Plate 4a.

4a. *L'Ecorché*. (Cf. Fig. 58.) Bronze, 1792.
Paris, École des Beaux-Arts

4b–c. *L'Ecorché*. (Cf. Fig. 58.) Bronze, 1776. Chatillon-sous-Bagneux,
Courty Collection

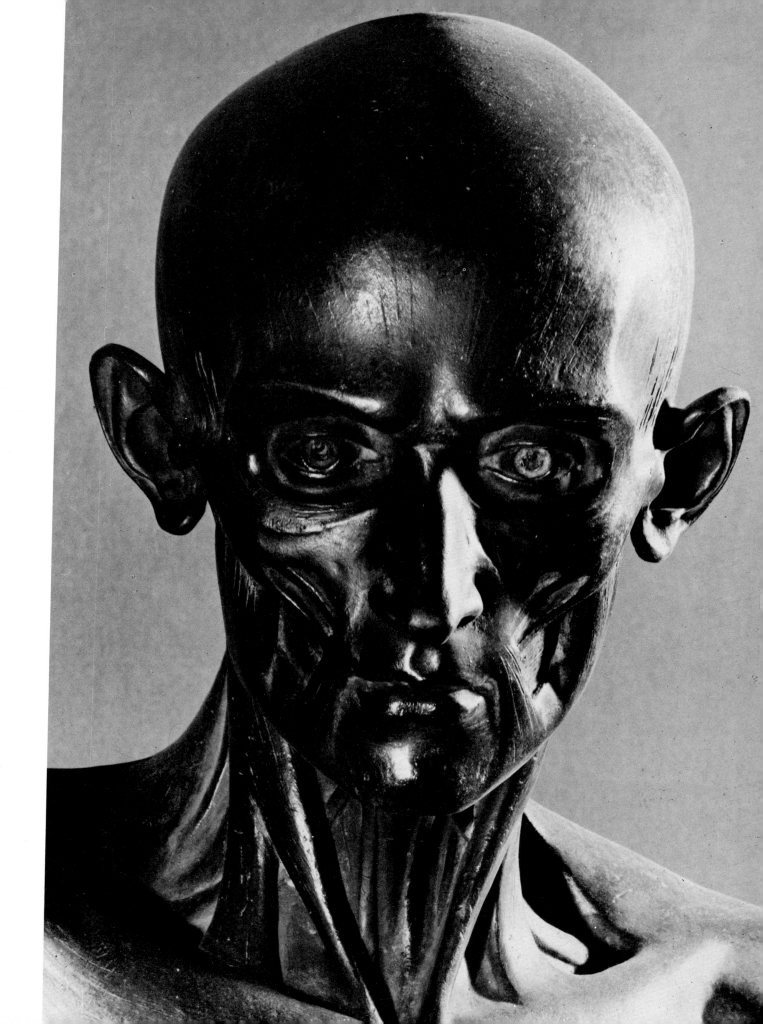

6. *St. John the Baptist.* (Cf. Fig. 59.) Plaster, about 1766–7. Gotha, Schlossmuseum

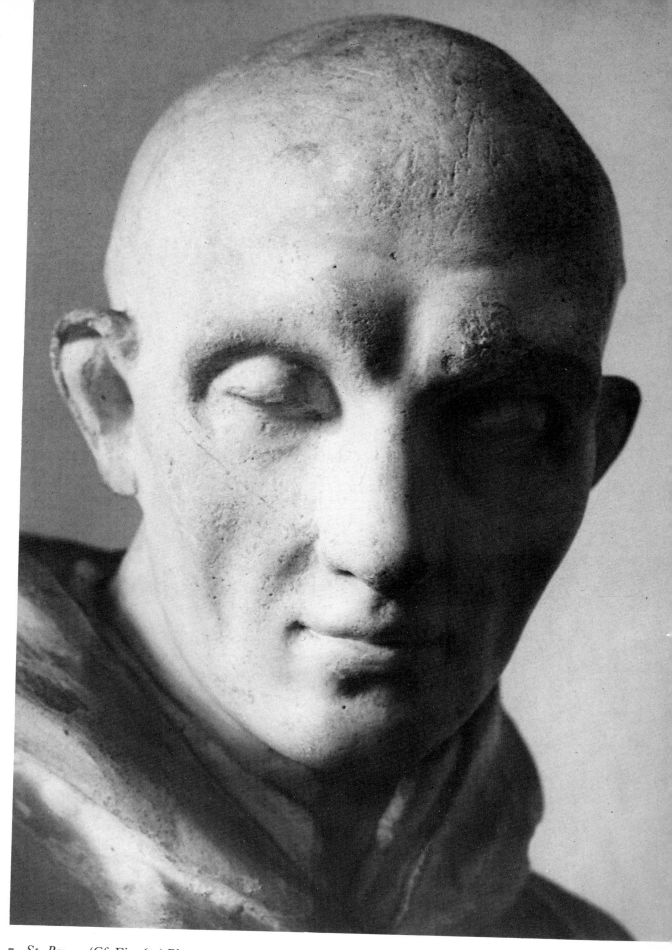

7. *St. Bruno.* (Cf. Fig. 60.) Plaster, about 1766–7. Gotha, Schlossmuseum

8. *A Priest of the Lupercalia*. Detail of Fig. 61. Plaster, about 1768. Gotha, Schlossmuseum

9. *Morpheus.* (Cf. Fig. 65.) Marble, 1777. Paris, Louvre

oa–b. *Morpheus.* (Cf. Fig. 65.) Marble, 1777. Paris, Louvre

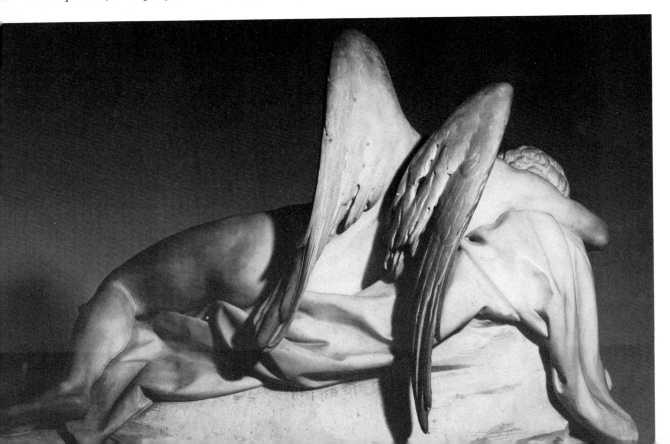

Madame de Charrière. (Cf. Fig. 66.)
Plaster, 1771.
Neuchâtel, Musée d'Art et d'Histoire

12a. *Denis Diderot.* (Cf. Fig. 70.) Terra cotta, about 1771. Paris, Louvre

12b. *Denis Diderot.* (Cf. Fig. 70.) Bronze, about 1781. Langres, Hôtel de Ville

Denis Diderot. Detail of Fig. 70. Marble, 1773. New York, Wrightsman Collection

14. *Frederick III, Duke of Saxe-Gotha*. Detail of Fig. 69. Plaster, 1773. Gotha, Schlossmuseum

15. *Empress Catherine II of Russia*. Marble, 1773. Leningrad, Hermita

16. *Empress Catherine II of Russia.* Detail of Plate 15

17a. *Justice mourning*. Detail from the Tomb of Prince Alexis Dmitrievitch Galitzin (Fig. 74). Marble, 1774. Moscow, Donskoy Monastery

17b. *Comtesse de Blot*. Detail from the Tomb of Comte d'Ennery (Fig. 132). Marble, 1781. Paris, Louvre

18. *Tomb of Prince Mikhail Mikhailovitch Galitzin.* Marble, 1774. Moscow, Donskoy Monastery

Military Genius. Detail of Plate 18

-21. *La petite Lise*. Details of Fig. 77. Marble, 1775. Leningrad, Hermitage

22. *Marquis de Miromesnil*. Detail of Fig. 81. Marble, 1777. New York, Frick Collection

23. *Anne-Robert-Jacques Turgot*. Detail of Fig. 83. Terra cotta, 17°
Boston, Museum of Fine Arts

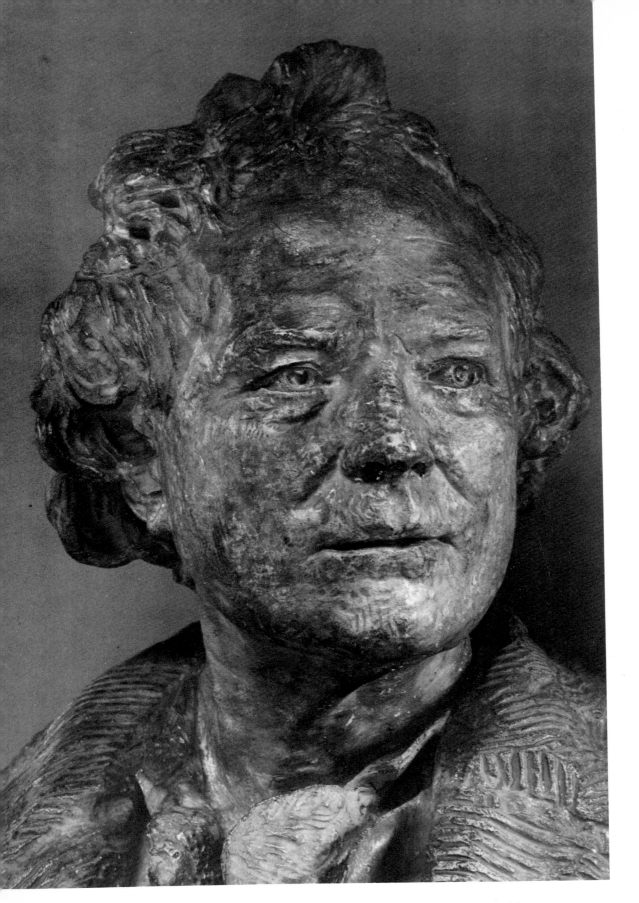

24. *Christoph Willibald von Gluck*. (Cf. Fig. 78.) Plaster, 1775. Schwerin, Staatliches Museum

Sophie Arnould as Iphigenia. Detail of Fig. 79. Marble, 1775. Paris, Louvre

27. '*Baroness de la Houze*'. Detail of Fig. 80. Marble, 1777. San Marino, Calif.,
Henry E. Huntington Library and Art Gallery

6. *A Lady*. Detail of Fig. 82. Plaster, about 1775.
Schwerin, Staatliches Museum

Overleaf: 28–29. *Comtesse du Cayla*. Details of Fig. 84. Marble, 1777.
New York, Frick Collection

Madame Adélaïde, aunt of Louis XVI. Detail of Fig. 87. Marble, 1777. Paris, Louvre

Monsieur, le Comte de Provence (later Louis XVIII). Detail of Fig. 85.
Plaster, 1776. Stockholm, National Museum

32. *Madame Victoire, aunt of Louis XVI*. Detail of Fig. 88. Marble, 1777. London, Wallace Collection

33. *Le baiser donné*. Detail of Fig. 86. Marble, 1778. New York, Wildenstein & Co.

34. *Comtesse de Jaucourt*. Detail of Fig. 89. Marble, 1777. Paris, Louvre

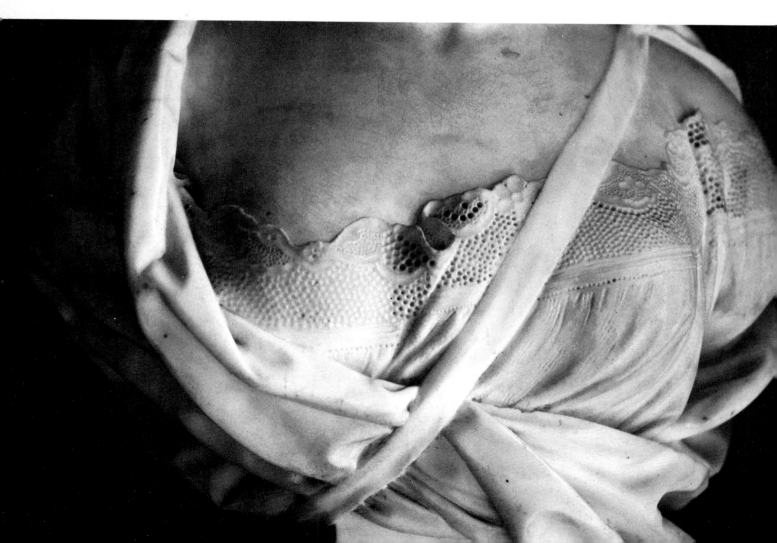

35. *Comtesse de Jaucourt*. Detail of Fig. 89. Marble, 1777. Paris, Louvre

36. *Alexandre Brongniart.* (Cf. Fig. 93.) Terra cotta, about 1777. Paris, Louvre

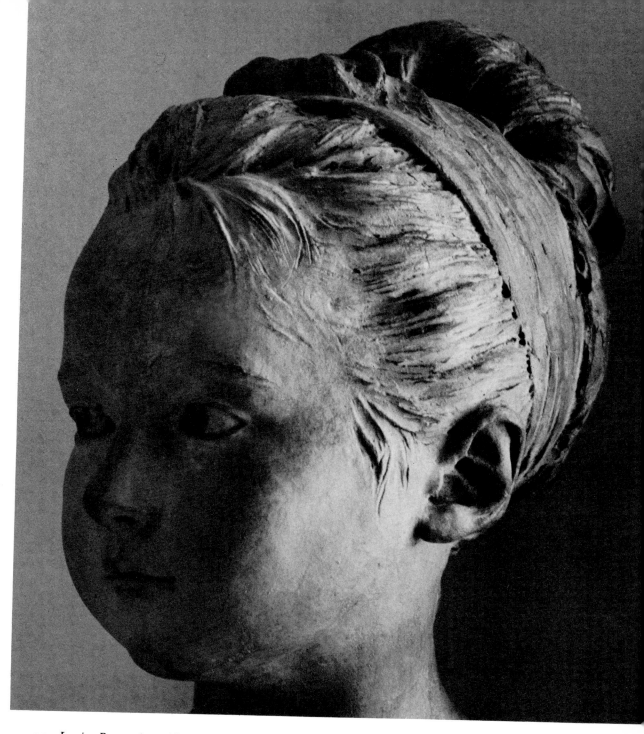

37. *Louise Brongniart*. (Cf. Fig. 94.) Terra cotta, about 1777. Paris, Louvre

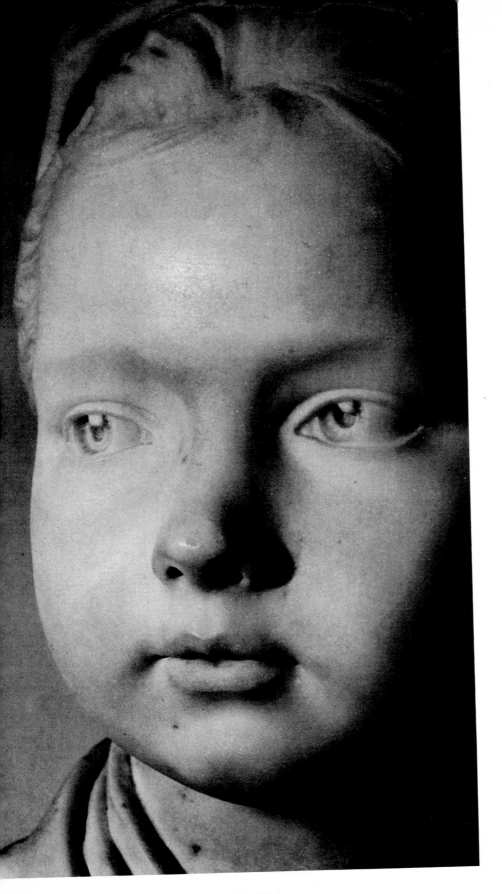

38. *Louise Brongniart*. Cf. Plate 37. Marble, 1779.
New York, Metropolitan Museum of Art

Diana. Detail of Fig. 103. Marble, 1778. Washington, D.C., National Gallery of Art

40a. *Diana*. Marble, 1780. Lisbon,
Calouste Gulbenkian Foundation, Museum

40b. *Diana*. Bronze, 1782. San Marino, Calif.,
Henry E. Huntington Library and Art Gallery

41. *Diana*. Terra cotta, 1778. New York, Frick Collection

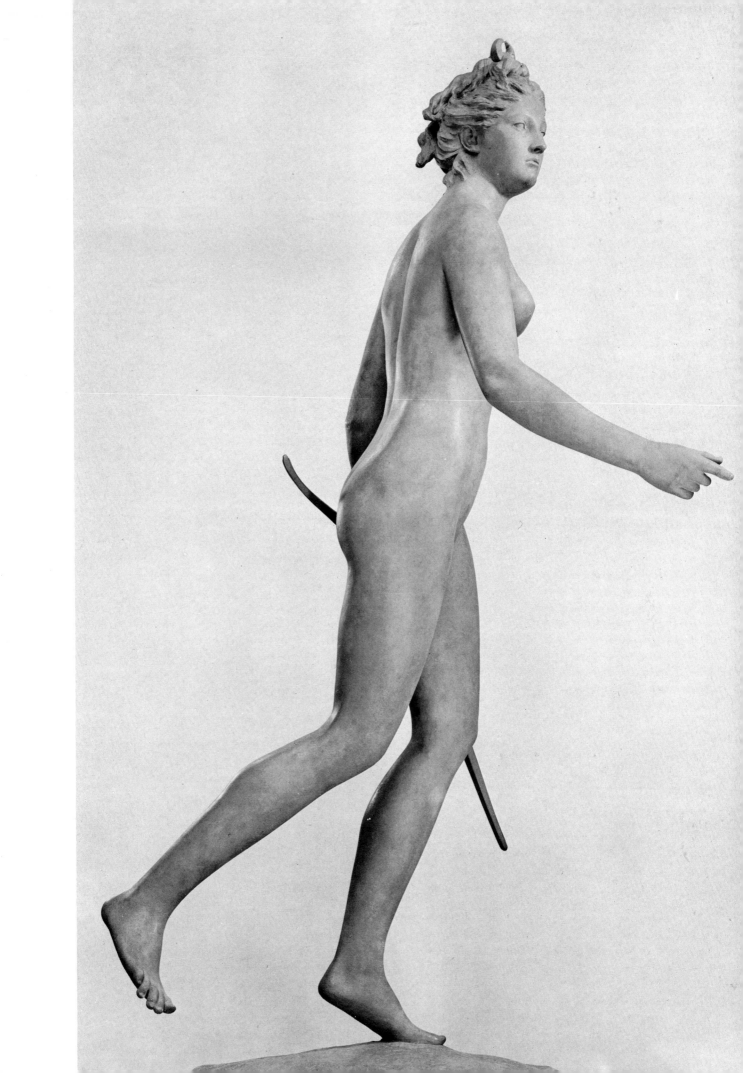

42. *Diana*. Detail of Fig. 100. Bronze, 1782. San Marino, Calif., Henry E. Huntington Library and Art Gallery

43. *Baron de Vietinghoff*. Detail of Fig. 91. Marble, 1791.
East Berlin, Staatliche Museen

46. *Molière*. (Cf. Plate 45.) Marble, 1778. Paris, Comédie Française

On the preceding pages:

44. *Aymard-Jean de Nicolay*. Detail of Fig. 104. Marble, 1779. Coll. Comte de Contades

45. *Molière*. Detail of Fig. 106. Plaster, 1778. Princeton, N.J., University Library

Molière. Detail of Fig. 106. Plaster, 1778. Princeton, N.J., University Library

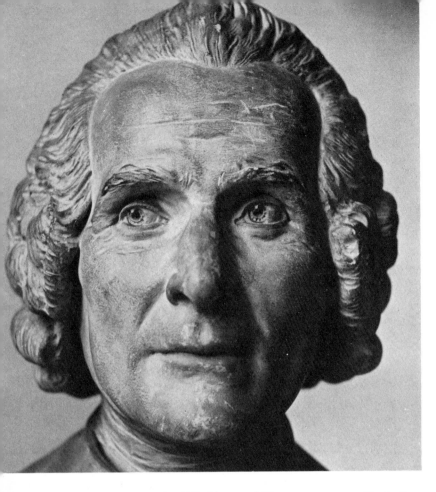

48a. *Jean-Jacques Rousseau.* (Cf. Fig. 107.) Terra cotta, 1779. Paris, Louvre

48b. *Jean-Jacques Rousseau.* Detail of Fig. 108.
Bronze, 1778. Paris, Louvre

49. *Jean-Jacques Rousseau.* (Cf. Fig. 107.)
Plaster, about 1778. Gotha, Schlossmuseum

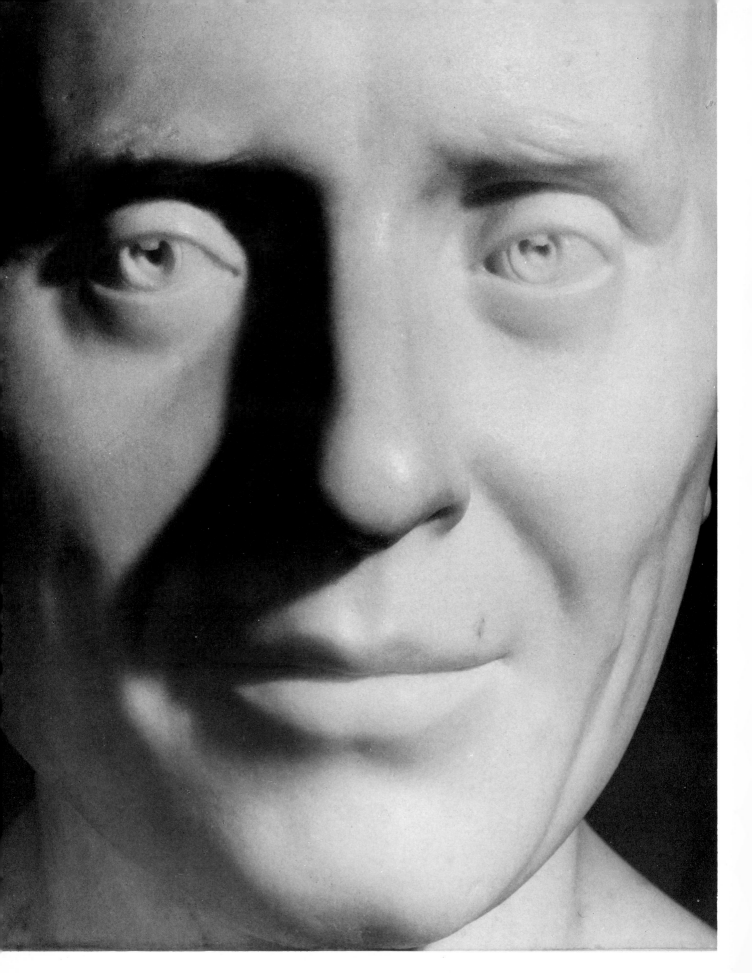

50. *Jean Le Rond d'Alembert*. Detail of Fig. 110. Marble, 1779. New Haven, Conn., Yale University Art Gallery

51. *Voltaire*. (Cf. Figs. 114–117.) Marble, 1778. Washington, National Gallery of Art, Widener Collection

52a. *Voltaire*. Detail of Fig. 116. Marble, 1778. Leningrad, Hermitage

52b. *Voltaire*. Bronze, 1778. Baltimore, Walters Art Gallery

53a. *Voltaire*. Detail of Fig. 114. Marble, 1778. New York, Metropolitan Museum of Art

53b. *Voltaire*. Detail of Fig. 117. Paris, Comédie Française

VOLTAIRE.

Voltaire. (Cf. Fig. 112.) Marble, 1781. Leningrad, Hermitage

Voltaire. (Cf. Fig. 111.) Marble, 1781. Paris, Comédie Française

56. *Voltaire*. Detail of
Plate 55. Marble, 17[...]
Leningrad, Hermita[...]

57a–b. *Voltaire*. Details of Plate 55. Marble, 1781. Leningrad, Hermitage

58. *Benjamin Franklin*. Detail of Fig. 118. Marble, 1778. New York, Metropolitan Museum of Art

59. *Benjamin Franklin*. Detail of Fig. 119. Plaster, 1786–1791 (?). Boston, Athenaeum

Overleaf:

60. *César-Gabriel, Duc de Choiseul-Praslin*. Detail of Fig. 120. Plaster, 1780. Paris, Louvre

61. *Duc de Choiseul-Praslin*. Cf. Plate 60. Marble, 1780. Paris, Louvre; on loan to the Château at Angers

62a. *Dr. Théodore Tronchin*. Detail of Fig. 125. Marble, 1781.
Geneva, Musée d'Art et d'Histoire

62b. *Charles Palissot de Montenoy*. Detail of Fig. 123. Terra cotta, 1779.
Paris, Institut de France, Bibliothèque Mazarine

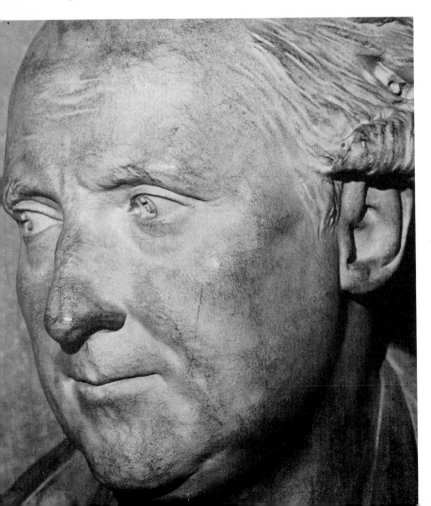

John Paul Jones. (Cf. Fig. 126.) Plaster, 1780. Boston, Museum of Fine Arts

64. *Anne Audéoud*. Detail of Fig. 128. Plaster, 1780. New York, Metropolitan Museum of Art

65. *A Negress*. (Cf. Fig. 129.) Plaster, about 1781. Soissons, Musée municipal

66. *Madame de Sérilly*. Detail of Fig. 127. Marble, 1782. London, Wallace Collection

67. *Maréchal de Tourville*. Detail of Fig. 130. Marble, 1781.
Versailles

68. *Tomb of Comte d'Ennery*. Marble, 1781. Paris, Louvre

69a–b. *Comtesse d'Ennery and her Daughter*. Details of Plate 68

70. *Comte d'Ennery*. Detail of Plate 68

71. *General Ivan Petrovitch Soltykov*. Detail of Fig. 133. Marble, 178[
Leningrad, Hermitage

3. *Comte de Buffon*. (Cf. Fig. 135.) Marble, 1783. Leningrad, Hermitage

2. *Antoine Louis*. Detail of Fig. 134. Marble, 1782.
   Paris, Ecole de Médecine

74. *Joseph and Etienne Montgolfier*. (Cf. Fig. 136.) Bronze, 1783. Paris, Musée de l'Air

75. *Jean Mauduit, called de Larive*. Detail of Fig. 138. Marble, 1784.
Paris. Comédie Française

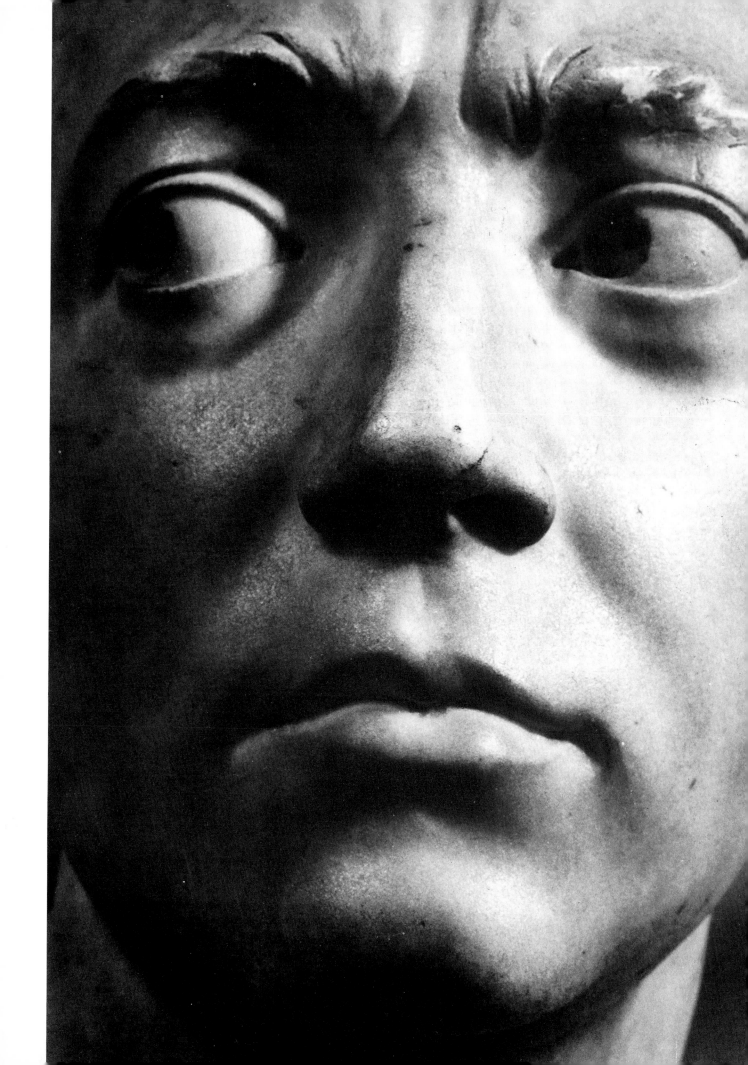

76a. *Jean de La Fontaine*. Detail of Fig. 139. Marble, 1783.
Philadelphia Museum of Art

76b. *Jean de La Fontaine*. (Cf. Fig. 139.) Plaster, about 1781.
Schwerin, Staatliches Museum

Jean de La Fontaine.
(Cf. Fig. 139.)
Plaster, about 1781.
Orléans,
Musée des Beaux-Arts

Prince Friedrich Franz I of Mecklenburg-Schwerin. Detail of Fig. 140. Terra cotta, 1782. Schwerin, Staatliches Museum

Princess Louise of Mecklenburg-Schwerin. Detail of Fig. 141. Terra cotta, 1782.
Schwerin, Staatliches Museum

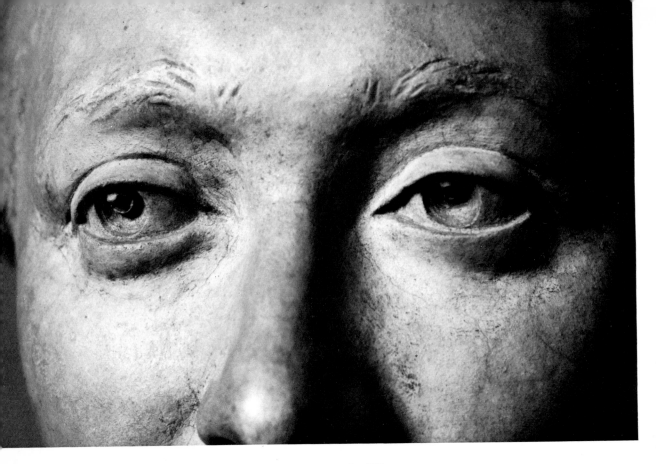

80a. *Prince Friedrich Franz I of Mecklenburg-Schwerin*. Detail of Plate 79

80b. *La Frileuse*. Detail of Plate 83b

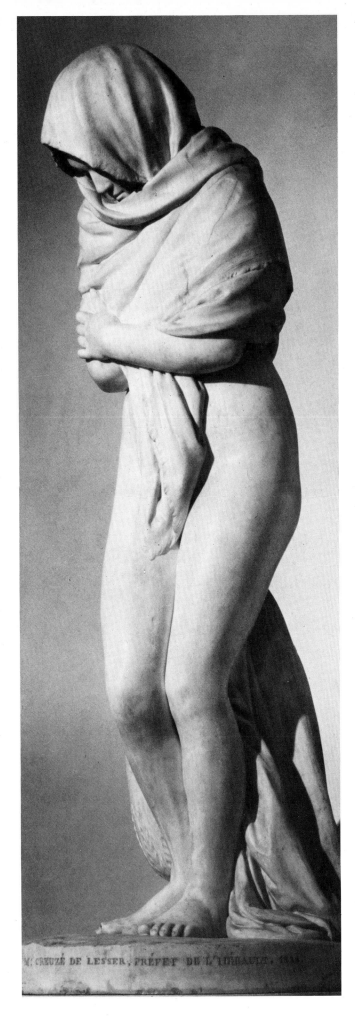

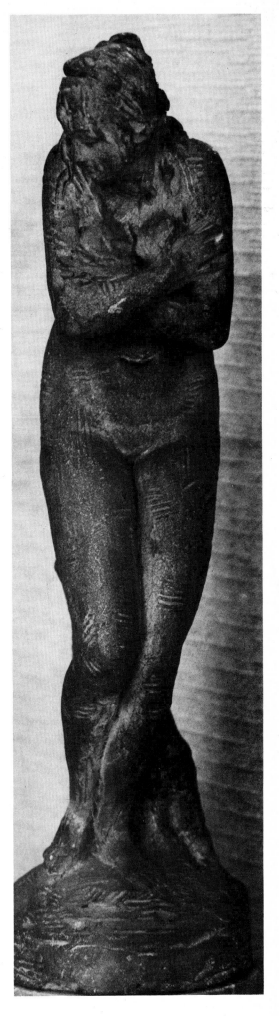

81a. *La Frileuse (Winter)*.
Marble, 1783. Montpellier, Musée Fabre

81b. *La Frileuse (Winter)*.
Terra cotta, about 1783. Paris, Louvre

82. *La Frileuse (Winter)*. Bronze, 1787.
New York, Metropolitan Museum of Art

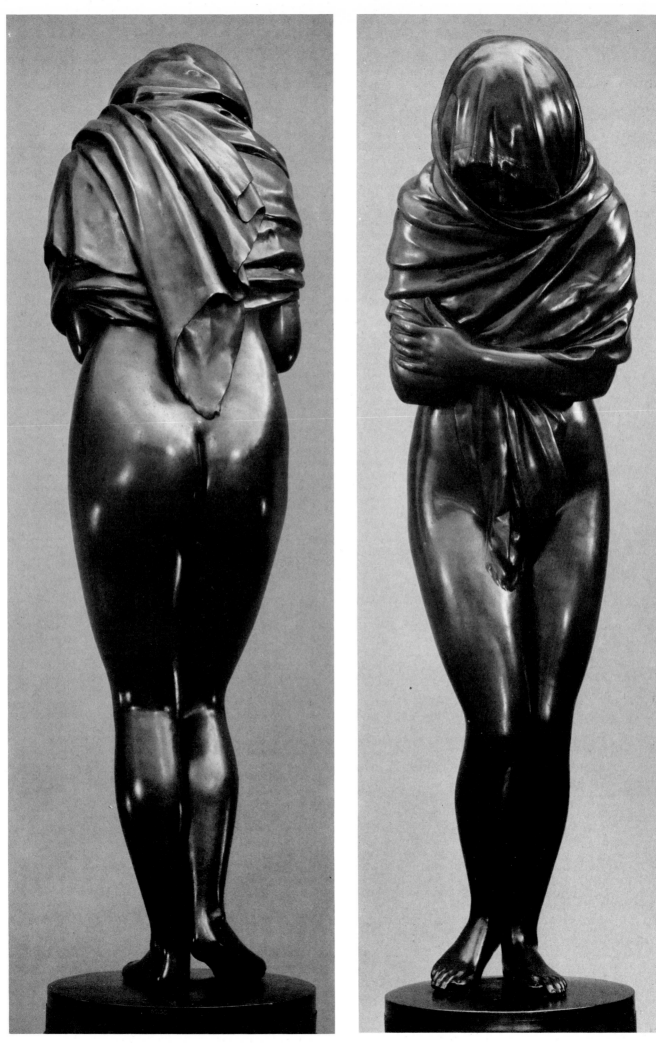

83a–b. *La Frileuse* (*Winter*). Bronze, 1787. New York, Metropolitan Museum of Art

85a. *Summer*. (Cf. Fig. 143.) Plaster, about 1785. Paris, Musée Nissim de Camondo

85b. *Summer*. (Cf. Fig. 143.) Marble, about 1785. Paris, Musée Nissim de Camondo

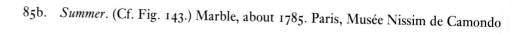

4. *La Frileuse* (*Winter*).
Detail of Plate 83b

87. *A Bather*. Detail of Plate 86

6. *A Bather*. Marble, 1782. New York, Metropolitan Museum of Art

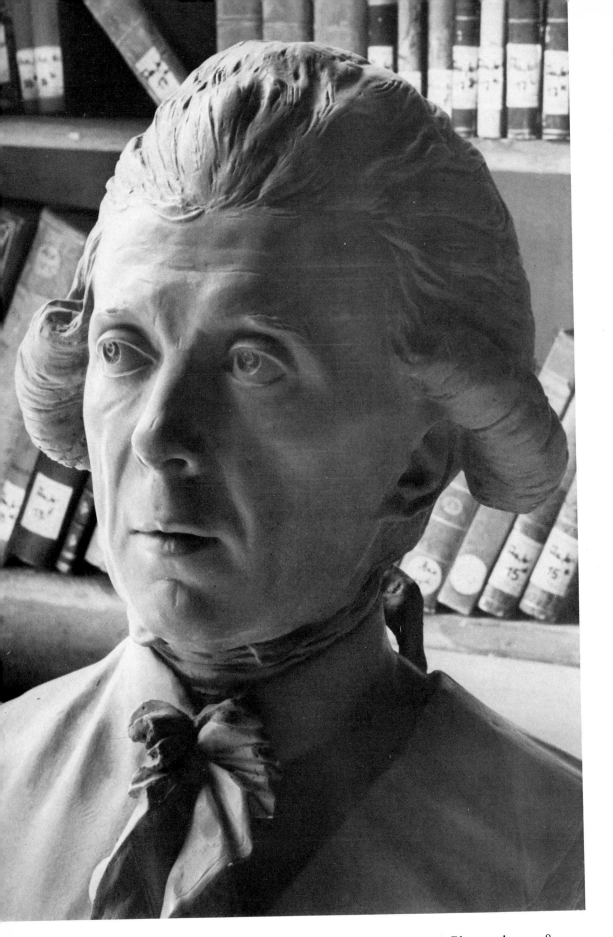

88. *Prince Henry of Prussia, brother of Frederick the Great.* Detail of Fig. 145. Plaster, about 1784.
Weimar, Landesbibliothek

89. *'Marquis de Biré.'* Detail of Fig. 148. Marble, 1786.
Boston, Museum of Fine Arts

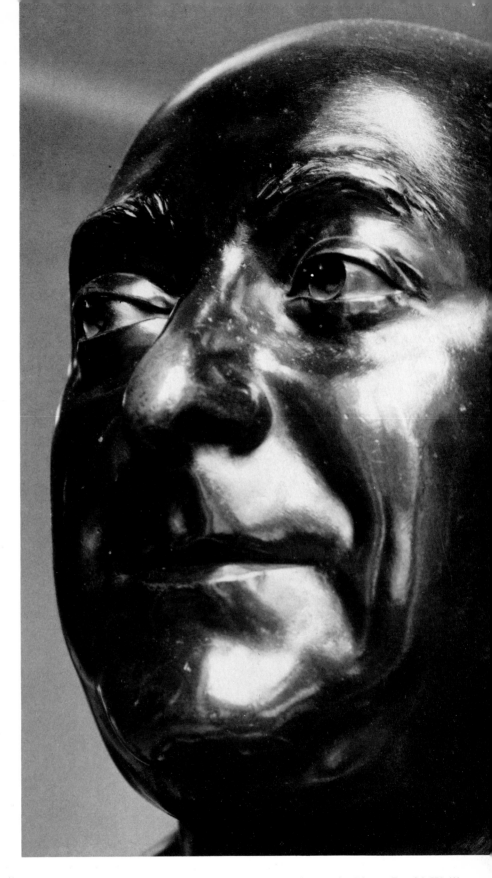

91. '*J.-Ch. Lenoir.*' Detail of Fig. 149. Bronze, 1786. Paris, Pierre David-Weill

o. '*Chrétien-Guillaume de Lamoignon de Malesherbes*'. Detail of Fig. 150.
Marble, 1784. Paris, Louvre

92. *Marquis de Condorcet.* (Cf. Fig. 151.) Marble, 1785. Philadelphia, American Philosophical Society

93. *Marquis de Condorcet*. Detail of Fig. 151. Plaster, about 1785. Paris, Louvre

95. *George Washington*. Detail of Fig. 156. Marble, about 1786. New York,
Mrs. Sarah Hunter Kelly

Comtesse de Sabran. Detail of Fig. 152. Plaster, about 1785.
Eisenach, Thuringian Museum

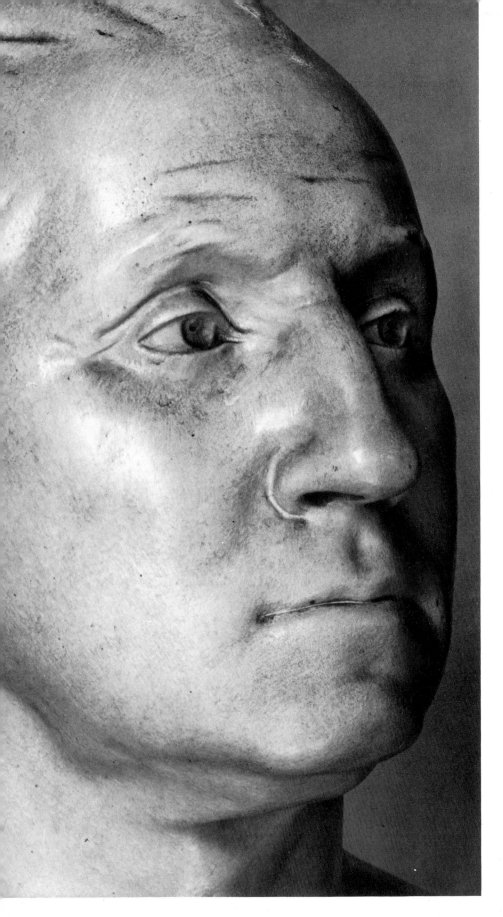

96. *George Washington*. Detail of Fig. 154. Plaster, about 1786. Boston, Athenaeum

97a. *George Washington*. Terra cotta, 1786. Paris, Louvre

97b. *George Washington*. Terra cotta, 1785. Mount Vernon, Va.,
The Mount Vernon Ladies' Association

98a–b. *George Washington*. Marble, signed 1788. Richmond, Virginia, Capitol

George Washington.
Marble, signed 1788.
Richmond, Virginia, Capitol

I. *George Washington*. Detail of Plate 99

103. *Pierre-André de Suffren*. Detail of Fig. 158. Marble, 1787. The Hague, Mauritshuis

2. *Louis XVI*. Detail of Fig. 159. Marble, 1790, Versailles

104. *Marquis de Lafayette*. Detail of Fig. 161. Plaster, about 1785. Boston, Athenaeum

106. *Marquis de Lafayette*. Detail of Fig. 162. Marble, 1787. Richmond, Virginia, Capitol

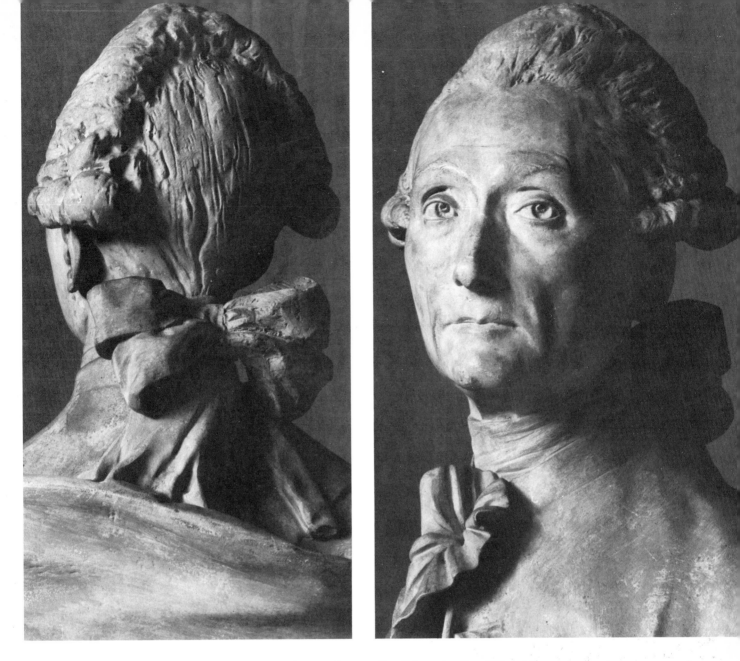

107a–b. *Duc de Nivernais.* Details of Fig. 164. Plaster, about 1787. Schwerin, Staatliches Museum

108. *A Vestal.* Detail of Fig. 167.
Marble, 1787.
New York, Wildenstein & C

9. *Comtesse d'Ennery
and her daughter.*
Detail of Plate 68

110. *Conte Cagliostro*. Detail of Fig. 166. Marble, 1786. Washington, National Gallery of Art, Samuel H. Kress Collection

111. *Madame Houdon, the artist's wife*. Detail of Fig. 172
Plaster, 1787. Paris, Louvre

112. *Sabine Houdon, the artist's eldest daughter,* (Cf. Figs. 177–8.) Plaster, 1791. Paris, Louvre

113. *Sabine Houdon at the age of four*. Detail of Fig. 178. Marble, about 1791. San Marino, Calif., Henry E. Huntington Library and Art Gallery

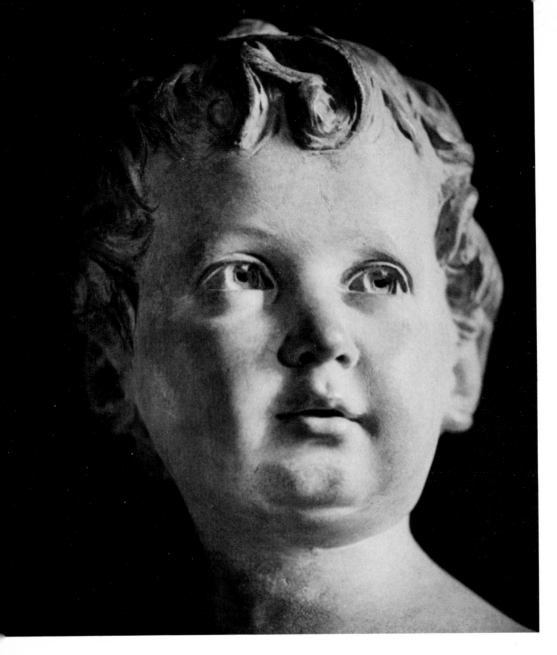

114. *Anne-Ange Houdon, the artist's second daughter, at the age of three.* Detail of Fig. 175.
Plaster, about 1791. Paris, Louvre

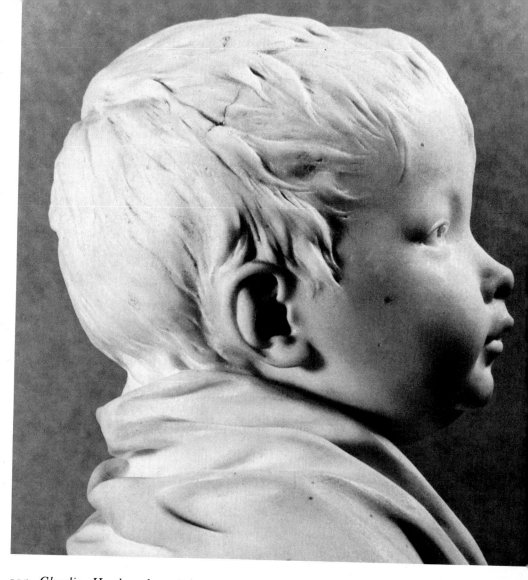

115. *Claudine Houdon, the artist's youngest daughter, at the age of one.* Detail of Fig. 176.
Marble, about 1791. Worcester, Mass., Worcester Art Museum

116. *Thomas Jefferson*. Detail of Fig. 168. Marble, 1789. Boston, Museum of Fine Arts

117. *Thomas Jefferson*. Detail of Fig. 168. Marble, 17
Boston, Museum of Fine Arts

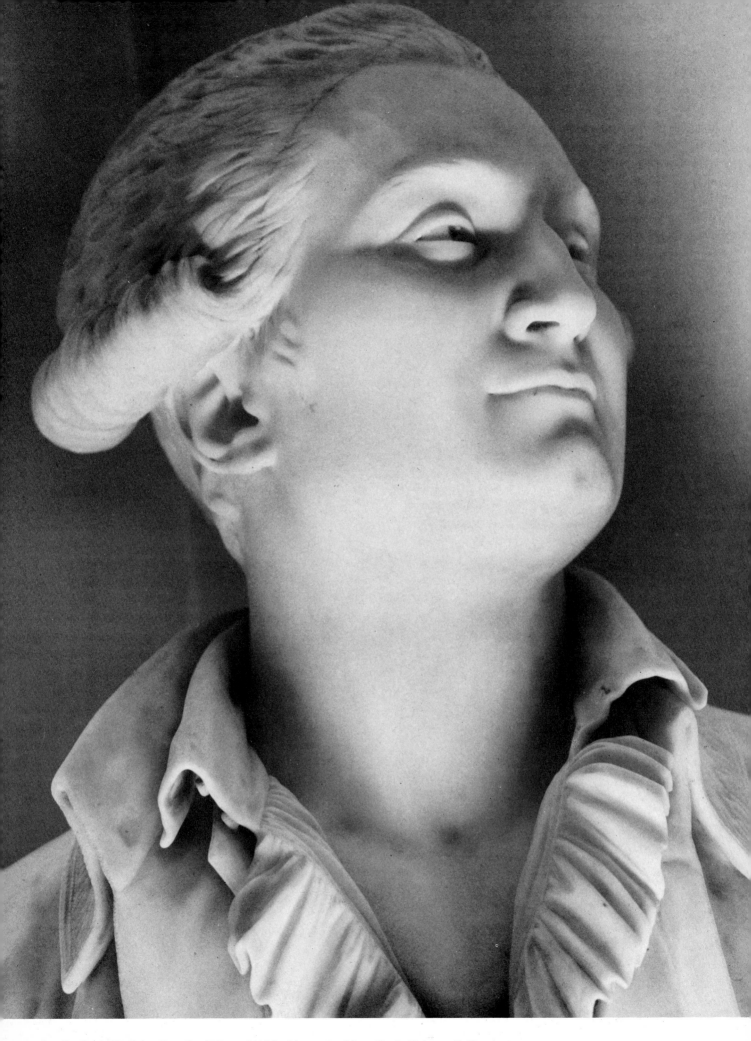

118. *Comte de Guibert*. Detail of Fig. 169. Marble, 1791. New York, Private Collection

119. *Jacques Necker*. Detail of Fig. 170. Marble, 1790. Geneva, Musée d'Art et d'Histoire

121. *Comte de Mirabeau.* Detail of Fig. 181. Terra cotta. 1791. Paris, Louvre

120. *Comte de Mirabeau.* Detail of Fig. 181.
Terra cotta, 1791. Paris, Louvre

122. *Apollo*. Bronze, 1790.
Lisbon, Calouste Gulbenki[an]
Foundation, Museum

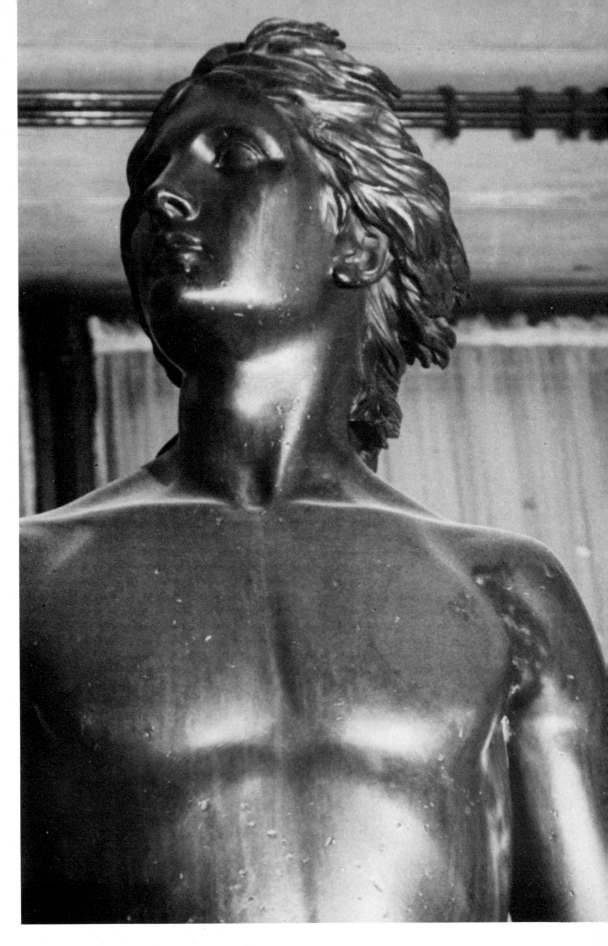

123. *Apollo*. Detail of Plate 122.

125. *Madame Houdon and Sabine Houdon*. Detail of Fig. 173. Terra cotta, 1798. Paris, Petit Palais

124. *Abbé Jean-Jacques Barthélémy*. Detail of Fig. 186.
Marble, about 1802. Paris, Bibliothèque Nationale

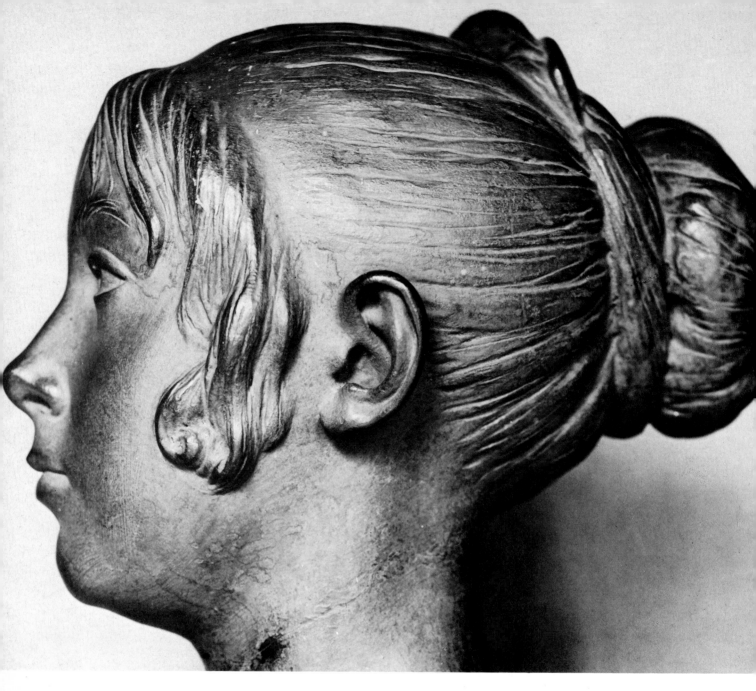

126. *Sabine Houdon, the artist's eldest daughter, at the age of fifteen*. Detail of Fig. 179. Plaster, about 1802. Formerly Paris, Perrin Houdon collection

127. '*Sabine Houdon at the age of twenty*.' Detail of Fig. 180. Marble, 1807. New York, Wildenstein & Co.

128a. *Mme Duquesnoy*. Detail of Fig. 190. Marble, about 1800. San Francisco, de Young Museum

128b. *Adrien-Cyprien Duquesnoy*. Detail of Fig. 191. Marble, about 1800. Paris, Louvre

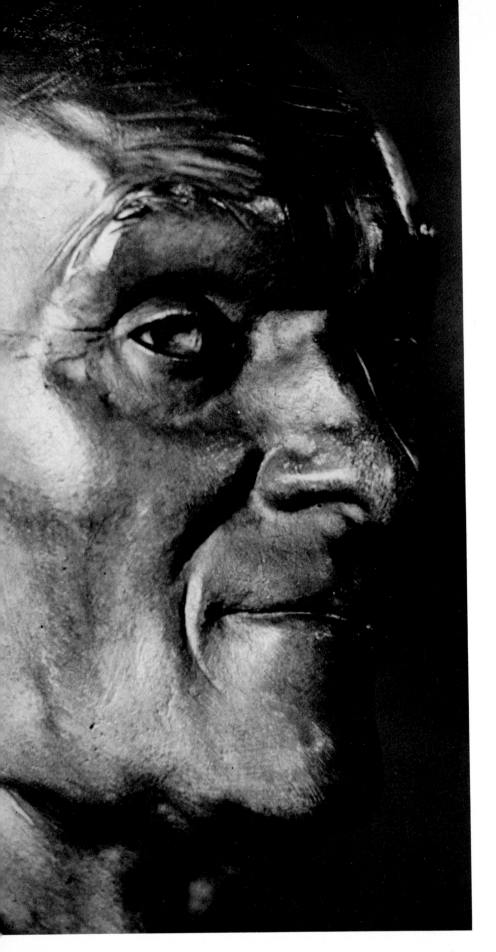

130. *Joseph-Jérôme Le François de Lalande.* Detail of Fig. 189. Plaster, about 1801. Paris, Observatoire

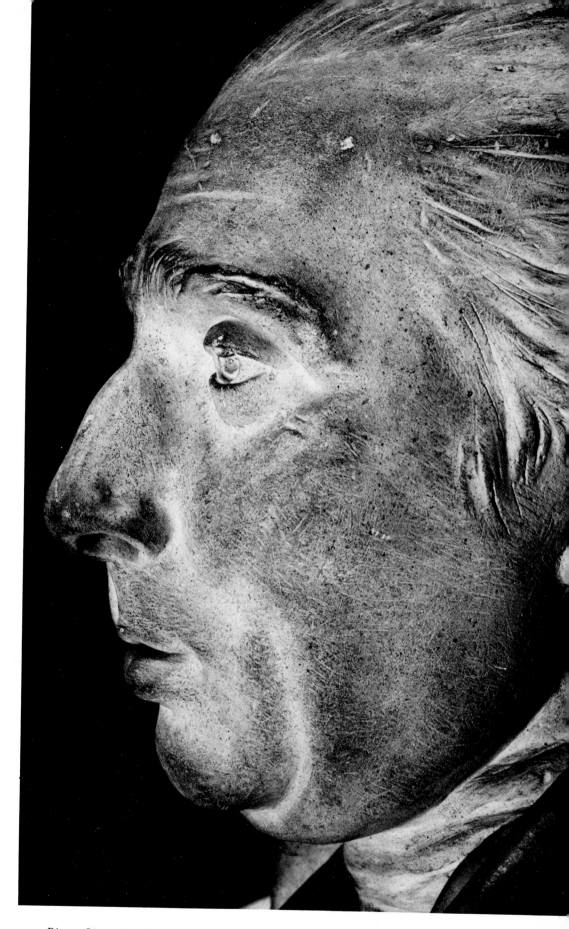

131. *Pierre-Simon Laplace*. Detail of Fig. 193. Plaster, about 1803.
Paris, Musée des Arts Décoratifs

132. *Joel Barlow*. Detail of Fig. 194. Marble, about 1804. Washington, D.C.,
The White House

133. *Robert Fulton*. Detail of Fig. 195. Marble, 1804.
Detroit, Institute of Arts

135. *Cicero*. Detail of Plate 134

134. *Cicero*. Plaster, 1804. Paris, Bibliothèque Nationale

136. *The Emperor Napoleon.* Detail of Fig. 201. Terra cotta, 1806. Dijon, Musée des Beaux-Arts

37. *The Emperor Napoleon.* Detail of Fig. 201. Terra cotta, 1806. Dijon, Musée des Beaux-Arts

138. *General Joubert*. Detail of Plate 139

139. *General Joubert*. Marble, about 1812. Versailles

40–141. *Voltaire*. Marble, about 1812. Paris, Panthéon

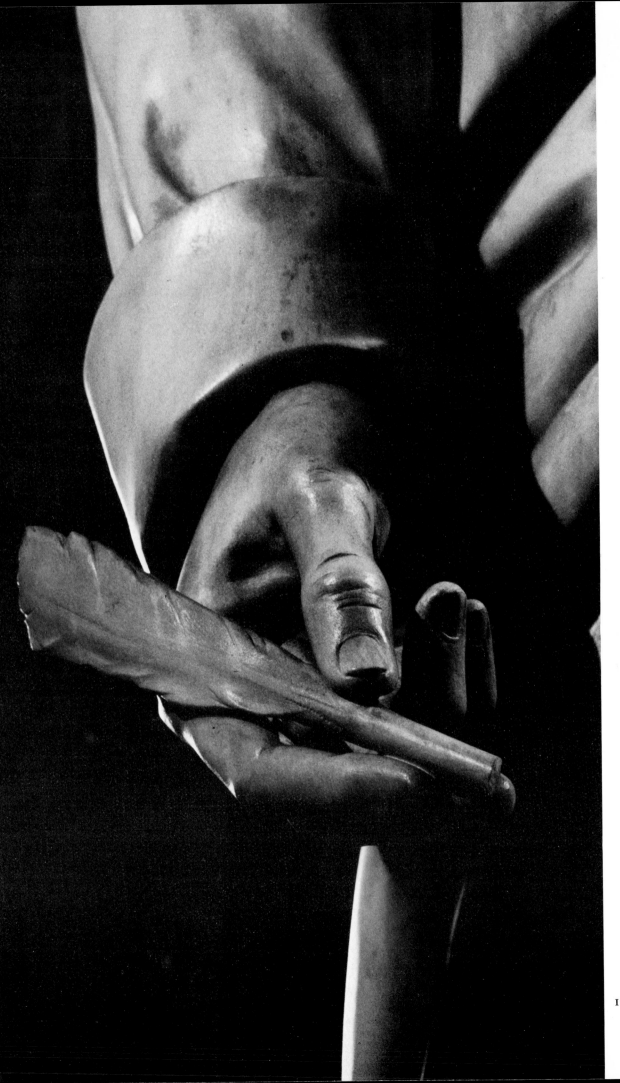

142. *Voltaire.*
Detail of Plate 140

143. (a) *Diderot*, New York (Fig. 70) – (b) *Tomb of Alexis Galitzin*, Moscow (Fig. 74) – (c) *Gluck*, Weimar (Fig. 78) – (d) *Marie Adélaïde Servat*, New York (Fig. 90) – (e) *'La petite Robert'*, Barnard Castle (Fig. 95) – (f) *Voltaire*, Leningrad (Fig. 116) – (g) *d'Alembert*, New Haven (Fig. 110) – (h) *Duc de Choiseul-Praslin*, Paris (Fig. 120) – (i) *Tomb of Comte d'Ennery*, Paris (Fig. 132) – (j) *Diana*, San Marino (Fig. 100) – (k) *Larive*, Paris (Fig. 138) – (l) *'Lenoir'*, Paris (Fig. 149) – (m) *Vestal*, New York (Fig. 167) – (n) *Jefferson*, Boston (Fig. 168) – (o) *Washington*, Richmond (Fig. 153)

144. (a) *Louis XVI*, Versailles (Fig. 159) – (b) *Comte de Guibert*, New York (Fig. 169) – (c) *George Washington*, Versailles (Fig. 157) – (d) *Fulton*, Detroit (Fig. 195) – (e) *Napoleon*, Dijon (Fig. 201) – (f) *'Sabine Houdon'*, New York (Fig. 180) – (g) seal on the bust of Voltaire, Baltimore (Fig. 113)

BIBLIOGRAPHY

Bibliographical Note

THE Bibliography is divided into four sections: I. Sources. This includes original documents, principally in the Archives Nationales in Paris and the Library of Congress in the United States. Also included are reprints of documents. Most of those in French collections are available in Réau, *Houdon*, Paris, 1964, but substantial additions have been made here in the listing of American documents relative to Houdon. II. Monographs and Catalogues on Houdon. The most important of these are obviously Réau, 1964, Giacometti, Dierks, Lami, Mansfeld, and Arnason, 1964. III. Periodicals and Bulletins. Here it should be noted that a large percentage of the periodical articles are minor notes that do not add very much to the literature. Obviously, most of the articles by Réau and Vitry are important. IV. General Works. The category of general works includes a miscellany of biographies, histories, museum catalogues, etc. which have been consulted. These are by no means complete. For the biographical notes on Houdon's sitters a wide variety of sources have been consulted— biographies of individuals, dictionaries, and encyclopedias—and only the most pertinent are listed. The same holds true of museum catalogues. It may be assumed that every major museum which owns works by Houdon has at some point published a catalogue or handbook; but only a few, which provide special or unique information, are listed. In the same way, a large number of general histories and other studies of The Enlightenment have been consulted at various points. Most of these are listed in the extensive bibliography of Peter Gay's monumental work, *The Enlightenment*.

I. *Sources*

NOTE: Most of the documents are reprinted or excerpted in Réau, *Houdon*, Paris, 1964. The *Livrets* of the Salons are reprinted here as Appendix 1; The List of Sculptures *c.* 1784, Appendix 2; Memorandum from Houdon to Bachelier 1794, Appendix 3; The Sculptures sold from Houdon's Studio 1795, Appendix 4; The Catalogue of the Auction from Houdon's Studio after his death, Appendix 5.

Archives Nationales, O^1678–845–845^9–847^7–1094–1097, fol. 150–1698–1698^6–1911–1914–1914^3–1915–1916–1916^4, 234–1917–1917^4, 393–1918, 63–1918^1–1918^2, 196, 211–1919^1, 118–1919^2, 194–1919^3, 254, 255–1919^5, 174–1922–$1921A^3$–$1922A^3$–1922–1925–$1925B$–1926^8, folios $9v^0$, $113v^0$, 115–1926^9, fol. 77–1926^{10}, fol. 59–1927–1931–1932–1933–1934^6–1935^2–1941–2086–O^2202–818–819–838–840–841–843–1840 O^3556–556 No. 5104–1387. Most pertinent documents are cited in the notes. Minutier Central, LXXI, file 35–AA 64 (438)–C 67 dos. 662–AF^{IV} 151 dos 901.

Actes de la Commune de Paris pendant la Révolution, ed. S. Lacroix; series I and II, Paris, 1894–1907.

American Philosophical Society, Philadelphia, Benjamin Franklin Papers (documents).

Archives du Musée des monuments français, Paris, 1883–97, vols. I and III.

Bachaumont, Louis de. *Mémoires secrets pour servir à l'histoire de la République des lettres en France de 1762 jusqu'à nos jours*, London, 1777–89 (3 vols).

— *Lettres sur les peintures, sculptures et gravures de MM. de l'Académie Royale, exposées au Salon du Louvre depuis 1757 jusqu'en 1779*, London, 1780.

— *Anecdotes échappées à l'observation anglaise et aux mémoires secrets, en forme de correspondance: pour servir de suite à ces ouvrages*, London, 1788.

Chinard, Gilbert, ed. *Houdon in America: a Collection of Document. in the Jefferson Papers in the Library of Congress*, Baltimore, 1930s Chinard gives the basic documents. See also papers of Franklin, Jefferson, and Washington below and under General Works.

The Diaries of George Washington, ed. John C. Fitzpatrick, New York, 1925 (vol. 2, entries of October 2, October 7, October 9, October 10, October 19, 1785).

Diderot, Denis. Œuvres complètes, ed. Jules Assézat and Maurice Tourneux, 20 vols, Paris, 1875–1877. *Mme de Vandeul*. Mémoires pour servir à l'histoire de la vie des ouvrages de Diderot. Régistre des délibérations du Conseil municipal de Langres, August 27, 1780 (in Diderot, Œuvres complètes).

The Papers of Benjamin Franklin, 1706–1771, ed. William B. Willcox, Yale, New Haven, 1959– (Vols 1–18).

Grimm, F. M., and Diderot, Denis. *Correspondance littéraire, philosophique et critique*, ed. M. Tourneux, Paris, 1877–82, reprint (16 vols).

Houdon, Jean-Antoine. *Letters in Reference to his Statue of Rousseau* (manuscripts in file, Library of Art and Archaeology, University of Paris).

— *Lettre à M. le Président de la Société des Amis de la Constitution*, Paris, June 5, 1791. (Reprinted in Délerot & Legrelle, p. 185 and in Réau, 1964, vol. 1, p. 67.)

— *Réflexions sur les Concours en général et sur celui de la statue de J.-J. Rousseau en particulier*, Paris, 1791. (Reprinted in Délerot & Legrelle, pp. 185–6 and in Réau, 1964, vol. 1, pp. 66–68.)

— *Lettre à Bachelier*, Paris, October 11, 1794, *Archives nationales* $O,^1$ $198,^2$ 196 (reprinted in Dierks, Gandouin, Réau, 1964, etc. See Appendix 3, p. 129 above.)

The Jefferson Papers 1760–1791, ed. Julian Boyd, Princeton University Press, 1950–(vols 1–19).

The Jefferson Papers Index, ed. Elizabeth J. Sherwood and Ida T. Hopper, Princeton University Press, 1954, 1958, 1973.

Jefferson, Thomas. Correspondence between Thomas Jefferson and Pierre Samuel du Pont de Nemours, ed. Dumas Malone, Boston, 1930.

The Thomas Jefferson Papers, ed. Julian P. Boyd, Princeton University Press, 1950–date.

La société des Jacobins, ed. A. Aulard, Paris, 1889–97 (6 vols).

Library of Congress, Washington D.C. *Benjamin Franklin Papers*: Franklin to [Houdon], June 20, 1785 (Series 2, vol. 27, p. 2651); *Thomas Jefferson Papers*: [July 1785], vol. 53, folios 8987–88, 8991; [July 1785], vol. 53, folios 8989–90, 8992; September 14, 1785, vol. 14, folio 2510; June 29, 1786, vol. 22, folios 3768–72; September 1786, vol. 24, folio 4214; [1786], vol. 234, folio 41899; July 3, 1786, vol. 50, folio 8486; [1789], vol. 53, folio 9050; September 8, 1796, vol. 100, folios 17212–13; *George Washington Papers*: Washington to Houdon, September 20, 1785 (Series 2, vol. 12, p. 231).

Livrets pub. by J. J. Guiffrey, Paris, 1870 et seq.: 1769, 1771, 1773, 1775, 1777, 1779, 1781, 1783, 1785, 1787, 1789, 1791, 1793, 1795, 1796, 1800, 1801, 1802, 1804, 1806, 1808, 1812, 1814. Copies of the original *Livrets* are in the Deloynes Collection, Cabinet des estampes, Bibl. Nationale (40 vols). (See Appendix 1, above.)

Von Manlich, Johann-Christian. Original manuscript in French of *Mémoires*, Munich Library. Translation by E. Stollreither: *Ein deutscher Maler und Hofmann. Lebenserinnerungen des Joh. Christian von Manlich*, Berlin, 1910. (Original text in French ed. by J. Delage, Paris, 1948.)

Massachusetts Historical Society Catalogue of Manuscripts, vol. 3, Boston, 1969.

Montaiglon, A. de. *Bibliographie des livrets et des critiques de Salons depuis 1673 jusqu'en 1851*, Paris, 1852.

Montaiglon, A. de, and Guiffrey, J. *Correspondance des directeurs de l'Académie de France à Rome, 1766–1804*, Paris, 1887–1908 (18 vols). Vol. XII, 1902 (1764–74); vol. XIII, 1904 (1776–79); vol. XV, 1906 (1785–90).

New York Historical Society's Dictionary of Artists in America, 1564–1860, ed. George C. Groce and David H. Wallace, Yale University Press, 1957.

Pidansat de Mairobert. *Lettres sur les peintures, sculptures et gravures de Mm. de l'Académie royale exposées au Salon du Louvre depuis MDCCLXVII jusqu'en MDCCLXXIX*, London, 1780.

Procès-verbaux de l'Académie royale de peinture et de sculpture, ed. A. de Montaiglon, vol. VIII (1888) and vol. X (1892), Paris.

Procès-verbaux de l'Académie des Beaux-Arts after 1795, ed. M. Bonnaire, Paris, 1937–43 (3 vols).

Procès-verbaux de la Commission temporaire des arts, ed. A. Tuetey, Paris, 1912–17 (2 vols).

Procès-verbaux du Comité d'instruction publique de la Convention nationale, ed. J. Guillaume, Paris, 1891–1907 (6 vols).

Réau, Louis, *Houdon, sa vie et son œuvre*, Paris, 1964, 4 vols in 2. (Most complete reprints of documents and bibliography.)

Saint-Aubin, G. de. *Explication des peintures, sculptures et gravures de Messieurs de l'Académie Royale*, Paris, 1769. (Catalogue of the Salon of 1769 annotated with drawings by Saint-Aubin. Photostat.)

— *Catalogue ed ventes et livrets de Salons illustrés par [Saint-Aubin]* Paris, 1910.

Seznec, Jean, and Adhémar, Jean. *Diderot Salons*, Oxford, vol. I, 1957; vol. II, 1960; vol. III, 1963; vol. IV, 1967.

Thiery, Luc Vincent. *Guide des amateurs et des étrangers voyageurs à Paris et aux environs de Paris, 1787 et 1788*, Paris, 1928.

The Papers of George Washington, University of Virginia, Charlottesville. Available in xerox. Not yet published.

The Writings of George Washington, ed. John C. Fitzpatrick, New York, 1931 (letters of September 26, October 7, October 30, December 5, 1785, and August 1, 1786).

Of contemporary journals, note particularly *Les affiches de Paris*, 1783–1804; *Journal de Paris*, 1777–1811; *Mercure de France*, 1672–1820.

II. *Monographs and Catalogues on Houdon*

Arnason, H. H. *Sculpture by Houdon*, Worcester, Mass., 1964 (exhibition catalogue).

Bapst, Germain. *Diana Huntress by Jean-Antoine Houdon*, Paris, 1915.

Bénézit, E. *Dictionnaire critique et documentaire des Peintres, Sculpteurs, Dessinateurs et Graveurs*, Paris, 1951, vol. IV.

Claparède, Jean. *Houdon et la Société des Beaux-Arts de Montpellier*, Paris, 1950.

Darl, Jacques. *Le buste de la Diane de Houdon*, Paris, 1906.

Délerot, E., and Lagrelle, A. *Notice sur J.-A. Houdon, de l'Institut (1741–1818)*, Versailles, 1856.

Dierks, Hermann. *Houdon's Leben und Werke*, Gotha, 1887. (Reprints letter to Bachelier, October 11, 1794, 'Réflexions sur les concours en général et sur celui de la statue de J. J. Rousseau en particulier', etc.)

Fermiani, Franco. *Spigolature houdoniane. In margine al busto di Napoleone I del Civico Museo Revoltella di Trieste*, Rome, 1971 (Univ. Studi Trieste).

Gandouin, Ernest. *Quelques notes sur J.-A. Houdon*, Paris, 1900. (Includes list of Salons, catalogue and list of works in sale of 1828. Reprints letter of Houdon to Bachelier, October 11, 1794.)

Giacometti, Georges. *Le statuaire Jean-Antoine Houdon et son époque (1741–1828)*, Paris, 1918–19 (3 vols). (Detailed catalogue, list of Salons. Reprints of documents and letters.)

— *La vie et l'œuvre de Houdon*, Paris, 1928 (2 vols). (See above.)

— *Un lévrier, terre-cuite originale par Houdon*, Paris, n.d.

Hart, Charles Henry, and Biddle, Edward. *Memoirs of the Life and Works of Jean-Antoine Houdon, the Sculptor of Voltaire and of Washington*, Philadelphia, 1911.

Centenaire de J.-A. Houdon, Versailles, April–May 1928 (exhibition catalogue).

Exposition du Centenaire de Houdon, Paris, Galerie Buvelot, 1928 (exhibition catalogue).

Century Association Exhibition, New York City. *Sculpture by Houdon; paintings and drawings by David*, February 19–April 10, 1947 (exhibition catalogue).

Jean-Antoine Houdon: Sein Werk in Deutschland. Deutsche Akademie der Künste, Berlin, 1955 (exhibition catalogue).

Jal, Augustin. *Dictionnaire critique de biographie et d'histoire*, 1864, originally in *La Pandore*, July 30, 1828, signed A. J., 3rd ed. 1872, p. 689.

Lami, Stanislas. *Dictionnaire des Sculpteurs de l'école française en dix-huitième siècle*, Paris, 1910 (2 vols) (Catalogue and bibliography, vol. I, pp. 408–36.)

Levron, Jacques. *Les œuvres de Houdon à Angers*, Paris, 1941.

McRae, Sherwin. *Washington, his person as represented by the artists, The Houdon statue, its history and value*. Published by the order of the Senate of Virginia, 1873. (Photostat, Frick Art Reference Library, New York.)

Maillard, Elisa. *Houdon*, Paris, 1931.

Mansfeld, Heinz. *Der Bildhauer Jean-Antoine Houdon. Seine Zeit, sein Werk in Deutschland*, Greifswald, 1955. (Unpublished Diss.)

Massengale, Jean Montague. *The Angers-Athenaeum Bust of Benjamin Franklin by Houdon*, New York University, 1965 (unpublished thesis).

Michel, André. *Statue de Washington par Houdon*, Paris, 1918.

Montaiglon, A. de, and Duplessis, J. *Houdon, sa vie et ses ouvrages*, Paris, 1855-6.

Quatremère De Quincy. *Notice historique sur la vie et les ouvrages de M. Houdon, sculpteur, Mém. de l'Académie des Beaux-Arts*, 1829 (reprinted in *Recueil des notices historiques lues dans les séances publiques de l'Académie royale des Beaux-Arts*, Paris. 1834, 2 vols).

Réau, Louis. *Houdon, biographie critique*, Paris, 1930.

— *Houdon, sa vie et son œuvre*, Paris, 1964. 4 vols in 2.

Roger-Milès, L. *Les Dianes de Houdon, et les caprices de la pudeur esthétique à la fin du XVIIIe siècle*, Paris, 1913.

Rostrup, Haavard. *J.-A. Houdon*, Copenhagen, 1942.

Sauerländer, Willibald. *Jean-Antoine Houdon: Voltaire*, Stuttgart, 1963 (Werkmonographien zur Bildenden Kunst in Reclams Universal Bibliothek).

Vollmer, Hans. *Houdon, Allgemeines Lexikon der bildenden Künstler*, Thieme-Becker, Leipzig, 1924, vol. 17.

III. *Periodicals, Bulletins, etc.*

Aldhoven, Karl. 'Houdon in Gotha' (in his *Gesammelte Aufsätze . . .*), Leipzig, 1911, pp. 139-45.

Ansaldi, Giulio R. 'Il Neoclassico e Houdon', *Fede e Arte*, vol. 14, 1966, pp. 116-27.

Arnason, H. H. 'Note on the Diana of Houdon', *The Art Quarterly*, vol. 2, no. 4, Autumn 1939, pp. 402e-402f.

— 'Jean-Antoine Houdon's Jean de la Fontaine', *Art News*, vol. 66, no. 10, February 1968, pp. 30-33, 69-70.

Aubert, Marcel. 'Le mausolée du comte d'Ennery par Houdon', *Revue des Beaux-Arts de France*, 1943; and Monuments Piot (with Ch. Picard), vol. XL.

— 'Le buste de Madame Adélaïde par Houdon', *Bulletin des Musées de France*, 1947.

Bapst, Germain. 'Le buste en marbre de Madame Pineu-Duval, née Sabine Houdon', 1917.

Baud-Bovy, Daniel. 'Les bustes de J.-J. par Houdon', *Semaine Littéraire*, Geneva, July 10, 1920.

Beaulieu, Michèle. 'Le buste de la cantatrice Sophie Arnould par Houdon', *Bulletin des Musées de France*, 1947.

Belleudy, Jules. 'Les portraits authentiques de Mirabeau', *Bulletin of the International Committee of Historical Sciences*, Paris, vol. 6, part 4, December 1934, pp. 361-70.

Benisovich, M. 'Houdon's Statue of Voltaire Seated', *Art Bulletin*, no. 30, March 1948, pp. 70-71.

Besterman, Theodore. 'The terra-cotta statue of Voltaire made by Houdon for Beaumarchais', *Studies on Voltaire and the eighteenth century*, vol. XII, 1960, pp. 21-7.

Biebel, Franklin M. 'Benjamin Franklin by Houdon', *Bulletin of the City Art Museum of St. Louis*, St. Louis, July 1936, pp. 51-5.

Biver, Marie-Louise. 'La colonne Napoléon et le camp de Boulogne-sur-Mer', *Revue Institut Napoléon*, 1965, pp. 76-83.

Bogyay, Thomas von. 'Nouveaux documents relatifs aux rapports de la cour de Gotha avec les artistes français', *Bulletin de la Société de l'histoire de l'art français*, 1935, pp. 126-35.

— 'Houdon à Weimar', *Gazette des Beaux-Arts*, June 1935, pp. 364-9.

— 'Studien zu Jean-Antoine Houdons Werk in Deutschland', *Zeitschrift für Kunstgeschichte*, vol. 27, no. 2, 1964, pp. 105-32.

— 'Houdon: sa vie et son œuvre by L. Réau', *Kunstgeschichte*, vol. 31, no. 1, 1968, pp. 70-77 (Review).

Böhme, Walter. 'Unbekannte Büsten Houdons. Die Büsten von Lalande und Bailly in Altenburg', *Jahrbuch der preussischen Kunstsammlungen*, 1926.

Bouvier, Auguste. 'Buste en marbre de J.-J. Rousseau par Houdon', *Musée de Genève*, 1956.

Bovy, Adrien. 'Les bustes de J.-J. Rousseau par Houdon', *Semaine Littéraire de Genève*, July 1920.

— 'Quelques bustes français conservés à Genève', *Actes du Congrès intern. d'histoire de l'art tenu à Paris*, 1921, vol. III, 1924, p. 590.

Breck, Joseph. 'Three busts by Houdon', *Bulletin of the Metropolitan Museum of Art*, New York, vol. 3, December 1912, pp. 224-5.

Brière, Gaston. 'Une lettre de J.-A. Houdon relative aux bustes de Napoléon et de Joséphine', *Bulletin de la Société de l'histoire de l'art français*, 1907.

— 'Le buste de Caumartin par Houdon', *Annales de l'Est et du Nord*, Nancy, 1908.

— 'La statue de Washington par Houdon', *Musées de France*, Paris, 1910, pp. 82-5.

— 'Notes sur quelques bustes de Houdon', *Archives de l'art français*, vol. 7, 1913, pp. 344-60.

Brière, Gaston, Vitry, Paul, *et al.* 'Notes critiques sur les œuvres de peinture et de sculpture réunies à l'Exposition des Cent Pastels du XVIIIe Siècle ouverte à La Galerie Petite en mai–juin 1908', *Bulletin de la Société de l'histoire de l'art français*, Paris, 1908, pp. 158-82. (Houdon, pp. 166-75.)

Buffenoire, Hippolyte. 'J.-J. Rousseau et Houdon', *Mercure de France*, Paris, July 1912, pp. 14-44.

— 'Jean-Jacques Rousseau et Houdon pendant la Révolution', *Mercure de France*, April 1, 1913.

Callatay, Édouard de. 'Les bustes genevois de Houdon', *Genava*, 1954.

Calosso, Achille Bertini. 'Il classicismo di Gian-Lorenzo Bernini e l'arte francese', *L'Arte*, 1921; French version in *Actes du III Congrès d'histoire de l'art*, 1924, p. 524.

— 'Il San Giovanni Battista di Giovanni Antonio Houdon', *Dedalo*, vol. 1, no. 4, 1922, pp. 289-306.

— 'Houdon a Roma', *Roma*, no. 6, June 1923, pp. 3-10.

Caso, Jacques de. 'Bibliographie de la sculpture en France 1770-1800', *Information de l'Histoire de l'Art*, vol. VIII, 1963, pp. 151-9.

Cecil, R. A. 'French 18th century sculpture formerly with the Hertford-Wallace Collection', *Apollo*, vol. 81, 1965, pp. 449-59.

Charageat, M. 'Le Fleuve et Le Sommeil, études en vue des morceaux de réception à l'Académie de Caffieri et de Houdon', *Musées de France*, no. 5, June 1950, pp. 106-16.

Chéramy, H. 'Houdon à l'Académie de France (1764-1768)', *Rome*, vol. XXa, no. 144, Paris, 1923, pp. 453-6.

Coppoler, Orlando Edoardo. 'Il ritratto di Cagliostro', *Archivio Storico Siciliano*, 1953.

Cott, Perry B. 'A Note on Houdon's Bust of Diana', *Studies in the History of Art* (Mél Suida), 1959, pp. 364-7.

Courajod, Louis. 'La Diane en bronze de Houdon du Musée du Louvre', *Archives de l'art français*, 1879-80, pp. 269-71.

Delarue, H. 'Le masque de J.-J. Rousseau', *Musée de Genève*, 1953.

Demmler, Theodor. 'Unbekannte Büsten Houdons', *Jahrbuch der preussischen Kunstsammlungen*, 1926.

Dowley, Francis H. 'D'Angiviller's Grands Hommes and the Significant Moment', *Art Bulletin*, vol. 39, 1957, pp. 260–3.

Du Bus, Charles. 'Molière dans l'art. Apropos des expositions Moliéresques de 1922', *Gazette des Beaux-Arts*, February 1922, pp. 77–84.

Du Pont de Nemours, Pierre Samuel. 'Lettres sur les salons de 1773, 1777, et 1779 adressées a la margrave Carolina Louise de Bade', *Archives de l'art français*, 1908, pp. 1–123 (p. 37 & footnote).

Feulner, Adolf. 'Eine Büste von Houdon' (Grimm), *Pantheon*, September 1928.

Frankfurter, Alfred M. 'Houdon: Thirteen Unfamiliar Busts', *Art News*, vol. 35, January 1937, pp. 15, 25. (Review of Houdon exhibition, Seligmann Gallery, New York.)

Frick, Helen C. 'Houdon and Rembrandt Peale', *Antiques*, vol. 26, no. 1, July 1934, pp. 8–10.

— 'Madame Jean-Antoine Houdon', *Art Bulletin*, vol. 29, September 1947, pp. 207–12.

— 'Un buste présumé de Lady Craven par Houdon', *Bulletin de la Société de l'histoire de l'art français*, 1948.

Fröhlich-Bume, L. 'Terrakotta-Skulpturen bei Mallet in Bourdon House, London', *Weltkunst*, vol. XXXIII, 1963, no. 20, pp. 19–20.

Furcy-Raynaud, Marc. 'Inventaire des sculptures exécutées au XVIIIᵉ siècle pour la direction des bâtiments du roi. Documents réunis', *Archives de l'art français*, vol. 14, 1927, pp. 156–63.

— 'Correspondance de M. d'Angiviller avec Pierre', *Nouvelles archives de l'art français*, vol. 21, 1905; vol. 22, 1906; pp. 126-7.

Gagneur, Adrien. 'Le mausolée de Victor Charpentier, marquis d'Ennery, par Houdon', *Mémoire de la Société de l'histoire du Vexin*, 1947.

Gardner, A. T. 'Huntington's Franklins', *Bulletin of the Metropolitan Museum of Art*, New York, vol. 15, Summer 1956, pp. 16, 19.

Gielly, Louis. 'Le buste de Théodore Tronchin par Houdon au Musée de Genève', *Genava*, 1929.

Gillet, Louis. 'Le buste de Rousseau de la collection de Girardin au Musée de Châalis', *Beaux-Arts*, December 15, pp. 326–8.

Gilou, Albert. 'Un vrai collectionneur ne devrait pas avoir plus d'une douzaine d'objets' (article on the collection of Sir Robert Abdy and his bust of Mme His), *Connaissance des arts*, October 1960.

Girod De L'Ain, Gabriel. 'Les Thellusson et les artistes', *Genava*, 1956.

Gordon, Katherine K. 'Mme du Pompadour, Pigalle and the Iconography of Friendship', *Art Bulletin*, vol. 50, 1968, pp. 209–62.

Grigant, P. 'A Marble Bust of Robert Fulton by Houdon', *Art Quarterly*, 1949, p. 257.

Hipkiss, Edwin J. 'Portrait Sculpture by Houdon', *Bulletin of the Boston Museum of Fine Arts*, vol. 32, no. 193, October 1934, pp. 70–74.

Hodgkinson, T. 'Houdon and Clodion, Masters of Elegance', *Apollo*, vol. 93, May 1971, pp. 394–9.

Hubert, Gérard. 'Une œuvre de Houdon identifiée: la statue du général Joubert à Versailles', *Gazette des Beaux-Arts*, 1956.

— 'Houdon, Réau', *Œil*, no. 144-7, December 1966 (Review).

Ingersoll-Smouse, Florence. 'Houdon en Amérique', *Revue de l'art ancien et moderne*, vol. 35, April 1914, pp. 278–98.

— 'Quelques documents et lettres relatifs au voyage (1785) et aux œuvres de Jean-Antoine Houdon aux États-Unis', *Bulletin de la Société de l'histoire de l'art français*, 1914, pp. 11–36.

— 'Catalogue provisoire des œuvres de Houdon conservées aux États-Unis', *Bulletin de la Société de l'histoire de l'art français*, 1914, pp. 31–7.

— 'Lettres inédites de J.-J. Caffieri', *Bulletin de la Société de l'histoire de l'art français*, 1913, pp. 202ff.

Joret, Charles. 'Houdon et le Duc de Weimar, Charles-Auguste', *Bulletin de la Société de l'histoire de Paris et de l'Ile de France*, January–June 1896, pp. 1–4.

Joubin, André. 'Études sur le Musée de Montpellier. Les Sculptures des XVIIᵉ et XVIIIᵉ siècles', *Revue de l'art ancien et moderne*, vol. 41, February 1922, pp. 117–24, 211–20, 277–83. March, 214–20; April, 277–83.

Jouin, Henry. 'Actes d'état civil concernant Houdon', *Archives de l'art français*, 1884, pp. 152–3.

Kaczmarzyk, D. 'New acquisitions of foreign sculpture in the Museum of Warsaw 1945–1957' (in Polish). *Roczn. Muz. Narod. Warszawie*, vol. v, 1960, pp. 335–57.

Lavoix, Henri. 'Les portraits de Molière', *Gazette des Beaux-Arts*, March 1872, pp. 230–50.

Léonardon, H. 'Un aide-sculpteur de Houdon et de F. Masson', *Bulletin de la Société des Sciences morales, des lettres et des arts de Seine-et-Oise*, July–September 1894, pp. 152–5.

Levallet-Haug, Geneviève. 'Le buste de Louis XVI par Houdon à Strasbourg détruit en 1870', *Bulletin de la Société de l'histoire de l'art français*, 1937.

— 'Houdon et la ville de Strasbourg', *Cahiers alsaciens d'archéologie, d'art et d'histoire*, 1958.

Levey, Michael. Review of *Houdon, sa vie et son œuvre* by Louis Réau, *Burlington Magazine*, March 1966.

Lotte, Maurice. 'Le mausolée de Victor Charpentier par Houdon', *Bulletin de la Société de l'histoire de l'art français*, 1920.

McAgy, J. 'Comte de Buffon: portrait bust', *Bulletin of the California Palace of the Legion of Honor*, San Francisco, vol. 1, June 1943, pp. 20–22.

Mansfeld, Heinz. 'Houdon, ein realistischer Porträtist', *Bildende Kunst*, 1956, pp. 381–4.

Mar, Léopold. 'Quelques renseignements inédits ou peu connus sur Houdon', *La curiosité universelle*, April 24, 1893.

Marcel, Henry. 'Essai sur l'iconographie de Mirabeau', *Revue de l'art ancien et moderne*, 1901, pp. 269–80.

Marmottan, Paul. 'Commandes de Napoléon aux peintres et sculpteurs', *Carnet de la Sabretache*, 1906, 1921.

Marquand, Allan. 'Two busts by Houdon in the collection of Henry C. Frick', *Art in America*, February 1917. pp. 65–72

Massengale, Jean Montague. 'A Franklin by Houdon Rediscovered', *Marsyas*, vol. XII, 1964–65, pp. 1–15. (Summary of thesis.)

Metz, Peter. 'Das Marmorbildnis der Dorothea von Rodde-Schlözer von Jean-Antoine Houdon', *Berliner Museen*, vol. VIII, no. 1, July 1958, pp. 1–14.

Michel, André. 'Exposition Universelle de 1889. La sculpture', *Gazette des Beaux-Arts*, July 1889, pp. 57–66, September 1889, pp. 281–309; Oct. 1889, pp. 389–406.

— 'Notes sur Houdon', *Journal des débats*, June 28, 1891.

— 'Les acquisitions du département de la sculpture du moyen-âge, de la renaissance et des temps modernes au Musée du Louvre', *Gazette des Beaux-Arts*, April 1903, pp. 299–311; May 1903, pp. 369–90.

— 'Houdon en Amérique' (on the bust of Paul Jones), *Journal des débats*, July 11, 1905.

— 'Les récentes acquisitions du département de la sculpture, moyen-âge, renaissance et temps modernes, au Musée du Louvre', *Gazette des Beaux-Arts*, May 1906, pp. 393–414.

— 'Les accroissements du département des sculptures . . . au Musée du Louvre', *Gazette des Beaux-Arts*, Paris, 1912, pp. 295–318.

— 'Les bustes d'Helvétius et de Malesherbes au Musée du Louvre', *Les musées de France*, 1912.

— 'La sculpture au Musée Jacquemart-André', *Gazette des Beaux-Arts*, 1914.

— 'La statue de Washington par J.-A. Houdon', *Les arts*, 1918.

Neugass, Fritz. 'Houdon und seine amerikanischen Auftraggeber', *Weltkunst*, vol. XXXIV, 1964, pp. 133–4.

Niclausse, Juliette. 'L'activité de Thomire comme ciseleur et fondeur au XVIIIe siècle', *Bulletin de la Société de l'histoire de l'art français*, 1940.

Nolhac, Pierre de. 'Les sculpteurs de Marie-Antoinette: Boizot et Houdon', *Les arts*, 1917.

Parker, Robert Allerton. 'The Centenary of Jean-Antoine Houdon', *International, Studio*, January 1928.

Petrusevic, N. B. 'The Statue of Voltaire by Houdon', *Leningrad*, 1970, 38 pp. (in Russian).

Phillip, Claude. 'The Voltaire of Houdon', *Art Journal*, 1906.

Phillips, John Goldsmith. 'Monsieur Houdon's Frileuse', *The Metropolitan Museum of Art Bulletin*, Summer 1963, pp. 29–36.

Picard, Charles. 'Houdon et l'antique', *Gazette des Beaux-Arts*, December 10, 1943, p. 5.

Picard, M. 'Un Buffon de Houdon', *Mémoires de l'académie de sciences, arts et belles-lettres de Dijon*, series 4, vol. 11, 1911, p. 60ff.

Pradel, Pierre. 'Une "Petite Frileuse" par Houdon', *Bulletin des Musées de France*, October 1946, pp. 12–13.

Preux, Baron de. 'Houdon dans son atelier par Boilly', *Gazette des Beaux-Arts*, October 1895, pp. 305–8.

Pudelko, George. 'A Marble Bust of John Paul Jones by Jean-Antoine Houdon', *Art in America*, vol. 27, October 1939, pp. 151–5.

Quarri, P. 'Sur un buste de Buffon au Musée de Dijon', *Annales de Bourgogne*, vol. XXX, 1958, pp. 133–4.

Raspail, Dr. Julien. 'Le masque mortuaire de J.-J. Rousseau', *Chronique médicale*, 1912.

Réau, Louis. 'Les œuvres de Houdon en Russie', *Bulletin de la Société de l'histoire de l'art français*, 1914, pp. 37–53.

— 'L'œuvre de Houdon en Russie', *Gazette des Beaux-Arts*, April–June 1917, pp. 129–54.

— 'Documents sur Houdon', *Bulletin de la Société de l'histoire de l'art français*, 1922, pp. 367–94. (La Frileuse, pp. 379–87.)

— 'Les bustes de Gerbier par Lemoyne et Houdon', *Bulletin de la Société de l'histoire de l'art français*, 1922.

— 'Documents sur Houdon: la statue de Tourville; la Frileuse; la Vierge de Pitié de la cathédrale de Verdun; le projet d'un monument au Parc de Bruxelles; le monument du poète Salomon Gessner à Zurich', *Bulletin de la Société de l'histoire de l'art français*, 1922 and 1923.

— 'Le premier salon de Houdon' (1769), *Gazette des Beaux-Arts*, January 1923, pp. 41–52.

— 'Le buste de Buffon du Musée de Dijon', *Gazette des Beaux-Arts*, 1923.

— 'Le buste de la Comtesse de Moustier par Houdon', *Bulletin de la Société de l'histoire de l'art français*, 1924, pp. 320–21.

— 'Houdon sous la révolution et l'empire', *Gazette des Beaux-Arts*, July–August 1924, pp. 59–86.

— 'Les relations artistiques entre la France et la Russie', *Mélanges Paul Boyer*, 1925.

— 'Un nouveau buste de Washington', *Gazette des Beaux-Arts*, 1926.

— 'Notes critiques sur les expositions du centenaire de Houdon', *Bulletin de la Société de l'histoire de l'art français*, 1928.

— 'Les expositions du centenaire de Houdon', *Gazette des Beaux-Arts*, June 1928, pp. 339–56.

— 'Un ambassadeur de l'art français dans les deux mondes: le sculpteur Houdon', *Revue de l'alliance française*, July 1928.

— 'Le buste en marbre de Franklin par J.-J. Caffieri', *Gazette des Beaux-Arts*, July–December 1928, pp. 167–72.

— 'Un recueil de lettres de Houdon à la Bibliothèque d'art et d'archéologie', *Bulletin de la Société des amis de la Bibliothèque*, no. 2, 1929.

— 'J.-B. Defernex, sculpteur du duc d'Orléans', *Gazette des Beaux-Arts*, June 1931.

— 'Un buste inédit de Houdon' (Mme Rodde, née Dorothea von Schlözer), *Gazette des Beaux-Arts*, August 1931, p. 25.

— 'Correspondance artistique de Grimm avec Catherine II', *Archives de l'art français*, 1931–2, pp. 1–206.

— 'L'iconographie de Houdon', *Gazette des Beaux-Arts*, March 1933, pp. 157–71.

— 'La sculpture française à Rome', *Bulletin de la Société de l'histoire de l'art français*, 1934, pp. 21–43.

— 'A propos du deuxième centenaire de la naissance de Houdon', *Gazette des Beaux-Arts*, 1941.

— 'Une œuvre inédite de Houdon: le buste en marbre de Mlle Servat', *Gazette des Beaux-Arts*, January 27, 1941.

— 'Une œuvre inédite de Houdon: le buste de Mlle Olivier', *Gazette des Beaux-Arts*, November 20, 1942.

— 'Houdon et la Belgique', *Apollo*, May 1943.

— 'La sculpture funéraire dans l'œuvre de Houdon: le mausolée du comte de Valbelle', *Gazette des Beaux-Arts*, November 1943.

— 'Un nouveau chef-d'œuvre de Houdon au Musée du Louvre: le mausolée du comte d'Ennery', *Pro arte*, May 1946.

— 'A Great French Sculptor of the 18th century: Jean-Antoine Houdon', *Connoisseur*, June 1948, pp. 74–77.

— 'A bust of Voltaire by Houdon', *Burlington Magazine*, March 1949.

— 'La vie intime de Houdon', *Bulletin de la Société de l'histoire de l'art français*, 1950, pp. 177–86.

— 'Bust of an unknown child by Houdon', *The Connoisseur*, October 1950.

— 'Les bustes français du XVIIIe siècle', *Médecine*, no. 98, pp. 17–24.

— 'Compléments au catalogue des bustes de Houdon', *Bulletin de la Société de l'histoire de l'art français*, 1952.

— 'La sculpture française en Hollande au XVIIIe siècle' (bust of Suffren), *Actes du Congrès d'Amsterdam*, 1952.

— 'La Diane et l'Apollon de Houdon à la Fondation Calouste Gulbenkian de Lisbonne', *Coloquio*, June 1960.

Réau, Louis, and Vallery-Radot, Pierre. 'Les deux écorchés de Houdon', *Aesculape*, July–August 1938, pp. 170–84.

Rocheblave, Samuel. 'Note sur le buste de Steven Hoogendijk par Houdon à la Société batave de Rotterdam', *Bulletin de la Société de l'histoire de l'art français*, 1923.

Rosenthal, Gertrude. 'The Basic Theories of French Classic Sculpture', *Journal of Aesthetics and Art Criticism*, vol. 1, no. 6, 1942, pp. 42–53.

Schwark, Günther. 'Houdon in deutschen Museen', *Belvedere*, 1930, pp. 48–51.

— 'Zwei unbekannte Houdon-Büsten in Deutschland', *Pantheon*, September 1930, pp. 407–9.

Seymour, Charles. 'Houdon's Washington at Mount Vernon Re-examined', *Gazette des Beaux-Arts*, March 1948, pp. 137–58.

— 'Houdon's Marble Bust of D'Alembert', *Yale University Art Gallery Bulletin*, vol. 25, no. 2, October 1959, pp. 4–15.

Staring, A. 'Houdon en Nederland', *Oud Holland*, 1940.

Steinmann, Ernst. 'J. Antoine Houdon im Grossherzoglichen Museum zu Schwerin', *Monatshefte für Kunstwissenschaft*, vol. 4, 1911, pp. 207–23.

Taylor, Francis Henry. 'Jean-Antoine Houdon, 1828–1928', *Pennsylvania Museum Bulletin*, vol. 24, October–November 1928, pp. 13–21.

Terrade, A. 'Quelques documents sur Houdon', *Versailles Illustré*, vol. 7, 1901–1902, pp. 20–24. (Typescript, Frick Art Reference Library, New York.)

Tourneux, Maurice. 'Les portraits de Diderot', *L'art*, 1878.

— 'Deux nouveaux portraits de Diderot au Musée du Louvre', *Musées de France*, 1912, pp. 1–3.

— 'Hommages rendus à Diderot par ses compatriotes (1780–81)', *Bulletin de la Société de l'histoire de l'art de France*, 1913, pp. 184–91.

Vaudoyer, Jean-Louis. 'Les Houdon d'Aix', *L'art et les artistes*, February 1925.

— 'Houdon portraitiste', *Illustration*, June 9, 1928.

Villard, A. 'Sur le buste du marquis de Méjanes', *Arts en Provence*, 1952.

Vitry, Paul. 'Un buste de négresse par Houdon au Musée de Soissons', *Revue de l'art ancien et moderne*, 1897.

— 'La sculpture française des XVIIe and XVIIIe siècles au Musée Wallace de Londres', *Les arts*, 7, August 1902, p. 18.

— 'La Collection de M. Jacques Doucet', *Les Arts*, no. 21, September 1903, pp. 2–19.

— 'Houdon animalier', *Les Arts*, June 1905.

— 'Houdon, portraitiste de sa femme et de ses enfants', *La Revue de l'art ancien et moderne*, vol. 19, May 1906, pp. 337–51.

— 'La "Diane" et l' "Apollon" de Houdon', *Les Arts*, no. 61, January 1907, pp. 9–16.

— 'Notes sur les différents logements et ateliers occupés par J.-A. Houdon', *Archives de l'art français*, vol. 1, 1907, pp. 217–20.

— 'Le Morphée de Houdon', *Revue de l'art ancien et moderne*, vol. 21, January–June 1907, pp. 149–56.

— 'La statue de la Philosophie de Houdon', *Archives de l'art français*, vol. 1, 1907, pp. 210–16.

— 'Une liste d'œuvres de J.-A. Houdon redigée par l'artiste lui-même vers 1784', *Archives de l'art français*, series 1, 1907, pp. 193–220.

— 'Quelques bustes français à l'exposition des cent pastels', *Revue de l'art ancien et moderne*, 1908.

— 'Les accroissements du département de la sculpture du moyen-âge, de la renaissance', *La Revue de l'art ancien et moderne*, vol. 23, February 1908, pp. 101–12; March 1908, pp. 205–17.

— 'Les monuments à J.-J. Rousseau de Houdon à Bartholémé', *Gazette des Beaux-Arts*, August 1912, pp. 97–117.

— 'Les projets de monuments à la mémoire de Jean-Jacques Rousseau', *Bulletin de la Société de l'histoire de l'art français*, 1912.

— 'Works of Houdon in America: I The Portrait Busts of his Wife and Children', *Art in America*, vol. 2, no. 3, April 1914, pp. 217–26.

— 'Works of Houdon in America: II La Baigneuse; La Vestale, Les Baisers', *Art in America*, vol. 2, no. 5, August 1914' pp. 368–79.

— 'Les collections Pierpont Morgan', *Gazette des Beaux-Arts*, May 1914, pp. 425–40.

— 'Le Saint Jean-Baptiste de Houdon', *Renaissance de l'art et des industries de luxe*, Paris, année 6, 1923, pp. 76–82.

— 'Un buste de Houdon au Musée de Berlin' (Vietinghoff), *Gazette des Beaux-Arts*, January 1927.

— 'L'exposition Houdon à la Bibliothèque municipale de Versailles', *Gazette des Beaux-Arts*, May 1, 1928.

— 'L'exposition du centenaire de Houdon à Versailles', *La Revue de l'art ancien et moderne*, June 1928, pp. 9–20.

— 'Le centenaire de Houdon', *Revue de l'art*, June and July 1928.

— 'Le centenaire de Houdon; deuxième exposition', *La Revue de l'art ancien et moderne*, July–August 1928, pp. 57–60.

— 'Houdon dessinateur', *Gazette des Beaux-Arts*, 1928.

— 'La tête de Négresse de Houdon du Musée de Soissons', *Bulletin des Musées de France*, January 1931, pp. 7–9.

— 'Un buste de la collection de M. de Camondo: La Négresse de Houdon', *Gazette des Beaux-Arts*, November 1931, pp. 307–11.

— 'Houdon and the Legion of Honor', *Légion d'Honneur*, April 1933.

— 'Le buste de la comtesse de Jaucourt au Louvre', *Bulletin des Musées français*, 1937.

Vuaflant, Albert. 'Houdon arbitre dans un concours entre sculpteurs flamands en 1779', *Bulletin de la Société de l'histoire de l'art français*, 1911.

Waldschmidt, Charles. 'La restauration de la Colonne de la Grande Armée', *Monuments de l'histoire français*, 1963, pp. 183–94.

Watson, F. J. B. 'From Antico to Houdon', *Apollo*, n.s. 90, Summer 1969, pp. 218–19.

Watson, Francis, 'Diderot and Houdon: A Little Known Bust', in *The Artist and the Writer in France*, Essays in Honour of Jean Seznec, Oxford 1974, pp. 15–20.

Weitenkampf, Frank. 'Notes on some Franklin busts', *Bulletin of the Metropolitan Museum of Art*, New York, vol. 1, March 1906, pp. 60–61.

Zimmerman, H. 'Eine unbekannte Bronzestatue Jean-Antoine Houdons' (La Frileuse), *Mitteilungsblatt der Westberliner Museen*, June 1957.

IV. *General Works*

The American Philosophical Society, Catalogue of Portraits and Other Works of Art in the Possession of, Philadelphia, 1961.

Aude, E. *Le marquis de Méjanes*, Paris, 1933.

Barère de Vinzac, Bertrand. *Mémoires de B. Barère . . . par mm Hippolyte, Carnot, . . . et David (d'Angers) précédés d'une notice historique par H. Carnot*, Paris, 1842 (4 vols).

Benot, Y. *Diderot et Falconet: le Pour et le Contre*, Paris, 1958.

Besterman, Theodore. *Voltaire*, London, 1969.

Blunt, Anthony. *Art and Architecture in France 1500–1700*, Baltimore, 1954. (The Pelican History of Art.)

Bottarius, J., and Foggini, N. *Musei Capitolini . . . cum animadversionibus*, Rome, 1750–82 (4 vols in 3), vol. 3, 'Statue', plate 23.

Bourdier, G. *L'iconographie de Buffon*, Paris, 1952.

Brinckmann, A. E. *Barockskulptur*, Berlin-Neubabelsberg, 1917.

Brion, M. *Pierre Puget*, Paris, 1930.

Buffenoire, Hippolyte. *Les portraits de Jean-Jacques Rousseau*, Paris, 1913.

Camondo, Musée Nissim de, Handbook, Paris, 1954.

Cassirer, Ernst. *The Philosophy of the Enlightenment*, Princeton, 1951.

de Champeaux, A. *Dictionnaire des bronziers*, Paris, n.d. (Manuscript, Library, Musée des Arts Décoratifs, Paris.)

Le Châtelier, G. *Louis-Pierre Deseine*, Paris, n.d. (1906).

Cobban, Alfred. *A History of Modern France*, Baltimore, 1961 (2 vols).

Cochin, *Mémoires*, ed. Ch. Henry, Paris, 1880.

Colin, O. *Edmé Bouchardon* (exhibition catalogue), Chaumont, 1962.

Comédie-Française, Régistre des délibérations de la, September 30, 1776.

Courajod, Louis. *Histoire de l'École des Beaux-Arts au XVIIIe siècle: l'École des élèves protégés*, Paris, 1874.

Dacier, Émile. *Le Musée de la Comédie-Française*, Paris, 1905.

— *Catalogues illustrés par Gabriel de Saint-Aubin*, Paris, 1910.

— *Gabriel de Saint-Aubin*, Paris, 1929–31.

Delpech, Jenine. *L'Amour le plus tendre* (Mme de Sabran), Paris, 1964.

Deshairs, L. *Le château de Maisons*, Paris, 1907.

— *Dijon, Architecture et décoration au XVIIIe siècle*, Paris, 1910.

Dilke, Lady Emilia Francis. *French Architects and Sculptors of the XVIIIth Century*, London, 1900.

Dunlap, William. *History of the Arts of Design in the United States*, 1834; new Ed. Boston, 1918 (3 vols).

Duquesnoy, Journal d'Adrien, ed. R. de Crévecœur, Paris, 1894.

Dussieux, Louis. *Mémoires inédits sur la vie et les ouvrages des membres de l'Académie Royale de Peinture et de Sculpture*, Paris, 1854.

— *Les artistes français à l'étranger*, 3rd Ed., Paris, 1876.

Eisen, Gustave. *Portraits of Washington*, New York, 1952.

Encyclopédie, ou Dictionnaire des sciences, des arts et des métiers, ed. Diderot and D'Alembert, Paris, 1751–80 (35 vols).

Fleury, Abram Joseph Bénard, called (1750–1822). *Mémoires de Fleury de la Comédie-Française*; ed. J. B. P. Lafitte, Paris, 1847 (2 vols).

Francastel, P. *Girardon*, Paris, 1928.

Freeman, Douglas Santhall. *George Washington, a Biography*, New York, 1948–57, vol. 6.

Furcy-Raynaud, M. *Correspondance de M. de Marigny* (N.A.A.F.), Paris, 1904–5.

— *Correspondance de M. d'Angiviller* (N.A.A.F.), Paris, 1906–7.

Gay, Peter. *The Enlightenment: An Interpretation*, Vol. I, New York, 1966; Vol. II, New York, 1969. (With extensive bibliography.)

— *The Enlightenment* (A Comprehensive Anthology), New York, 1973.

Gombrich, E. H. *Art and Illusion*, New York and London, 1960; fourth ed. 1972.

— *Art, Perception, and Reality*, Baltimore and London, 1970.

Goncourt, J. and E. De. *L'Art au XVIIIe siècle*, Paris, 1880–2.

Gonse, Louis. *Les chefs-d'œuvre des Musées de France*, Paris, 1904.

Gougenot, L. *Vie de Coustou le jeune* (Société des Bibliophiles François, Mélanges, no. 4), Paris, 1903.

Guiffrey, J. *Notes et documents inédits sur les expositions du XVIIIe siècle*, Paris, 1873.

— *Les Caffieri*, Paris, 1877.

Gulbenkian, Catalogue de la Collection, Lisbon, 1960.

Hampson, Norman. *A Cultural History of the Enlightenment*, New York, 1968.

Hautecœur, Louis. *Rome et la renaissance de l'antiquité à la fin du dix-huitième siècle*, Paris, 1912.

Hildebrandt, E. *Leben, Werke und Schriften des Bildhauers E. M. Falconet*, Strassburg, 1908.

— *Malerei und Plastik des achtzehnten Jahrhunderts in Frankreich*, Wildpark-Potsdam, 1924.

Honour, Hugh. *Neo-Classicism*, Baltimore, 1968. (Penguin.)

Ingersoll-Smouse, Florence. *La Sculpture Funéraire en France au XVIIIe siècle*, Paris, 1912.

Jal, Augustin. *Dictionnaire critique de biographie et d'histoire*, Paris, 1864.

Jefferson, Thomas. *Correspondence between Thomas Jefferson and Pierre Samuel du Pont de Nemours*, ed. Dumas Malone, Boston, 1930.

— *The Thomas Jefferson Papers*, ed. Julian P. Boyd, Princeton University Press, 1950–date.

— *The Jefferson Papers Index*, ed. Elizabeth J. Sherwood and Ida T. Hopper, Princeton University Press, 1954, 1958.

Jones, H. Stuart, M.A. *A Catalogue of the Ancient Sculptures Preserved in the Municipal Collections of Rome*, London, 1912.

Kalnein, Wend Graf, and Levey, Michael. *Art and Architecture of the Eighteenth Century in France*, Baltimore, 1972. (The Pelican History of Art.)

Keller-Dorian, G. *Antoine Coysevox*, Paris, 1920.

Kimball, Marie. *Jefferson: The Scene of Europe 1784–1789*, New York, 1950.

Lafayette, Marquis de. *Mémoires*, Paris, 1837.

Lami, S. *Dictionnaire des sculpteurs de l'école française sous le Règne de Louis XIV*, Paris, 1907.

— *Dictionnaire des sculpteurs de l'école française au XVIIIe siècle*, Paris, 1910–11.

Lapauze, Henry. *Histoire de l'Académie de France à Rome*, 1924 (2 vols).

de Launay, Louis. *Une grande famille de savants: les Brongniart*, Paris, 1940.

Legrand. *Les collections artistiques de la Faculté de médecine*, Paris, 1911.

Lenoir, Alexandre. *Catalogue du Musée royal des monuments français*, Paris, 1816.

Levitine, George. *The Sculpture of Falconet*, Greenwich, Conn., 1972.

Louvre, les sculptures moyen-age, renaissance, temps modernes au Musée du Louvre, Paris, 1957.

Luc-Benoist, *La Sculpture française*, Paris, 1945.

Malone, Dumas. *Jefferson and His Times*, Boston, 1948–date (4 vols).

Marmottan, Paul. *Le Peintre Louis Boilly*, Paris, 1913.

Mondain-Monval, Jean. *Les collections de la Comédie-Française*, Paris, 1897.

Morant, Henry de. *Sculptures du XVIIIe siècle au Musée des Beaux-Arts d'Angers*, 1950. (Exhibition catalogue.)

Morgan, John Hill, and Fielding, Mantle. *Life Portraits of Washington and their Replicas*, Philadelphia, 1931.

Morison, Samuel Eliot. *John Paul Jones: A Sailor's Biography*, Boston, 1959.

Morris, Richard (Columbia University). *The Wright Plaque of Washington*, 1961 (unpublished manuscript).

Neo-Classicism (exhibition catalogue), Arts Council, London, 1972.

Niclausse, Juliette. *Thomire, fondeur-ciseleur: sa vie, son œuvre*, 1947.

Niklaus, Robert. *A Literary History of France. The Eighteenth Century 1715–1789*, New York and London, 1970.

Novotny, Fritz. *Painting and Sculpture in Europe 1780–1880*, Baltimore, 1960. (The Pelican History of Art.)

Pascal, A. *Pierre Julien, sculpteur, sa vie et son œuvre*, Paris, 1904.

Panofsky, Erwin. *Tomb Sculpture*, New York, 1964.

Perey, L. *Un petit-neveu de Mazarin: le duc de Nivernais*, Paris, 1891.

Plan, P. P. *J.-J. Rousseau raconté par les gazettes de son temps*, Paris, 1912.

Pope-Hennessy, John. *The Portrait in the Renaissance*, New York and London, 1966.

Pope-Hennessy, John, and Hodgkinson, Terence. *The Frick Collection Catalogue*, New York, 1970, vol. IV.

Pevsner, Nikolaus. *Academies of Art Past and Present*, Cambridge, England, 1940.

Raspail, Dr. Julien. *Le mystère de la mort de J.-J. Rousseau*, Paris, 1911.

Réau, Louis. *Correspondance de Falconet avec Catherine II*, Paris, 1921.

— *Étienne-Maurice Falconet*, Paris, 1922.

— *Histoire de l'expansion de l'art français, 1924–1933* (4 vols).

— *Histoire de la peinture française au XVIIIᵉ siècle*, Paris–Brussels, 1925-6.

— *L'Art français aux États-Unis*, Paris, 1926.

— *Une Dynastie de sculpteurs au XVIIIᵉ siècle, Les Lemoyne*, Paris, 1927.

— *Catalogue de l'art français dans les musées russes*, Paris, 1929.

— *L'Europe française au siècle des lumières*, Paris, 1938.

— *Les Sculpteurs français en Italie*, Paris, 1945.

— *Le rayonnement de Paris au XVIIIᵉ siècle*, Paris, 1946.

— *J.-B. Pigalle*, Paris, 1950.

— *L'art au XVIIIᵉ siècle. Époque Louis XVI*, Paris, 1952.

Rich, Jack C. *The Materials and Methods of Sculpture*, New York, 1947.

Rocheblave, S. *Jean-Baptiste Pigalle*, Paris, 1919.

Rodin, Auguste. *On Art and Artists*, New York, 1957.

Rosenblum, Robert. *Transformations in Late Eighteenth Century Art*, Princeton, 1967.

Sellers, Charles Coleman. *Benjamin Franklin in Portraiture*, New Haven, 1962, pp. 304–16.

Smith, Preserved. *The Enlightenment 1687–1776* (vol. II), New York and London, 1934.

Souchal, F. *Les Slodtz*, Paris, 1967.

Stein, Henri. *Augustin Pajou*, Paris, 1912.

Swan, Mabel Munson. *The Athenaeum Gallery 1827–1873*, Boston, 1940.

Thieme, U., and Becker, F. *Allgemeines Lexikon der bildenden Künstler*, Leipzig, 1908–50.

Thirion, H. *Les Adam et Clodion*, Paris, 1885.

Vallon, F. *Falconet, Diderot et Catherine II*, Grenoble, 1930.

Mme Vigée-Lebrun. *Souvenirs*, Paris, 1835.

Vitry, Paul. *Le château de Maisons-Laffitte*, Paris, 1912.

— *La sculpture française classique de Jean Goujon à Rodin*, Paris, 1934.

— *La sculpture française du XVIᵐᵉ au XIXᵐᵉ siècle*, Paris, 1938.

Waetzoldt, Wilhelm. *Die Kunst des Porträts*, Leipzig, 1908.

Wark, R. R. *Sculpture in the Huntington Collection*, Los Angeles, 1954.

— *Sculpture in the Huntington Collection*, San Marino, California, 1959.

Washington, George. *The Diaries of George Washington 1748–1799*. ed. John C. Fitzpatrick, Boston, 1925 (4 vols).

— *The Writings of George Washington*, Washington, D.C., U.S. Government Printing Office, 1931–44 (39 vols).

Weber, Gerold. *Edmé Bouchardon*, Vienna, 1965.

Weinshinker, Anne Betty, *Falconet, his writings and his friend Diderot*. Geneva, 1966.

Wilson, Arthur M. *Diderot*, New York, 1972.

Wittkower, Rudolf. *Gian Lorenzo Bernini*, London, 1966.

Zaretskaya, Z., and Kosareva, N. *La Sculpture française des XVII–XX siècles au Musée de l'Ermitage*, Leningrad, 1963.

SOURCES OF PHOTOGRAPHS

H. H. Arnason: Figs. 13, 17, 23, 24, 41, 43, 44, 46, 51–53, 55, 56, 61, 62, 64, 65, 67, 68, 70, 72, 74–77, 79, 82, 83, 86, 87, 90, 91, 93, 94, 96, 101–104, 106, 108, 109, 111, 114–117, 119–121, 123, 124, 126, 129, 130, 132–134, 139–142, 144, 145, 147–151, 153–158, 160–164, 166, 167, 170, 172, 174–176, 180–182, 185, 186, 189, 192–194, 196, 198–201, 203, 204, 207, 208; Plates 1–3, 4bc, 6–10, 12b–21, 23–26, 31–39, 43–49, 51–63, 66–81, 85ab, 87–93, 95–97a, 98–101, 103–112, 114–121, 123–125, 127–142, 143a,b,c,f,h,i,k,l,m,o, 144a,c,e,f.

Aix-en-Provence, Studio Raphaël: Fig. 122

Angers, J. Evers: Figs. 183, 187

Baltimore, Walters Art Gallery: Fig. 113, Plate 144g

Barnard Castle, Bowes Museum: Plate 143e

Berlin, German Academy: Figs. 69, 78, 99, 107, 152

Berlin-Dahlem, Staatliche Museen: Fig. 26

Boston, Museum of Fine Arts: Plate 143n

Detroit, Institute of Arts: Fig. 195, Plate 144d

Florence, Alinari: Fig. 29

Geneva, Musée d'Art et d'Histoire: Fig. 125

Glasgow, City Art Gallery: Fig. 135

Karlsruhe, Kunsthalle: Plate 94

Leipzig, G. Reinhold: Fig. 171

Lisbon, Gulbenkian Foundation, Museum: Plate 122

London, Courtauld Institute of Art: Figs. 63, 71, 138, 168

London, Heim Gallery: Plate 144b

London, Phaidon Press: Figs. 54, 95, 206

London, Victoria and Albert Museum: Fig. 34

London, Wallace Collection: Figs. 88, 127

Mount Vernon, Ladies' Association: Plate 97b

Neuchâtel, Leo Hilber: Fig. 66, Plate 11

New Haven, Conn., Yale University Art Gallery: Fig. 110, Plates 50, 143g

New York, Frick Collection: Figs. 81, 84, Plates 22, 28, 29, 41

New York, Metropolitan Museum of Art: Figs. 118, 128, 177, Plates 64, 82–84, 86

New York, Taylor and Dull: Fig. 169

New York, Wildenstein & Co.: Plate 143d

Paris, Archives Photographiques: Figs. 3, 20, 21, 31, 131, Plate 12a

Paris, Bulloz: Figs. 1, 4, 5, 11, 16, 19, 22, 25, 27, 47, 49, 50, 105, 136, 165, 173, 179, Plate 126

Paris, Giraudon: Figs. 2, 7–10, 12, 14, 15, 18, 28, 30, 32, 33, 35–40, 42, 45, 48, 57, 58, 112, 143, 159, 184, 191, Plates 4a, 5, 40a, 102

Paris, Musée des Arts Décoratifs: Fig. 205

Paris, Musée du Louvre: Fig. 6

Paris, Vizzavona: Fig. 89

Paris, P. Willi: Fig. 98

Potsdam-Sanssouci, Schlösser: Fig. 146

Providence, Rhode Island School of Design: Fig. 73

Rome, Anderson: Figs. 59, 60

San Francisco, M. H. De Young Museum: Fig. 190

San Marino, Huntington Library and Art Gallery: Figs. 80, 100, 178, Plates 27, 40b, 42, 113, 143j

Stockholm, National Museum: Fig. 85, Plate 30

Warsaw, National Museum: Fig. 137

INDEX OF LOCATIONS

INDEX OF NAMES

Subjects of portraits by Houdon are given in italics

Pineu-Duval, Henri-Jean, 98, 106
Pineu-Duval, Sabine, *see* Houdon, Sabine
Pingré, 8
Pompadour, Madame de, 6, 7, 37
Pope, Alexander, 57
Potemkin, 42
Potocki, Count, 86
Poussin, Nicolas, 2, 9, 16, Fig. 41
Préameneu, Comte Félix-Julien-Jean Bigot de, 103, 120 (note 253), Fig. 202
Primaticcio, Francesco, 1, 43
Provence, Comte de, *see* Louis XVIII
Provence, Comtesse de, 38
Puget, Pierre, 2, 3, 6, Figs. 14, 16

Quesnay, Blaise-Guillaume, 56
Quesnay, François, 56

Rabache, Anne, 10
Racine, Jean, 25
Ramey, Claude, Fig. 52
Raphael, 2
Réau, Louis, viii–ix
Réaumur, René Antoine Ferchault de, Fig. 24
Récamier, Madame, 9, Fig. 53
Reiffenstein, 25
Richardson, Samuel, 30, 50, 108 (note 55)
Richelieu, Cardinal 1, 2, 3, 27, Figs. 5, 10
Richier, Ligier, 1, 14, Fig. 1
Rigaud, Hyacinthe, 66
Rilliet, Madame, 109 (note 70)
Riquetti, Honoré-Gabriel-Victor, Comte de Mirabeau, *see* Mirabeau, Comte de
Robert, Adèle, 42
Robert, Hubert, 2, 9, 16, 42, 63
Robespierre, Maximilien Marie Isidore, 96
Rochette, Désiré-Raoul, 106, 111 (note 105)
Rodde-Schlözer, Dorothea von, 96, 99, 102, 119 (note 244), 120 (note 252), Fig. 192, Plate 129
Rodin, Auguste, 68, 70, 106, 107 (note 2), 113 (note 145)
Roland, Philippe-Laurent, 95, 102, 106, 119 (note 249)
Roland, Madame, 108 (note 55)
Roslin, Alexander, 111 (note 108)
Rosso Fiorentino, Giovanni Battista, 1
Rotrou, Jean de, 8, 65, 67, Fig. 44
Rousseau, Jean-Jacques, 7, 10, 14, 18, 22, 23, 26, 34, 36, 46, 47, 48–9, 67, 70, 86, 87, 95, 100,

113 (note 140), 118 (notes 231, 236) Figs. 107, 108, Plates 48a–b, 49
Rozier, Jean-François Pilâtre de, 86
Rubens, Peter Paul, 2
Rude, François, 88, 106

Sabran, Comtesse de, 72, 86, Fig. 152, Plate 94
Sagonne, Comte Mansard de, 110 (note 95)
Saint-Aubin, Gabriel de, 12, 15, 17, 42, 43, 59, 64, 66, 109 (note 70), 110 (note 94), 115 (note 177), Fig. 92
Saint-Gaudens, Augustus, 111 (note 105)
Salm-Dyck, Princess, 96, 98, 119 (note 239), Fig. 188
Sarrazin, Jacques, 1
Saxe, Maréchal de, 7, 27, 29, 37, 62, Fig. 38
Saxe-Gotha, *see* Ernest Louis II; Frederick III; Louisa-Dorothea; Maria-Charlotte
Saxe-Weimar, Anna-Amalia, Duchess of, 114 (note 174)
Séguir, 14
Sergel, Johan Tobias, 115 (note 178)
Sérilly, Madame de, 58, 63, 67, 72, Fig. 127, Plate 66
Servat, Marie Adélaïde, 40–1, Fig. 90, Plate 143d
Short, William, 71–2
Shubin, F. I., 108 (note 40)
Slodtz, René-Michel (Michel Ange), 5–6, 10, 11, 14, 15, 27, 29, 35–6, 78, 107 (note 5), Figs. 25, 29
Soltykov, Ivan Petrovitch, 63, 64, 67, 114 (note 161), Fig. 133, Plate 71
Soltykov, Nicholas Ivanovitch, 63, 64
Staël, Madame de, 88
Stanislas-Auguste Poniatowski, King of Poland, 66
Stosch, Philipp, 5, Fig. 26
Stouf, Jean-Baptiste, 9, 55, 104
Stroganov, Count, 22, 25, 52, 53
Suffren, Pierre-André de, 79, 81, 116 (note 197), Fig. 158, Plate 103
Sully, Duc de, 59

Taylor, Charles W., 55
Theis, Constance-Marie de, *see* Salm-Dyck, Princess
Thélusson, Madame de, 96, 118 (note 233)
Thomire, Pierre-Philippe, 69, 78, 93, 114 (note 176)

Thorvaldsen, Bertel, 9, 94
Thouret, Michel-Augustin, 118 (note 234)
Tourville, Maréchal de, 8, 56, 59, 60, 61, 63, 69, 77, 106, 113 (note 158), Fig. 130, Plate 67
Triplett, William, 75
Tronchin, Théodore, 57, 64, 109 (note 70), Fig. 125, Plate 62a
Turgot, Anne-Robert-Jacques, Baron de l'Aulne, 31, 32–3, 38, 45, 46, 57, 88, Fig. 83, Plate 23

Valbelle, Comte de, 56, 57, Figs. 121, 122
Vallon, Fig. 122
Vandeul, Albert de, 42
Vandeul, Madame de, 23, 107 (note 3)
Vassé, L.-C., 27, 43
Vernet, Carl, 98
Victoire, Madame, Aunt of Louis XVI, 38, 39, 40, 79, Fig. 88, Plate 32
Vien, Joseph-Marie, 16
Vietinghoff, Baron de, 41, 110 (notes 84, 85), 112 (note 117), Fig. 91, Plate 43
Vieuzac, Barère de, 78–9
Vigée-Lebrun, Madame, 8, 72
Villevielle, Marquis de, 49
Vitry, Paul, viii
Voltaire, François Marie Arouet de, vii, 7, 9, 10, 18, 19, 20, 22, 23, 34, 36, 44, 46, 47, 48, 49–50, 53, 55, 58, 62, 63, 64, 65, 67, 70, 73, 86, 87, 94, 95, 96, 101, 103, 105–6, 112 (notes 118–30), 117 (note 215), 118 (note 236), Figs. 39, 111, 112, 113, 114, 116, 117, 204, Plates 51, 52a–b, 53a–b, 54, 55, 56, 57a–b, 140–2, 143f, 144g

Warin, Jean, 1, Fig. 5
Washington, George, vii, 10, 27, 39, 47, 48, 50, 53, 54, 55, 58, 66, 69, 72–8, 80, 86, 91, 105, 113 (note 140), 115 (notes 189, 191), Figs. 153, 154, 155, 157, Plates 95, 96, 97a–b, 98a–b, 99, 100, 101, 144c
Watt, James, 101
Wellington, Arthur Wellesley, Duke of, 102
West, Benjamin, 76
Winckelmann, Johann Joachim, 24
Winters, Jonathan, 54
Wright, Joseph, 115 (note 189)

Zurbarán, Francisco, 15
Zuylen, Isabelle de Tuyll de, *see* Charrière, Madame de